Improving Workplace Quality

Bulletin of Comparative Labour Relations

VOLUME 97

Founding Editor

The series started in 1970 under the dynamic editorship of Professor Roger Blanpain (Belgium), former President of the International Industrial Relations Association. Professor Blanpain, Professor Emeritus of Labour Law, Universities of Leuven and Tilburg, was also General Editor of the International Encyclopedia of Laws (with more than 1,600 collaborators worldwide) and President of the Association of Educative and Scientific Authors Authors. He passed away in October 2016.

General Editor

In 2015 Frank Hendrickx, Professor of labour law at the Faculty of Law of the University of Leuven (Belgium) joined as a co-Editor. Frank Hendrickx has published numerous articles and books and regularly advises governments, international institutions and private organisations in the area of labour law as well as in sports law. He is the Editor-in-Chief of the European Labour Law Journal and General Editor of the International Encyclopaedia of Laws.

Introduction

The Bulletins constitute a unique source of information and thought-provoking discussion, laying the groundwork for studies of employment relations in the 21st century, involving among much else the effects of globalization, new technologies, migration, and the greying of the population.

Contents/Subjects

Amongst other subjects the Bulletins frequently include the proceedings of international or regional conferences; reports from comparative projects devoted to salient issues in industrial relations, human resources management, and/or labour law; and specific issues underlying the multicultural aspects of our industrial societies.

Objective

The Bulletins offer a platform of expression and discussion on labour relations to scholars and practitioners worldwide, often featuring special guest editors.

The titles published in this series are listed at the end of this volume.

BULLETIN OF COMPARATIVE LABOUR RELATIONS - 97

Improving Workplace Quality

New Perspectives and Challenges for Worker Well-Being

Editors

William Bromwich & Olga Rymkevich

Contributors

Tindara Addabbo
Maddalena Cannito
Giorgio Gallizioli
Elena Gerasimova
Avinash Govindjee
Wendy Greene
Trina Jones
Nikita L. Lyutov
Ubaldo Macchitella
Daniela Oliva
Marius Olivier
Giorgio Luigi Risso
Elena Sarti
Carla Spinelli
Fabrizio Starace
Elena Sychenko
Marco Tufo

General Editor

Frank Hendrickx

Founding Editor

Roger Blanpain

Wolters Kluwer

Published by:
Kluwer Law International B.V.
PO Box 316
2400 AH Alphen aan den Rijn
The Netherlands
Website: www.wolterskluwerlr.com

Sold and distributed in North, Central and South America by:
Wolters Kluwer Legal & Regulatory U.S.
7201 McKinney Circle
Frederick, MD 21704
United States of America
Email: customer.service@wolterskluwer.com

Sold and distributed in all other countries by:
Quadrant
Rockwood House
Haywards Heath
West Sussex
RH16 3DH
United Kingdom
Email: international-customerservice@wolterskluwer.com

Printed on acid-free paper.

ISBN 978-90-411-8628-7

e-Book: ISBN 978-90-411-8644-7
web-PDF: ISBN 978-90-411-8645-4

Printed in the United Kingdom.

Notes on Contributors

Tindara Addabbo – Associate Professor, Marco Biagi Department of Economics, University of Modena and Reggio Emilia (Italy)

William Bromwich – Associate Professor, Marco Biagi Department of Economics, University of Modena and Reggio Emilia (Italy)

Maddalena Cannito – Ph.D. candidate, Department of Culture, Politics and Society, University of Turin (Italy)

Giorgio Gallizioli – Formerly European Commission official, currently responsible for the Sports and Leisure Clubs Association at the European Commission (Belgium)

Elena Gerasimova – Associate Professor, Head of the Labour Law and Social Security Law Department. National Research University Higher School of Economics; Director, Centre for Social and Labour Rights, Moscow (Russia)

Avinash Govindjee – Executive Dean, Faculty of Law, Nelson Mandela Metropolitan University, South Africa; Consulting Attorney: Cliffe Dekker Hofmeyr; Senior Commissioner: Commission for Conciliation, Mediation and Arbitration (South Africa)

D. Wendy Greene – Professor of Law, Cumberland School of Law, Samford University (USA)

Trina Jones – Professor of Law, Duke University School of Law (USA)

Nikita Lyutov – Head of the Department of Labour and Social Security Law, Kutafin Moscow State Law University, Professor of Labour and Social Security Law, National Research University Higher School of Economics

Ubaldo Macchitella – European Commission official, Directorate-General Human Resources and Security, Brussels (Belgium)

Daniela Oliva – Director of Training and Labour Policy, Bologna Institute for Social Research (Italy)

Marius Olivier - Adjunct Professor, Faculty of Law, University of Western Australia; Extraordinary Professor, Faculty of Law, Northwest University, South Africa; Director: International Institute for Social Law and Policy (South Africa)

Giorgio Risso Luigi – Public Employment Services Official, Regional Agency for Labour Market Policies (Italy)

Olga Rymkevich – Senior Researcher, Marco Biagi Foundation, University of Modena and Reggio Emilia (Italy)

Elena Sarti – Research Collaborator, Marco Biagi Foundation, University of Modena and Reggio Emilia (Italy)

Carla Spinelli – Associate Professor of Labour Law, Aldo Moro University of Bari (Italy)

Fabrizio Starace – Director of the Department of Mental Health and Substance Abuse, AUSL Modena (Italy)

Elena Sychenko – Associate Professor, State Institute of Economics, Finance, Law and Technology (Russia)

Marco Tufo – Ph.D. candidate, Marco Biagi Foundation, University of Modena and Reggio Emilia (Italy)

Summary of Contents

Notes on Contributors v

Editors' Preface xv

Part I
Discrimination in the Workplace 1

Chapter 1
To Be Aggrieved by "Misperception Discrimination" in the Workplace
D. Wendy Greene 3

Chapter 2
Work-Life Balance and the Use of Child-Care Leave by Fathers Serving in the Military: The Case of *Konstantin Markin v. Russia*
Elena Gerasimova 55

Chapter 3
Disability and Age Discrimination in Employment: Compliance of Russian Law with International Labour Standards
Nikita L. Lyutov 67

Chapter 4
Psychosocial Risk of Harassment at Work: Comparative Research of French and Italian Experience and Possible Implications for Russia
Elena Sychenko 81

Chapter 5
Low-Wage Workers and Employment Benefits in the United States: A Bleak Forecast
Trina Jones 93

PART II
Company Welfare and Work-Life Balance 117

CHAPTER 6
The Use of Paternity Leave in the Private Sector: The Role of Company-Level Welfare Provisions
Maddalena Cannito 119

CHAPTER 7
Flexibility Tools For Part-Time Work: The Italian Jobs Act
Carla Spinelli 147

CHAPTER 8
Well-Being at and Through Digital Work?
Marco Tufo 157

PART III
Health, Well-Being and Workers' Integration in the Labour Market 191

CHAPTER 9
Improving Return to Work and Disability Management in the Developing World: Pointers Emanating from International Instruments, Standards and Guidelines
Marius Olivier & Avinash Govindjee 193

CHAPTER 10
Fit@work: The Comprehensive Health and Well-Being Programme of the European Commission
Ubaldo Macchitella & Giorgio Gallizioli 219

CHAPTER 11
Company-Level Welfare and Public Policies in Care Services
Daniela Oliva & Giorgio Luigi Risso 235

CHAPTER 12
The Adverse Impact of Unemployment on Mental Health in the Province of Modena, Italy
Tindara Addabbo, Elena Sarti & Fabrizio Starace 253

Table of Contents

Notes on Contributors v

Editors' Preface xv

PART I
Discrimination in the Workplace 1

CHAPTER 1
To Be Aggrieved by "Misperception Discrimination" in the Workplace
D. Wendy Greene 3
§1.01 Introduction 3
§1.02 Title VII of the 1964 Civil Rights Act: Its Prohibitions and Protections 7
§1.03 The Evolution of an Actuality Requirement in Title VII Cases 12
[A] Express Adoption of an Actuality Requirement 14
[1] Butler v. Potter 14
[2] Burrage v. FedEx Freight, Inc. 16
[3] Burrage II 20
§1.04 Towards Unity: The Methods Behind the Actuality Madness 23
[A] Nothing Borrowed: Courts' Refusal to Apply the ADA's Perception Theory to the Title VII Context 23
[B] Something Borrowed: A Rigid Application of the Protected-Class Approach in McDonnell Douglas 26
[C] Something New?: An "Anti-anticlassificationist Interpretation" of Title VII 29
[D] Something Old, Something New?: What Lies Beneath the Actuality Requirement 33
§1.05 (Mis)Perceptions Are Protected under Title VII 44
[A] Protection for Misperception Discrimination Plaintiffs: *EEOC v. WC & M Enterprises* and Longstanding EEOC Directives 45
[1] EEOC Directives 45

[2] EEOC v. WC & M Enterprises 47
[B] Misperception Discrimination Plaintiffs Are Protected: More Recent Developments 49
[C] Towards Title VII Protection for All "Persons Aggrieved" Categorical Discrimination: *Thompson v. American Stainless, LP* 50
§1.06 Conclusion 53

CHAPTER 2
Work-Life Balance and the Use of Child-Care Leave by Fathers Serving in the Military: The Case of *Konstantin Markin v. Russia*
Elena Gerasimova 55
§2.01 Introduction 55
§2.02 The Case of Konstantin Markin in Courts of General Jurisdiction and the Constitutional Court of Russian Federation 57
§2.03 *Konstantin Markin v. Russia* in the ECtHR 58
§2.04 Reaction to the ECtHR's Decision in Russia 60
§2.05 Decision of the Grand Chamber of the ECtHR 62
§2.06 Priority of the ECtHR or of the Constitution of Russia: Changes to the Russian Law 64

CHAPTER 3
Disability and Age Discrimination in Employment: Compliance of Russian Law with International Labour Standards
Nikita L. Lyutov 67
§3.01 Introduction 67
§3.02 'The Law in the Books' 69
§3.03 The International Legal Framework 71
§3.04 Discrimination Against Persons with Disabilities 73
§3.05 Age Discrimination 76
§3.06 Conclusion 78

CHAPTER 4
Psychosocial Risk of Harassment at Work: Comparative Research of French and Italian Experience and Possible Implications for Russia
Elena Sychenko 81
§4.01 Introduction 81
§4.02 Human Dignity as a Basis of Anti-harassment Protection 82
§4.03 Protection from Moral Harassment at Work in France 84
[A] Legal Definition of Harassment 84
[B] Obligations of Employer and Employees for Prevention and Investigation of Acts of Harassment 85
[C] Trade Union Rights in the Sphere of Anti-harassment Protection 85
[D] Possibility of Mediation at the Enterprise Level 86
[E] Reverse Burden of Proof 86
[F] Protection of Harassment Victim 86

[G] Possibility of Criminal Liability for Harassment at Work 87
[H] Developed Jurisprudence on Harassment 87
§4.04 The Protection from Mobbing at Work in Italy 88
§4.05 Prerequisites for the Elaboration of Anti-harassment Protection in Russia 90
§4.06 Conclusions 92

Chapter 5
Low-Wage Workers and Employment Benefits in the United States: A Bleak Forecast
Trina Jones 93
§5.01 Introduction 93
§5.02 Demographic Characteristics of Low-Wage Workers 94
§5.03 The Benefits Gap 96
[A] Flexible Work Arrangements and Part-Time Work 98
[B] Leave 99
[C] Healthcare and Retirement Benefits 100
§5.04 Employer Incentives 102
[A] *Advantages v. Disadvantages of Extending Employment Benefits* 102
[B] Competition (The Law of Supply and Demand) 105
[C] Skills, Value, and Class Bias 106
§5.05 A Bleak Future Forecast 108
[A] The Decline of Organized Labor 108
[B] Legislative Action and Inaction 111
§5.06 Conclusion 114

Part II
Company Welfare and Work-Life Balance 117

Chapter 6
The Use of Paternity Leave in the Private Sector: The Role of Company-Level Welfare Provisions
Maddalena Cannito 119
§6.01 Introduction 119
§6.02 Decentralized or Company-Level Welfare 120
§6.03 Corporate Social Responsibility, Company-Level Welfare and Work-Life Balance 121
[A] Main Initiatives of Company-Level Welfare for Work-Life Balance in Italy 124
[B] Company-Level Welfare in Piedmont 126
§6.04 Parental Leave in Italy 128
[A] The Legislation 128
[B] Some Data on the Use of Parental Leave in Italy 130

§6.05 Parental Leave and Work-Life Balance Measures: Focus on Male Workers 131
[A] Company-Level Welfare Provisions and Male Workers 131
[B] Acceptance of the Use of Parental Leave by Men in Private Firms 133
§6.06 Objectives and Methods 134
§6.07 The Use of Parental Leave by Fathers in Family-Friendly Companies in Piedmont 136
[A] Company-Level Welfare Policies and Parental Leave: The Management Point of View 136
[B] Parental Leave and the Work Environment: The Point of View of Fathers 140
§6.08 Conclusions 144

CHAPTER 7
Flexibility Tools For Part-Time Work: The Italian Jobs Act
Carla Spinelli 147
§7.01 The Definition of Part-Time Employment and the Regulation of Working Conditions 147
§7.02 Part-Time Work Flexibility in the Employer's Interest 149
[A] Supplementary Work and Overtime 149
[B] 'Flexibility Clauses' 151
[1] The Worker's Right to 'Reconsider' 152
§7.03 Tools of Flexibility Provided in the Interest of the Part-Time Worker: Transferring from Full-Time to Part-Time and Vice Versa 153
§7.04 Concluding Remarks 155

CHAPTER 8
Well-Being at and Through Digital Work?
Marco Tufo 157
§8.01 Introduction 157
§8.02 From the Social to the Legal Dimension of Telework 159
§8.03 The Guidelines from Sectoral Social Dialogue 161
§8.04 The EFA on Telework: Voluntary ... 162
§8.05 ...and 'Autonomous' Agreements 166
§8.06 The Implementation of the EFA on Telework 167
[A] The 'Legislation Cluster' 168
[B] The 'Collective Agreements Cluster' 171
[C] The 'Soft Law Cluster' and the 'Incomplete Implementation Cluster' 175
§8.07 What Is the Applicable Law? 177
§8.08 The Evolution of Digital Work: 'Crowdworking' and 'Working on Demand via Apps' 181
§8.09 Smart Working 183
§8.10 Conclusion 184

PART III
Health, Well-Being and Workers' Integration in the Labour Market 191

CHAPTER 9
Improving Return to Work and Disability Management in the Developing World: Pointers Emanating from International Instruments, Standards and Guidelines
Marius Olivier & Avinash Govindjee 193
§9.01 Introduction 193
§9.02 Rationale 194
§9.03 International Law 196
[A] Background 196
[B] The Importance of International Law for RTW, also in Malaysia and South Africa 196
[C] UNCRPD 198
[D] ILO 200
[E] ISSA (International Social Security Association) 203
[F] Analysis 205
§9.04 Regional Developments 205
§9.05 Challenges 207
§9.06 Developing World Experiences 209
[A] Malaysia 209
[B] South Africa 212
§9.07 Improving Effective Implementation: International Standards and Guidelines 213
§9.08 Conclusion 215

CHAPTER 10
Fit@work: The Comprehensive Health and Well-Being Programme of the European Commission
Ubaldo Macchitella & Giorgio Gallizioli 219
§10.01 The Context 219
§10.02 Objectives, Rationale and Description of the EC Programme *Fit@work* 223
§10.03 *Fit@work*: The First Year of Life 225
§10.04 A Comprehensive Programme, Spanning Different Organizational Levels 226
§10.05 The Key Role of the SLCA in Encouraging Physical Activity 229
§10.06 Organizational Challenges Ahead 230
[A] Enhancing the *Fit@work* Activities in the DGs 230
[B] Increasing the Cooperation Among Different Units and Services 231
[C] Defining Key Performance Indicators 232
§10.07 Conclusion 233

CHAPTER 11
Company-Level Welfare and Public Policies in Care Services
Daniela Oliva & Giorgio Luigi Risso 235
§11.01 Introduction 235
§11.02 The Family Assistance Project 236
[A] Introduction 236
[B] The Regional Model 237
[C] The Common Characteristics of the Family Care Projects 239
[D] Quantitative Results 242
[E] Considerations on the Experimentation with the Two Projects 243
§11.03 The Gender Community Network 245
[A] The Background 245
[B] Services Implemented 246
[C] The Gender Community Network 246
[D] Results 247
[E] Development of the Projects 248
[F] Some Considerations on the Gender Community Network 248
§11.04 Some Considerations on the Two Projects 251

CHAPTER 12
The Adverse Impact of Unemployment on Mental Health in the Province of Modena, Italy
Tindara Addabbo, Elena Sarti & Fabrizio Starace 253
§12.01 Introduction 253
§12.02 Literature Review 254
§12.03 Data 255
§12.04 Descriptive Evidence 256
§12.05 Multivariate Analysis 258
§12.06 Concluding Remarks 260

Editors' Preface

The volume presents a selection of contributions mostly from the fourteenth annual conference in commemoration of Prof Marco Biagi on *Wellbeing at and through Work* held in Modena (Italy) on 17–18 March 2016. The papers, which form the chapters in this volume, cover a number of countries and a wide range of issues in relation to quality of work and employee well-being including discrimination, harassment, disability, and work-life balance addressing them in an interdisciplinary perspective. Moreover, a number of regulatory approaches ranging from legislative interventions to voluntary measures are analysed in an attempt to cast light on the problem of well-being at work.

Certain legal problems of discrimination are highlighted by **Wendy Greene** with respect to the USA. In particular, her legal analysis is concentrated on the questionable interpretation by the courts of Title VII of the 1964 Civil Rights Act aiming to protect employees from any form of discrimination on the basis of race, colour, sex and religion. The focus of the chapter is on 'misperception discrimination' by which employees suffer discrimination based on false assumptions about their ethnic or national origin. The author draws attention to the evident discrepancies and sometimes paradoxes deriving from the courts' interpretation which may be potentially harmful for employees.

In a similar vein **Elena Gerasimova** considers the role of the national courts in shaping anti-discriminatory policies and business culture in Russia. She focuses her analysis on the impact of a landmark court ruling, *Konstantin Markin v. Russia,* which demonstrates highly controversial aspects and attitudes to this problem as well as the general weakness of international law in the face of national sovereignty and the primacy of national legislation.

Also in relation to Russia, **Nikita Lyutov** investigates the problems of discrimination legislation with particular reference to age and disability discrimination, and its compliance with the international labour standards. While highlighting a significant gap in the legislation and case law and the reasons for this lack of provisions, the author outlines some constructive ways to harmonize domestic law with international standards.

A further dimension of well-being concerning harassment at work is addressed by another Russian scholar, **Elena Sychenko**, who provides a comparative analysis of the regulatory approaches to this problem in France and Italy. By highlighting the lack of attention to this matter in Russia, the author argues that this problem is not sufficiently taken into consideration even in the European countries with a sounder anti-discrimination legislative framework.

Another crucial aspect of worker well-being linked to the conciliation of work and family life is at the centre of **Trina Jones's** analysis exploring the effects of work-life balance policies on low-wage workers in the US. The author argues that for a number of reasons these workers have limited access to such benefits compared to their higher-wage counterparts. In this regard the author provides some interesting insights into a complex question concerning advantages and disadvantages of these policies, advocating the extension of these benefits to low-wage workers.

Maddalena Cannito reflects on the use of parental leave as a means to improve employee well-being and the prospects for its more effective implementation in Italy. The author argues that legislative measures alone are likely to be insufficient and should be supported by a range of measures aimed to encourage fathers to take parental leave. Even though the research is limited to the Piedmont region, it provides useful insights into the general situation at national level in relation to parental leave, in particular paternity leave, in Italy.

The legal aspects of the regulation of part-time work as a way to allow better conciliation of work and family needs are examined by **Carla Spinelli** in light of recent Italian labour law reforms aimed at the rationalization and simplification of the regulation of non-standard employment contracts.

Again with regard to non-standard forms of employment, in particular digital work, **Marco Tufo** provides a detailed assessment of the approaches towards its legal regulation at national and international level, highlighting the advantages and disadvantages of these new forms of employment and their possible impact on employee well-being.

Marius Olivier and **Avinash Govindjee** consider the relation between disabilities and worker well-being by examining different strategies for the return to work of people with disabilities, with a focus on emerging countries such as South Africa and Malaysia. By providing a critical overview of the existing international provisions in this regard and its implementation at national level, they draw attention to the need for in-depth research into the proper adaption of these measures and best practices implemented in the developed countries to the particular institutional contexts of countries emerging on the global scene.

The chapter by **Ubaldo Macchitella** and **Giorgio Gallizioli** shows how the approaches to well-being at work may be creative and not necessarily limited to statutory provisions. In particular the authors reflect on innovative measures adopted by the European Commission for its employees within the programme *Fit@work* aiming to encourage a healthy lifestyle and to create a healthy work environment by promoting active participation in sport.

Other examples of creative approaches to well-being at work, achieved by means of partnerships between private and public welfare institutions, are outlined in the chapter by **Daniela Oliva** and **Giorgio Risso** examining two care services projects successfully implemented in Turin and Bologna. Their research brings to mind some of the experimental programmes promoted by Marco Biagi in Modena and Milan, aimed at improving the working conditions of care workers, against the backdrop of demographic changes in society with increasing numbers of individuals in the older age cohorts in need of care services in the home. Also in this instance, it is evident that Marco Biagi's research work was both innovative and far-sighted.

Finally an interesting econometric analysis of the link between mental health, well-being and unemployment is proposed by Tindara **Addabbo, Fabrizio Starace** and **Elena Sarti** in relation to Modena (Italy). The study provides a breakdown on the basis of sex, age and education considering also the effects of the economic crisis and the series of major earthquakes which took place in Modena (Italy) in May 2011.

Several of the contributions in this volume adopt a wide-ranging international and comparative perspective while others focus on more specific regional experiences, but it is evident that a common set of problems in relation to employee well-being can be identified in various countries and at different levels. One important indication that emerges from the case studies is that many problems can be solved not just through legislation, but also by means of original and creative solutions and practices that need to be properly analysed by researchers and promoted by policy-makers.

William Bromwich
Olga Rymkevich

PART I Discrimination in the Workplace

CHAPTER 1

To Be Aggrieved by "Misperception Discrimination" in the Workplace

D. Wendy Greene[*]

§1.01 INTRODUCTION

John has a caramel brown complexion, green eyes, and dark, wavy hair.[1] Since he began working for his employer, John's co-workers have consistently aimed derogatory names and comments at him. Everyday they call him a "wetback" and "an illegal," and they instruct him "to go back to Mexico." Instead of John, his co-workers call him "Juan Valdez." At least once, John also arrived to his work cubicle only to be greeted with pictures of a man named "Juan" with a noose around his neck and an attached note that reads, "Go back where you came from!" John has complained to his supervisor about his co-workers' comments and the picture depicting his lynching. He

---

* Visiting Professor of Law, University of Kentucky College of Law and Professor of Law, Cumberland School of Law at Samford University. B.A., cum laude, Xavier University of Louisiana; J.D., Tulane University Law School; LL.M., The George Washington University School of Law. Wendy.greene@samford.edu. This chapter is an excerpt from and amendment to D. Wendy Greene, *Categorically Black, White, or Wrong: "Misperception Discrimination" and the State of Title VII Protection*, 47 U. Mich. J. L. Ref. 87 (2013). Many thanks to the Fourteenth Marco Biagi Conference organizers, Professors William Bromwich, Susan Bisom Rapp, and Iacopo Senatori for the invitation to present my work during this incredible annual gathering and Professors Mario Barnes, Trina Jones, Camille Gear Rich, Terry Smith and Angela Onwuachi-Willig for their collegiality, friendship, and partnership in developing the conference panel, "Workplace Discrimination as an Occupational Injury." As always, I am especially grateful for a host of family and friends who extend unwavering support to my endeavors. Special thanks to Professor Deleso Alford, Anika Calloway, Doris Glymph Greene, Kimberly Greene, and Cheryl Réné Washington for lifting me up throughout this leg of the journey. Special thanks to Riley Murphy, J.D., for his excellent research assistance.

1. John's narrative is fictional, yet based upon a composite of actual misperception discrimination cases. *See, e.g.*, *Burrage v. FedEx Freight, Inc.*, No. 4:10-CV-2755, 2012 WL 1068794 (N.D. Ohio Mar. 29, 2012); *Daniels v. Essex Grp., Inc.*, 937 F.2d 1264 (7th Cir. 1991).

has explained, to no avail, that his co-workers are harassing him because they misperceive him to be of Mexican origin. To John's knowledge, he does not have any Mexican ancestry; he, his parents, and his grandparents have self-identified as Black,[2] non-Hispanic. Even when he reported the offensive conduct to his supervisor, his supervisor responded, "Well, you do look Mexican," and continued to call him "Juan Valdez" alongside other employees.

John believes that he is the victim of racial harassment and is thinking seriously about suing his employer for racial discrimination. Seemingly, John is experiencing what this chapter deems "categorical discrimination"—invidious, differential treatment on the basis of race or another protected characteristic[3]—and he should have a colorable claim of discrimination under Title VII of the 1964 Civil Rights Act.[4] However, a disturbing, counterintuitive development is transpiring within the federal judiciary. It is quite plausible that a court would conclude that, based upon his specific allegations of race-based invidious treatment, John *cannot* seek relief under the federal antidiscrimination laws that prohibit race discrimination in the workplace.

Though it is commonly understood that Title VII makes it unlawful for employers to treat individuals invidiously and differentially *on the basis of* race, religion, sex, national origin, and color,[5] a number of federal courts have rejected this interpretation of Title VII's scope in cases of "misperception discrimination."[6] In cases like John's, courts have imposed an "actuality requirement" for Title VII protection. According to

2. Professor Kimberlé Crenshaw has explained that "Black" deserves capitalization because "Blacks, like Asians [and] Latinos . . . constitute a specific cultural group and, as such, require denotation as a proper noun." Kimberlé Williams Crenshaw, *Race, Reform, and Retrenchment: Transformation and Legitimation in Antidiscrimination Law*, 101 Harv. L. Rev. 1331, 1332 n.2 (1988) (citing Catharine A. MacKinnon, *Feminism, Marxism, Method, and the State: An Agenda for Theory*, 7 Signs: J. Women in Culture & Soc'y 515, 516 (1982)). Additionally, Professor Neil Gotanda contends that the capitalization of Black is appropriate as it "has deep political and social meaning as a liberating term." Neil Gotanda, *A Critique of "Our Constitution is Colorblind,"* 44 Stan. L. Rev. 1, 4 n.12 (1991). I agree with both Professors Crenshaw and Gotanda, and for both reasons, throughout this article when I reference people of African descent individually and collectively, the word Black will be represented as a proper noun.
3. John could also assert claims of national origin and/or color discrimination under Title VII of the 1964 Civil Rights Act.
4. Though this article primarily addresses discrimination cases arising under Title VII, it is important to note that it is equally plausible that a plaintiff like John would not have a colorable race or national origin discrimination claim under similar federal antidiscrimination laws like §1981 of the Civil Rights Act of 1866, which has been interpreted to prohibit intentional race discrimination in the employment context. *See Leonard v. Katsinas* (a §1981 race discrimination case in which the court held that in order to maintain their lawsuit, plaintiffs would have to "prove" that they were Native American at trial).
5. *See, e.g.*, *Taken v. Okla. Corp. Comm'n*, 125 F.3d 1366, 1369 (10th Cir. 1997) ("The principal goal of Title VII is to eliminate discrimination in employment based on differences of race, color, religion, sex or national origin.") (citing *Trans World Airlines, Inc. v. Hardison*, 432 U.S. 63, 71 & n.6 (1977)); *Lightner v. City of Wilmington*, 545 F.3d 260, 264 (4th Cir. 2008) ("Title VII prohibits discrimination on the basis of specifically enumerated grounds: 'race, color, religion, sex, or national origin.' [The statute's] purpose to eliminate these invidious forms of discrimination is clear.") (citation omitted).
6. Though this Article delineates that all discrimination is the manifestation of one's perceptions, related animus, or stereotypes about the victim of discrimination, I have coined the term, "misperception discrimination," to simply refer to instances whereby the plaintiff alleges that the defendant misperceived her identity, or rather that the defendant's perceptions do not correlate

these courts, only intentional discrimination claims based upon an individual's actual protected status are cognizable under Title VII. Therefore, John can benefit from Title VII's protection against intentional race discrimination only if he is in fact of Mexican descent or if he brings forth specific allegations of invidious, differential treatment because of his Black, non-Hispanic ancestry.[7] This result is illogical and inequitable. John's case does not present claims of discrimination that are any less injurious or remediable than if he were to maintain a conventionally framed employment discrimination case in which he alleged discriminatory treatment because of his self-identified Black, non-Hispanic racial identity. Accordingly, this chapter posits that plaintiffs in misperception discrimination cases, like plaintiffs in conventionally framed cases, are asserting allegations of invidious, differential treatment on the basis of Title VII's proscribed characteristics. In other words, they have been subjected to "categorical discrimination." Thus, misperception discrimination plaintiffs are likewise entitled to statutory protection against unlawful discrimination in the workplace.

This chapter argues that courts' adoption of an actuality requirement in Title VII cases is categorically wrong. It represents a counterproductive, contrary, and disconcerting position within antidiscrimination law that, if left unexamined and unchallenged, can easily result in a wholesale lack of relief for victims of discriminatory treatment of the very nature that Congress meant to eliminate from the workplace. Moreover, in light of increased immigration, cultural diversity, interracial marriage, and transracial adoption, as well as the formal recognition of multiracial identity and more fluid self-characterizations of racial, ethnic, religious, and gender identity, claims stemming from misperceptions about the plaintiff's protected status may become as commonplace as traditional claims of discrimination based upon an individual's self-classified identity. Consequently, continued application of an actuality requirement in intentional discrimination cases not only fails to respond to these real and ongoing demographic changes in American society, but can also engender pervasive discrimination on the basis of race, religion, national origin, color, and sex in contemporary workplaces. This may leave many individuals unprotected against categorical discrimination within Title VII's meaning and reach.

Additionally, imposition of an actuality requirement in categorical discrimination cases not only inflicts obvious injury on discrimination plaintiffs but also yields

---

with the plaintiff's self-perception or self-ascribed identity, and the plaintiff suffered invidious, differential treatment stemming from the defendant's perceptions. *See infra* section 1.02[A].

7. Though less oft-discussed, one who may identify as Hispanic and/or of Mexican ancestry may also have African ancestry and therefore identify as Afro-Mexican, Afro-Chicana, Afro-Hispanic, or Afro-Latina. *See generally* Tanya Katerí Hernández, *Afro-Mexicans and the Chicano Movement: The Unknown Story*, 92 Cal. L. Rev. 1537 (2004). Therefore, classification as "Black" and "Mexican" are not mutually exclusive racial or ethnic identities. Indeed, individuals of Mexican ancestry may also have African ancestry. *See generally* Taunya Lovell Banks, *Mestizaje and the Mexican Mestizo Self: No Hay Sangre Negra, So There Is No Blackness*, 15 S. Cal. Interdisc. L.J. 199 (2006) (discussing the marginalization of Afro-Mexicans and African ancestry within the paradigm of Mexico's mixed-race or "mestizaje" identity despite Mexico's dealings with African slavery); Laura E. Gómez, *Manifest Destinies: The Making of the Mexican American Race* 50 (N.Y. Univ. Press 2007) ("During the first century of Spanish conquest of Mexico, there were about as many African slaves brought to Mexico as Spaniards who emigrated there . . . [and] [o]ver time, African slaves mixed with Spaniards, Indians, and mestizos (people of Indian and Spanish ancestry) in Mexico to produce a racially mixed population.").

unexpected repercussions for antidiscrimination law theory, policy, and praxis, which this chapter illuminates and aims to remedy. Overall, this chapter seeks to cease this narrow interpretation of antidiscrimination law generally and Title VII more specifically, which has also been employed in conventionally framed discrimination cases. Section 1.02 of this chapter briefly outlines Title VII's protections and prohibitions. Section 1.03 details the development of an express espousal of an actuality requirement in intentional discrimination cases in which plaintiffs contended that their employers' misperceptions about their race, national origin, and/or religion motivated adverse employment actions, such as harassment or termination. Section 1.03 also highlights the often unacknowledged harm of workplace discrimination—namely psychological and emotional injuries—that employees suffer regardless of whether an employer accurately or mistakenly perceives an employee's identity.

Section 1.04 investigates courts' reasoning for adopting an actuality requirement and argues that these judicial decisions are based on an unsettling misinterpretation of Title VII. Primarily, these courts have reasoned that, unlike the Americans with Disabilities Act (ADA), which expressly affords protection to individuals discriminated against because of their perceived identity, Title VII protects against discrimination because of an individual's actual identity. Yet, by adopting an actuality requirement in Title VII cases, federal courts have patently disregarded the indelible nexus between employer perception and the resulting invidious, differential treatment, a relationship that courts recognize in ADA cases. Per these courts, to recognize misperception discrimination in the Title VII context would expand statutory protection to a new class of individuals whom Congress did not intend to protect. Indeed, this chapter makes clear Title VII does not embody protected classes; any prospective, current, or former employee is protected against unlawful racial, religious, national origin, sex, or color discrimination engaged in by a covered employer.

Seemingly, the actuality requirement advanced in misperception discrimination cases also derives from a literal interpretation of the plain language of Title VII's substantive provision, which prohibits discrimination "because of *such* individual's race, sex, national origin, color, and religion."[8] More precisely, however, section 1.04 continues by positing that the development of an actuality requirement is the product of an excessively rigid application of the protected-class approach first adopted by the US Supreme Court in *McDonnell Douglas v. Green.*[9] Courts' intransigence represents a disturbing interpretative methodology that this Article terms an "anti-anticlassificationist" interpretation of Title VII. This approach rejects one of the conventionally accepted purposes of Title VII: to prohibit all decision-making on the

8. 42 U.S.C. §2000e-2(a) (2006) (emphasis added).
9. *See McDonnell Douglas Corp. v. Green*, 411 U.S. 792, 802 (1973) (holding that the plaintiff, who identified himself as Black, established the initial element of a prima facie case of intentional race discrimination by demonstrating that he belonged to a "racial minority" group). Thereafter, lower courts interpreted the initial prima facie element articulated in *McDonnell Douglas* as requiring a showing of membership within a protected class or a protected group. *See generally* Nancy Levit, *Changing Workforce Demographics and the Future of the Protected Class Approach*, 16 Lewis & Clark L. Rev. 463 (2012) (providing a critique of the protected class approach in light of demographic changes within American workplaces).

basis of Title VII's proscribed traits, whether benign or invidious, in furtherance of a norm of individual fairness.[10]

Section 1.05 unveils under-examined Fifth Circuit precedent of *EEOC v. WC & M Enterprises*[11] and EEOC guidance. Both of these precedents recognize misperception discrimination cases, reject an actuality requirement in Title VII intentional discrimination cases, and embrace the fact that subjective perceptions about a discrimination victim's protected status animate the invidious, differential treatment from which she suffers. Section 1.05[B] briefly explores the most recent Title VII cases wherein federal district courts have recognized misperception discrimination claims and the attendant harm of workplace discrimination regardless of whether the discriminatory conduct stems from an accurate or mistaken belief concerning the plaintiff's identity. Section 1.05[C] further illustrates that the harm that misperception discrimination plaintiffs suffer due to the discrimination suffered at the hands of a covered employer should be recognized and that an actuality requirement in intentional discrimination cases should cease to be adopted. In this part, the article posits that the Supreme Court in *Thompson v. North American Stainless, LP*[12] implicitly denounced a showing of actuality as a prerequisite to maintain a Title VII action. Consequently, *all* categorical discrimination plaintiffs—despite the fact that the alleged discriminatory treatment they experienced may have emanated from their self-ascribed or mistaken identity—have standing to maintain a cause of action under Title VII. In both instances, plaintiffs assert claims of discrimination clearly "within the zones of interests protected by Title VII" and are "persons aggrieved" by a covered employer's unlawful employment practices. Thus, satisfying an actuality requirement should not be required for plaintiffs in conventionally framed *or* misperception discrimination cases to vindicate their statutory rights to be free from racial, religious, color, national origin, and sex discrimination in the workplace.

§1.02 TITLE VII OF THE 1964 CIVIL RIGHTS ACT: ITS PROHIBITIONS AND PROTECTIONS

In 1964, during the heart of the modern civil rights movement, Congress enacted the Civil Rights Act, which is one of the most notable pieces of civil rights legislation to date. Title VII of the 1964 Civil Rights Act proscribes discrimination on the basis of race and color[13] and was designed to address pervasive racial discrimination in the sector of

10. Though legal academics have proposed and identified a number of perspectives appropriated by courts when interpreting Title VII and other antidiscrimination laws, the anticlassificationist and antisubordinationist approaches are largely represented within these academic debates as the chief, conventional methodologies used to interpret antidiscrimination laws. *See generally* Jack M. Balkin & Reva B. Siegel, *The American Civil Rights Tradition: Anticlassification or Antisubordination?*, 58 U. Miami L. Rev. 9 (2003).
11. 496 F.3d 393 (5th Cir. 2007).
12. 131 S. Ct. 863 (2011).
13. Civil Rights Act of 1964, Pub. L. No. 88-352, §703, 78 Stat. 241, 255 (codified as amended at 42 U.S.C. 2000e-2 (2006)).

private employment.[14] Congress also forbade discrimination based upon sex, national origin, and religion.[15] Accordingly, in Section 703(a) of Title VII, Congress made it unlawful for an employer employing twenty-five or more employees:[16]

> to fail or refuse to hire or to discharge any individual, or otherwise to discriminate against any individual with respect to his compensation, terms, conditions, or privileges of employment, because of such individual's race, color, religion, sex, or national origin; or to limit, segregate, or classify his employees or applicants for employment in any way which would deprive or tend to deprive any individual of employment opportunities or otherwise adversely affect his status as an employee, because of such individual's race, color, religion, sex, or national origin.[17]

Title VII further provides that an employer violates the Act whenever a plaintiff "demonstrates that race, color, religion, sex, or national origin was a motivating factor for any employment practice."[18] Therefore, Title VII expressly protects individuals against race, color, religion, sex, or national origin discrimination both before and during the employment relationship.[19]

Title VII also protects applicants and employees who have opposed an unlawful employment practice or participated in an investigation[20] related to such discrimination from employer retaliation.[21] Specifically, Title VII prohibits an employer from retaliating "against any of his employees or applicants for employment . . . because he has opposed any practice made an unlawful employment practice by this subchapter, or because he has made a charge, testified, assisted, or participated in any manner in

14. Juan F. Perea, *Ethnicity and Prejudice: Reevaluating "National Origin" Discrimination Under Title VII*, 35 Wm. & Mary L. Rev. 805, 806 & n.6 (1994) (citing 110 Cong. Rec. 2556 (1964) (remarks of Congressman Celler) ("You must remember that the basic purpose of Title VII is to prohibit discrimination in employment *on the basis* of race or color.") (emphasis added)).
15. Civil Rights Act §703; *see also* Perea, *supra* note 14.
16. Title VII originally defined an "employer" as any entity "engaged in an industry affecting commerce who has twenty-five or more employees for each working day in each of twenty or more calendar weeks in the current or preceding calendar year." Civil Rights Act §701, 78 Stat. at 253. This was later changed to fifteen or more employees. *See* 42 U.S.C. §2000e(b) (2006).
17. Civil Rights Act §703(a) (codified at 42 U.S.C. §2000e-2(a)).
18. 42 U.S.C. §2000e-2(m). *But see id.* §2000e-2(e) (providing that an employer does not violate Title VII when its consideration of national origin, religion, or sex in an employment decision is a "bona fide occupational qualification reasonably necessary to the normal operation of the particular business or enterprise").
19. *See Robinson v. Shell Oil Co.*, 519 U.S. 337, 346 (1997) (holding that former employees were also included under the statutory term "employees" and are thereby able to maintain an actionable retaliation against former employers who are covered under the Title VII).
20. At least five federal courts of appeals require a claimant to file a charge of discrimination with the EEOC or a similar enforcement agency or participate in investigatory proceedings before the EEOC or parallel state or local enforcement agency for the extension of protection under the participation clause. *See Abbott v. Crown Motor Co.*, 348 F.3d 537, 543 (6th Cir. 2003); *EEOC v. Total Sys. Servs., Inc.*, 221 F.3d 1171, 1174 n.2 (11th Cir. 2000); *Byers v. Dallas Morning News*, Inc. 209 F.3d 419, 428 (5th Cir. 2000); *Brower v. Runyon*, 178 F.3d 1002, 1005–07 (8th Cir. 1999); *Vasconcelos v. Meese*, 907 F.2d 111, 113 (9th Cir. 1990).
21. The Supreme Court held that an employer's action against a plaintiff constitutes unlawful retaliation when such an action is considered "materially adverse" or materially injurious or harmful to an objectively reasonable employee in the plaintiff's position. *Burlington N. & Santa Fe Ry. Co. v. White*, 548 U.S. 53, 67–73 (2006).

an investigation, proceeding, or hearing under this subchapter."[22] An individual who claims that an employer has discriminated against her because of a prohibited basis enumerated in the statute is a "person aggrieved" under Title VII and is permitted to file a charge of discrimination with the Equal Employment Opportunity Commission (EEOC).[23] If the EEOC decides not to sue the employer, Title VII permits an individual aggrieved by a prohibited employment practice to initiate a civil action against the employer.[24] Though Congress did not provide a statutory definition of a "person aggrieved," a little over a decade after Title VII's enactment, the Supreme Court made clear that Title VII was "design[ed] as a comprehensive solution for the problem of *invidious* discrimination in employment."[25] A "person aggrieved" includes, at a minimum, an individual who suffers invidious, differential treatment: (1) on the basis of Title VII's protected categories; or (2) in retaliation for protected conduct at the hands of a covered employer.[26] As this Article later demonstrates, such a person is thereby entitled to assert her statutory right to protection from discrimination on the basis of Title VII's proscribed grounds.

However, a band of federal district courts and at least one federal court of appeals have adopted an actuality requirement in Title VII cases of intentional discrimination emanating from an employer's misperceptions about the plaintiff's racial, ethnic, or religious identity.[27] By extension, this actuality requirement also applies to Title VII intentional discrimination cases on the basis of color or sex.[28] Misperception

22. 42 U.S.C. §2000e-3(a) (2006).
23. *Id.* §2000e-5(b).
24. *Id.* §2000e-5(b), (f)(1).
25. *Johnson v. Ry. Express Agency*, Inc., 421 U.S. 454, 459 (1975) (emphasis added).
26. *See Thompson v. Am. Stainless Steel*, LP, 131 S. Ct. 863, 869–70 (2011) (holding that the employee protected against retaliation need not be the applicant or the employee who opposed the discriminatory conduct or participated in a proceeding relating to alleged discrimination under Title VII); *infra* section 1.05[C].
27. *See, e.g.*, *Sears v. Jo-Ann Stores, Inc.*, No. 3:12-1322, 2014 U.S. Dist. LEXIS 58148 (M.D. Tenn. Apr. 25, 2014); *Yousif v. Landers McClarty Olathe KS*, LLC, No. 12-2788-CM, 2013 U.S. Dist. LEXIS 154504 (D. Kan. Oct. 28, 2013); *Guthrey v. Calif. Dep't of Corr. & Rehab.*, No. 1:10-CV-02177-AWI-BAM, 2012 U.S. Dist. LEXIS 89174 (E.D. Cal. Jun. 27, 2012); *Burrage v. FedEx Freight, Inc.*, No. 4:10-CV-2755, 2012 WL 1068794 (N.D. Ohio Mar. 29, 2012); *El v. Max Daetwyler Corp.*, No. 3:09-CV-415, 2011 WL 1769805 (W.D.N.C. May 9, 2011), *aff'd*, 451 Fed. App'x 257 (4th Cir. 2011); *Adler v. Evanston Nw. Healthcare Corp.*, No. 07-C-4203, 2008 WL 5272455 (N.D. Ill. Dec. 16, 2008); *Lopez-Galvan v. Mens Warehouse*, Civil No. 3:06-CV-537, 2008 WL 2705604 (W.D.N.C. Jul. 10, 2008); *Berrios v. Hampton Bays Union Free Sch. Dist.*, No. CV 02-3124, 2007 U.S. Dist. LEXIS 101366 (E.D.N.Y. Mar. 12, 2007); *Uddin v. Universal Avionics Sys. Corp.*, CIVA 1:05-CV-1115-TWT, 2006 WL 1835291 (N.D. Ga. Jun. 30, 2006); *EEOC v. WC & M Enter.*, Inc., No. Civ.A. H-04-3372, 2005 WL 2106090 (S.D. Tex. 2005), *rev'd*, 496 F.3d 393 (5th Cir. 2007); *Butler v. Potter*, 345 F. Supp. 2d 844 (E.D. Tenn. 2004); *see also McIntosh v. Ill. Dep't. of Emp't. Sec.*, No. 05-C-7044, 2007 WL 1958577 (N.D. Ill. Jul. 2, 2007) (holding that a plaintiff who was born in the United States and self-identified as African-American could not support her national origin discrimination claim on the ground that she was misperceived as Hispanic because she spoke Spanish in the workplace unless the plaintiff could demonstrate she was "actually" Hispanic since speaking Spanish did not necessarily signify her "actual" country of origin or race). Examination of available court documents and opinions reveals that the parties involved did not present the EEOC guidance on misperception discrimination to the courts, and the courts did not investigate *sua sponte* the EEOC's guidance on this issue.
28. In *Uddin v. Universal Avionics Systems Corp.*, for example, the court adopted an actuality requirement in a Title VII case alleging religious and misperception of race and national origin

discrimination plaintiffs have alleged that they suffered a hostile work environment and other adverse employment actions, such as termination, because their employers have misperceived their identities. The Supreme Court has articulated various frameworks for courts to use in such intentional discrimination cases. In *McDonnell Douglas v. Green Corp.*,[29] the US Supreme Court promulgated a tripartite analytical framework to be utilized in disparate treatment cases in which the plaintiff is unable to proffer "direct"[30] evidence or an admission from the defendant that the proscribed characteristic is the reason for the adverse employment action. According to the Supreme Court, plaintiffs can raise a rebuttable presumption of discrimination by first putting forth a prima facie case that establishes that, more likely than not, a proscribed criterion was the reason for the alleged adverse employment action.[31] In *McDonnell Douglas*, the Court held that plaintiffs could establish a prima facie case of race discrimination by demonstrating:

> (i) that he belong[ed] to a racial minority; (ii) that he applied and was qualified for a job for which the employer was seeking applicants; (iii) that, despite his qualifications, he was rejected; and (iv) that, after his rejection, the position remained open and the employer continued to seek applicants from persons of complainant's qualifications.[32]

According to *McDonnell Douglas*, once a plaintiff raises a viable prima facie case, the burden shifts to the defendant-employer to rebut the presumption of discrimination

---

discrimination. 2006 WL 1835291 at *6. The court dismissed the plaintiff's discrimination claims on the basis of race and national origin yet denied summary judgment on plaintiff's religious discrimination claim. *Id.* at *4–7. In furtherance of a prima facie actuality mandate, the *Uddin* court granted the plaintiff his day in court on the religious discrimination claim and on a color discrimination claim, which the court raised *sua sponte*. *Id.* at *7, *6 n.3. According to the court, Mr. Uddin established a presumption of color and religious discrimination because he was "in actuality" Muslim, his skin complexion was "in actuality" dark, and he was replaced by a white Christian. *Id.* at *6. In so doing, the *Uddin* court extended an actuality requirement to Title VII color discrimination claims.

29. 411 U.S. 792 (1973). *See Lapsley v. Columbia University-College of Physicians & Surgeons*, 999 F. Supp. 506, 514 (S.D.N.Y. 1998), for a discussion of the original conception for the *McDonnell Douglas* framework. In 1989, the Supreme Court developed an additional analytical framework for disparate treatment cases in *Price Waterhouse v. Hopkins*, 490 U.S. 228 (1989). Per *Price Waterhouse*, if the plaintiff proves that a protected characteristic was a substantial factor in the challenged employment action, the burden shifts to the defendant to prove that it would have made the same decision even had it not considered the protected characteristic. *Id.* at 250. After *Price Waterhouse*, Congress adopted an amended "mixed motive" analytical framework for proving disparate treatment cases. *See* Civil Rights Act of 1991, Pub. L. No. 102-166, §107, 105 Stat. 1071, 1075 (codified at 42 U.S.C. §2000e-2(m) (2006)). The plaintiff must prove that a protected characteristic was a motivating factor for the challenged employment action. *See* 42 U.S.C. §2000e-2(m). Upon a plaintiff making this showing, the defendant bears the burden of proving that it would have taken the same action even had it not considered the protected characteristic. *Id.* §2000e-5(g)(2)(B). The Supreme Court, however, has not expressly overruled *McDonnell Douglas*. Therefore, in this Article, I limit my discussion of proving discrimination via circumstantial evidence to the *McDonnell Douglas* framework.
30. "The classic notion of 'direct evidence' is evidence that, if believed, proves the ultimate question at issue *without drawing any inferences*." Michael J. Zimmer et al., *Cases and Materials on Employment Discrimination* 29 (7th ed. 2008).
31. *See McDonnell Douglas*, 411 U.S. at 802.
32. *Ibid.*

by producing, through admissible evidence, a "legitimate, nondiscriminatory reason" for the alleged adverse employment action.[33] Once the employer has produced a legitimate, nondiscriminatory reason for the adverse employment action, it is incumbent upon the plaintiff to demonstrate that the employer's alleged motivation is a pretext. That is, the plaintiff must present persuasive evidence either that the employer's asserted reason is false or that the employer's underlying motivation for the adverse employment action was, more likely than not, discriminatory.[34]

Though not expressly contemplated in Title VII's statutory language, the Supreme Court, in *Meritor Savings Bank v. Vinson*, interpreted Section 703(a) as prohibiting not only "economic" or "tangible" employment actions like a denial of benefits or termination, but also intangible employment actions such as creating a racially or religiously hostile work environment.[35] Although characterized as intentional discrimination, hostile work environment or harassment claims are not analyzed pursuant to the *McDonnell Douglas* framework. To assert an actionable hostile work environment claim under Title VII, a plaintiff must demonstrate that the discriminatory conduct is both subjectively and objectively sufficiently "severe or pervasive 'to [...] create an abusive working environment.'"[36] Therefore, the plaintiff must not only perceive the work environment as hostile or abusive, but the environment must also be one that a "reasonable person would find hostile or abusive."[37] The plaintiff must also show that the harassing conduct was unwelcome and because of a protected characteristic.[38] Some lower courts expressly require that plaintiffs demonstrate membership within a protected category.[39]

At the outset, some courts are rigidly applying the first prong, known as the "membership prong," of the aforementioned legal frameworks to hold that misperception discrimination plaintiffs are not protected under Title VII. These courts reason that the invidious, differential treatment the plaintiffs allegedly suffered was not caused by their actual identity. Implicitly, these courts are characterizing misperception discrimination plaintiffs as persons who are not aggrieved by an unlawful employment practice under the statute even though they allege that they are the intended target of

33. *Ibid.*
34. *See Tex. Dep't of Cmty. Affairs v. Burdine*, 450 U.S. 248, 254, 256 (1981) (holding that a plaintiff may succeed in an intentional discrimination case "either directly by persuading the court that a discriminatory reason more likely motivated the employer or indirectly by showing that the employer's proffered explanation is unworthy of credence"); *Reeves v. Sanderson Plumbing Prods., Inc.*, 530 U.S. 133, 147–48 (2000) ("Proof that the defendant's explanation is unworthy of credence is simply one form of circumstantial evidence that is probative of intentional discrimination. [...] [and] a plaintiff's prima facie case, combined with sufficient evidence to find that the employer's asserted justification is false, *may* permit the trier of fact to conclude that the employer unlawfully discriminated.") (emphasis added).
35. *See* 477 U.S. 57 (1986).
36. *See id.* at 67 (quoting *Henson v. City of Dundee*, 682 F.2d 897, 904 (11th Cir. 1982)).
37. *See Harris v. Forklift Sys. Inc.*, 510 U.S. 17, 21 (1991).
38. *Meritor*, 477 U.S. at 68.
39. *See, e.g., Harvil v. Westwood Comms.*, L.L.C., 433 F.3d 428, 434 (5th Cir. 2005) (requiring that a hostile work environment plaintiff demonstrate that she: (1) belongs to a protected group; (2) was subjected to unwelcome harassment; (3) experienced harassment because of a protected trait; and (4) was subjected to harassment that affected a term, condition, or privilege of employment).

discrimination on the basis of Title VII's proscribed grounds.[40] These courts have effectively concluded that such plaintiffs do not have standing to initiate a Title VII claim and cannot benefit from Title VII's protection against workplace discrimination.[41] Indeed, such an outcome is categorically wrong. It contravenes the reach and purpose of Title VII's proscriptions against religious, racial, ethnic, color, and sex discrimination, and impairs one's statutory right to be free from such workplace discrimination. Thus, the following sections critically appraise the development and negative consequences of this misinterpretation of Title VII and proffer persuasive legal precedent and EEOC prescriptions for its cessation.

§1.03 THE EVOLUTION OF AN ACTUALITY REQUIREMENT IN TITLE VII CASES

Though in the making for nearly twenty years,[42] the imposition of an actuality requirement in Title VII intentional discrimination cases is nascent. However, an actuality requirement gained momentum in the federal judiciary within the past decade in categorical discrimination cases involving misperceptions about the plaintiff's race, national origin, and religion.[43] A number of federal courts have imposed an actuality requirement in Title VII intentional race, national origin, and religious discrimination cases.[44] These courts have mandated this requirement primarily in cases of categorical discrimination that derive from an employer's misperceptions about the plaintiff's race, national origin, or religion.[45] Misperception discrimination cases expose a variety of categorical discrimination manifesting in contemporary American society[46] and

40. *See infra* section 1.03[D].
41. *See infra* section 1.05. *See also* E. Christi Cunningham, *The Rise of Identity Politics I: The Myth of the Protected Class in Title VII Disparate Treatment Cases*, 30 Conn. L. Rev. 441, 461–69 (1998) (illustrating how lower courts have applied the membership prong as a standing requirement in Title VII intentional sex, religious, and race discrimination cases).
42. *See Perkins v. Lake Cnty. Dep't of Util.*, 860 F. Supp. 1262, 1262–63 (N.D. Ohio 1994) (defendant-employer arguing that the court should adopt an actuality requirement in Title VII intentional discrimination cases based upon the notion that plaintiff did not prove successfully that he was actually Native American; therefore, the plaintiff was unable to meet a preliminary showing of protection against race and national origin discrimination under Title VII, and thus, the plaintiff could not assert an actionable discrimination claim).
43. *See* cases cited *supra* note 27; *see also Leonard v. Katsinas*, No. 05-1069, 2007 WL 1106136, at *9 (C.D. Ill. Apr. 11, 2007) (holding in a conventionally framed race discrimination case under §1981 that discrimination plaintiffs must satisfy an actuality requirement and thus prove their racial identity at trial).
44. *See* cases cited *supra* note *27*.
45. *See* cases cited *supra* note *27*; *see also* Leonard, 2007 WL 1106136, at *9 (holding in a conventionally framed race discrimination case under §1981 that discrimination plaintiffs must satisfy an actuality requirement and prove their racial identity).
46. Misperceptions about an individual's race, color, religion, sex, or national origin engender not only discrimination in the workplace but also violent hate crimes that are at times fatal. *See, e.g.*, *Martinez v. State*, 980 S.W.2d 662, 666 (Tex. App. 1998) (upholding the enhancement of the defendant's criminal sentence for capital murder under the Texas Hate Crimes Act where the defendant misperceived the minor victim as Black and such misperception motivated the defendant's victimization of the child, which caused the child's death). Moreover, based upon media reports, an individual who opened fire on Sikhs in their house of worship in Wisconsin,

workplaces that is no different in legal substance or injurious effect from the invidious, differential treatment based upon a plaintiff's self-ascribed identity alleged in conventionally framed cases. Additionally, these discrimination cases of mistaken identity foreshadow the framing of discrimination claims to come. With increased immigration, cultural diversity, interracial marriages, and transracial adoptions, as well as more formal recognition of mixed-race classifications and more fluid conceptualizations of gender, racial, and cultural identity,[47] courts will likely encounter more discrimination cases where an alleged dissonance exists between the employer's categorization of an employee and the employee's self-identification.

Fundamentally, misperception discrimination claims are not exceptional. Discrimination plaintiffs claim to suffer invidious or adverse treatment motivated by the discriminator's conscious or unconscious perceptions about their race, color, religion, sex, or national origin,[48] which are informed by personal, temporal, and broader social contexts. In conventionally framed discrimination cases, the employer's perception of the plaintiff's identity simply happens to comport with her self-perception.[49] Conversely, in misperception discrimination cases framed as instances of mistaken identity, the employer's perception of the plaintiff's protected status and the plaintiff's self-ascribed identity are at odds. Both types of discrimination cases reflect the socially constructed nature of identity classification. External perceptions of one's identity are oftentimes uncontroverted and, presumably, fixed and logical.[50] Simultaneously, external perceptions of one's identity are oftentimes contestable, seemingly illogical, and formulated independently of any awareness of an individual's self-selected identity.[51]

Nonetheless, an employer's misperception of an individual's protected status does not negate an employer's related animus, stereotyping, stigmatization, or the attendant malicious treatment. Regrettably, a number of federal courts have ignored the fact that such perceptions and the invidious, differential treatment activated by them are at the crux of intentional discrimination. This section examines *Butler v.*

---

killing six and injuring numerous others, misperceived the victims as Muslims. Though not yet confirmed, quite plausibly, the assassin's misperception motivated his targeted act of violence. *See* Samuel G. Freedman, *If the Sikh Temple Had Been a Mosque*, N.Y. Times (Aug. 10, 2012), http://www.nytimes.com/2012/08/11/us/if-the-sikh-temple-had-been-a-muslim-mosque-on-religion.html?_r=3.

47. *See* Kevin R. Johnson, *The Legacy of Jim Crow: The Enduring Taboo of Black-White Romance*, 84 Tex. L. Rev. 739, 739–40 (2006) (positing that the increase in interracial relationships and the growing acceptance of interracial intimacy, mixed-race identity, and transracial adoption over the past half-century have drastically altered "notions about race and races"; as a result, "racial mixture promises to transform the entire civil rights agenda in the United States"). *See generally* Levit, *supra* note 9.
48. *See, e.g.*, *Wal-Mart Stores, Inc. v. Dukes*, 131 S. Ct. 2541, 2548 (2011) (clarifying that the "basic theory of [the class action plaintiffs in their Title VII intentional sex discrimination case] is that a strong and uniform 'corporate culture' permits bias against women to infect, perhaps subconsciously, the discretionary decisionmaking of each of Wal-Mart's managers").
49. *See, e.g.*, *Price Waterhouse v. Hopkins*, 490 U.S. 228 (1989); *McDonnell Douglas Corp. v. Green*, 411 U.S. 792 (1973).
50. *See infra* section 1.03[D].
51. *See infra* note 208.

Potter:[52] the first reported Title VII misperception discrimination case wherein a federal district court expressly adopted an actuality requirement. The second, a more recent case, *Burrage v. FedEx Freight, Inc.*,[53] marks an intractable formation of the actuality requirement in Title VII jurisprudence and illuminates the under-appreciation of the psychological and emotional harms of intentional discrimination regardless of whether it emanates from an employer's accurate or mistaken perception of an employee's identity.

[A] Express Adoption of an Actuality Requirement

[1] Butler v. Potter

Butler v. Potter is the first reported case wherein a federal district court expressly held that a showing of actuality was required for Title VII protection against categorical discrimination.[54] In *Butler v. Potter*, a former carrier with the US Postal Service, Jesse Butler, who identified as a "white, Caucasian"[55] male, alleged, among other claims, that his supervisor harassed him on the basis of race or national origin in violation of Title VII.[56] According to Mr. Butler, his supervisor "accused" him of being "Arab, Indian or Middle Eastern" because of his facial features—namely, his "prominent nose"[57]—and harassed him accordingly.[58] With only a passing reference to Title VII's substantive provision, Section 703(a), the court endorsed the legal argument of the US government[59] that "Title VII protects those persons that belong to a protected class, and says nothing about protection of persons who are *perceived* to belong to a protected

52. 345 F. Supp. 2d 844 (E.D. Tenn. 2004).
53. No. 4:10-CV-2755, 2012 WL 1068794 (N.D. Ohio Mar. 29, 2012).
54. *Butler v. Potter*, 345 F. Supp. 2d 844 (E.D. Tenn. 2004).
55. *Butler*, 345 F. Supp. 2d at 846.
56. *Ibid.*
57. *Id.* at 850. *See generally* D. Wendy Greene, *Title VII: What's Hair (and Other Race-Based Characteristics) Got to Do With It?*, 79 U. Colo. L. Rev. 1355, 1365–66 (illustrating that an individual's physical characteristics, like skin color, cranial structure, and the shape of one's nose or lips, have been racialized historically and contemporarily).
58. *Butler*, 345 F. Supp. 2d at 846.
59. In this case, attorneys with the US Department of Justice, Office of US Attorney in Knoxville, Tennessee, represented the Postmaster General of the United States Postal Service in his representative capacity. *See id.* at 846. Interestingly, governmental attorneys for two federal agencies during the George W. Bush administration played a critical role in developing conflicting jurisprudence on the issue of whether a showing of actuality is required for Title VII intentional discrimination cases involving misperceptions about the plaintiff's protected status. In 2004, in *Butler v. Potter*, the US Department of Justice argued successfully for the imposition of an actuality requirement in an intentional race/national origin discrimination case under Title VII. In 2007, the EEOC argued successfully before the Fifth Circuit in *EEOC v. WC & M Enterprises* that actuality is not required for Title VII protection against intentional national origin discrimination emanating from an employer's misperceptions about the plaintiff's ethnic identity. *See infra* section 1.05[A].

class."[60] In so holding, the court also summarily adopted the federal government's legal reasoning. The court declared that discrimination in Title VII cases would not be conceptualized by the court as a phenomenon animated by employer perception: "Congress has shown, through [...] the Americans with Disabilities Act, that it knows how to enact legislation that protects persons who are wrongly perceived to be in a protected class."[61] The court further intimated that since neither Mr. Butler nor the federal government proffered controlling legal precedent that expressly recognized a perception theory of discrimination in the Title VII context, it was obligated to hold that Butler's misperception discrimination claim was not actionable.[62]

Seemingly, the *Butler* court was amenable to forgoing a showing of actuality had the litigants presented persuasive or controlling legal authority to this effect.[63] Nonetheless, since *Butler*, a number of federal district courts have expressly adopted an actuality requirement in categorical discrimination cases involving allegations of misperceptions about the plaintiff's religion, race, or national origin, and one federal court of appeals has sanctioned this prerequisite for statutory protection.[64] In doing so, most courts have simply rehashed the reasoning the *Butler* court advanced.[65] For example, in *Lewis v. North General Hospital*, a federal district court in New York held that a plaintiff's Title VII case failed as a matter of law where an employer allegedly discriminated against the plaintiff based upon his misperceived religious identity.[66] Citing to *Butler* for support, the *Lewis* court proclaimed: "protections of Title VII do not extend to persons who are *merely* perceived to belong to a protected class."[67]

More recent misperception discrimination cases[68] reveal a more intractable disposition. Indeed, in the case discussed next, *Burrage v. FedEx Freight, Inc.*,[69] a federal district court in the Northern District of Ohio went to great lengths to ensconce an actuality requirement for categorical discrimination plaintiffs.

60. *Butler*, 345 F.Supp.2d at 850 (citation omitted). Defense counsel also supported its argument for an actuality requirement (and thus disavowal of a perception theory in the Title VII context) by referencing the Rehabilitation Act of 1973, which preceded the Americans with Disabilities Act (ADA) in proscribing disability discrimination. *See ibid.*
61. *Ibid.*
62. *Ibid.*
63. *Ibid.* (noting that neither plaintiff nor defendant put forth controlling authority that legitimates a holding that Title VII embraces a perception theory like the ADA and thus does not require a showing of actuality in intentional discrimination cases).
64. *See* cases cited *supra* note 27.
65. *See Adler v. Evanston Nw. Healthcare Corp.*, No. 07-C-4203, 2008 WL 5272455, at *4 (N.D. Ill. Dec. 16, 2008); *Lopez-Galvan v. Mens Warehouse*, Civil No. 3:06-CV-537, 2008 WL 2705604, at *7 (W.D.N.C. Jul. 10, 2008); *McIntosh v. Ill. Dep't. of Emp't. Sec.*, No. 05-C-7044, 2007 WL 1958577, at *5 (N.D. Ill. Jul. 2, 2007); *Leonard v. Katsinas*, No. 05-1069, 2007 WL 1106136, at *8 (C.D. Ill. Apr. 11, 2007); *Uddin v. Universal Avionics Sys. Corp.*, No. 1:05-CV-1115-TWT, 2006 WL 1835291, at *6 (N.D. Ga. Jun. 30, 2006); *EEOC v. WC & M Enter., Inc.*, No. Civ.A. H-04-3372, 2005 WL 2106090, at *4 (S.D. Tex. 2005) *rev'd*, 496 F.3d 393 (5th Cir. 2007).
66. 502 F. Supp. 2d 390, 401 (S.D.N.Y. 2007).
67. *Ibid.* (emphasis added).
68. *See, e.g., Burrage v. FedEx Freight, Inc.*, No. 4:10-CV-2755, 2012 WL 1068794 (N.D. Ohio Mar. 29, 2012); *El v. Max Daetwyler Corp.*, No. 3:09-CV-415, 2011 WL 1769805, at *5–6 (W.D.N.C. May 9, 2011).
69. *Burrage*, 2012 WL 1068794.

[2] Burrage v. FedEx Freight, Inc.

Born of an African-American father and a white mother,[70] Nathaniel Burrage claimed that his supervisors and several co-workers at FedEx harassed him because they misperceived him as Mexican.[71] According to Burrage, for approximately three years his supervisor and co-workers referred to him as Mexican and "cheap labor" in a "derogatory and pervasive manner" and directed the Spanish terms "Andale, Andale" and "Arriba, Arriba" toward him.[72] Burrage alleged that after informing his supervisor of his Black and white parentage, Burrage's supervisor retorted that he "looked Mexican."[73] Burrage claimed that he attempted to explain that being called Mexican offended him because one of his ex-girlfriends requested that he deny to her family that he was Black and pretend to be Mexican.[74] His supervisor laughed at his account and continued to call him Mexican.[75]

Burrage also alleged that, on one occasion, FedEx dockworkers pointedly questioned him about the veracity of a dehumanizing graffiti statement on a trailer that read, "Mexicans were 'proof that American Indians had sex with buffalos.'"[76] Burrage also claimed that one day after greeting one of his supervisors, the supervisor replied, "I don't talk to Mexicans."[77] According to Burrage, he complained to supervisory level FedEx employees, including the supervisor who allegedly called him "Mexican" on several occasions and told Burrage that he did not speak to Mexicans, about the race-based references aimed at him by both supervisors and co-workers.[78] In doing so, he confided that their conduct left him feeling "degraded," "embarrassed and [a]shamed," and disinterested in working.[79]

Burrage filed a Title VII claim against FedEx, alleging that he suffered harassment on the basis of his race and/or color.[80] The court granted FedEx's summary judgment motion on several grounds.[81] First, like the *Butler* court, the *Burrage* court reasoned that Burrage failed to satisfy a prima facie element of a Title VII intentional race discrimination claim, which required actual membership within the racial group of which the harassers perceived the plaintiff to be a member.[82] In other words, since

70. *Id.* at *2 n. 2.
71. *Id.* at *1–2.
72. *Id.* at *1–2, *4.
73. *Id.* at *1–2.
74. *Ibid.*
75. *Ibid.*
76. *Id.* at *2.
77. *Id.* at *3.
78. *Id.* at *2.
79. *Ibid.*
80. *Id.* at *1. Burrage also filed a complaint pursuant to Ohio state law. *Ibid.*
81. *See id.* at *8–9 (holding that Burrage failed to demonstrate a basis for employer liability because he did not satisfy an actuality requirement, he did not notify sufficiently the employer of alleged racial harassment, and he failed to take advantage of the reporting process outlined in the employer's anti-harassment policy of which he was aware).
82. Burrage did not satisfy the first element of a hostile work environment claim within this jurisdiction. Per the court, an employee asserting that he suffered a hostile work environment on the basis of race or color in violation of Title VII must first establish that "he is a *member of a protected class*." *Id.* at *4. (emphasis added).

Burrage was not actually Mexican as his co-workers and supervisors allegedly perceived him to be, he could not satisfy a prima face case of race discrimination. Indeed, the court held that "Title VII protects only those who are *actually* in a protected class, and not those who are *perceived* to be in a protected class."[83] The court further pronounced that "[c]laims based on perceived class membership are not legally viable under Title VII, and the Court *will not expand* the reach of Title VII to cover that which Congress *chose* not to protect."[84]

According to the court, Burrage did not present an actionable Title VII race discrimination claim because none of the "alleged harassing events were based upon his race (African-American) or had a racial character or purpose."[85] The *Burrage* court reasoned:

> [a]t best, the references to Burrage as "the Mexican" and "cheap labor," and the use of the Spanish terms "andale" and "ariba," [sic] represent the very unfortunate employment of offensive stereotypes of Hispanics, and can be said to arise out of a misperception that Burrage was of Hispanic descent; or at worst, they amount to incomprehensible name calling. They cannot *reasonably* be considered to have referred to the fact that Burrage's race was African-American or that his skin color was brown.[86]

Therefore, the court did not simply impose an actuality requirement on plaintiffs in order to receive statutory protection and ensure that an employer's invidious, differential treatment of the plaintiff on Title VII's proscribed bases would be deemed remediable. It cemented an artificial line between protection and non-protection under Title VII by holding that the discrimination that one suffers does not become actionable until the discriminatory treatment corresponds with her actual protected status. Indeed, the court expressly held that Burrage's racial harassment claim failed because "Burrage [did not] maintain that his supervisors and co-workers began to use any terms that were . . . related to his status as an African-American, *upon learning of his true race*."[87]

By the court's reasoning, only if Burrage were in fact Mexican or began suffering derogatory comments or references related to his self-ascribed and self-reported racial identity as biracial or Black would the court recognize Burrage's statutory right to be free from racial harassment.[88] Instead of being called "Mexican," "cheap labor," and having "andale," and "arriba" directed at him in a deprecating manner by supervisors and co-workers, Burrage would have to put forth allegations that he was called pejorative terms alluding to his self-ascribed racial identity, like "zebra,"[89]

83. *Id.* at *5. (emphasis added).
84. *Id.* at *8. (emphasis added).
85. *Id.* at *5. Notably, the court classified Burrage as African American rather than mixed-race although Burrage self-identified as Black and mixed-race. *Id.* at *1, *6.
86. *Id.* at *6. (emphasis added). Logically, one may question whether courts will begin deciphering which racially derogatory terms are associated with a particular racial group.
87. *Id.* at *8 n. 8 (emphasis added).
88. Based upon Burrage's self-identification.
89. *See Madison v. IBP, Inc.*, 149 F. Supp. 2d 730, 752 (S.D. Iowa 1999), for a race discrimination suit brought under Title VII, §1981, and a state antidiscrimination law in which a white female

"Euronigger,"[90] "half-breed,"[91] "Buckwheat,"[92] "nigger,"[93] or "monkey."[94] Alternatively, according to the court, Burrage could only benefit from Title VII's protection against a racially hostile work environment once the employer uncovered his mixed-race heritage and subjected him to dehumanizing graffiti in the workplace that specifically targeted interracial Black-white relationships, biracial children, and/or Blacks more generally, rather than the dehumanizing graffiti about individuals of Mexican ancestry (who may or may not be of African descent).[95]

The court displayed an equally myopic and intransigent adherence to an actuality requirement in its analysis of Burrage's color discrimination claim. The court acknowledged the plausibility of FedEx employees aiming "offensive stereotypes of Hispanics"[96] at Burrage because of their "misperception that Burrage was of Hispanic descent."[97] Remarkably, however, the court concluded that his being called "Mexican" in a racially subordinating manner and being subjected to offensive stereotypes about Hispanics could not "reasonably be considered to have referred to the fact that [...] his skin color was brown."[98]

First, in failing to acknowledge the obvious nexus between Burrage's theories of race and color discrimination, the court held that Burrage's Title VII color discrimination claim was not actionable because the alleged remarks of Burrage's

plaintiff contended that she endured racial insults aimed at her marriage to a Black man and their children, whom a co-worker called "zebras," "monkeys" and "fucking nigger babies."

90. *See, e.g., Moore v. Bd. of Educ.*, 300 F. Supp. 2d 641, 643 & n. 2 (N.D. Ill. 2004) (minor plaintiff who self-identified as "African American and Caucasian" asserting a denial of equal protection under the Fourteenth Amendment because a public school high school teacher allegedly made several public, racially discriminatory comments related to plaintiff's biracial identity, which included calling him "Euronigger").

91. *See Wheaton v. North Oakland Medical Center*, 130 F. App'x 773, 777 (6th Cir. 2005), for a Title VII race discrimination case in which a white female plaintiff supported her hostile work environment claim with testimony that co-workers made insulting comments about her long-term relationship with a Black man and that a co-worker called their daughter a "half breed."

92. *See Daniels v. Essex Group, Inc.*, 937 F.2d 1264, 1266 (7th Cir. 1991), for a Title VII race-based hostile work environment case in which a Black male plaintiff testified that his co-workers nicknamed him "Buckwheat."

93. *See, e.g., id.* at 1267 (Black male plaintiff testifying during the trial of his Title VII race-based hostile work environment case that his co-worker called him "nigger" and "dumb nigger"). As seen in *Madison v. IBP, Inc.*, this pejorative term unfortunately has been used to demean individuals racialized as non-white more generally, as a co-worker of a race discrimination plaintiff called the plaintiff's children, who were of Black and white parentage, "niggers." 149 F. Supp. 2d at 752.

94. *See Madison*, 149 F. Supp. 2d at 752 (race discrimination plaintiff contending that co-worker called her biracial children "monkeys").

95. *But see Daniels*, 937 F.2d at 1268 (Seventh Circuit affirming that a racial harassment claim can be supported by racially offensive comments not aimed at a plaintiff's or a co-worker's "actual" race in light of evidence proffered that plaintiff's co-worker, Randy Heron, was called "Reinaldo Gonzalez" because he "looked Mexican" and that "Reinaldo" was scrawled on a wall in the workplace alongside references to the Ku Klux Klan).

96. *Id.* at *6.

97. *Ibid.*

98. *Ibid.*

co-workers and supervisors did not have a "color-related character or purpose."[99] According to the court's reasoning, Burrage needed to proffer express statements of FedEx employees that his skin color rather than his general physical appearance (which plausibly encompasses his skin color) spawned the comments "andale," "arriba," "cheap labor," and "Mexican," as well as his supervisor's persisting belief that Burrage "looked Mexican." Moreover, although the court expressly recognized the often indistinguishable nature of race and national origin discrimination,[100] it depicted Burrage's Title VII case as one "where issues of national origin and race are [not] so intertwined that it is difficult to separate the two for purposes of analysis."[101] The court characterized Burrage's hostile work environment case as one of national origin discrimination, deeming it "a separate and distinct form of discrimination" from race or color discrimination.[102] In the court's estimation, the alleged comments directed at Burrage were unequivocally based upon national origin and not upon race or color.[103] Consequently, the court held that Burrage could not "recast a national origin claim into one of race or color."[104] The court criticized Burrage's quite cogent argument that "'but for' his skin color, he would not have been perceived as Mexican or Hispanic,"[105] as "circular logic." Meanwhile, the court itself engaged in flawed reasoning in order to circle back to and fortify its initial decree: "Title VII protects only those who are *actually* in a protected class."[106] The court would not recognize categorical discrimination cases emanating from an employer's misperceptions about a plaintiff's race, color, or national origin under Title VII unless Congress commanded the court to do so.

In light of its express actuality requirement, it appears that the court strategically framed Burrage's race and color discrimination claims as theoretically distinguishable from his claim of national origin discrimination in order to effectively render Burrage's hostile work environment claim irremediable under Title VII. To present an actionable Title VII claim of national origin discrimination, Burrage would have to undermine his allegations and, once again, satisfy a superfluous condition by demonstrating that he was actually of Mexican descent. What if Burrage or a like plaintiff uncovered during the litigation of his employment discrimination case that he descended from Mexican ancestors or discovered that he was adopted and that his natural mother or father was of Mexican descent?[107] What if his supervisors also began aiming derogatory comments

---

99. *See id.* at *5 (contrasting Burrage's allegations with the aphorism "the blacker the berry, the sweeter the juice" proffered in support of a Title VII color discrimination claim that survived summary judgment).
100. *See id.* at *7 (acknowledging that discrimination on the basis of national origin or race "certainly overlap").
101. *Ibid.*
102. *See id.* at *6 ("[C]omments supporting one type of discrimination can[not] provide the sole support for a claim for a separate and distinct form of discrimination.").
103. *See id.* at *7 (cursorily citing to federal court opinions in Title VII discrimination cases as support for its treatment of race, national origin, and color discrimination as unrelated, discrete concepts).
104. *Ibid.*
105. *Ibid.*
106. *Id.* at *5. (emphasis added).
107. *See*, for example, *Wood v. Freeman Decorating Services, Inc.*, No. 3:08-CV-00375-LRH-RAM, 2010 WL 653764, at *4-5 (D. Nev. Feb. 19, 2010), for a Title VII intentional race/national

at Burrage related to his Black or multiracial identity or making deprecating references about his skin color? According to the court's holding and rationale, such ancestral evidence and offensive comments could magically transform non-cognizable claims of national origin, race, or color discrimination into cognizable claims of discrimination under Title VII.

Such a line of demarcation between statutory protection and non-protection is nonsensical and contrived. There is no plausible reason for the court to protect Burrage against a racially hostile work environment if the employer repeatedly called him a "half-breed" or "Buckwheat" rather shouting at him "andale" in a demeaning way or calling him "cheap labor" Likewise, there is no reason for a court to extend Title VII protection to an employee who self-identifies as Hispanic and whom an employer calls "cheap labor" and directs "andale" or "arriba" in a derogatory manner but to fail to extend the same protection to Burrage who suffers the same invidious treatment in the workplace.

[3] Burrage II

Following this grant of summary judgment in favor of FedEx, Burrage sought the court's reconsideration of its opinion. However, in *Burrage II,* the federal district court affirmed its holding, categorizing Burrage's allegations of discrimination as mere "teasing." According to the court:

> [i]f anything, the fact that [Burrage's] supervisors and co-workers continued to employ the same ethnic slurs after plaintiff disavowed them of the notion that he was Mexican takes [his] evidence even further beyond the protections of Title VII, as it amounts to mere teasing. [S]imple teasing, offhand comments, and isolated incidents (unless extremely serious) will not amount to discriminatory changes in the terms and conditions of employment.[108]

In *Burrage II,* the court completely dismissed Burrage's claims that he felt feeling "degraded," "embarrassed and [a]shamed," and disinterested in working[109]--all common psychological harms resulting from workplace discrimination. Numerous studies have confirmed that employees who are the victims of employment discrimination are at "increased risk for work-related injury or illness" than those employees who are not the targets of an employer's harassment and/or those employees who witness workplace discrimination.[110] For example, a number of studies have concluded that

---

origin discrimination case in which the plaintiff maintained that he began to self-identify as Native American after his adopted mother informed him that his biological parents were Native American though his birth certificate classified him as white and he self-classified as white and as Hispanic at earlier points in his life. *See also* Defendant's Motion to Dismiss, *Wood v. Freeman Decorating Servs., Inc.*, No. 3:08-CV-00375-LRH-RAM, 2009 WL 4836455 (D. Nev. Jul. 30, 2009).

108. *Burrage v. FedEx Freight, Inc.*, 2012 WL 6732005 *4 (N.D. Ohio Dec. 28, 2012).

109. *Ibid.*

110. Cassandra A. Okechukwu, Kerry Souza, Kelly D. Davis, and A. Butch de Castro, *Discrimination, Harassment, Abuse, and Bullying in the Workplace: Contribution of Workplace Injustice to Occupational Health Disparities*, 57 Am. J. Ind. Med. 573 (2014) (page 7 of author

"perceived discrimination is related to well-being, or lack of it such as life [and job] satisfaction, chronic health problems, psychological distress, depression, and generalized anxiety."[111] Indeed, episodes of racial discrimination that include "focal events involving battery or public humiliation may provide the significant life event precipitating Posttraumatic Stress Disorder (PTSD)."[112] Moreover, victims of workplace discrimination may suffer other serious psychological injuries like acute stress disorder,[113] panic disorder,[114] agoraphobia,[115] and somatoform disorder[116] especially where they "must tolerate a hostile work environment over a protracted time."[117] A more recent national origin misperception discrimination case, *Arsham v. Mayor & City Council of Baltimore*,[118] illustrates the harmful consequences of workplace discrimination regardless of whether the differential treatment is based upon an employer's mistaken or accurate perception of the employee's identity. Ms. Arsham, who identified as Persian, alleged that her supervisor misperceived her as a being a member of the Parsee ethnic group, which according to Arsham is an ethnic group originating in India and considered to be one of the lower castes of Indian ethnic groups.[119] While expressing his disdain for Parsees, her supervisor relayed to her his belief that she was a Parsee.[120] Though he did not aim racial epithets at Arsham, he treated her more harshly and less favorably than her colleagues because of his misperception of her ethnic identity and associated animus. According to Arsham, her supervisor disciplined her every time she requested leave, treated her absences from work as unpaid leave dissimilarly to her colleagues, and yelled at her during meetings.[121] Arsham also alleged that her supervisor denied her permission to visit project sites and did not invite her to project meetings wherein information shared was within the scope of her

manuscript) (reporting studies that "found observing [workplace injustice like bullying and sexual harassment] was linked to poor psychological well-being [of employees who were not the targets of the workplace injustice], even after controlling for one's own experiences.").

111. Tyrone A. Forman, *The Social Psychological Costs of Racial Segmentation in the Workplace: A Study of African Americans' Well-Being*, 44 J. of Health and Social Behavior 332, 333 (2003).
112. Jane Goodman-Delahunty and William E. Foote, *Compensation for Pain, Suffering and Other Psychological Injuries: The Impact of Daubert on Employment Discrimination Claims*, 13 Behavioral Sciences and the Law 183, 194 (1995).
113. When a person experiences dissociative symptoms, e.g., feeling "as if he or she is an observer to the events rather than a participant." *Id.* at 192.
114. When a person "develop[s] an overwhelming fear of particular situations." Employees who are the victims of discrimination may experience "panic attacks with a full range of physical symptoms [that] may arise when the person approaches the workplace or even enters the car to go to work." *Id.* at 193.
115. "Agoraphobia may be diagnosed if the panic disorder becomes so pervasive that the employee is unable to leave home." *Id.* at 193.
116. When "a worker copes with stress [resulting from workplace discrimination] by developing multiple physical symptoms [...] which may intensify with the duration of the stress and exacerbate following significant events." *Id.* at 194.
117. *See id.* at 193.
118. 85 F.Supp.3d 841 (D. Md. 2015).
119. *Id.* at 844.
120. *Ibid.*
121. *Id.* at 844–45.

responsibilities and critical to her professional success.[122] Additionally, the Human Resources Manager was instructed to monitor only Arsham's time and a junior colleague was assigned to approve Arsham's requests for leave when her supervisor was not present.[123] Lastly, management called in security personnel to monitor events where Arsham was present despite claims that she had not exhibited violent behavior.[124] Overall, Arsham complained that her supervisor sought to "sabotage her efforts at [professional] success" because of her gender and perceived ethnic identity yet he did not exhibit the same behavior toward her co-workers.[125] Arsham explained that the ethnic and gender-based discrimination she suffered at the hands of her supervisor engendered feelings of humiliation, embarrassment, and severe emotional distress (of which her employer was made aware by her psychologist), ultimately resulting in a suicide attempt six months prior to termination of her employment.[126]

Despite the serious psychological injuries that can result from being the target of workplace discrimination, it is not uncommon for courts to categorize in particular derogatory and subordinating racialized comments in the workplace as harmless, playful jokes that cannot amount to actionable intentional discrimination, as seen in the court's ultimate holding in *Burrage II:*

> [w]hen considered in a light most favorable to plaintiff, the evidence only shows that Jamiot teased him initially because he may have perceived Burrage to be Hispanic, and later Jamiot and others in the workplace teased Burrage because they found it funny that someone would want to introduce him as Mexican, or that they simply thought it was funny to compare him to Mexicans. This evidence fails to demonstrate a triable issue over whether Burrage was subjected to a hostile workplace on the basis of his race and/or color.[127]

In so doing, the court focused more on the *court's perception* of the intent of Burrage's supervisor and co-workers and simply disregarded Burrage's claims that he did not experience his supervisor's and employee's targeted, racialized treatment as "funny" or mere "teasing," but rather as humiliating, stigmatizing and depressing.[128] Consequently, the *Burrage* court sends a signal to employers that they need not respect their employees' requests *to management* that they cease subjecting the employee to conduct implicating her race or ethnicity, which the employee finds not only offensive but also injurious to her emotional and psychological well being. Indeed, ["b]y condoning less than egregious forms of humiliation,"[129] the decision and reasoning of

122. *Ibid.*
123. *Id.* at 844.
124. *Id.* at 845.
125. *Ibid.* Arsham alleged unlawful national origin and sex discrimination under Title VII and Maryland antidiscrimination laws. She also brought claims of intentional and/or negligent infliction of emotional distress under state law. *Id.* at 841.
126. *Id.* at 845.
127. *Burrage*, 2012 WL 6732005, at *4.
128. *See* D. Wendy Greene, *Title VII: What's Hair (and Other Race-Based Characteristics Got to do With It?*, 79 U. Colo. L. Rev. 1355, 1376 (2008) (arguing that in intentional race discrimination cases courts should shift the concentration from an employer's intent to the stigmatizing effects of an employer's conduct on the plaintiff).
129. Catherine L. Fisk, *Humiliation at Work*, 8 William & Mary J. of Women and L. 73, 73 (2001).

the court exemplify the way in which "the law systematically underestimates the corrosive effect of workplace humiliation."[130]

§1.04 TOWARDS UNITY: THE METHODS BEHIND THE ACTUALITY MADNESS

Section 1.03 described the development of the actuality requirement imposed in Title VII intentional discrimination cases and the harms of workplace discrimination that are often dismissed and underappreciated. This section argues that such courts' interpretative methodology in cases of categorical discrimination marks the arrival of a peculiar "anti-anticlassificationist" interpretation of Title VII, an intransigent statutory reading that negates express legislative objectives and conventional understandings of the meaning and scope of antidiscrimination law. This section explores the myriad underlying justifications for this anti-anticlassificationist interpretation adopted in misperception discrimination cases.

[A] Nothing Borrowed: Courts' Refusal to Apply the ADA's Perception Theory to the Title VII Context

Without exploring Title VII's purpose or meaning or even referencing the EEOC's express guidance on misperception discrimination,[131] a band of federal district courts and one federal appellate court have concluded that cases involving invidious, differential treatment motivated by an employer's misperceptions about an employee's race, religion, or national origin (and by extension, color or sex) are beyond Title VII's scope.[132] Moreover, these courts did not acknowledge the fact that the alleged invidious, differential treatment the plaintiffs experienced is inherently connected to the defendant-employer's perceptions of the plaintiffs' racial, ethnic, or religious identity or status.[133] Notably, in these intentional discrimination cases, the focal point for courts when adopting an actuality requirement (and rejecting a perception theory of discrimination) is an antidiscrimination statute Congress enacted nearly three decades *after* Title VII, the Americans with Disabilities Act (ADA).[134] The recurring, express justification that courts proffer for imposing an actuality requirement is a facial

130. *Id.* at 73.
131. *See infra* section 1.05[A].
132. *See, e.g., Burrage v. FedEx Freight, Inc.*, No. 4:10-CV-2755, 2012 WL 1068794, at *5-6 (N.D. Ohio Mar. 29, 2012); *El v. Max Daetwyler Corp.*, No. 3:09-CV-415, 2011 WL 1769805, at *5-6 (W.D.N.C. May 9, 2011) *aff'd*, 451 Fed. App'x 257 (4th Cir. 2011); *Adler v. Evanston Nw. Healthcare Corp.*, No. 07-C-4203, 2008 WL 5272455, at *4 (N.D. Ill. Dec. 16, 2008); *Lopez-Galvan v. Mens Warehouse*, Civil No. 3:06-CV-537, 2008 WL 2705604, at *7 (W.D.N.C. Jul. 10, 2008); *McIntosh v. Ill. Dep't. of Emp't. Sec.*, No. 05-C-7044, at *5 (N.D. Ill. Jul. 2, 2007); *Uddin v. Universal Avionics Sys. Corp.*, CIVA 1:05-CV-1115-TWT, 2006 WL 1835291, at *6 (N.D. Ga. Jun. 30, 2006); *EEOC v. WC & M Enter., Inc.*, No. Civ.A. H-04-3372, 2005 WL 2106090, at *4 (S.D. Tex. 2005) *rev'd*, 496 F.3d 393 (5th Cir. 2007).
133. *See infra* sections 1.03[A] and 1.03[C].
134. Americans with Disabilities Act of 1990, Pub. L. No. 101-336, 104 Stat. 327 (codified as amended at 42 U.S.C. §§12101-12213 (2012)).

difference among the substantive provisions of the Americans with Disabilities Act and Title VII of the 1964 Civil Rights Act.[135]

In 1990, Congress enacted the Americans with Disabilities Act to respond to the discrimination that disabled individuals experienced in the American workplace as well as the lack of access in places of public accommodation.[136] With the ADA, Congress expressly covered claims stemming from misperceptions about an individual. The Act made it unlawful for employers to discriminate against individuals whom they "regard[ed] as" disabled even if they did not suffer an actual disability.[137] In 2008, Congress further enacted the ADA Amendments Act (ADAAA) with the express purpose of ensuring that courts construe "the definition of disability [...] in favor of broad coverage of individuals [...] to the maximum extent permitted."[138] Like the ADA, the ADAAA prohibits covered employers[139] from discriminating against an individual who has an actual disability, a record of a disability, or who is regarded as having a disability.[140]

As outlined in section 1.01, Title VII does not expressly include "regarded as" language in its substantive provision like the ADA. Instead, Title VII prohibits covered employers from discriminating against an individual "because of *such individual's* race, color, religion, sex, or national origin."[141] Accordingly, courts have reasoned that since the ADA expressly includes a "regarded as" or perception theory of discrimination in its substantive provision and Title VII does not, discrimination claims based upon an employer's misperception about the plaintiff's race, national origin, religion (and, by extension, color and sex) are not cognizable under Title VII.

Yet, in their groundbreaking article, *By Any Other Name?: On Being "Regarded as" Black and Why Title VII Should Apply Even If Lakisha and Jamal are White*, Professors Angela Onwuachi-Willig and Mario Barnes argue that if courts viewed the substantive provisions in the ADA and Title VII as mutually reinforcing rather than distinct concepts, a more precise and nuanced understanding of the operation of discrimination

135. *See Leonard v. Katsinas*, No. 05-1069, 2007 WL 1106136, at *12 (C.D. Ill. Apr. 11, 2007) (distinguishing the plain language of §1981 and the ADA to hold that the plaintiffs must prove their "actual" race at trial in order to maintain their §1981 race discrimination claim). Accordingly, the adoption of the actuality requirement is not limited to the Title VII context and thus implicates the available federal protection against race discrimination and quite plausibly broader state level protection under antidiscrimination statutes that mirror the plain language of Title VII's substantive provision.

136. Americans with Disabilities Act §2, 104 Stat. at 328–29 (codified as amended at 42 U.S.C. §12101).

137. *Id.* §3, 104 Stat. at 329–30 (codified as amended at 42 U.S.C. §12102).

138. ADA Amendments Act of 2008, Pub. L. No. 110-325, §§2–4, 122 Stat. 3553, 3553–56 (codified at 42 U.S.C. §§12101–02).

139. The ADA defines an "employer" as a "a person engaged in an industry affecting commerce who has fifteen or more employees for each working day in each of twenty or more calendar weeks in the current or preceding calendar year, and any agent of such person." Americans with Disabilities Act §101, 104 Stat. at 330 (codified as amended at 42 U.S.C. §12111).

140. ADA Amendments Act §4, 122 Stat. at 3555 (codified at 42 U.S.C. §12102).

141. 42 U.S.C. §2000e-2(a) (2006) (emphasis added).

would be revealed.[142] At the heart of invidious, differential treatment are perceptions or misperceptions that observable or ascertainable characteristics signify an individual's physical and mental capability, morality, and self-worth, among other individual characteristics.[143] Indeed, the Third Circuit acknowledged the interdependency between perceptions and discrimination in its declaration that "[d]iscrimination stems from a reliance on immaterial outward appearances that stereotype an individual with imagined, usually undesirable, characteristics thought to be common to members of the group that shares these superficial traits."[144]

Professors Onwuachi-Willig and Barnes also poignantly observe that, notwithstanding the fact that Title VII does not expressly include "regarded as" language, "*nothing* [...] prevents a court from using doctrinal analyses and understandings from other antidiscrimination statutes to assist in understanding the operation of discriminatory conduct within the Title VII context."[145] Nonetheless, when ascertaining the operation of discrimination in the Title VII context, a number of federal courts have successively found *something* preventing them from appropriating the ADA's express acknowledgement of discrimination as a perception-based phenomenon. It appears that courts have manipulated a seemingly logical comparative construal of the ADA's and Title VII's plain language to substantiate the unqualified dismissal of discrimination cases.

Regrettably, courts have relied upon the mere presence of the ADA's "regarded as" language to deny protection to individuals whose allegations unequivocally implicate protected characteristics and their invidious use, despite the fact that Congress sought to eliminate such considerations in employment decisions. Courts have boldly declared that "Title VII protects those persons that belong to a protected class. [...] [since] Congress has shown, through [...] the Americans with Disabilities Act, that it knows how to enact legislation that protects persons who are wrongly perceived to be in a protected class."[146] In doing so, courts have contrasted the substantive provisions of the ADA and Title VII in a way that does not acknowledge that Title VII has "long-shared [sic] with the ADA an identical congressional and

---

142. *See* Angela Onwuachi-Willig & Mario L. Barnes, *By Any Other Name?: On Being "Regarded as" Black, and Why Title VII Should Apply Even if Lakisha and Jamal are White*, 2005 Wis. L. Rev. 1283, 1325–43.
143. According to Professor Robert Post:

> [p]rejudice against a stigmatizing characteristic, such as race or sex, can manifest itself through invidious judgments of the "differential worth" of persons who display the characteristic, or it can manifest itself through "faulty" judgments about the capacities of such persons. American antidiscrimination law understands itself as negating such prejudice by eliminating or carefully scrutinizing the use of stigmatizing characteristics as a ground for judgment.

Robert Post, Prejudicial Appearances: The Logic of American Antidiscrimination Law, 88 Cal. L. Rev. 1, 9 (2000) (quoting Paul Brest, The Supreme Court, 1975 Term—Foreword: In Defense of the Antidiscrimination Principle, 90 Harv. L. Rev. 1, 7 (1976), and Gordon W. Allport, The Nature of Prejudice 9 (1954)).
144. *Bennun v. Rutgers State Univ.*, 941 F.2d 154, 173 (3d Cir. 1991).
145. Onwuachi-Willig & Barnes, *supra* note 142 at 1328. (emphasis added).
146. *Butler v. Potter*, 345 F. Supp. 2d 844, 850 (E.D. Tenn 2004).

judicial philosophy—namely, that employer perception or stereotype is an appropriate justification for imposing employment discrimination liability, even when that perception or stereotype is erroneous and inaccurate."[147] Furthermore, some courts have simply dismissed the fact that employers' subjective perceptions, related animus, stigmatization, and stereotypes are the impetuses for resulting invidious, differential treatment in all cases, whether such categorical discrimination is on the grounds of disability, race, national origin, sex, religion, or color.

[B] Something Borrowed: A Rigid Application of the Protected-Class Approach in McDonnell Douglas

Title VII provides that it is unlawful for an employer to discriminate "because of *such individual's* race, color, religion, sex, or national origin."[148] Courts have routinely held that this substantive statutory provision prohibits discrimination *on the basis of* race, color, sex, national origin, and religion.[149] Nonetheless, as previously discussed, a number of federal courts have concluded that this proscription affords statutory protection only to individuals who are discriminated against on the basis of their actual race, color, religion, sex, or national origin.[150]

It is unlikely that the courts are simply engaging in a strict, literal interpretation of Title VII's plain language. Courts like the *Butler* court have merely referenced Title VII's substantive provision by citation.[151] Equally significant, courts make no mention of Congress's interpretive memoranda issued during Congress's enactment of Title VII or Congress's more recent expression of Title VII's proscriptions.[152] For example, an oft-cited bipartisan interpretive memo, which Senators Clifford Case and Joseph Clark, the floor managers of the Civil Rights Act of 1964, entered into the congressional record, explains that "[t]o discriminate is to make a distinction, to make a difference in treatment or favor, and those distinctions or differences in treatment or favor which are prohibited by section [703] are those which are based on any five of the forbidden criteria: race, color, religion, sex, and national origin."[153]

Moreover, as previously mentioned, in 1991 Congress amended Title VII and, in doing so, clarified that an employer violates the Act when a plaintiff "demonstrates that race, color, religion, sex, or national origin was a motivating factor for any employment practice."[154] A faithful construal of this more recent statutory amendment and of congressional intent in enacting Section 703 would permit claims of invidious, differential treatment *on the basis of* Title VII's proscribed characteristics regardless of whether such treatment derives from the plaintiff's self-ascribed or mistaken

147. Craig Robert Senn, *Perception Over Reality: Extending the ADA's Concept of "Regarded As" Protection under Federal Employment Discrimination Law,* 36 Fla. St. U. L. Rev. 827, 827 (2009).
148. 42 U.S.C. §2000e-2(a) (2006) (emphasis added).
149. *See supra* note 5 and accompanying text.
150. *See* cases cited *supra* note 27.
151. *See, e.g.*, Butler, 345 F. Supp. 2d 844.
152. *See* cases cited *supra* note 27.
153. 110 Cong. Rec. 7213 (1964) (emphasis added).
154. 42 U.S.C. §2000e-2(m) (2006).

identity.[155] Nevertheless, no express deconstruction of Title VII's original and more recent statutory language or of Title VII's purpose and meaning emerges in the opinions of cases like *Butler*.[156] Therefore, it does not appear that courts are attempting to employ an exacting interpretation of Title VII's plain language to conclude that Title VII only protects individuals against discrimination because of their actual protected status and, thus, that misperception discrimination plaintiffs are a class of individuals that Congress did not intend to cover.

It does appear, however, that courts are engaging in a literal application of the protected-class approach first articulated in *McDonnell Douglas v. Green*. *McDonnell Douglas* was a conventionally framed Title VII intentional discrimination case in that the plaintiff alleged that his former employer discriminated against him because of his self-ascribed racial identity. The Supreme Court held that the plaintiff established the first element of his prima facie case of racial discrimination because he demonstrated that he was a member of a racial minority (i.e., because he was Black).[157] Accordingly, a plaintiff may satisfy an initial prima facie element by demonstrating that she is a member of a protected class, which generally amounts to a simple attestation by the plaintiff of her relevant identity. For example, the plaintiff in a race discrimination case may allege that she is white or, in a sex discrimination case, the plaintiff may allege that she is a woman.[158] Since *Vinson v. Meritor Savings Bank*,[159] wherein the Supreme Court recognized a harassment theory of discrimination under Title VII, some lower courts have closely followed *McDonnell Douglas* and have also required Title VII harassment plaintiffs to prove membership within a protected class.[160]

However, this rigid application of the *McDonnell Douglas* formula is misplaced. The Supreme Court made clear that the elements of a prima facie case were not meant to be applied in formulaic fashion. In *McDonnell Douglas v. Green*, the court cautioned lower courts against perfunctorily applying the framework developed therein to assess Title VII intentional discrimination cases based upon circumstantial evidence. In doing so, the court explained that "facts necessarily will vary in Title VII cases, and the specification . . . of the prima facie proof required from [the plaintiff] is not necessarily applicable in every respect to differing factual situations."[161] In *Furnco Construction Corporation v. Waters*, the Supreme Court reiterated that the *McDonnell Douglas* test "was never intended to be rigid, mechanized, or ritualistic. Rather, it is merely a

155. *See infra* section 1.05.
156. *See* cases cited *supra* note 27.
157. *McDonnell Douglas Corp. v. Green*, 411 U.S. 792, 802 (1973).
158. *But see* section 1.05[B] (demonstrating that courts' actuality requirement will engender identity litigation as an initial matter in conventionally framed intentional discrimination cases as well as those deriving from misperceptions about the plaintiff's identity).
159. 477 U.S. 57, 64–67 (1986).
160. *See, e.g.*, *Burrage v. FedEx Freight, Inc.*, No. 4:10-CV-2755, 2012 WL 1068794, at *4 (N.D. Ohio Mar. 29, 2012) (holding that a Title VII hostile work environment plaintiff must first establish membership within a protected class); *Harvil v. Westwood Comms., L.L.C.*, 433 F.3d 428, 434 (5th Cir. 2005) (requiring a hostile work environment plaintiff to demonstrate that she "is a member of a protected group").
161. *McDonnell Douglas*, 411 U.S. at 802 n.3.

sensible, orderly way to evaluate the evidence in light of the *common* experience as it bears on the critical question of discrimination."[162]

Consequently, *McDonnell Douglas*'s initial prima facie element, that a plaintiff demonstrates she is a member of a protected class, may simply be the manifestation of the facts of the case at hand. The plaintiff in *McDonnell Douglas* self-identified as Black and the employer perceived him as such (or, at least, did not challenge the plaintiff's racial identity).[163] It is also quite probable that when articulating this membership prong, the Supreme Court did not contemplate that a Title VII discrimination plaintiff's allegations of invidious, differential treatment may not comport with her self-ascribed identity. The Court may have conceptualized certain identities, like racial and gender identities, in static terms. The development of a membership prong in *McDonnell Douglas* may have also been a function of the lack of clarity at the time concerning whether Title VII was solely meant to redress discrimination against non-whites, or if all individuals regardless of their racial classification would be protected against discrimination engaged in by covered employers.[164] Nevertheless, based upon the Court's express directive that lower courts fluidly apply the elements it set forth in *McDonnell Douglas*, it is illogical to conclude that the first prong of the *McDonnell Douglas* framework must be construed as an absolute bar against misperception discrimination claims.

Professor Natasha Martin acutely observes, however, that:

> [d]iscrimination law confronts identity as if it were static, and this approach has been shown to be inadequate in capturing the complexity of identity and the perceptions of employees in contemporary work settings. The protected-class approach under Title VII has focused largely on the physical embodiment of the identity category—the immutable aspects of an individual's identity.[165]

Courts' unyielding devotion of the *McDonnell Douglas's* membership prong in cases of misperception discrimination reflects the criticality to the protected-class approach of identity as an immutable quality. Thus, the convergence of the legal construction of immutability and the protected-class approach is entrenched in anti-discrimination law.[166] As a consequence, courts have effortlessly and rigidly applied

162. *Furnco Constr. Corp. v. Waters*, 438 U.S. 567, 577 (1978) (emphasis added).
163. *See McDonnell Douglas*, 411 U.S. 792.
164. *See McDonald v. Santa Fe Trail Transp. Co.*, 427 U.S. 273, 278–79 (1976) (clarifying three years after McDonnell Douglas that the legislative history, EEOC statutory interpretations, and dicta in *Griggs* affirm that Title VII is "not limited to discrimination against members of any particular race" and thereby holding that Title VII prohibits racial discrimination against whites as well nonwhites).
165. Natasha T. Martin, *Diversity and the Virtual Workplace: Performance Identity and Shifting Boundaries of Workplace Engagement*, 16 Lewis & Clark L. Rev. 605, 642 (2012).
166. *See* Sharona Hoffman, *The Importance of Immutability in Employment Discrimination Law*, 52 Wm. & Mary L. Rev. 1483, 1509 (2011) (arguing that "the concept of immutability has been a fixture in both constitutional and statutory analysis of discrimination issues. . . . [and] is a unifying principle that satisfactorily explains the protected classifications [covered in employment discrimination statutes]"). *But see* Jessica A. Clarke, *Inferring Desire*, 63 Duke L.J. 525, 618–619 (2013) (explaining that in order for plaintiffs to benefit from protection against sexual orientation discrimination under current and future state and local laws there is a "temptation to require a plaintiff to prove she is a member of a protected class (i.e., lesbian, gay, bisexual,

this membership prong in misperception discrimination cases. In doing so, courts have instituted an onerous burden on plaintiffs, and set aside reason and established legal precedent in the process.

[C] Something New?: An "Anti-anticlassificationist Interpretation" of Title VII

By creating an artificial, unresolved tension between the "regarded as" language in the ADA and the "such individual" language in Title VII and strictly adhering to a protected-class approach, courts deny purposive effect to Title VII's proscription against invidious, differential treatment in the workplace.[167] This interpretative dissonance prods Congress to amend Title VII, yet engenders destructive implications that impede Title VII's meaning and scope in the meantime. Courts' inflexible posture in defining Title VII's reach in combating workplace discrimination marks the arrival of a new interpretative perspective within antidiscrimination jurisprudence, which this Article describes as "anti-anticlassificationist."

It is important to note that courts' interpretative methodology largely shapes the scope of antidiscrimination law's prohibitions and protections. Professor Jessica Roberts aptly explicates that:

> the antidiscrimination principle is often described in terms of two sometimes competing, sometimes complementary, interpretations: antisubordination and anticlassification. These two versions of the antidiscrimination principle employ differing accounts of the meaning of equality. The antisubordination principle roughly holds that covered entities should not act in a way that reinforces the social status of subjugated groups [...] Its complement, the anticlassification principle, maintains that covered entities should not consider certain classes of forbidden traits under any circumstance, adopting a formal equal treatment model of equality.[168]

In *The Anticlassification Turn,*[169] Professor Bradley Areheart explains that, at least facially, Title VII's substantive disparate treatment provision is "anticlassificationist" in nature.[170] Areheart submits that the Supreme Court evidenced its early antisubordinationist commitments by interpreting Title VII to embody a disparate

---

or transgender) as a part of her prima facie case of discrimination" and cautioning against applying a protected class/immutability approach that results in the adjudication of one's sexual orientation because "courts rely on narrow, self-identification and reputation based definitions [of sexual orientation], which distract from the purpose of remedying discrimination, require a plaintiff who desires the law's protection to 'out' herself," and fail to acknowledge the fluidity and multidimensionality of sexual orientation).

167. *But see Culpepper*, 421 F.2d at 891 n.3. During a speech made to lawyers shortly after Title VII's enactment, the Honorable Griffin B. Bell of the Fifth Circuit Court of Appeals implored that the judiciary's approach in interpreting and enforcing Title VII be "generous" in order to "make [Title VII] work." *Ibid.* Judge Bell also proclaimed "[w]e want to fill in these gaps, and we want to stay within the intent of Congress in making it work." *Ibid.*

168. Jessica L. Roberts, *The Genetic Information Nondiscrimination Act as an Antidiscrimination Law*, 86 NOTRE DAME L. REV. 597, 626–29 (2011).

169. Bradley A. Areheart, *The Anticlassification Turn in Employment Discrimination Law*, 63 ALA. L. REV. 955 (2012).

170. *Id.* at 969.

impact theory of discrimination in *Griggs v. Duke Power Company*.[171] Areheart argues, however, that the Supreme Court's recent decision in *Ricci v. DeStefano*,[172] a Title VII race discrimination case, solidifies the Supreme Court's shift from an antisubordinationist interpretation of Title VII to an anticlassificationist approach, which "shields individuals from all forms of disparate treatment based upon a forbidden trait" in furtherance of a norm of individual fairness.[173]

Assuming that the prevailing posture of the Supreme Court (and other members of the federal judiciary) is to interpret Title VII through an anticlassificationist lens, it is notable that a number of federal judges have rejected this perspective in Title VII misperception discrimination cases. Through an express, strict application of the protected-class approach and an implicit, literal interpretation of Title VII's statutory language, a divergent anti-anticlassificationist interpretation of Title VII emerges. Such an anti-anticlassificationist methodology is marked by a paucity of meaningful statutory interpretation, which effectively frustrates the orthodox aim of the elimination of Title VII's proscribed traits in all decision-making in furtherance of a norm of individual fairness. Indeed, no deliberation of Title VII's arguable goal of prohibiting any consideration of race, religion, sex, color, or national origin from employment decision-making surfaces in the court opinions decreeing an actuality mandate.[174]

Similarly, courts have not expressly acknowledged that underlying misperception discrimination plaintiffs' allegations is an employer's targeted unfair treatment on the basis of Title VII's proscribed characteristics. Also notably lacking is an acknowledgement that Title VII should be interpreted in a manner effectuating fair and equal treatment rather than maintaining invidious, differential treatment in the workplace. Moreover, courts in previously mentioned misperception discrimination cases do not expressly consider potential negative consequences, both practical and policy oriented, that an anti-anticlassificationist statutory interpretation will produce.

Courts' anti-anticlassificationist interpretation and attendant actuality requirement fail to acknowledge the interrelated operation of human categorization based upon conscious and unconscious perceptions and resulting invidious (or even favorable), differential treatment. Based upon one's discernible characteristics, like skin color, hair texture, behavior, dress, accent, speech, language, and names,[175] everyone is perceived by an observer at any given moment as a particular race, color, ethnicity, or gender.[176]

Professor Gear Rich further elucidates that:

> the same way that people develop a lexicon of morphological traits that they use to identify a person's race or ethnicity, they also develop a taxonomy of voluntary

171. *See id.* at 993; *Griggs v. Duke Power Co.*, 401 U.S. 424, 431 (1971) (adopting a disparate impact theory of discrimination in Title VII cases to redress "not only overt discrimination but also practices that are fair in form, but discriminatory in operation").
172. 129 S. Ct. 2658 (2009).
173. *See* Areheart, *supra* note 169, at 963, 993–95.
174. *See* cases cited *supra* note *27*.
175. *See, e.g.*, *El-Hakem v. BJY Inc.*, 415 F.3d 1068, 1073 (9th Cir. 2005) (observing that an individual's non-physical traits like a name could serve as a proxy for race or ethnicity).
176. *See generally* Camille Gear Rich, *Performing Racial and Ethnic Identity: Discrimination by Proxy and the Future of Title VII*, 79 N.Y.U. L. Rev. 1134 (2004).

> behaviors that signify race and ethnicity. That is, in the same way that we associate skin color, eye color, or nose shape with particular races or ethnic groups, we also maintain beliefs about the dialects, aesthetics, and mannerisms that signal one's race or ethnic status.[177]

Based upon his empirical study of sighted and blind peoples' conceptualizations of race, Professor Osagie Obasogie likewise concludes that the majority of blind respondents, similarly to sighted respondents, correlated race primarily with physical traits like skin color.[178] According to Professor Obasogie, generally "both blind and sighted people understand race in visual terms, suggesting that there is a significant shared social experience that not only gives race its meaning but makes it perceptible in the first place."[179] More than half of the blind respondents participating in Professor Obasogie's study also reported that audible characteristics such as an individual's accent, tone of voice, and speech pattern served as a secondary set of characteristics appropriated to categorize one's race.[180] However, Professor Obasogie surmises that:

> these audible clues did not stand in for the visual cues a sighted person might rely upon, nor did they become primary in how blind respondents conceived race. Rather, voice and accent remained secondary measures used to give a sense of what is thought to be the primary characteristic of race: visual cues.[181]

In addition to audible characteristics, for a number of the blind respondents, an individual's skin texture, hair texture, and bodily aroma were also significant factors in the respondents' categorization of an individual's race.[182]

Accordingly, despite omnipresent attestations of colorblindness,[183] gender-blindness,[184] and post-racialism,[185] it is essentially impossible for any one person to

---

177. *Id.* at 1158.
178. Osagie K. Obasogie, *Do Blind People See Race? Social, Legal, and Theoretical Considerations*, 44 Law & Soc'y Rev. 585, 595–96 (2010).
179. *Id.* at 597.
180. *Id.* at 599.
181. *Ibid.*
182. *See id.* at 600–01.
183. Professor John Powell argues that a "colorblind, race-neutral position currently occupies center stage in the American debate on race, both in politics and in the law." John A. Powell, *An Agenda For the Post-Civil Rights Era*, 29 U.S.F. L. Rev. 889, 893 (1995); *see also* Athena D. Mutua, *Introducing ClassCrits: From Class Blindness to a Critical Legal Analysis of Economic Inequality*, 56 Buff. L. Rev. 859, 876 (2008) (arguing that the colorblind rhetoric "ignores, cements, and blinds itself to the historical factors that determine, shape and continue to structure the racial caste system that law and society constructed in the first place").
184. According to Professor Lucinda Finley:

> [t]he insistence that the law should be blind to stereotyped, not "real," differences of gender, just as it should be color-blind, is often prescribed as the proper antidote to . . . "girls and boys each have their proper place" separate spheres thinking [fundamental to the Supreme Court's decision in *Plessy v. Ferguson*, which affirmed the constitutionality of the separate-but-equal doctrine].

Lucinda M. Finley, *Sex-Blind, Separate But Equal, or Anti-Subordination? The Uneasy Legacy of* Plessy *v.* Ferguson *for Sex and Gender Discrimination*, 12 Ga. St. U. L. Rev. 1089, 1108 (1996) (citing *J.E.B. v. Alabama*, 114 S. Ct. 1419, 1422 (1994)).

185. In 2008, a sea of media pundits, politicians, and average Americans proclaimed that the election of President Barack Obama demarcated a post-racial moment in United States history.

escape being perceived and, thus, categorized by an observer through the lens of race, ethnicity, religion, color, and gender, which are proscribed characteristics in employment decision-making under Title VII. According to Professor Linda Hamilton Krieger:

> people categorize objects in their environment in a particular way because it proves useful in understanding their environment and predicting future events. It would be difficult to argue credibly that racial, ethnic, or gender distinctions have no utility in understanding American society or negotiating experience within it. [...] [Therefore] [a]s a theoretical matter, the notion that racial, ethnic, or gender distinctions could be ignored in the priming of schematic expectancies is, at best, implausible. As an empirical matter, it is simply insupportable. Because gender, ethnic, and racial distinctions are often perceptually apparent, and because these categories are made salient by our social and cultural context, we can expect race, ethnic, and gender-based schemas to be implicated in the processing of information about other people. Once activated, the content of a schema will profoundly affect how we interpret a person's subsequent behavior, what about that behavior we remember, and how we use the behavior in judging the person later.[186]

Such external observations and attendant categorizations are beyond an individual's control, and are typically irrelevant to one's ability to perform her job duties, but serve as the central basis for pervasive, systematic, and purposeful exclusion of individuals from (and marginalization within) employment opportunities in the American workforce. For that reason, Congress deemed it necessary to proscribe invidious, differential treatment on certain bases with the enactment of Title VII.[187] Consequently, Title VII protects everyone who is an employee of or seeks employment with a covered entity against race, color, sex, national origin, and religious discrimination. Any individual who suffers invidious, differential treatment at the hands of a covered employer is therefore able to seek relief under Title VII.

Judges' anti-anticlassificationist interpretation of Title VII, which expressly denies statutory protection to certain individuals alleging that they are the victims of invidious, differential treatment on the basis of proscribed characteristics, is categorically wrong. Such judicial interpretation contravenes the express purposes of Title VII:

See generally Berta Esperanza Hernández-Truyol, *Narratives of Identity, Nation, and Outsiders Within Outsiders: Not Yet a Post-Anything World*, 14 *Harv. Latino L. Rev.* 325, 325–36 (2011) (acknowledging that "[t]he present conceptualization of a post-racial America became mainstream for many when Barack Obama took office as the 44th President of the United States in 2008" and noting that immediately following his election, "all of the major news outlets began debating whether his victory brought an official end to the acknowledged pernicious and longstanding racial and ethnic stigmas that have pervaded this country"). Professor Sumi Cho maintains that "post-racialism is yet distinct as a descriptive matter [from colorblindness], in that it signals a racially transcendent event that authorizes the retreat from race. Colorblindness, in comparison, offers a largely normative claim for a retreat from race that is aspirational in nature." Sumi Cho, *Post-Racialism*, 94 Iowa L. Rev. 1589, 1597–98 (2009).

186. Linda Hamilton Krieger, *The Content of Our Categories: A Cognitive Bias Approach to Discrimination and Equal Employment Opportunity*, 47 Stan. L. Rev. 1161, 1201–02 (1995).

187. *See Perkins v. Lake Cnty. Dep't. of Util.*, 860 F. Supp. 1262, 1276 (N.D. Ohio 1994) (explicating that a Title VII plaintiff need not prove her racial identity in order to assert an actionable claim of race or national origin discrimination in light of Title VII's express purpose: to "address [invidious treatment based upon] perceived differences which do not have a basis in fact between races and ethnic groups").

to afford "statutory rights against invidious discrimination in employment"[188] and to eliminate such treatment from the workplace.[189] Indeed, rather than dismantle categorical, inequitable treatment against an individual on the basis of race, sex, color, national origin, and religion, courts' misinterpretation of Title VII allows unchecked invidious, differential treatment in the workplace.[190]

[D] Something Old, Something New?: What Lies Beneath the Actuality Requirement

The mere presence of the ADA's "regarded as" language has enabled courts to perpetuate such invidious, differential treatment by embracing the argument that Title VII, unlike the ADA, only prohibits discrimination based upon an individual's actual protected status. However, such a facial difference between the two statutes does not adequately explain the dearth of thoughtful deconstruction by the courts regarding Title VII's substantive provision, purpose. Courts' distinction between the substantive provisions in Title VII and the ADA, in addition to an unyielding, literal application of the protected-class approach, which translates into an unorthodox, anti-anticlassificationist interpretation of Title VII's proscriptions, causes one to pause. On its face, the imposition of an actuality requirement in cases of categorical discrimination is perplexing and problematic. Understandably, questions abound relating to the development of and rationale for the adoption of this puzzling legal prerequisite in cases of invidious, differential treatment.

The previously examined cases offer little to draw upon to definitively deduce courts' justifications for employing an anti-anticlassificationist interpretation of Title VII. Therefore, this section contemplates more obscure and more obvious explanations, new and old, for this categorically wrong movement in antidiscrimination law. Namely, this section observes the ways in which the actuality requirement reflects lawmakers' understandings of identity classification, the operation of discrimination, and antidiscrimination litigation. It also considers courts' divergent treatment of the ADA's and Title VII's statutory language and purpose as well as courts' rigid application of antidiscrimination law's protected-class approach.

Perkins v. Lake County Department of Utilities, the first reported Title VII case in which an employer argued for the imposition of an actuality requirement before a federal district court, was a case of intentional race/national origin discrimination.[191]

188. *Johnson v. Ry. Express Agency, Inc.*, 421 U.S. 454, 457–58 (1975).
189. *See McKennon v. Nashville Banner Pub'g Co.*, 513 U.S. 352, 358 (1995) (acknowledging that Title VII and the ADEA share a mutual purpose of "elimination of discrimination in the workplace.") (quoting *Oscar Mayer & Co. v. Evans*, 441 U.S. 750, 756 (1979)).
190. *See infra* section 1.05[A].
191. *Perkins*, 860 F. Supp. 1262. Essentially, the *Perkins* court rejected an anti-anticlassificationist interpretation of Title VII (which would later be adopted by some courts in parallel contexts), noting that imposing an actuality requirement was inconsistent with the aims of Title VII and the operation of discrimination. The court observed that in its experience deciding employment discrimination cases, it "never encountered an instance in which an employer admittedly first checked the pedigree of an employee before engaging in discriminatory conduct." 860 F. Supp. at 1273. Accordingly, the court found it incongruous for the plaintiff to first prove that he was

Ten years after *Perkins*, *Butler v. Potter*—the first reported Title VII case in which a federal district court expressly adopted an actuality requirement—was also an intentional race/national origin discrimination case.[192] Therefore, one simple observation may explain the derivation of an actuality requirement: this mandate reflects an age-old conceptualization of racial identity as biological, fixed, and inherent, as well as courts' longstanding treatment of "race and ethnicity as biological, morphological concepts and discrimination as a reaction to a set of biologically fixed traits."[193]

Since the founding of the United States, securing race as a static, predictable, and biological trait has functioned as a principal and shared aspiration (and arguably fascination) among academic, social, political, and legal communities alike.[194] Conceptualizations of permanent, inheritable race, racial hierarchies, racial purity and superiority were espoused to justify and effectuate racial oppression and exclusion in a plethora of manifestations including racial colonization,[195] racial

actually Native American in a case alleging invidious, differential treatment. *Ibid.* The court reasoned that antidiscrimination legislation like Title VII sought "to equalize the footing of all employees without regard to the employer's *subjective* perceptions and preconceived ideas" rather than provide benefits on the basis of race, sex, national origin, religion, and color. *Id.* at 1278 (emphasis added). The *Perkins* court further explained that it was "unnecessary, and indeed inappropriate, to attempt to measure [the plaintiff's] percentage of Indian blood or to examine his documentable connection to recognized existing tribes" for the maintenance of the plaintiff's categorical race discrimination case. *Ibid. But see Leonard v. Katsinas*, No. 05-1069, 2007 WL 1106136 (C.D. Ill. Apr. 11, 2007) (requiring racial discrimination plaintiffs to prove that they were Native American for an actionable §1981 claim). Though the *Perkins* court did not adopt an actuality requirement it did apply a "reasonable basis" test which mandates that a plaintiff proffer objective evidence that supports the notion that the employer reasonably believed that the plaintiff was a member of a protected category. *Ibid.* According to the court, an "objective basis may consist of physical appearance, language, cultural activities, or associations, so long as any or all of those objective factors lead the employer to believe that a given employee is a member of that protected class, and to deal with him/her on that basis." *Ibid.* I contend, however, that satisfying the court's reasonable basis test is not as simple as it seems. To maintain a Title VII race or national origin discrimination case, the objective characteristics that a plaintiff would rely upon are not objective but rather determined subjectively, relationally, and contextually and thus are contestable. For example, an individual who self-identifies as Native American could describe her skin color as light brown, one observer could describe the individual's skin color as medium brown and characterize her as Hispanic, and another observer could describe the same individual as having a fair skin color and characterize her as white. Plausibly, the two observers may not find the respective opinion of the other a reasonable assessment of the individual's skin color and race. *But see generally* Ken Nakasu Davison, Note and Comment, *The Mixed-Race Experience: Treatment of Racially Mischaracterized Individuals Under Title VII*, 12 Asian L.J. 161, 184 (2005) (endorsing the *Perkins* court's reasonable belief requirement by reasoning "it avoids the complicated and often indeterminate task of establishing a plaintiff's actual racial background"). Furthermore, the *Perkins* court's rationale for a reasonable basis test in race discrimination cases is grounded in a fixed, physical construction of indigeneity and Blackness. *See Perkins*, 860 F. Supp. at 1278 & n. 20. For additional commentary on the *Perkins* court's express ruminations on the static and immutable physicality of Blackness, *See* D. Wendy Greene, *Determining the (In)Determinable: Race in Brazil and the United States*, 14 Mich. J. Race & L. 143, 184 (2009).

192. 345 F. Supp. 2d 844 (E.D. Tenn. 2004).
193. Rich, *supra* note 176, at 1134.
194. *See generally* Christian B. Sundquist, *The Meaning of Race in the DNA Era: Science, History and the Law*, 27 TEMP. J. SCI. TECH. & ENVTL. L. 231 (2008).
195. D. Wendy Greene, *On Race, Nationhood, and Citizenship*, 34 T. MARSHALL L. REV. 421, 425 (2009) (reviewing Laura E. Gómez, *Manifest Destinies: The Making of the Mexican American*

slavery,[196] racial segregation,[197] racial violence[198] as well as exclusionary race-based immigration policies[199] and property ownership qualifications.[200] According to Professor Christian Sundquist:

> [t]he meaning of "race" has been vigorously contested throughout history. Early theories of race assigned social, intellectual, moral and physical values to perceived physical differences among groups of people. The perception that race should be defined in terms of genetic and biological difference fuelled the "race science" of the eighteenth and nineteenth centuries, during which time geneticists, physiognomists, eugenicists, anthropologists and others purported to find scientific justification for denying equal treatment to non-white persons.[201]

As Professor Sundquist explains, post-World War II academic, legal, and scientific communities have consistently repudiated scientific notions of race and, conversely, have embraced a conceptualization of race as a social construct.[202] For example, legal scholar Ian Haney Lopez explains that:

> [t]here are no genetic characteristics possessed by all Blacks but not by non-Blacks; similarly, there is no gene or cluster of genes common to all Whites but not to non-Whites. One's race is not determined by a single gene or gene cluster, as is,

---

Race (N.Y. Univ. Press 2007)) ("Grounded in notions of white racial superiority, Euro-American politicians and military leaders espoused 'Manifest Destiny' as the rationale for, and the method by which, to expand United States borders westward [to colonize Mexico] and abroad and create a Euro-American dynasty consisting of predominantly Euro-Americans.").

196. *See* Greene, *supra* note 191 at 164 ("[W]hite slave owners, philosophers, and politicians, like Thomas Jefferson, articulated formal defenses of slavery in concert with the country's philosophical origins [which espoused liberty, equality and natural rights of men], yet grounded in the presumption of whites' natural superiority and Blacks' innate inferiority.").
197. *See, e.g.*, *Brown v. Bd. of Educ.*, 347 U.S. 483, 494–95 (1954) (holding state-sanctioned racially segregated public schools unconstitutional).
198. Throughout American history and United States, notions of white supremacy and white racial purity permeated the social fabric and fueled the lynching of racial minorities—largely men racialized as non-white because of their ethnicity, color, race, or religion—when they transgressed (or were perceived to transgress) socially and legally constructed racial boundaries, which served as a form of extra-legal criminal enforcement. *See generally* Barbara Holden-Smith, *Lynching, Federalism, and the Intersection of Race and Gender in the Progressive Era*, 8 Yale J.L. & Feminism 31, 31–39 (1996).
199. In 1790 and 1870, Congress enacted express race-based prerequisites for naturalized United States citizenship. *See* Act of Mar. 26, 1790, ch. 3, 1 Stat. 103 (permitting only free whites to become naturalized US citizens); Act of Jul. 14, 1870, ch. 254, §7, 16 Stat. 254, 256 (repealed 1952) (extending naturalized US citizenship to individuals of "African nativity").
200. *See, e.g.*, Rose Cuison Villazor, *Blood Quantum Land Laws and the Race Versus Political Identity Dilemma*, 96 Cal. L. Rev. 801, 808–09 (2008) (describing the US government's early twentieth century adherence to blood quantum laws, which dictated that individuals with less than "one-half American Indian blood" or ancestry could not own property after the enactment of the Dawes Severalty Act, which divided indigenous owned land as well as commanded that "[m]ixed-blood" American Indians could only sell their property to "full-blood" American Indians with the permission of the federal government).
201. Christian B. Sundquist, *Science Fictions and Racial Fables: Navigating the Final Frontier of Genetic Interpretation*, 25 Harv. Blackletter L.J. 57, 57 (2009).
202. *See* Sundquist, *supra* note 194 at 252–56 (illustrating that post-World War II, the United Nations established the Educational, Scientific and Cultural Organization, UNESCO, to develop a formal statement on race to "scientifically debunk the biological conception of race" and drew upon leaders within the scientific community in doing so).

for example, sickle cell anemia. Nor are races marked by important differences in gene frequencies, the rates of appearance of certain gene types.[203]

Though a scientific notion of race has largely been condemned, and a social constructionist view of race has been endorsed within a variety of intellectual communities,[204] a fixed, biological, and inherent notion of racial/ethnic identity remains salient. This has continued despite the existence and recognition of "multi-raciality,"[205] and even for those who subscribe to the conception that race is a social construct.[206] Generally speaking, an individual, consciously or unconsciously, perceives her self-classified race, much like her sex, as a primary component within her macro identity (e.g., profession, religion, age, etc.) that is static and indisputable. According to Omi and Winant, "at the level of experience, of everyday life, race is an almost indissoluble part of our identities. Our society is so thoroughly racialized that to be without racial identity is to be in danger of having no identity. To be raceless is akin to being genderless."[207] Even those individuals who consciously and acutely subscribe to an ideal that race is a malleable social construct, and whose experiences bear this out, are not exempt from this default understanding of one's self-identity.[208] Accordingly, it is important to remember that lawyers advanced and adopted the actuality

203. Ian F. Haney López, *The Social Construction of Race: Some Observations on Illusion, Fabrication, and Choice*, 29 Harv. C.R.-C.L. L. Rev. 1, 11 (1994).

204. Namely, Professor Sundquist argues that post-World War II, federal courts in the United States have "generally embraced the modern rejection of biological theories of race [and] [i]nstead . . . have focused on racial 'markers' such as ancestry, physical appearance, language, outsider perception, and self-identification to determine race." Sundquist, *supra* note 194, at 256. However, with the meteoric rise of genetic ancestry tests, "contemporary society has unquestionably assumed that race has some genetically-determinable essence." *Id.* at 257.

205. In its recognition of "multi-raciality," and thus the fluidity of race and socio-legally constructed status based upon racial difference, the colonial Virginia legislature in 1662 attempted to promulgate a fixed racial and social status for mixed-race children of white and Black parentage by codifying that such children's racial and social status followed the mother's status. *See* Edmund Morgan, American Slavery American Freedom 333 (1975).

206. *See, e.g., Saint Francis Coll. v. Al-Khazraji*, 481 U.S. 604, 613 (1987) (observing the socially constructed and fluid nature of race while implicitly adhering to a biological notion of race in its affirmation of the lower court's holding that §1981 "'at a minimum,' reaches discrimination against an individual 'because he or she is genetically part of an ethnically and physiognomically distinctive sub-grouping of *homo sapiens*.'"); *see also Abdullahi v. Prada*, 520 F.3d 710 (7th Cir. 2008) (Judge Posner appealing to both fluid, social constructionist and fixed, biological notions of race in recognizing that mutable, ethnic characteristics like one's accent can animate invidious treatment akin to racism).

207. Michael Omi & Howard Winant, *On the Theoretical Concept of Race, in* Race and Representation in Education 5 (Cameron McCarthy & Warren Crichlow eds., 1993). Indeed, Justice Sandra Day O'Connor noted the improbability of an individual navigating through contemporary American society without the micro and macro operation of race shaping her experiences. *Grutter v. Bollinger*, 539 U.S. 306, 333 (2003) ("Just as growing up in a particular region or having particular professional experiences is likely to affect an individual's views, so too is one's own, unique [racialized] experience . . . in a society, like our own, in which race unfortunately still matters.").

208. Indeed, to substantiate this point, a personal narrative is illustrative. I—a native South Carolinian of known Native American, European, and African ancestry who self-identifies as Black and American—actively embrace and recognize the socially constructed nature of race. In fact, the contextual and fluid nature of racial classification has borne out in my own personal experiences domestically and abroad. For example, on numerous occasions observers have

mandate in intentional race discrimination cases. The lawyers arguing and adjudicating these cases are human beings whose understandings of racial identity were likely shaped by broader social, political, legal, and economic forces as well as specific personal experiences.

With this in mind, it is more fathomable that this legal position and resulting statutory imperative, the actuality requirement, could take shape. When confronted with a discrimination claim emanating from misperceptions about a plaintiff's race, a lawyer who represents either a plaintiff or an employer, or a judge deciding such a case, may simply be unable to rationalize the proposition that a plaintiff's race was mistaken. Similarly, a lawyer or judge might outright disbelieve that a plaintiff's race could be mistaken, based on her own preset conceptualizations of race and sex as fixed, indisputable constructs. The development of a legal principle in conformity with a lawmaker's conscious or unconscious default understanding of racial identity as a provable, unmistakable, fixed construct could reflexively emerge.[209]

For example, the plaintiff in *LaRocca v. Precision Motorcars, Inc.*, like Burrage, alleged that he was harassed by his supervisor, who perceived him as Mexican, even though the supervisor was aware that the plaintiff self-identified as Italian-American.[210] Essentialist, fixed notions of race or ethnicity undergirded the court's decision to recognize LaRocca's misperception discrimination claim. The court treated the plaintiff's darker skin complexion as a physical characteristic indicative of Italian ancestry.[211] Accordingly, the court held that LaRocca's claim of national origin harassment was actionable, as his actual national origin, or rather his innate ethnic characteristic, triggered the alleged invidious treatment.[212] In other words, but for LaRocca's dark brown skin color, a physical characteristic presumably inherent to his

classified me as Ethiopian and Hispanic, namely with ethnic origins in both Spanish and Portuguese speaking countries. When an observer begins to address me in their native language or simply inquires, for example, whether I am Brazilian, Ethiopian, or Dominican (and they express shock when I answer in the negative), admittedly my immediate reaction is one of curiosity. I wonder which of my physical markers or behaviors could have engendered the observer's perceptions. I recognize that my wonderment stems from an embedded construction of my racial and ethnic identity as a Black American without Hispanic, Iberian, or Ethiopian roots and my daily conscious and unconscious operation through this lens. Intellectually, however, I am aware that this external classification of my race and ethnicity is a contextual, subjective, and relational determination. When I have shared these experiences with others, many listeners have affirmed the observer's misclassification of my race and ethnicity, implicitly appealing to a notion of fixed, physical racial and ethnic attributes in doing so. Listeners, even those who also embrace a social constructionist view of race, have expressed that due to my skin color, hair texture, or the shape of my nose and eyes, it is plausible that observers could perceive me as Brazilian or as Ethiopian. Equally as many listeners cannot fathom my racial or ethnic classification as anything other than what I have self-reported: an externally reinforced self-perception which has been informed by broader historical and contemporary constructions of race and ancestry in the United States as well as my family's relatively fixed identity as Black Americans—or Americans of African descent without any known Hispanic, Iberian, or Ethiopian ancestry or specific knowledge of our African country of origin.

209. This understanding could also easily extend to sex misperception discrimination claims.

210. *LaRocca v. Precision Motorcars, Inc.*, 45 F. Supp. 2d 762 (D. Neb. 1999). Specifically, LaRocca claimed that his supervisor called him a "spic" and a "wetback." *Id.* at 766.

211. *Id.* at 770.

212. *Ibid.*

Italian ancestry, LaRocca's supervisor would not have perceived him as Mexican and harassed him accordingly.[213] Thus, by treating LaRocca's brown skin complexion as a physical proxy for his Italian ancestry, the court implicitly appealed to a notion that fixed, physical racial characteristics exist.

Hence, the underlying reasoning for the advancement of an actuality requirement in *Perkins* and its eventual adoption in *Butler*, both race/national origin discrimination cases, are quite plausibly the product of conscious or subliminal conceptualizations about race on the part of defense counsel and judges alike. Without any patent reflection of the logic undergirding the development of an actuality requirement or its natural consequences, a number of federal district courts after *Butler* merely regurgitated the court's holding and rationale and imposed this onerous and unnecessary mandate in categorical race and national origin discrimination cases.[214] The requirement was subsequently extended to religious discrimination cases.[215]

Although a simple inability to visualize race as anything other than a fixed, biological construct is the most obvious explanation for the initial adoption of an actuality requirement in Title VII race and national origin cases, a number of other possible explanations for its continued implementation exist. More generally, judges deciding misperception cases may have decided not to view discrimination as a perception-based phenomenon in Title VII cases, though expressly acknowledged in the ADA, for fear that doing so will open the proverbial Pandora's Box. Courts may be fearful that individuals with deceitful motives will be encouraged to disingenuously frame employment discrimination claims as stemming from misperceptions about their respective identities. For example, a plaintiff may insincerely claim that an employer misperceived her as Native American and appropriate racially offensive comments about Native Americans and/or differential treatment of Native Americans in the workplace, arguably not intentionally aimed at the plaintiff, to support her discrimination claim.[216]

It is also plausible that lawyers arguing and judges deciding these cases are incorrectly conceptualizing the alleged discrimination emanating from misperceptions about one's race or religion, for example, as less injurious than discrimination implicating one's actual racial or religious identity. They may believe that the plaintiff endures minimal, ancillary harm rather than a direct, personal offense since the

213. *Ibid.* Though the court accepted the plaintiff's contention that his supervisor misperceived him as Mexican during his employment, the court viewed the supervisor's misperception as an "isolated incident" which was corrected; therefore, the harassment the plaintiff suffered was not due to his misperceived ethnic identity but rather his actual ethnic identity. *Id.* at 770–71. Accordingly, the court held that the plaintiff's Title VII and §1981 hostile work environment claims were actionable since the supervisor developed and acted upon a "reasonable" perception of the plaintiff's ethnic identity due to one of his physical characteristics—his darker skin color—which is supposedly inherent to individuals of Italian descent, i.e., the plaintiff's actual national origin. *Id.* at 770–71, 776–77. In so holding, the court implicated an actuality requirement.

214. *See* cases cited *supra* note *27*.

215. *See El v. Max Daetwyler Corp.*, No. 3:09-CV-415, 2011 WL 1769805 (W.D.N.C. May 9, 2011) aff'd, 451 Fed. App'x 257 (4th Cir. 2011).

216. *See, e.g., Defendant's Motion to Dismiss, Wood v. Freeman Decorating Servs., Inc.*, No. 3:08-CV-00375-LRH-RAM, 2009 WL 4836455 (D. Nev. Jul. 30, 2009).

invidious treatment is ostensibly not animated by, or is unrelated to, her self-ascribed racial or religious identity. Accordingly, courts may be viewing misperception discrimination cases as third-party discrimination cases, which are cases wherein the plaintiffs are seeking redress for the unlawful discrimination that other individuals have suffered rather than any discrimination that they have endured directly. Prototypical third-party cases are sex discrimination cases initiated by male plaintiffs on behalf of women or race discrimination cases brought on behalf of non-white employees by white plaintiffs.[217] Some courts have not recognized these third-party claims, reasoning that an employer's discrimination against individuals based on Title VII's proscribed bases indirectly harms third-party claimants, as such discrimination is unrelated to the plaintiffs' protected status. Correspondingly, these courts have held that Title VII protects an individual against proscribed discrimination specifically aimed at her because of her protected status.[218]

It is not a far-fetched possibility that courts may be conceptualizing misperception discrimination claims as akin to these third-party discrimination claims. For example, in *Wood v. Freeman Decorating Services, Inc.*, counsel for the defendant-employer argued that the plaintiff, who alleged suffering a racially hostile work environment, did not have standing under Title VII because he could not prove his self-proclaimed Native American identity.[219] To undermine the veracity of Mr. Wood's racial classification as Native American, the defendant-employer proffered evidence that Wood self-identified as Hispanic on a military admissions form on which American Indian was a choice.[220] Additionally, the defendant-employer argued that Wood could not provide any documentation that he was Native American. The only proof he could offer was his adopted mother's hearsay admissions to him that his natural

217. *See generally* Camille Gear Rich, *Marginal Whiteness*, 98 CAL. L. REV. 1497 (2010) (categorizing third-party race discrimination claims initiated by white plaintiffs as "interracial solidarity" claims and providing a more nuanced conceptualization of the injuries suffered by whites because of an employer's minority-targeted discrimination and thus arguing for the legal recognition of such claims).

218. *See, e.g.*, *Jackson v. Deen*, No. 4:12-CV-139, 2013 WL 4078292, at *2, *6–7 (S.D. Ga. Aug. 12, 2013) (holding that a female plaintiff, one who self-identified as white yet was arguably misperceived as African American or mixed-race, did not have standing under Title VII and §1981 to challenge the derogatory comments and treatment aimed at her African-American co-workers though she claimed she was personally affected by the alleged racially discriminatory and subordinating work environment. The court held that the plaintiff was "not an aggrieved party under Title VII because her interests are not those arguably sought to be protected by [the] statute" since none of the "racially offensive comments were either directed toward [her] or made with intent to harass her." Notably, in so holding, the court relied upon the Supreme Court's decision in *Thompson v. North American Stainless Steel*, later discussed in section 1.05[C]; *Childress v. City of Richmond*, 134 F.3d 1205, 1207, 1209 (4th Cir. 1998) (en banc) (Luttig, J., concurring) (finding that since plaintiffs "assert[ed] only the rights of third-parties to be free from race or sex-based discrimination in the workplace," white male plaintiffs did not have standing under Title VII to sue for sex and race-based hostile work environment claim based upon the alleged harassment of Black and female employees) *cert. denied*, 524 U.S. 927 (1998).

219. Defendant's Motion to Dismiss, *Wood v. Freeman Decorating Servs., Inc.*, No. 3:08-CV-00375-LRH-RAM, 2009 WL 4836455 (D. Nev. Jul. 30, 2009).

220. *Ibid.*

parents were Native American.[221] The defense further contended that Wood's self-classification as Native American was an insincere and self-serving attempt to capitalize on alleged racially offensive conduct toward, and statements about, Native Americans in the workplace.[222]

As a result, the defendant-employer sought the dismissal of Mr. Wood's Title VII case and asserted that his hostile work environment claim failed as a matter of law because he was unable to show that "he was subjected to racially derogatory comments based on *his* race."[223] In support of its contention that Title VII intentional discrimination cases are actionable only when the alleged invidious, differential treatment is related to the plaintiff's protected status, the defendant-employer cited to Title VII third-party sex and race discrimination cases wherein courts held that the plaintiffs did not have standing to bring a discrimination action on behalf of other individuals since the alleged discrimination was not because of the plaintiffs' sex or race, respectively.[224] Notably, however, the court held that Mr. Wood's race discrimination claim was actionable. Yet, in doing so, the court relied in part upon a case wherein the court upheld a third-party discrimination claim.[225] Thus, some other courts may also be viewing misperception discrimination cases as akin to third-party cases.

Additionally, the emergence of an anti-anticlassificationist interpretation of Title VII could be the result of a haphazard, mechanical application of the protected-class approach despite the Supreme Court's caveats to the contrary.[226] Conversely, to the extent that courts misconstrue claims of misperception discrimination as radically different from conventionally framed claims of discrimination, courts' anti-anticlassificationist interpretation could also be the manifestation of what Professor Jed Rubenfeld describes as an "anti-antidiscrimination agenda," whereby courts cite textual grounds to quash a plaintiff's theory of discrimination "perceived to take antidiscrimination ideology too far"[227] by "extend[ing] antidiscrimination ideas to unusual contexts."[228]

Similarly, Title VII misperception discrimination claims may fall victim to judicial biases against employment claims more generally.[229] Professor Michael Selmi asserts that, in part, judges' "general misperception [...] that employment cases are easy—not difficult—to win, and the volume of employment discrimination cases is said to reflect an excessive amount of costly nuisance suits" accounts for employment discrimination

221. *Ibid.*
222. *Ibid.*
223. *Ibid.*
224. *Ibid.*
225. *See Wood v. Freeman Decorating Servs., Inc.*, No. 3:08-CV-00375-LRH-RAM, 2010 WL 653764, at *4 (D. Nev. Feb. 19, 2010).
226. *See supra* section 1.03[B].
227. Jed Rubenfeld, *The Anti-Antidiscrimination Agenda*, 111 Yale L.J. 1141, 1142–43 (2002).
228. *Id.* at 1143.
229. *See, e.g.*, Michael Selmi, *Why Are Employment Discrimination Cases So Hard to Win?*, 61 La. L. Rev. 555 (2001).

cases' relative lack of success.[230] Selmi maintains that judicial biases against discrimination lawsuits, though different depending on the particular cause of action, also explain employment discrimination cases' high rate of failure.[231] For example, before Congress amended the Americans with Disabilities Act in 2008,[232] in response to what they viewed as an expansive act, courts "trimmed [the Act's] scope as a way of ferreting out some of the more extravagant claims, but in the process have excluded many claims that were clearly intended to fall within the statute's ambit."[233] Moreover, as it pertains to race discrimination cases, "which are generally the most difficult claim for a plaintiff to succeed on, courts often seem mired in a belief that the claims are generally unmeritorious, brought by whining plaintiffs who have been given too many, not too few, breaks along the way."[234] Accordingly, the reproduction of an anti-anticlassificationist statutory interpretation and attendant actuality requirement in previously mentioned intentional discrimination cases may be indicative of pervasive judicial bias against employment discrimination cases and a concerted attempt to restrain further expansion of Title VII's scope and the resulting litigation.

This latter possibility, indeed, appears more supportable in cases like *Burrage*, wherein the courts boldly proclaimed that categorical discrimination claims deriving from misperceptions would not be recognized until Congress expressly instructed the courts otherwise by amending Title VII. Meanwhile, the *Burrage* court advanced tenuous analytical reasoning to ensure that actionable claims of invidious, differential treatment comport with an individual's self-classified or provable protected status in the meantime.

In doing so, such an anti-anticlassificationist interpretation of Title VII creates a legal fiction that the only rightful beneficiaries of Title VII's protections against workplace discrimination are individuals who allege invidious, differential treatment on the basis of their self-ascribed identity. Courts are mistaken in their belief that by recognizing misperception discrimination cases, statutory protection will be extended to a new class of individuals. Fundamentally, the only class of individuals unable to benefit from Title VII's proscriptions consists of those discriminated against by entities not covered by Title VII.[235] Nonetheless, courts like *Burrage* have denied Title VII protection to misperception discrimination plaintiffs, even at the expense of undermining longstanding legal principles as well as Title VII's meaning and purpose, and despite the risk of engendering paradoxical, "absurd results"[236] for categorical

230. *Id.* at 556.
231. *Ibid.*
232. *See infra* section 1.03[A].
233. Selmi, *supra* note 229, at 556.
234. *Ibid. See generally* Wendy Parker, *Lessons in Losing: Race Discrimination in Employment*, 81 Notre Dame L. Rev. 889 (2006).
235. For example, employers with less than fifteen employees are expressly exempted from Title VII coverage. *See* 42 U.S.C. §2000e(b) (2006). Businesses and enterprises on or in close proximity to Native American reservations that afford an employment preference to Native Americans are also exempt from Title VII coverage. *See id.* §2000e-2(i).
236. Per time-honored Supreme Court jurisprudence, the prevailing rule courts are to apply when interpreting statutes is that the "plain language" of the statute governs except when giving effect to the plain language produces "absurd or glaringly unjust" results. *See United States v. Rodgers*, 466 U.S. 475, 484 (1984) (quoting *Sorrells v. United States*, 287 U.S. 435, 450 (1932)).

discrimination cases on the basis of an individual's race, color, sex, national origin, and religion.

Title VII extends protection and relief to individuals suffering invidious, differential treatment perpetrated by a covered employer because of the statute's forbidden criteria, regardless of whether such categorical discrimination derives from an accurate or inaccurate categorization of an individual's racial, ethnic, gender, or religious identity. Although it is likely presumed that everyone will self-identify as a member of a particular socially constructed racial group, or as male or female, not everyone will (or does) classify as a member of a singular racial, ethnic, color, or religious group or even classify themselves as simply male or female.[237] Moreover, one's racial, religious, ethnic, and gender self-identification can change throughout the course of her life. This lack of fixed classification or membership within a protected class does not render an individual unprotected from invidious, differential treatment in the workplace on Title VII's proscribed bases. Correspondingly, differential, invidious treatment based upon the statute's forbidden criteria that does not neatly comport with an individual's actual self-identification, yet is specifically aimed at the individual, is not beyond Title VII's remedial scope. Indeed, Congress and the Supreme Court made clear that the purpose of Title VII is to protect all Americans from categorical discrimination engaged in by covered employers *on the basis* of race, color, national origin, sex, and religion.[238]

Despite specific contentions that the plaintiff conceivably suffered invidious, differential treatment on the basis of proscribed characteristics under Title VII, several federal courts have decreed that Title VII plaintiffs are only protected against unlawful discrimination if they experience invidious, differential treatment occasioned by the defendant's accurate classification of the plaintiff's racial, religious, ethnic, color, or gender identity. In doing so, these courts have afforded employers a minimalist defense even in otherwise viable cases of discrimination resulting from an employer's subjective perceptions or misperceptions of an individual's race, color, national origin, religion, or sex. Essentially, employers need not deny the allegations of discriminatory treatment on the basis of proscribed characteristics. Rather, employers can effectively defend a case of categorical discrimination on the grounds that the alleged invidious,

---

See John F. Manning, *The Absurdity Doctrine*, 116 Harv. L. Rev. 2387, 2398–408 (2003), for the origins of the absurdity doctrine in addition to the seminal Supreme Court cases in which the Court appropriated the absurdity doctrine when literal application of a statute's plain language led to nonsensical results. Professor Manning posits that the absurdity doctrine "rests on a judicial judgment that a particular statutory outcome, although prescribed by the text, would sharply contradict society's 'common sense' of morality, fairness, or some other deeply held value." *Id.* at 2405–06.

237. For example, some individuals may not classify themselves in singular racial terms like Black and white but rather as mixed-race or multiracial due to their diverse racial or ethnic heritage. Similarly, individuals may not identify as either female or male due to their intersex identity. *See generally* Ilana Gelfman, *Because of Intersex: Intersexuality, Title VII, and the Reality of Discrimination "Because of . . . (Perceived) Sex,"* 34 N.Y.U. Rev. L. & Soc. Change 55 (2010).

238. *See McDonald v. Santa Fe Trail Transportation Co.*, 427 U.S. 273, 280 (1976), in which the court held that Title VII and §1981 prohibited discrimination against white men and women. The court proclaimed that its holding was in accordance with "uncontradicted legislative history to the effect that Title VII was intended to 'cover white men and white women and all Americans.'" *Id.* at 280 (quoting Congressman Celler's remarks at 110 Cong. Rec. 2578 (1964)).

differential treatment did not relate to the individual's actual or self-ascribed race, religion, national origin, color, or sex. However, whether invidious treatment derives from a plaintiff's actual or misperceived status is irrelevant and should not bear on the viability of her discrimination case.

As Professor Craig Robert Senn clarifies:

> employers who [are either "accurate discriminators" or "erroneous discriminators"] are identical in discriminatory intent and action. An "accurate discriminator" and an "erroneous discriminator" are each motivated to act based on a protected trait, and each actually manifests that intent in the form of a tangible, adverse employment action. Of course, the difference between these employers is the *accuracy* of the perception of protected status—one subset's employers happened to be "right" while the other subset's employers happened to be "wrong." But, the "erroneous discriminators" are—to be blunt—still discriminators.[239]

Indeed, as one federal district court in a recent misperception race discrimination case opined, it is "as offensive as it is incorrect" for an employer to contend that it is blameless on the issue of discrimination simply because the employer's perception of the plaintiff's race and resulting negative treatment did not align with the plaintiff's actual racial identity.[240] Unfortunately, in a series of intentional discrimination cases, federal courts reached the opposite result. These courts have endorsed the patently erroneous prescription that an individual's statutory right to be free from racial, religious, ethnic, color, and sex discrimination under Title VII is not conditioned upon whether an employer conceivably discriminated against an individual on the basis of a proscribed characteristic but rather upon the precision with which an employer's perception corresponds to an individual's self-ascribed or provable racial, religious, ethnic, color, or gender identity and whether the employer treats her accordingly.[241]

239. Senn, *supra* note 147, at 856.

240. *Boutros v. Avis Rent a Car Sys., LLC*, No. 10-C-8196, 2013 WL 3834405, at *7 (N.D. Ill. Jul. 24, 2013). In this case, the plaintiff, who identified as Assyrian, alleged that he suffered a hostile work environment and was terminated because the defendant-employer misperceived him as Arab. *Id.* at *6–7. The court dismissed the employer's defense that it could not be held liable for unlawful race discrimination under Title VII because it was not aware of the plaintiff's racial identity. *Id.* at *7.

241. As seen in *Burrage*, such a condition will have a deleterious effect on individuals who self-classify as mixed-race or multi-racial. Indeed, Professor Sharona Hoffman observes that "[t]he growing population of individuals of mixed 'racial' backgrounds makes the question of 'race' identity in American society increasingly complex and the idea that there are fixed 'racial' categories increasingly outdated." Sharona Hoffman, *Is There a Place for "Race" as a Legal Concept?*, 36 Ariz. St. L.J. 1093, 1141 (2004). In employment discrimination cases involving plaintiffs like Burrage who identify as mixed-race, courts generally place such plaintiffs into a monoracial category and analyze the case accordingly. Professor Nancy Leong critiques the "judicial erasure" of mixed-race plaintiffs and the particular animus and resulting discrimination that mixed-race individuals endure. *See* Nancy Leong, Judicial Erasure of Mixed-Race Discrimination, 59 Am. U. L. Rev. 469 (2010). *See generally* Davison, *supra* note 191 at 176 (2005) (arguing that courts' emphasis on whether a plaintiff's employment discrimination claim "fits within traditional notions of race" rather than on employer's intent is not only misplaced but is also especially problematic for mixed-race individuals, as the "tendency to mischaracterize a person's race is heightened for mixed-race people" because "[they] are often not easily identifiable based on stereotypical indicators"); Scott Rives, Comment, *Multiracial Work: Handing Over the Discretionary Judicial Tool of Multiracialism*, 58 UCLA L. Rev. 1303,

This prima facie actuality requirement indicates a divergence from assessing the "critical question of discrimination"[242] in Title VII intentional discrimination cases. Not only does an actuality requirement leave a Title VII plaintiff wanting for protection against discrimination, but it may also leave her unprotected against retaliation for opposing such discriminatory treatment.

§1.05 (MIS)PERCEPTIONS ARE PROTECTED UNDER TITLE VII

Within the federal judiciary, the adoption of an actuality requirement is the predominant trend in misperception discrimination cases arising under Title VII.[243] Additionally, as the previous section illustrated, some federal courts in conventionally framed discrimination cases have even allowed an actuality defense, and, as a result, imposed an actuality requirement on plaintiffs. In so doing, courts have ignored the central purposes of Title VII in part because of the ADA's "regarded as" language. This language has made it relatively easy and facially logical for courts to argue that Title VII, unlike the ADA, requires discrimination be based upon an individual's actual protected status. Furthermore, adopting an actuality requirement would be an easy enterprise for courts if they were not provided with legal authority or EEOC guidance on the issue of misperception discrimination.

However, this trend has not been universal. Certain federal courts and the EEOC have resisted an anti-anticlassificationist interpretation of Title VII, thereby refusing to impose an actuality requirement.[244] At present, there is a split amongst federal appellate courts and a near even split amongst federal district courts that have addressed directly the viability of misperception discrimination cases. The remainder of this Article presents Title VII jurisprudential support and EEOC directives which avow all individuals alleging categorical discrimination on the basis of Title VII's proscribed characteristics are already entitled to statutory protection and have standing

1310 (2012) (arguing that mixed-race plaintiffs should be accorded the task of "fram[ing] race as he or she desires for the initial complaint").

242. *Furnco Constr. Corp. v. Waters*, 438 U.S. 567, 577 (1978) (emphasis added).

243. *Compare* cases cited *supra* note *27* (adopting an actuality requirement), *with* cases cited *infra* note 244 (declining to adopt an actuality requirement).

244. *See Perkins*, 860 F. Supp. at 1273 (declining to adopt an actuality requirement yet adopting a reasonable basis test in a Title VII race/national origin discrimination case); *EEOC v. WC & M Enter.*, 496 F.3d 393, 401 (5th Cir. 2007); *Capek v. BNY Mellon, N.A.*, No. 15CIV4155LTSAJP, 2016 WL 2993211, at *1 (S.D.N.Y. May 23, 2016); *Arsham v. Mayor & City Council of Balt.*, 85 F. Supp. 3d 841, 849–50 (D. Md. 2015); *Kallabat v. Mich. Bell Tel. Co.*, No. 12-CV-15470, 2015 U.S. Dist. LEXIS 78944 (E.D. Mich. Jun. 18, 2015); *Boutros v. Avis Rent a Car Sys., LLC*, No. 10-C-8196, 2013 WL 3834405, at *7 (N.D. Ill. Jul. 24, 2013); *Henao v. Wyndham Vacation Resorts, Inc.*, No. 10-00772 SOM/BMK, 2013 WL 704895, at *7 (D. Haw. Feb. 26, 2013) (citing *EEOC v. WC & M Enterprises*); *Smith v. Specialty Pool Contractors*, No. 02:07-CV-1464, 2008 WL 4410163, at * 6 (W.D. Penn. Sept. 24, 2008) (citing *Fogelman v. Mercy Hosp., Inc.*, 283 F.3d 561, 567 (3d Cir. 2002)); *Wood v. Freeman Decorating Servs., Inc.*, No. 3:08-CV-00375-LRH-RAM, 2010 WL 653764, at *4 (D. Nev. Feb. 19, 2010) (pronouncing that "plaintiffs who are not members of [a] protected class have standing to challenge racially discriminatory conduct in their own right when they are the direct target of discrimination.") (quoting *RK Ventures, Inc. v. City of Seattle*, 307 F.3d 1045, 1055 (9th Cir. 2002) (citing *Estate of Amos v. City of Page*, 257 F.3d 1086, 1093–94 (9th Cir. 2001))).

to maintain a claim of discrimination, regardless of whether their identity was correctly perceived. First, Section A examines underappreciated EEOC directives and Fifth Circuit precedent in *EEOC v. WC & M Enterprises*, both of which affirm that misperception discrimination cases are cognizable under Title VII. Section B highlights the most recent cases wherein federal district courts have recognized misperception discrimination claims under Title VII.

Lastly, Section C explains that the Supreme Court has implicitly rejected an actuality requirement in Title VII cases and, thus, has articulated a more cohesive notion of statutory protection in a recent Title VII retaliation case, *Thompson v. North American Stainless, LP*. In their offer of practical solutions *within* Title VII's ambit, the following sections cover new and important ground towards extending protection to all victims of invidious, differential treatment on the basis of race, color, national origin, religion, or sex.

[A] Protection for Misperception Discrimination Plaintiffs: *EEOC v. WC & M Enterprises* and Longstanding EEOC Directives

[1] EEOC Directives

For over thirty years, the EEOC has issued interpretive directives on matters of employment discrimination involving misperception. Only the Fifth Circuit and a few other federal courts have expressly taken note of such directives in Title VII misperception discrimination cases.[245] In concluding that references to national origin directed at the plaintiff are sufficient to establish a prima facie case of national origin discrimination, the Fifth Circuit relied upon the EEOC Guidelines published in 1980, which state:

> [i]n order to have a claim of national origin discrimination under Title VII, it is not necessary to show that the alleged discriminator knew the *particular* national origin group to which the complainant belonged. [To prove a national origin claim], it is enough to show that the claimant was treated differently than others because of his or her foreign accent, appearance, or physical characteristics.[246]

In 2002, the EEOC reinforced its earlier guidance by enumerating that unlawful national origin discrimination under Title VII embodies:

> [e]mployment discrimination against an individual based on the employer's belief that he is a member of a particular national origin group, for example, discrimination against someone perceived as being Arab based on his speech,

245. *See, e.g.*, *EEOC v. WC & M Enter.*, 496 F.3d 393, 401 (5th Cir. 2007); *Henao v. Wyndham Vacation Resorts, Inc.*, No. 10-00772 SOM/BMK, 2013 WL 704895, at *7 (D. Haw. Feb. 26, 2013); *Arsham v. Mayor & City Council of Baltimore*, 85 F.Supp.3d 841, (D. Md. 2015); *Capek v. BNY Mellon, N.A.*, No. 15CIV4155LTSAJP, 2016 WL 2993211, at *3 (S.D.N.Y. May 23, 2016).

246. WC & M Enter., 496 F.3d at 401. (quoting 45 Fed. Reg. 85632, 85633 (Dec. 29, 1980)) (emphasis in original).

mannerisms, and appearance, *regardless of how he identifies himself or whether he is, in fact, of Arab ethnicity.*[247]

However, the EEOC did not simply limit its guidance on misperceptions to the context of national origin discrimination. The EEOC has specifically stated in its Compliance Manual that unlawful race discrimination under Title VII constitutes "discrimination against an individual based on a belief that the individual is a member of a particular racial group, *regardless of how the individual identifies himself.* Discrimination against an individual based on a perception of his or her race violates Title VII *even if that perception is wrong.*"[248] In light of increased workplace religious, ethnic, and racial discrimination post-9/11, the EEOC fortified its position that discrimination claims resulting from misperceptions about an individual's racial, religious, or ethnic identity are cognizable under Title VII. According to EEOC guidelines issued in 2002 in response to post-9/11 discrimination, Title VII prohibits "[h]arassing or otherwise discriminating because of the perception or belief that a person is a member of a particular racial, national origin, or religious group *whether or not that perception is correct.*"[249]

In the wake of terrorist attacks in Paris, France,[250] San Bernardino, California,[251] among other places and resulting backlash[252] against Muslims, Middle Eastern Americans, and those perceived as such, in August 2016 the EEOC re-emphasized its commitment to enforce Title VII against claims of harassment, intimidation, and discrimination based upon an individual's perceived religious and/or ethnic identity through its public restatement of guidance on national origin discrimination.[253] Accordingly, the EEOC made clear that the extension of Title VII protection to race,

247. EEOC Compl. Man. §13-II(B) (2002) (emphasis added).
248. EEOC Compl. Man. §15-II (2006) (emphasis added).
249. *Employment Discrimination Based on Religion, Ethnicity, or Country of Origin*, US Equal Opportunity Comm'n, http://www.eeoc.gov/laws/types/fs-relig_ethnic.cfm (last visited Aug. 2, 2013) (emphasis added). The EEOC has also expressed in its official publication, which provides guidance to employers on complying with the various antidiscrimination laws the agency enforces, that discrimination based on misperceptions about an individual's race constitutes unlawful discrimination under Title VII. According to the EEOC, "discrimination [occurs] against an individual based on a belief that the individual is a member of a particular racial group, regardless of how the individual identifies himself. Discrimination against an individual based on a perception of his or her race violates Title VII even if that perception is wrong." EEOC Compl. Man. §15-II (2006) (emphasis added). The EEOC provides parallel guidance for national origin discrimination. *See* EEOC Comp. Man. §13-II(B) (2002) ("Employment discrimination against an individual based on the employer's belief that he is a member of a particular national origin group, for example, discrimination against someone perceived as being Arab based on his speech, mannerisms, and appearance, regardless of how he identifies himself or whether he is, in fact, of Arab ethnicity.").
250. *See* Andrew Higgins and Kimiko De Freytas-Tamura, *Attacks in Paris*, N.Y.Times (Nov. 19, 2015), http://www.nytimes.com/news-event/attacks-in-paris.
251. *See* Michael S. Schmidt and Richard Pérez-Peña, *F.B.I. Treating San Bernardino Attack as Terrorism Case*, N.Y. Times (Dec. 4. 2015), http://www.nytimes.com/2015/12/05/us/tashfeen-malik-islamic-state.html?_r = 0.
252. *See* Laurie Goodstein, *Muslims in America Condemn Extremists and Fear Anew for Their Lives*, N.Y.Times (Dec. 4, 2015), http://www.nytimes.com/2015/12/05/us/muslims-in-america-condemn-extremists-and-fear-anew-for-their-lives.html?action = click&contentCollection = U.S.& module = RelatedCoverage&region = Marginalia&pgtype = article.
253. At https://www.eeoc.gov/eeoc/newsroom/wysk/religion_national_origin_2016.cfm.

religion, and national origin discrimination is not contingent upon a plaintiff's showing that the alleged discrimination was induced by her actual racial, religious, or ethnic identity. Instead, a plaintiff is protected when race, religion, or national origin is the basis for a covered employer's invidious, differential treatment. In its directives on religious, national origin, and racial discrimination, the EEOC acknowledges the nexus between employer perceptions of an individual's identity and the actualization of invidious, differential treatment. Furthermore, according to the EEOC, the plaintiff need not demonstrate that the employer is aware of the plaintiff's self-ascribed racial, ethnic, or religious identity nor must the plaintiff demonstrate that her identity comports with the employer's perception in order to assert an actionable claim of discrimination.

[2] EEOC v. WC & M Enterprises

In its prosecution of a Title VII case in *EEOC v. WC & M Enterprises*, the EEOC presented its above regulations on misperception discrimination to the Fifth Circuit, which proved to be influential to the successful outcome of the case.[254] The plaintiff-intervenor, Mohommed Rafiq, like Foad Afshar,[255] alleged that beginning September 11, 2001 and lasting until the end of his employment, he experienced post-9/11 discrimination.[256] Specifically, he contended that he experienced harassment because of his religion and national origin in violation of Title VII.[257] Rafiq, born in India, was a practicing Muslim.[258] According to Rafiq, upon reporting to work on the afternoon of September 11, his co-workers and supervisors were watching media reports of the terrorist attacks and inquired sarcastically about his whereabouts prior to his arrival.[259] Rafiq felt as if "[his] supervisors and colleagues were implying that [he] had participated in some way in the terrorist attacks against the United States."[260] Thereafter, his co-workers and supervisors repeatedly called him "Taliban" despite his requests that they cease doing so and his complaints to management.[261] According to Rafiq, he was subjected to mocking inquiries and comments about his Islamic faith and religious practices.[262]

Furthermore, on numerous occasions, Rafiq's supervisors and co-workers allegedly called him "Arab."[263] Rafiq also recalled an incident when, allegedly after inquiring about his mandatory attendance at a United Way event, his supervisor responded, "This is America. That's the way things work over here. This is not the

254. 496 F.3d 393 (5th Cir. 2007).
255. *See supra* section 1.02[A].
256. 496 F.3d at 396–97.
257. *Ibid.*
258. *Id.* at 396.
259. *Ibid.*
260. *Ibid.*
261. *Ibid.*
262. *Ibid.*
263. *Id.* at 397.

Islamic country where you come from."[264] His supervisor issued a written reprimand stating that Rafiq was acting like a "Muslim extremist" and he could no longer work with him due to his "militant stance."[265] Days later, Rafiq reported to management another harassing altercation involving a different supervisor. Two days after issuing his complaint, Rafiq was terminated.[266]

Rafiq sued his former employer on the basis of religion and national origin discrimination in violation of Title VII, and the EEOC decided to litigate Rafiq's case on his behalf.[267] Similar to other federal district courts in misperception discrimination cases, the court granted the defendant-employer's summary judgment motion with respect to Rafiq's national origin discrimination claim.[268]

Like *Burrage* and a series of other federal district court cases,[269] the court held in *WC & M Enterprises* that the EEOC could not assert a national origin discrimination claim because none of the alleged harassing comments referred to Rafiq's actual birthplace of India.[270] However, on appeal, the Fifth Circuit overruled the district court's conclusion that actuality is required in Title VII intentional discrimination cases. The Fifth Circuit declared that "a party is able to establish a discrimination claim [under Title VII] based on its own national origin *even though the discriminatory acts do not identify the victim's actual country of origin*."[271] The Fifth Circuit deferred to the EEOC's longstanding guidance on national origin discrimination[272] and held that alleged derogatory comments related to national origin, or rather the alleged statements specifically referencing co-workers' and supervisors' perception (or misperception) of Rafiq's country of origin, were sufficient to assert a cognizable claim of national origin discrimination.[273]

It is also important to note that the Eleventh Circuit endorsed the Fifth Circuit's holding by observing that "a harasser's use of epithets associated with a different ethnic or racial minority than the plaintiff will not necessarily shield an employer from liability for a hostile work environment."[274] The fact that two federal courts of appeal have taken seriously the EEOC's guidelines on misperception discrimination and rejected an anti-anticlassificationist interpretation of Title VII suggests that this will be

264. *Ibid.*
265. *Ibid.*
266. *Ibid.*
267. *Ibid.*
268. *See ibid.*
269. *See* cases cited *supra* note *27*.
270. *EEOC v. WC & M Enter., Inc.*, No. Civ.A. H-04-3372, 2005 WL 2106090, at *4 (S.D. Tex. 2005) (holding that the EEOC's national origin discrimination claim failed as a matter of law because none of the comments referring to Rafiq's national origin specifically targeted India, Rafiq's birthplace).
271. *WC & M Enter.*, 496 F.3d at 401 (emphasis added).
272. *See also Eriksen v. Allied Waste Sys., Inc.*, No. 06-13549, 2007 WL 1003851, at *6 (E.D. Mich. Apr. 2, 2007) (relying on the EEOC's guidance to conclude that "national origin discrimination is not based on the actual national origin of the plaintiff, but rather on the perceived characteristics of the plaintiff leading the alleged discriminator to treat the plaintiff differently").
273. *WC & M Enter.*, 496 F.3d at 401–03.
274. *Jones v. UPS Ground Freight*, 683 F.3d 1283, 1299 (11th Cir. 2012) (citing *WC & M Enter.*, 496 F.3d at 401).

the natural disposition of courts when deciding future misperception discrimination cases. However, as previously discussed, a number of federal district courts and at least one federal court of appeals have adopted an antithetical posture, which courts may be inclined to follow.[275] Consequently, divergent readings of Title VII's scope and meaning in misperception discrimination cases within the federal judiciary have produced a legal tension (that may soon engender a federal circuit split), which is in need of a resolution.

[B] Misperception Discrimination Plaintiffs Are Protected: More Recent Developments

In 2015, a federal district court in Maryland recognized a national origin misperception discrimination claim as actionable under Title VII in *Arsham v. Mayor & City Council of Baltimore.*[276] Applying the line of reasoning lawyers and judges asserted in previous misperception discrimination cases, the City argued that "Title VII does not protect an individual from discrimination based on the individual's perceived national origin.."[277] Calling the City's contention "superficially logical, but fundamentally abhorrent," the court explained that the "the obvious corollary of this argument is that it is lawful for an employer to discriminate against an individual based upon the employer's mistaken perception of the individual's actual national origin because only the latter is specifically outlawed as a basis for discrimination [in contradistinction to the ADA]."[278] The *Arsham* court rejected the City's position, opining that "Congress may not have thought it necessary to revise Title VII to conform to the wording of the ADA if it was aware of the EEOC's published 'Guidelines on Discrimination Because of National Origin,' which include the Commission's definition of national origin discrimination" and encompasses misperception discrimination.[279] The court deferred to the EEOC's guidance while also relying upon the Fifth Circuit's holding in *EEOC v. WC & M Enterprises* and other persuasive sources cited herein[280] to conclude that non-recognition of Arsham's misperception discrimination claim would unfairly "shield the employer from liability for discrimination that is no less injurious to the employee than if the employer guessed correctly regarding the employee's national origin."[281]

In 2016, citing to *Arsham*, in *Capek v. BNY Mellon*, a federal district court in New York also held that misperception discrimination claims are actionable under Section 1981 of the 1866 Civil Rights Act.[282] In Capek, the plaintiff, a twenty-five year veteran

275. *See supra* text accompanying note 28.
276. 85 F.Supp.3d 841 (D. Md. 2015). For a complete discussion of the facts in *Arsham, see* section 1.02[A][3].
277. 85 F.Supp.3d at 845.
278. *Ibid.*
279. *Id.* at 846.
280. *See id.* at 846–49. The Court also noted that "in analyzing this issue, the Court found helpful" the complete version of this article, *Categorically Black, White or Wrong: "Misperception Discrimination" and the State of Title VII Protection*. *Id.* at 849 fn.1.
281. *Id.* at 845.
282. *Capek v. BNY Mellon*, No. 15 Civ. 4155 (LTS) (AJP), 2016 WL 2993211 (S.D.N.Y. 2016). Significantly, the court also recognized Capek's retaliation claim.

and high ranking employee with BNY Mellon, a global financial services corporation, alleged that her manager misperceived her as Jewish.[283] Based upon this misperception, her manager restricted her cultivation of business opportunities to the Jewish community and unlike her colleagues, Capek's manager did not channel non-Jewish clients to Capek.[284] Capek alleged that she lost significant incentive pay because of her manager's segregative employment practice deriving from his mistaken belief she was Jewish, about which she complained to her manager.[285] When Capek expressed her discontent with this practice, her manager "justified his conduct by stating that he makes decisions based on what he believes will be 'a good fit' for the client and that there are 'cultural sensitivities in the buying environment.'"[286] According to Capek, upon realizing that she was not Jewish, her manager responded, "all this time I thought you were Jewish.'"[287] Like the *Arsham* court, the *Capek* court, rejected the defendant-employer's argument that Section 1981's statutory language does not permit misperception discrimination claims. It, too, was persuaded by the "weight of the authority in other circuit and district courts, which [held] that claims of discrimination based on mistaken 'perception' are cognizable even under Title VII."[288] Furthermore, the *Capek* court pronounced "[t]hat an employer discriminates against an employee based upon a mistaken belief regarding that employee's race (or any of the characteristics protected under Title VII) does not make the practices less damaging to the employee nor does it make the discrimination itself less worthy of redress."[289] Thus, the Fifth Circuit's holding in *EEOC v. WC & M Enterprises*, the EEOC's guidance alongside more recent judicial decisions recognizing misperception discrimination cases, like *Arsham* and *Capek*, solidify that asserting a remediable claim of unlawful discrimination is not contingent upon a plaintiff's demonstration that an employer discriminated against her because of her actual protected status. Furthermore, misperception discrimination plaintiffs are no less aggrieved by unlawful workplace discrimination than plaintiffs in conventionally framed discrimination cases. Indeed, the *Arsham* court fully appreciated the severe psychological and emotional distress that ultimately triggered a suicide attempt caused by the workplace discrimination Arsham suffered due to her supervisor's misperceptions about her ethnic identity and held that she articulated a plausible claim of intentional infliction of emotional distress.[290]

[C] Towards Title VII Protection for All "Persons Aggrieved" Categorical Discrimination: *Thompson v. American Stainless, LP*

The previous sections have demonstrated that the actuality requirement is not an inherent or stable prerequisite for Title VII protection and that misperception

283. *Id.* at *1.
284. *Ibid.*
285. *Ibid.*
286. *Ibid.*
287. *Ibid.*
288. *Id.* at *3.
289. *Ibid.*
290. 85 F.Supp.3d at 850.

discrimination plaintiffs can, too, suffer loss of employment, differential workplace conditions, harassment, and resulting severe emotional and psychological distress. Consequently, misperception discrimination plaintiffs endure the same occupational injuries stemming from invidious, differential treatment engaged in by a covered employer as plaintiffs in conventionally framed cases. As previously discussed in section 1.01, Title VII provides that "persons aggrieved" may seek statutory protection and relief. Yet, Congress did not define which individuals are "persons aggrieved" by practices proscribed under the Act, such as race, color, sex, national origin, and color discrimination;[291] retaliation for opposing unlawful discrimination on these grounds; and retaliation for participation in proceedings related to such discrimination.[292]

However, in *Thompson v. North American Stainless, LP*, the Supreme Court demarcated the scope of Title VII's "persons aggrieved" language.[293] Under similar factual circumstances to *Fogleman*, the Court concluded that the plaintiff in *Thompson* alleged a cognizable claim of retaliation on different, yet related, grounds.[294] The petitioner, Thompson, and his fiancée worked simultaneously for the defendant-employer.[295] Thompson's fiancée sued the defendant-employer for sex discrimination under Title VII.[296] Three weeks later, the defendant-employer terminated Thompson.[297] According to Thompson, even though he did not engage in statutorily protected activity[298] (e.g., Thompson did not file a claim of discrimination nor did he oppose the discrimination his fiancée allegedly experienced), Thompson's former employer terminated him in retaliation against his fiancée because of her protected conduct.[299] Therefore, Thompson's termination constituted unlawful retaliation under Title VII.[300]

291. Congress also did not define the term "discrimination." This Article demonstrates that the term discrimination was primarily intended to cover invidious, differential treatment. However, the Supreme Court has also interpreted unlawful intentional discrimination or disparate treatment to envelop an employer's benign consideration of a protected classification in an employment decision that infringes upon the legitimate expectations of an employee. *See Ricci v. DeStefano*, 557 U.S. 557, 583 (2009); *see also Trans World Airlines, Inc. v. Hardison*, 432 U.S. 63, 78-83 (1977), wherein the Supreme Court held that an employer's duty to accommodate an employee's religious observances and practices cannot override other employees' legitimate expectations established pursuant to a nondiscriminatory collective bargaining agreement or other valid employment contract. The court reasoned that accommodating one employee's religious obligations by denying another employee her shift preferences and depriving the employee her contractual rights under a collective bargaining agreement constitute "unequal treatment" or discrimination that "Title VII does not contemplate." *Id.* at 81.
292. *See supra* section 1.01.
293. *Thompson v. N. Am. Stainless, LP*, 131 S. Ct. 863, 863 (2011).
294. It is important to note that *Thompson* did not advance the perception theory the Third Circuit adopted in *Fogleman*. *But see* Gerri L. Plain, *I'll Get You My Pretty . . . and Your Little Associate Too—the Expansion of Employee Protection in Title VII Retaliation Claims*, 42 CUMB. L. REV. 549, 564 (2012) (positing that the Supreme Court implicitly adopted the perception theory in *Thompson*).
295. *Thompson*, 131 S. Ct. at 867.
296. *Ibid.*
297. *Ibid.*
298. *See ibid.*
299. *Ibid.*
300. *Ibid.*

The Supreme Court interpreted Title VII's "persons aggrieved" language to hold that Thompson's retaliation claim was actionable under the statute. The court pronounced that "the term 'aggrieved' in Title VII . . . enable[s] [a] suit by *any* plaintiff with an interest 'arguably [sought] to be protected by [Title VII],' while excluding plaintiffs . . . whose interests are unrelated to the statutory prohibitions in Title VII."[301] Moreover, the Court reasoned that Thompson was a person aggrieved with standing to sue his former employer for unlawful retaliation because he was not an "accidental victim" of the employer's retaliatory animus against his fiancée.[302] According to the court:

> injuring [Thompson] was the employer's intended means of harming [Thompson's fiancée]. Hurting him was the unlawful act by which the employer punished her. In those circumstances, we think Thompson well within the zone of interests sought to be protected by Title VII. He is a person aggrieved with standing to sue.[303]

The Court allowed Thompson to maintain his retaliation action even though he did not actually engage in protected activity. In doing so, the Supreme Court implicitly denounced a showing of actuality as a prerequisite to maintain a Title VII action. Therefore, at a minimum, an individual who alleges that she is the victim of a covered employer's categorical discrimination on the basis of protected characteristics or protected conduct is a "person aggrieved" under Title VII and has standing to sue. In both instances, such plaintiffs are asserting claims that clearly fall "within the zone of interests protected by Title VII."[304] Thus, to maintain an action under Title VII, plaintiffs need not demonstrate that a covered employer's invidious, differential treatment was animated by their actual protected status or protected activity. Plaintiffs must allege that they suffered categorical discrimination on Title VII's proscribed grounds.

Unequivocally, a categorical discrimination plaintiff contends that she suffered employment-related harms of central importance to Congress when it enacted Title VII of the 1964 Civil Rights Act. Plaintiffs in misperception and conventionally framed discrimination cases are asserting parallel claims "within the zone of interests protected by Title VII"[305] in that they are seeking to remedy invidious, differential treatment on the basis of Title VII's proscribed characteristics. Furthermore, plaintiffs like Mr. Burrage and Mr. Butler, who experience invidious, differential treatment because of their misperceived identities, are no more accidental victims of an employer's categorical discrimination than plaintiffs alleging discrimination because of their

301. *Id.* at 870 (emphasis added) (quoting *Nat'l Credit Union Admin. v. First Nat. Bank & Trust Co.*, 522 U.S. 479, 495 (1998)).
302. *Ibid.*
303. *Ibid.*
304. *Ibid.*
305. *Ibid.*

self-ascribed identities. Rather, both sets of plaintiffs are intended victims[306] of discrimination that emanated from the employer's perceptions about their race, religion, color, sex, or national origin. Therefore, such plaintiffs should not be forced to satisfy an actuality requirement to vindicate their rights to be free from discrimination in the workplace, as they are "persons aggrieved."

§1.06 CONCLUSION

This Article unearths an alarming movement within antidiscrimination law, theory, and praxis. Some courts have employed an anti-anticlassificationist interpretation of Title VII in misperception and conventionally framed discrimination cases and in the process have imposed upon plaintiffs an unnecessary actuality requirement to benefit from Title VII protection. Per these federal courts, plaintiffs in misperception discrimination cases are automatically deemed unprotected because the discriminatory treatment they suffer is not on the basis of their actual protected status. In doing so, courts have also failed to recognize or are dismissive of the psychological and emotional injuries the alleged discrimination may cause. However, rather than protect individuals against invidious, differential treatment engaged in by covered employers, courts' anti-anticlassificationist interpretation of Title VII fosters irremediable race, color, sex, national origin, and religious discrimination in the workplace. Significantly, a number of federal courts have recognized misperception discrimination claims as cognizable, appreciating that the occupational injuries these plaintiffs suffer are no less harmful or remediable than those suffered by plaintiffs in conventionally framed intentional discrimination cases. Thus, courts should no longer apply an actuality requirement in misperception discrimination cases; misperception discrimination plaintiffs *are persons aggrieved by and protected against* unlawful race, color, sex, national origin, and religious discrimination in the workplace.

306. *See ibid.* (holding that the plaintiff who did not engage in protected conduct but was allegedly terminated because of his fiancée's protected activity was a "person aggrieved with standing to sue" his former employer under Title VII because he was "not an accidental victim of . . . the employer's unlawful act").

CHAPTER 2

Work-Life Balance and the Use of Child-Care Leave by Fathers Serving in the Military: The Case of *Konstantin Markin v. Russia*

Elena Gerasimova[*]

§2.01 INTRODUCTION

In the course of the reforms of the 1990s the Russian legislature repealed the model contract of working mothers that had previously existed in law, when a special provision for child-care leave was available only to women. In both law and legal practice, the concept of gender equality began to gain ground.

Article 19 (1) of the Constitution of the Russian Federation[1] (RF) lays down the principle of equal rights for citizens before the law and the judicial system. Article 19 (3) of the Constitution of the RF safeguards equal human rights and freedoms for citizens regardless of gender and a range of other characteristics. Russia is a signatory to a substantial number of international agreements prohibiting discrimination in general, and also to specific agreements targeting discrimination in employment relations, including the fundamental conventions.[2] A separate clause prohibiting discrimination is included in Article 3 of the Labour Code of the Russian Federation (LC

* Ph.D., National Research University Higher School of Economics, Associate Professor, Head of the Labour Law and Social Protection Law Department; Director of the Centre for Social and Labour Rights, Moscow, B. Trehsvyatitelsky pereulok, b.3, room 238, egerasimova@hse.ru, gerasimova@trudprava.ru.
1. Constitution of the Russian Federation. Approved on 12 Dec. 1993 in a nationwide plebiscite.
2. ILO Equal Remuneration Convention No. 100 (adopted in 1951) and ILO Convention No. 111 Concerning Discrimination in Respect of Employment and Occupation (adopted in 1958).

RF).[3] In order to make work compatible with family obligations, the LC RF also contains Chapter 41 entitled 'Specific labour standards for women and persons with family obligations', which currently contains twelve articles regulating various employment conditions for women, pregnant women, and persons with family obligations.

The long-standing Soviet tradition of integrating women into the life of society at large and into the labour force along with a series of legal proclamations prohibiting discrimination has worked against a proper understanding of the essential features of discrimination, while fostering the attitude that the issue had been settled in a satisfactory manner. Even though there is a lack of awareness of the fact in Russian society, many of its legal standards and judicial practices are discriminatory. Gender stereotypes are in full force, aided and abetted in recent years by advocacy of a patriarchal way of life and its associated values.

Child-care leave is one of the most important entitlements that make holding down a job compatible with starting a family. Russian law entitles the mother to child-care leave until the child reaches the age of three.[4] This leave may be used, partially or in full, by the child's father, grandmother or grandfather, or by other relatives or foster parents who are directly engaged in caring for the child.[5] With a duration of three full years, this leave in Russia is among the longest anywhere in the world. Until the child is a year and a half, the worker also receives a monthly financial allowance amounting to 40% of his or her average wage.[6]

However, this provision does not apply without restriction to all military personnel, but only to women in the armed forces. According to the Federal Law 'On the status of those in military service', pregnancy, maternity and child-care leave is granted only to women in the military. In addition, according to Russian law, only women in the military[7] or those in the military caring for children lacking a father (or mother) have the right to social entitlements and compensation.

A man serving in the military under contract may, if he so requests, be granted up to three months of additional (ordinary) leave in the event of the death of his wife in childbirth, or if he is caring for one of several children under the age of 14 (or under the age of 16 for a child with disabilities) lacking maternal care (in the event of the mother's death or severe injury, loss of parental custody, extended hospitalization, and other circumstances that preclude caring for a child).[8]

---

3. Labour Code of Russian Federation (LC RF), *Sobraniye Zakonodatelstva Rossiyskoy Federazii (SZ RF)* of 7 Jan. 2002, No. 1, Item 3 as amended by the Federal Law of 2 May 2014 No.116-FZ, SZ RF of 12 May 2014, No. 19, Item 2321.
4. LC RF *supra* n. 3, at s. 1, Art. 256.
5. *Id.* at s. 2 Art. 256.
6. Federal Law of 19 May 1995, No. 81-FZ *On state financial aid to citizens with children*, SZ RF of 22 May 1995, No. 21, Item 1929, Arts 13–15.
7. Federal Law of 27 May 1998, No. 76-FZ *On the status of military personnel*, Point 13, Art. 11.
8. Regulations of the Military Service Act by the Decree of the President of the Russian Federation of 16 Sep. 1999, No. 1237, Points 5 and 7, Art. 32.

It follows from these provisions that men serving in the military are also barred from receiving the monthly benefit payments that apply only to women in the military.[9]

This usage was in place for many years, without being called into question. However, the principle underlying its application was not discussed in advance or analysed. Only after the serviceman Konstantin Markin took his case to court was there any discussion of the justification for it.

§2.02 THE CASE OF KONSTANTIN MARKIN IN COURTS OF GENERAL JURISDICTION AND THE CONSTITUTIONAL COURT OF RUSSIAN FEDERATION

Konstantin Markin was an officer serving under contract as head of a shift for a section of a military division. He applied for the child-care leave that is granted in the case of a child under the age of 3, but his application was rejected on the grounds that this leave did not apply to fathers in the military.

In accordance with the prevailing legal standard, Markin was initially granted three months of additional ordinary leave, but that order was rescinded because of a lack of required documentation. Markin filed a suit in court with a claim for restoration of the ordinary leave that had been denied. The decision of the Pushkin Garrison Military Court of 9 March 2006 was that Markin was entitled to thirty-nine days of unused additional leave, but on 17 April 2006 that decision too was reversed on appeal to the Military Court of the Leningradskiy Command, which rejected Markin's request.

Markin had filed another suit at the same time, requesting that he be granted the child-care leave that applies to children under the age of three, but that claim was also rejected on the grounds that only women in the military qualify for this kind of leave (by decision of the Pushkin Garrison Military Court of 14 March 2006 and judgment of the Military Court of the Leningradskiy Command of 27 April 2006).

Markin then applied to the European Court of Human Rights (ECtHR) and subsequently to the Constitutional Court of the RF claiming that the provisions of the law that had been cited against his claim violated the Constitution of the RF inasmuch as they discriminated against and impeded the right of men serving in the military under contract to care for their children.

It should be noted that, after communication about the case from the ECtHR,[10] the head of the military unit granted parental leave to Markin until the third birthday of his youngest son, and in October 2006 Markin received financial aid amounting to

9. Federal Law of 19 May 1995 *supra* n. 6 at Part 1, Art. 13, paras 3 and 7 and Part 1, Art. 15, paras 2 and 3; Regulations on the determination and payment of state financial aid to citizens with children by the Decree of the President of the RF of 30 Dec. 2006 No. 865, Point 35, Subpoints b and e, and Point 44, paras 2 and 3. This document was annulled on 1 Jan. 2010; however, a new document (Order of the Ministry of Health and Social Development of Russia of 23 Dec. 2009 No. 1012 'On the manner and conditions applicable to determining and paying state financial aid to citizens with children') contains analogous provisions.
10. *See*: Oleg Anishik, *Konstantin Markin v. Russia': The Grand Chamber of the European Court Has Issued its Judgment*, (http://europeancourt.ru/2012/03/22/9768/); Kirill Koroteev, *The Conflict That Wasn't. Commentary on the Decision of the European Court of Human Rights in the 'Konstantin Markin v. Russia' Case*, 4 Comparative Constitutional Review, 122–130 (2012).

RUB 200,000, equivalent to approximately EUR 5,900, 'in view of [his] difficult family situation, the necessity of taking care of three minor children and the absence of other sources of income' (as stated in a letter from the head of military unit).[11] Subsequently, in December 2006, the Military Court of the Pushkin Garrison[12] criticized the head of the military unit for granting leave to Markin.

The Constitutional Court of the RF issued a judgment in the negative,[13] citing Article 1 §2 of ILO Convention No. 111 which provides that 'any distinction, exclusion or preference in respect of a particular job based on the inherent requirements thereof shall not be deemed to be discrimination.' The Constitutional Court of the RF stated that 'Inasmuch as military service entails unavoidable specific requirements that preclude any pervasive non-performance of their duties by military service persons without resulting in harm to the public interest, denial of leave for child-care to men in military service under contract does not constitute an infringement of constitutional rights and freedoms, including those guaranteed by Article 38 (part 2) of the Constitution. [...] Moreover, this limitation is consistent with the voluntary character of entering into a contract to serve in the military.'[14]

The Constitutional Court of the RF upheld the legislation with this reasoning: 'By extending the right to child-care leave as an exception only to female military personnel, the legislature proceeded, in the first place, from the extremely limited participation of women in military service, and, in the second place, from the distinctive maternal social role performed by women in society.' The Court found no incompatibility with either the equality of human and citizens' rights and freedoms or with equality of rights for men and women.[15]

§2.03 *KONSTANTIN MARKIN V. RUSSIA* IN THE ECtHR

Markin also appealed to the ECtHR for protection of his human rights. On 7 October 2010 the Chamber of the ECtHR issued a judgment[16] in favour of Markin (Application # 30078/06), and in March 2012 the Grand Chamber upheld this decision.

It fell to the Chamber of the First Section of the ECtHR to consider Markin's application after the Constitutional Court of the RF had already issued its decision, and the Chamber found infringement of Article 14 (prohibiting discrimination) of the

11. *Konstantin Markin v. Russia* [FS], Application no. 30078/06 (7 Oct. 2010) §16, http://hudoc.ECHR.coe.int/eng#{%22appno%22:[%2230078/06%22],%22itemid%22:[%22001-100926%22]} Accessed on 20 Nov. 2016.
12. *Id.* §17.
13. Judgment of the Constitutional Court of the RF of 15 Jan. 2009 No. 187-O-O 'Rejection of the claim by Mr Konstantin Alexandrovich Markin to the effect that his constitutional rights are infringed by provisions of Articles 13 and 15 of the Federal Law *On state financial aid to citizens with children*, Articles 10 and 11 of the Federal Law *On the status of military personnel*, Article 32 of the Decree on military service, and Points 35 and 44 of the Decree on determining and paying state financial aid to citizens with children', accessed in *Consultant Plus* (a commercial legal database).
14. Judgment of the Constitutional Court of the RF of 15 Jan. 2009 No. 187-O-O, Point 2.2.
15. *Id.* at Point 2.3.
16. *Konstantin Markin v. Russia* [FS], *supra* n. 11 at §16.

European Convention on Human Rights in conjunction with Article 8 (establishing the right to respect for private and family life) bringing a series of arguments to bear not only on the justifications presented to the ECtHR by the Government of the RF in the application, but also on the justifications employed by the Constitutional Court of the RF.

According to the categories employed in international law, section I, Article 8 of the European Convention on Human Rights refers to civil (or personal) rights. However, in practice the ECtHR applies a broader interpretation of that Article than merely the right to respect for family life. In 1998 the ECtHR held that it was applicable to financial aid during parental leave in that such support facilitates family life and has a direct impact on its arrangement.[17] In this way Article 8 was extended to cover what by its legal properties is a social right to receive financial aid relating to the birth of a child (or children). In 2009 an infringement of Article 8 (infringement of gender equality in entitlement to financial aid) was found in a Hungarian law which granted financial maternity aid to fathers only in the event of the mother's death.[18]

This way of interpreting Article 8 was also applied by the ECtHR in the Markin case. First, the Chamber took exception with the Constitutional Court of the RF by stating that 'society has moved towards more equal sharing between men and women of the responsibility for the upbringing of children and that men's caring role has gained recognition'. The Chamber could not 'overlook [...] developing views and associated legal changes [...] on this issue' and added: 'Nor can the reference to the traditional perception of women as primary child-carers provide sufficient justification for the exclusion of the father from the entitlement to take parental leave if he so wishes.'[19]

Second, the First Section Chamber emphasized that impeding the relations of military personnel of either gender with a newborn child would require a higher standard of justification that was absent in this case; and it went on to observe that, although maintaining national defence is a legitimate interest of the state, there must be a 'reasonable relationship of proportionality between the means employed and the aim pursued.'[20] The Chamber maintained that the Government of Russia had not provided any justification in this connection.[21]

Third, the Chamber took up the issue of the proportionality of the infringement of rights to the harm to national security arising if those rights were not restricted, concluding that 'the core argument of the Constitutional Court in support of the limitation of the rights of servicemen was that [...] the taking of parental leave by servicemen on a large scale would have a negative effect on the fighting power and operational effectiveness of the armed forces' but maintained that this argument is unconvincing. The Chamber noted the lack of substantiation of damage to national security and observed that 'the Constitutional Court based its decision on a pure

17. *Petrovic v. Austria*, Case № 156/1996/775/976 (27 Mar. 1998).
18. *Weller v. Hungary*, Case № 44399/05 (31 Mar. 2009).
19. *Konstantin Markin v. Russia* [FS], *supra* n. 11 at § 49.
20. *Id.* §55.
21. *Id.* §§53–55.

assumption, without attempting to probe its validity by checking it against statistical data or by weighing the conflicting interests of maintaining the operational effectiveness of the army, on the one hand, and of protecting servicemen against discrimination in the sphere of family life and promoting the best interests of their children, on the other.'[22]

Fourth, the Chamber emphasized that 'the different treatment of men and women in this sphere [...] was founded on the traditional gender roles, that is on the perception of women as primary child-carers and men as primary breadwinners, and these gender prejudices cannot be considered to amount to sufficient justification for the difference in treatment.'[23] The Chamber was 'particularly struck by the Constitutional Court's intimation that a serviceman wishing to take personal care of his children was free to resign from the armed forces, and servicemen are thereby forced to make a difficult choice between caring for their new-born children and pursuing their military career, no such choice being faced by servicewomen.'[24]

The Chamber ultimately found a violation under Article 14 in conjunction with Article 8 and recommended that the Government of Russia take measures to amend provisions in the law in order to put an end to discrimination against male military personnel as far as their entitlement to parental leave is concerned.[25]

§2.04 REACTION TO THE ECtHR'S DECISION IN RUSSIA

This decision of the ECtHR's First Section Chamber prompted discussion and strong objections by many in the Russian legal community, mostly because the decision criticized not only the laws of the RF, but also the judgment of 15 January 2009 of the Constitutional Court of the RF. The decision was taken as serious interference by the ECtHR with the authority of the Constitutional Court of the RF, and it gave impetus to a discussion of the relationship between national and supranational institutions. Questions were raised about whether the instructions of the ECtHR on required amendments to the law constituted a 'direct encroachment on national sovereignty that clearly exceeds the rights and powers stipulated by the Convention and, in turn, also clearly exceeds the authority inherent in the Convention itself',[26] and about both the acceptability of a single legal model as elaborated by the European Convention on Human Rights and the limitations on the ECtHR in interpreting the Convention.[27] A question also came up in connection with the subsequent decision of the ECtHR of 7 October 2010 about how to apply it when the issue of the constitutionality of the regulations which did not satisfy the ECtHR had already been decided by the Constitutional Court of the RF. There was also concern about what would happen with the judgment of the Constitutional Court of the RF of 15 January 2009.

22. *Id.* § 57.
23. *Id.* § 58.
24. *Id.* § 58.
25. *Id.* §§66, 67.
26. Valerii Zorkin, *A Limit to Acquiescence*, Rossiiskaya Gazeta (29 Oct. 2010).
27. Aliya Nurtdinova, *The Right to Respect for Family Life and Its Protection by the European Court of Human Rights*, 2 Journal of Constitutional Jurisprudence, at 1–8.

That discussion clearly highlighted the differences between the Constitutional Court of the RF and the ECtHR in understanding regulations prohibiting discrimination, in relating discrimination to the standards set by the Constitution of the RF for protecting maternity and childhood (Part 1, Article 38 of the Constitution of the RF), and in the limitations on restricting the human rights and freedoms of citizens (Part 3, Article 55 of the Constitution of the RF).

In his comments on the decision of the ECtHR, V.D. Zorkin, chairman of the Constitutional Court of Russia, called attention to:

> the kind of legal basis underlying these findings of the ECtHR about discrimination in the application of the laws that accommodate family life. The ECtHR affirms that the regard for women as primary care-givers for children is 'gender prejudice' and therefore criticizes the conclusions of the Constitutional Court on the special social role of women in society because of maternity. As an aside, the conclusions of the Constitutional Court based on the standard in part 1, Article 38 of the Constitution, according to which maternity and childhood along with the family are brought under the protection of the state, also are in keeping with the findings of modern scientific research in the fields of paediatrics and child psychology.[28]

S.P. Mavrin, the Deputy Chair of the Constitutional Court of the RF, in discussing compliance with the ECtHR's decision, observed that it would be possible in one of the two ways: either by eliminating child-care leave for servicewomen with children under the age of three, or by extending that right to servicemen as well. In this case, as he indicated, it is vital to recognize that, in contrast with servicewomen who mostly serve in posts that 'are not part of what we may call combat-ready forces', it may be said that 'the majority of servicemen fulfil their military duties in units that maintain a state of military readiness connected, by the way, with such things as servicing strategic nuclear weapons that are often placed at sites in hard-to-reach places.' For this reason, he maintains that 'an unanticipated abandonment of such a military posting can hardly be regarded as having no particular impact on Russia's security.'[29]

With this as a justification, Mavrin concluded that 'in view of its responsibility to the present and future generations of Russians, the national legislature has no path that does not violate the Constitution of its own nation for the sake of implementing in its legal system the measures that follow from the decision of the ECtHR in the Markin case.'[30] At the same time any appeal against the judgment of the Constitutional Court of the RF in the Markin case was ruled out by reference to the federal law 'On the

28. Valerii Zorkin, *supra* n. 26.
29. Sergey Mavrin, *Decisions of the European Court on Human Rights and the Russian Legal System* (Presentation and the 13th International Forum on Constitutional Jurisprudence entitled *The European Convention for the Protection of Human Rights and Fundamental Freedoms in the 21st Century: Problems and Prospects for its Application*, 20 Nov. 2010), http://pravo.ru/news/view/42649/). On the justification for excluding military service personnel from the scope of application of workers' rights *see also*: Aliya Nurtdinova, *The Right to Respect for Family Life and Its Protection by the European Court of Human Rights* at 5.
30. Sergey Mavrin, *supra* n. 29.

Constitutional Court of the Russian Federation'[31] which makes that Court's decision final and beyond appeal.

It should be noted that, instead of considering the possibility of excluding certain specific categories of military personnel from the list of those that may be granted child-care leave, the Constitutional Court of the RF rejected any such possibility for all categories of men in the military.

§2.05 DECISION OF THE GRAND CHAMBER OF THE ECtHR

The Government of Russia appealed to the Grand Chamber of the ECtHR against the decision of the ECtHR of 7 October 2010, and on 22 March 2012 the Grand Chamber issued its decision in favour of Konstantin Markin.[32] In this decision the analysis of the circumstances of the case centred on the issues of granting equal amounts of child-care leave to mothers and fathers and on the justification for denying that right to fathers in military service.

In discussing the nature of child-care leave and to whom it should be granted, the Government of Russia argued that during the three years of child-care leave, a serviceman's skills would deteriorate to such an extent that he could return to his post only after expensive retraining, while the absence from work of a serviceman's wife would be less of a burden for society.[33] Furthermore 'servicewomen were exceptionally granted an entitlement to parental leave', because according to scientific studies, there is 'a special biological and psychological connection between the mother and the newborn child.' Another argument was that 'given that there were few women in the army, their absence from service would have no impact on fighting capacity. [...] In view of the above, the present case concerned a justified positive discrimination of women.'[34]

The ECtHR Grand Chamber emphasized that:

> in contrast to maternity leave which is intended to enable the woman to recover from the childbirth and to breastfeed her baby if she so wishes, parental leave and parental leave allowances are intended to enable a parent concerned to stay at home to look after an infant personally. [...] The Court is therefore not convinced by the Government's argument concerning the special biological and psychological connection between the mother and the newborn child in the period following the birth, which is said to be confirmed by modern scientific research.

The ECtHR Grand Chamber concluded that 'as far as the role of taking care of the child during the period corresponding to parental leave is concerned, men and women are "similarly placed"'.[35]

31. Federal Constitutional Law dated 21 Jul. 1994, No. 1-FKZ *On the Constitutional Court of the Russian Federation*, Collected Statutes of the Russian Federation, No. 13 at 1,447 (25 Jul. 1994).
32. *Konstantin Markin v. Russia* [GC], Application no. 30078/06 (22 Mar. 2012).
33. *Id.* §115.
34. *Id.* §116.
35. *Id.* §132.

Regarding the justification for denying men in the military the right to child-care leave, the Grand Chamber stressed that any restrictions on Convention rights are justified only if they 'satisfy the test of necessity in a democratic society'.[36]

The Grand Chamber elaborated on its position in adding that:

> in respect of restrictions on the family and private life of military personnel, especially when the relevant restrictions concern 'a most intimate part of an individual's private life', there must exist 'particularly serious reasons' before such interferences can satisfy the requirements of Article 8 § 2 of the Convention. In particular, there must be a reasonable relationship of proportionality between the restrictions imposed and the legitimate aim of protecting national security. Such restrictions are acceptable only where there is a real threat to the armed forces' operational effectiveness.[37]

The ECtHR Grand Chamber found that 'the Government's reference to positive discrimination is misconceived, and the different treatment of servicemen and servicewomen as regards entitlement to parental leave was clearly not intended to correct the disadvantaged position of women in society or "factual inequalities" between men and women.'[38] The ECtHR affirmed that such a distinction 'has the effect of perpetuating gender stereotypes and is disadvantageous both to women's careers and to men's family life.'[39]

Concerning the proper scope of any 'distinction, exclusion or preference in respect of a particular job based on the inherent requirements thereof, which shall not be deemed to be discrimination',[40] the Grand Chamber held that it 'may be justifiable to exclude from the entitlement to parental leave any personnel, male or female, who may not easily be replaced in their duties owing to such factors as, for example, their hierarchical position, rare technical qualifications or involvement in active military actions.' But the Grand Chamber could not regard as legitimate 'a general and automatic restriction applied to a group of people on the basis of their sex.'[41]

In the hearings of the Grand Chamber, as in the earlier hearings, the Government of the RF failed to present proof of any deleterious effect on Russia's defence readiness that would result from granting child-care leave to Markin. The ECtHR further noted that the duties performed by the plaintiff might be assumed by other service personnel - either male or female - during child-care leave. In this connection, the ECtHR added that it is 'significant that equivalent posts in the applicant's unit were often held by servicewomen and that he himself was frequently replaced in his duties by servicewomen.'[42]

It is indicative that the hearings of the Grand Chamber of the ECtHR in this case referred far less to the judgment of the Constitutional Court of the RF than was the case

36. *Id.* §136.
37. *Id.* §137.
38. *Id.* §141.
39. *Id.* §141.
40. *Article 1 of ILO Convention No. 111 Concerning Discrimination in Respect of Employment and Occupation.*
41. *Konstantin Markin v. Russia* [GC], *supra* n. 11 at §148.
42. *Id.* § 149.

in the first hearings. However, this was the result not so much of a turn toward diplomacy on the part of the ECtHR, but rather of the significant number of clarifications and arguments presented by the Government of Russia in the second hearings, which the ECtHR therefore could address instead of making the case hinge on the logic of the Constitutional Court of the RF.[43]

§2.06 PRIORITY OF THE ECtHR OR OF THE CONSTITUTION OF RUSSIA: CHANGES TO THE RUSSIAN LAW

The decision of the ECtHR on this matter, concerning bringing Russian law into compliance with the European Convention for the Protection of Human Rights and Fundamental Freedoms, was not heeded by the Russian Federation. *Konstantin Markin* was not the first case in which a violation of the Convention was ascertained in conjunction with an earlier decision of the Constitutional Court of the RF that there had been no violation of the Constitution.[44] However, *Konstantin Markin* was the case that prompted debate in Russia about compliance with the decisions of the ECtHR and the priority of the Constitution of the RF over international agreements.

On 14 July 2015 the Constitutional Court of the RF in responding to a query from four factions of the State Duma declared that compliance with decisions of the ECtHR may not take precedence over the Constitution of the RF.[45] The Constitutional Court of the RF indicated that the European Convention for the Protection of Human Rights and Fundamental Freedoms and the legal standing of the ECtHR based upon it must yield to the supremacy of the Constitution. If the ECtHR should issue an interpretation of the Convention that stands in contradiction to the Constitution of the RF, then by virtue of the supremacy of the Russian Constitution, it will be obligatory to disregard the literal stipulations of the ECtHR. The Constitution may be enforced by the Constitutional Court of the RF through hearings to verify the constitutionality of laws and regulations that the ECtHR pronounces incompatible with the Convention; or the Constitutional Court may hold hearings to interpret the Constitution upon a query from the President or the Government of the RF when governmental agencies believe that compliance with a specific stipulation from the ECtHR to Russia would entail violation of the Basic Law. If the Constitutional Court of the RF concludes that a decision of the ECtHR is incompatible with the Constitution, then that decision is not binding.

In December 2015 amendments to that effect[46] of the Federal Constitutional Law 'On the Constitutional Court of the Russian Federation' were proposed by representatives of each of the factions in the State Duma and adopted.

43. Koroteev, *supra* n. 10 at 127.
44. *Kimlya and Others v. Russia*, Applications №76836/01 (1 Oct. 2009); *OAO Neftyanaya kompaniya YUKOS v. Russia*, Application №14902/04 (20 Sep. 2011); *Republican Party of Russia v. Russia*, Application №12976/07 (12 Apr. 2011). *See also*: Koroteev, *supra* n. 10 at 128–129.
45. Judgment of the Constitutional Court of the RF of 14 Jul. 2015, No. 21-P, Collected Statutes of the Russian Federation, No. 51 (2015) at 4,658.
46. Federal Constitutional Law dated 14 Dec. 2015, No. 7-FKZ, Collected Statutes of the Russian Federation, No. 51 at 7,229.

As many specialists[47] have noted, the decision of the ECtHR in *Konstantin Markin v. Russia* has made a significant contribution to the discussion of gender discrimination and the gender stereotypes that underlie it. Although the case has not brought about a change in the legal approach to child-care leave for fathers in the military, its impact on the formulation of gender policy and the understanding of positive gender discrimination in Russia has been great. For example, after the *Markin* decision the Constitutional Court of the RF handed down a decision in the *Ostaev* case at the end of 2011 that established that a father who was the only caregiver for a child with disabilities under the age of 18 or the only caregiver for a child under 3 and who also was caring for three or more minor children could not be dismissed from his job by his employer.[48] The Plenum of the Supreme Court of the RF also issued a judgment[49] specifying the special labour regulations that apply to women and individuals with family obligations in which the issue of gender discrimination came under consideration for the first time.

47. Koroteev, *supra* n. 10 at 129; Alexandra Timmer, *Gender Justice in Strasbourg*, Strasbourg Observers (22 Mar. 2012), http://strasbourgobservers.com/2012/03/22/gender-justice-in-strasbourg/; Grigory Vaypan, *Acquiescence Affirmed, Its Limits Left Undefined: The Markin Judgment and the Pragmatism of the Russian Constitutional Court* vis-à-vis *the European Court of Human Rights*, II No. 3 at 130–140 (2014).
48. Judgment of the Constitutional Court of the RF of 15 Dec. 2011, No. 28-P, Collected Statutes of the RF, No. 52 at 7,639 (26 Dec. 2011).
49. Judgment of the Plenum of the Supreme Court of the RF of 28 Jan. 2014, 4 Bulletin of the Supreme Court of the RF (April 2014).

CHAPTER 3

Disability and Age Discrimination in Employment: Compliance of Russian Law with International Labour Standards

Nikita L. Lyutov[*]

§3.01 INTRODUCTION

This chapter focuses on two grounds of employment discrimination in Russia, age and disability, in order to show how the norms on discrimination correspond to international labour standards on the matter. The aim is not to present an encyclopaedic overview of all aspects of the topic of discrimination, but rather to concentrate on the most significant areas in which Russian law and practices diverge from international labour standards. This chapter concludes by offering the reader several suggestions about how to harmonize Russian domestic law on employment discrimination of people with disabilities and older people with international labour standards while giving due respect to national legal and societal traditions and the current economic environment.

Equality of treatment was one of the mainstays of propaganda during the Soviet period of Russian history. The very nature of the socialist economy favoured equality in employment. With total state ownership of the enterprise and no practical freedom to negotiate the conditions of employment contracts, there was no economic motivation for employers to discriminate.[1] At the same time, political and societal motives for

* Head of the Department of Labour and Social Security Law, Kutafin Moscow State Law University; Professor of Labour and Social Security Law, National Research University Higher School of Economics.

1. This was the case during the 'classical' period of the socialist era from roughly 1930s to the beginning of 1980s. Later on, in the second half of the 1980s but still prior to the collapse of the Soviet Union, there was a brief period of transformation towards a market economy while

discrimination were in place in the Soviet era, especially on grounds such as political or religious convictions, or sexual orientation.

During the socialist period, the country was isolated from the Western legal tradition by the Iron Curtain. As a result, some legal concepts were used differently to the way they functioned in countries with market economies. Instead of anti-discrimination regulation, there was a principle of 'uniformity and differentiation in labour law,' which meant that labour legislation was applied equally to everyone, but some specific categories of employees (young people, women, people with family responsibilities, people with disabilities) were given preferential consideration by the legislators, and special norms were provided for them.[2] For some workers belonging to the protected categories these special norms were themselves discriminatory.[3] In fact, such a system functioned as the equivalent of a prohibition against discrimination including elements of affirmative action. After the collapse of the socialist system and the transition to a market economy with new privately owned enterprises, this approach to equality turned out to be insufficient because employers found economic motivations to discriminate against workers that were reinforced by the traditional stereotypes favouring discrimination.

This chapter focuses on two aspects of employment discrimination law: disability and age. It analyses how modern Russian employment law addresses the problem of age and disability discrimination, as well as the major discrepancies that exist between Russian law and international labour standards[4] on these matters, and what could be done to make these two sets of standards more compatible with each other. However, this chapter does not claim to deal with all the problems relating to the issue of employment discrimination.

Although any legal analysis must be responsive to the practical situation and employ a 'law plus' perspective, the primary aim here is to offer some ways to fill the legal gaps in protection from employment discrimination in Russia.

---

socialist ideology was still in place. This period was accompanied by so much legal and economic uncertainty that it is impossible to find any reliable information on discrimination in employment for those years.

2. *See*: Marina A. Bocharnikova, Tatiana Iu. Korshunova, *Differentsiatsiia pravovogo regulirovaniia trudovykh otnoshenii: teoreticheskie aspekty (Differentiation of labour relations legal regulation: theoretical aspects)*, 2 Rossiiskii ezhegodnik trudovogo prava (Russian Yearbook of Labour Law) 239 (2007); Aleksandr M. Kurennoi (ed.), *Trudovoe pravo Rossii (Russian Labour Law)* 27–28 (Pravovedenie, Moscow, 2008); Andrei M. Lushnikov, Marina V. Lushnikova, *Kurs trudovogo prava: uchebnik v 2-kh tomakh,* (The course of labour law: Tutorial in 2 volumes) vol.1 (Statut, Moscow, 2009), 526ff.
3. These categories include women, people with family responsibilities, and certain other categories. *See* for example: Nikita L. Lyutov, *Russian Law on Discrimination in Employment: Can it be Compatible with International Labour Standards?*, 4(3) Russian Law Journal 32–41. (2016) Available at: <http://www.russianlawjournal.org/jour/article/view/177/136>.
4. Although the term 'international labour standards' may be understood in different ways, the author prefers to use its most frequently accepted sense, which includes both binding international treaties and soft law. *See* examples of such usage: Jean-Claude Javillier, *Droit du Travail* 108 (L.G.D.J., Paris, 1999); Keith D. Ewing, *International Labour Standards*, in Michael J. Morley, Patrick Guningle, David G. Collins (eds.), *Global Industrial Relations* (Routledge, London and New York, NY, 239–253 (2006); Lee Swepston, *International Labour Law*, in Roger Blanpain (ed.), *Comparative Labour Law and Industrial Relations in Industrialized Market Economies*, IX Ed., 139ff. (Wolters Kluwer, Austin, Boston, Chicago, IL, 2007).

§3.02 'THE LAW IN THE BOOKS'

Russia is a party to both of the International Labour Organization (ILO) fundamental Conventions on discrimination[5] and has ratified other major international treaties on the matter.[6] The principle of equality is laid down in the Russian Constitution,[7] and there is a specific article concerning the prohibition of discrimination in employment in the Labour Code.[8] Separate articles of the Labour Code contain provisions on equality in the process of concluding employment contracts and in the payment of wages.[9] Since 2011, discrimination has been considered an administrative (non-criminal) offence, punishable by a fine with a maximum limit of RUB 100,000 (about EUR 1,600).[10] There is even an article in the Penal Code on 'The infringement of the principle of equality of rights and freedoms of human beings and citizens' laying down a serious sanction, a maximum of five years of imprisonment, for the most serious cases of discrimination.[11]

---

5. The ILO Equal Remuneration Convention, 1951 (No. 100), International Labour Organization (hereinafter 'ILO'), NORMLEX Information System on International Labour Standards. Available at <http://www.ilo.org/dyn/normlex/en/f?p=NORMLEXPUB:1:0> (hereinafter 'Normlex Database') and Discrimination (Employment and Occupation) Convention, 1958 (No. 111) (hereinafter 'ILO Convention No. 111'), Normlex Database.
6. Article 2, para. 1, International Covenant on Civil and Political Rights, 1966, The United Nations Office of the High Commissioner for Human Rights site, available at <http://www.ohchr.org/Documents/ProfessionalInterest/ccpr.pdf>; Art. 2, para. 2, International Covenant on Economic, Social and Cultural Rights, 1966, The United Nations Office of the High Commissioner for Human Rights site, available at <http://www.ohchr.org/EN/ProfessionalInterest/Pages/CESCR.aspx>; International Convention on the Elimination of All Forms of Racial Discrimination, 1965, The United Nations Office of the High Commissioner for Human Rights site, available at <http://www.ohchr.org/Documents/ProfessionalInterest/cerd.pdf>; Convention on the Elimination of All Forms of Discrimination against Women (CEDAW), 1979, The United Nations Office of the High Commissioner for Human Rights site, available at <http://www.ohchr.org/Documents/ProfessionalInterest/cedaw.pdf>; Convention on the Rights of Persons with Disabilities, 2006, The Council of Europe site, available at <http://www.un.org/disabilities/documents/convention/convoptprot-e.pdf>; Art. 1 of the European Social Charter, The Council of Europe site, available at <http://conventions.coe.int/Treaty/en/Treaties/Html/035.htm> covering the right to work, which is interpreted by the European Committee on Social Rights as including the prohibition of discrimination (see further), and several others.
7. Article 19 of the Constitution of Russia contains the provisions that: '1. All people shall be equal before the law and the courts. 2. The State shall guarantee the equality of rights and freedoms of man and citizen, regardless of sex, race, nationality, language, origin, property and official status, place of residence, religion, convictions, membership in public associations, and also of other circumstances. All forms of limitations of human rights on social, racial, national, linguistic or religious grounds shall be banned. 3. Men and women shall enjoy equal rights and freedoms and have equal opportunities to exercise them.' (translation by the author). 'Konstitutsiia Rossiiskoi Federatsii' with subsequent amendments (12 Dec. 1993) (hereinafter 'RF Constitution') *SZ RF* (2014) No. 31 item 4398.
8. Trudovoi Kodeks Rossiiskoi Federatsii (Labour Code of the Russian Federation with subsequent amendments), Art. 3 (hereinafter 'RF Labour Code') *SZ RF* (2002) No. 1 (Part 1) item 3.
9. Articles 64 and 132 of the RF Labour Code.
10. Article 5.62, Kodeks Rossiiskoi Federatsii ob administrativnykh pravonarusheniiakh (hereinafter RF Administrative Code with subsequent amendments), *SZ RF* (2002) No. 1 (Part 1) item 1.
11. Article 136, Ugolovnyi Kodeks Rossiiskoi Federatsii (hereinafter RF Penal Code with subsequent amendments) *SZ RF* (1996) No. 25 item 2954.

Special norms on what is called 'affirmative action' or 'positive action' in Western labour law and 'differentiation norms' (*normy differentsiatsii*) in Russian legal doctrine[12] also exist.

There is a provision on quotas for employing disabled persons in accordance with a 1995 Russian Federal Law,[13] which contains the requirement that employers with more than 100 workers establish such quotas ranging from 2% to 4% of the total number of workers in the company, the exact percentage within that range to be set by regional governments of the Russian Federation. An additional quota of up to 3% of the total number of workers has been introduced for employers with a number of workers ranging from thirty-five to 100 by a Federal Law adopted in 2013.[14] Another article of this law may be interpreted as providing a kind of 'reasonable accommodation' requirement for disabled persons similar to the requirements that are common in industrialized economies. Until quite recently the norms on reasonable accommodation were almost entirely restricted to the status of 'law in the books' in Russia. Nevertheless, the situation has begun to change in the last few years.[15]

Any disputes concerning discrimination in employment, as well as labour disputes on other quite serious grounds, can be resolved only through direct appeal to the courts and without any recourse to the internal procedures of a company that are applied to less important grievances.[16] This underlines the importance of disputes about discrimination in employment from the legislative point of view. Another reason for such a system can be seen in how labour inspectorates have the authority to examine complaints of clear violations of labour law, while the courts resolve labour disputes that require broader legal expertise to reach a judgment. Discrimination cases are regarded as sensitive, debatable and matters for judgment, therefore they are not entrusted to the inspectorates. At the same time this results in problems for victims of discrimination as they try to defend themselves. They have no right to file a complaint about discrimination to the State Labour Inspectorate as they could in the case of other infringements of other labour rights.

---

12. *See* more on the balance between 'differentiation' and discrimination: Andrei M. Lushnikov, *Problemy diskriminatsii v pravovom regulirovanii otnoshenii v sfere truda i sotsial'nogo obespecheniia* (*Problems of Discrimination in the Legal Regulation of Relations in the Sphere of Labour and Social Security*) in Kantemir N. Gusov (ed.), *Problemy differentsiatsii v pravovom regulirovanii truda i sotsial'nogo obespecheniia* 14–15 (*Problems of Differentiation in Legal Regulation and Social Security*) (Prospect, Moscow, 2009); Kantemir N. Gusov, *Edinstvo i differentsiatsiia trudovogo prava: nekotorie voprosy, supra*, (*Unity and Differentiation of Labour Law: Some Questions*) 31–36; Alexander M. Kurennoi, *Differentsiatsiia ili discriminatsiia? (Differentiation or Discrimination?)*, supra, 47–50.
13. Article 21, para. 1, Federal'nyi Zakon *O sotsial'noi zashchite invalidov v Rossiiskoi Federatsii* (Federal Law *On social protection of the disabled in the Russian Federation*) (24 Nov. 1995) No. 181-FZ with subsequent amendments, *SZ RF* (1995) No. 48 item 4563.
14. Federal'nyi Zakon *O vnesenii izmeneniia v statiu 21 Federal'nogo zakona 'O sotsial'noy zashchite invalidov v Rossiiskoy Federatsi'i"* (Federal Laws '*On amendments to the article 21 of the Federal Law*' and '*On social protection of the disabled in the Russian Federation*') (2 Jul. 2013) No. 183-FZ, *SZ RF* (2013) No. 27 item 3475.
15. *See* s. 9 further.
16. Article 391, para. 3, RF Labour Code.

As a result there is a well-developed set of legal norms in Russia that are intended to protect against discrimination. Nevertheless, such a purely normative description of the situation can provide information only about the 'law in the books' rather than about the actual ways that discrimination is approached in practice.

§3.03 THE INTERNATIONAL LEGAL FRAMEWORK

Any comparative analysis of national and international law supposes, first of all, that some basis for comparison should be defined. The plain text of binding international legal norms on prohibition of discrimination does not contain many rules that a national law could theoretically contradict. It is difficult to imagine any national legal norm in the modern world that would contain a statement such as 'discrimination is allowed'. More specific and important international requirements on the prohibition of discrimination are contained either in the soft law norms or in the decisions concerning Member States by international monitoring bodies. The legal status of these acts of interpretation is unclear. The Russian Constitution contains the statement that 'international treaties of the Russian Federation and core principles and norms of international law shall form a part of the Russian legal system'.[17] This means that Russian domestic courts have the right to use in their practice only ratified international treaties and those 'core principles and norms' which are not identical with, but close to, the 'peremptory norms of general international law (*jus cogens*)' as established by the Vienna Convention on the Law of Treaties, 1969.[18] There is no legal definition of the 'core principles and norms of international law' that are mentioned in the Constitution. However, the Supreme Court gives such definition[19] in a way that clearly quotes the definition of the Vienna Convention.

17. Article. 15, para. 4, RF Constitution.
18. Article 53, Vienna Convention on the Law of Treaties (23 May 1969) (hereinafter '*The Vienna Convention*'), United Nations Treaty Series. Vol. 1155, No. 18232.
19. Paragraph1, Postanovlenie Plenuma Verkhovnogo Suda Rossiiskoi Federatsii *O primenenii sudami obshchei iurisdiktsii obshchepriznannykh printsipov i norm mezhdunarodnogo prava i mezhdunarodnykh dogovorov Rossiiskoi Federatsii* (para. 1 of the Russian Federation Supreme Court Plenary Ruling on the application by the courts of general jurisdiction of generally recognized principles and norms of international treaties of the Russian Federation) No. 5 (10 Oct. 2003); 12 *Biulleten' Verkhovnogo Suda RF (Bulletin of the Supreme Court of the Russian Federation)* (2003). The Supreme Court provides two separate definitions: 'the core principles of international law' and 'the core norm of the international law'. Nevertheless, one definition is linked to another. The core principles are defined as 'the basic peremptory *norms* (italicized by the author – N.L.) of international law accepted and recognized by the international community of states as a whole from which no derogation is permitted'. In its turn, the core norm of international law is defined as 'the rule of behaviour that is accepted by the international community of states as binding' (translation is made by the author). The definition of 'principles' is made through the definition of norms and both of them textually rely on the wording of the Art. 53 of the Vienna Convention where the peremptory norm of general international law is defined as: 'a norm accepted and recognized by the international community of States as a whole as a norm from which no derogation is permitted and which can be modified only by a subsequent norm of general international law having the same character'.

The most detailed requirements of international law are contained in the observations of the ILO Committee of Experts on Application of Conventions and Recommendations (CEACR) and in the case law of the European Committee of Social Rights (ECSR) that is authorized to interpret the provisions of the European Social Charter (ESC). As is clear from the above quotation from the Russian Constitution, these case law rulings cannot be directly applied by the Russian domestic courts,[20] and this situation is the same in nearly every country.[21] The status of decisions by these international institutions has not been clarified in any international treaty. However, such rulings may be considered as sources of international law, if they are treated as international custom. Two conditions for this should be satisfied: the existence of repeated practice and the co-called *opinio juris sive necessitatis*,[22] i.e. the state's treatment of such acts as binding instruments must be proven.[23] Further analysis deals with domestic provisions on discrimination in employment as compared to both ratified treaties and the case law of international monitoring bodies on the matter.

This chapter does not attempt an analysis of the different sources of international law from the point of view of their specific legal content and interaction with national

20. The Constitutional Court of Russia cited the practice of CEACR once (*see* para. 3.2, Postanovlenie Konstitutsionnogo Suda Rossiiskoi Federatsii 'Po delu o proverke konstitutsionnosti Federal'nogo zakona '"O vnesenii izmenenii *v* Kodeks Rossiiskoi Federatsii ob administrativnykh pravonarusheniiakh i Federal'nyi zakon 'O sobraniiakh, mitingakh, demonstratsiiakh, shestviiakh i piketirovaniiakh' *v* sviazi s zaprosom gruppy deputatov Gosudarstvennoi Dumy i zhaloboi grazhdanina E.V. Savenko" (para. 3.2 of Ruling of the Russian Federation Constitutional Court: 'In the case about the verification of constitutionality of the Federal Law "On amendments to the Russian Code of administrative offences" and the Federal law "On assemblies, rallies, demonstrations, processions and picketing" in connection with inquiry of group of representatives of the State Duma and the complaint of the citizen E.V. Savenko' (12 Feb. 2013) No. 4-P, *SZ RF* (2013) No. 8 item 868). However, it does not follow from the text of this ruling that the Constitutional Court treats it as binding source.
21. The only exception that is known to us is the Ukrainian law which expressly names the practice of the ECtHR among the sources of domestic law. (Zakon Ukrainy 'Pro vykonannia rishen' ta zastosuvannia praktyky Evropeis'kogo sudu z prav liudyny' (23 Feb. 2006) No. 3477-IV, Vidomosti Verkhovnoi Rady Ukrainy (News of the Verkhovna Rada) (2006) No. 30 item 260). *See* more about monistic and dualistic approaches to the international law at: Eileen Denza, *The Relationship Between International and National Law*, in Malcolm D. Evans (ed.), *International Law* 411–438 (Oxford University Press, Oxford, 2010); Colin Warbrick, Dominic McGoldrick, *International Law in English Courts: Recent Cases* 52(3) International and Comparative Law Quarterly 815–824 (2003); Roger O'Keefe, *Customary International Crimes in English Courts* 72 British Yearbook of International Law 293 (2001); Fiona De Londras, *Dualism, Domestic Courts, and the Rule of International Law*, in Mortimer Sellers, Tadeusz, Tomaszewski (ed.), *Ius Gentium: The Rule of Law in Comparative Perspective* 217ff (Wien, Springer, 2009), available through SSRN at < http://papers.ssrn.com/sol3/Delivery.cfm/SSRN_ID1715502_code634962.pdf?abstractid = 1393293&mirid = 1 >; Pierre-Hugues Verdier, Mila Versteeg, *International Law in National Legal Systems: An Empirical Investigation*, 109 American Journal of International Law 514–533 (2015).
22. *See* more about the *opinio juris* requirement: Alina Kaczorowska, *Public International Law*, 4th ed. 39–41 (Routledge, London and New York, NY, 2010); Sean D. Murphy, *Principles of International Law* 80–81 (Thomson-West, 2006), Frederic L. Kirgis, *Custom on a Sliding Scale* 81 American Journal of International Law 146 (1987); Hugh Thirlway, *The Sources of International Law*, 1-272 (Oxford University Press, Oxford, 2014).
23. *See*: Nikita L. Lyutov, *Effektivnost' norm mezhdunarodnogo trudovogo prava.* Monografiia, (*The Effectiveness of Norms of the International Labour Law*, monograph) 50–62 (Prospect, Moscow, 2014).

law. There is abundant literature on these issues covering both international law in general[24] and, more specifically, international labour law.[25] As stated above, Russian legislation and practice are to be compared with international labour standards, which are understood as instruments that include both binding norms and soft law.

§3.04 DISCRIMINATION AGAINST PERSONS WITH DISABILITIES

The ESC contains a requirement for Member States to take adequate measures for placing disabled persons in employment.[26] Russia has ratified this provision, which is interpreted by the ECSR as the obligation for national legislators to directly prohibit discrimination in employment on the basis of disability as well as to prohibit dismissal on the basis of disability.[27] Although the ILO has failed to adopt the protocol to Convention No. 111 that would specify that differential treatment based on disability is discriminatory,[28] there is a special 1983 ILO Convention containing such a direct prohibition[29] to which Russia is a party.

---

24. Reino A. Müllerson, *Monitoring Compliance with International Human Rights Standards* in William E. Butler (ed.), *Control over Compliance with International Law*, 125–138 (Martinus Nijhoff Publishers, Dordrecht, The Netherlands, 1991); Bruno Simma and Philip Alston, *The Sources of Human Rights Law: Custom, Jus Cogens and General Principles*, 17 Australian Yearbook of International Law, 82–108 (1992); Reino A. Müllerson, *Ordering Anarchy: International Law in International Society*, 1–387 (Martinus Nijhoff Publishers, The Hague, 2000); Rebecca M. M. Wallace, *International Law*, 25–38 (Sweet & Maxwell ltd., London, 2006); Mary E. O'Connel, *The Power and Purpose of International Law*, 9 (Oxford University Press, Oxford, 2008).
25. Constance Thomas, Martin Oelz and Xavier Beaudonnet, *The Use of International Labour Law in Domestic Courts: Theory, Recent Jurisprudence, and Practical Implications*, in Jean-Claude Javillier and Bernard Gernigon (eds.), *Les normes internationales du travail: un patrimoine pour l'avenir Mélanges en l'honneur de Nicolas Valticos* 249–286 (International Labour Office, Geneva, 2004); Bob Hepple, *Does Law Matter? The Future of Binding Norms* in George P. Politakis (ed.), *Protecting Labour Rights as Human Rights: Present and Future of International Supervision*. Proceedings of the International Colloquium on the 80th Anniversary of the ILO Committee of Experts on the Application of Conventions and Recommendations 221–231 (Geneva: 24–25 Nov. 2006), (International Labour Office, Geneva, 2007); Tony Royle, *The ILO's Shift to Promotional Principles and the 'Privatization' of Labour Rights: An Analysis of Labour Standards, Voluntary Self-Regulation and Social Clauses*, 26(3) The International Journal of Comparative Labour Law and Industrial Relations 249–271 (2010); Antonio García-Muñoz Alhambra, Beryl ter Haar and Attila Kun, *Soft on the Inside, Hard on the Outside: An Analysis of the Legal Nature of New Forms of International Labour Law*, 27(4) The International Journal of Comparative Labour Law and Industrial Relations 337–363 (2011); Manfred Weiss, *International Labour Standards: A Complex Public-Private Policy Mix*, 29(1) The International Journal of Comparative Labour Law and Industrial Relations 7–20 (2013).
26. Article 15, para. 2 of the ESC.
27. Council of Europe. *Conclusions of the European Committee of Social Rights*, 2003, Slovenia, 503, ECSR Database.
28. *See* the discussion from the International Labour Conference, 83rd Session 1996. *Report of the Committee of Experts on the Application of Conventions and Recommendations (Articles 19, 22 and 35 of the Constitution)*. Special Survey on Equality in Employment and Occupation in respect of Convention No. 111, 120–122 (ILO, Geneva, 1996).
29. Article 4, ILO Vocational Rehabilitation and Employment (Disabled Persons) Convention (1983) (No. 159), Normlex Database. Convention No. 159. *See also* the CEACR opinion about its requirements from the International Labour Conference, 86th Session 1998. *Report of the Committee of Experts on the Application of Conventions and Recommendations (Articles 19, 22*

Russian legislation does not directly mention the use of disability as a justification for differential treatment as discriminatory.[30] Nevertheless, the list of discriminatory justifications is open-ended and includes any differences not based on the 'occupational qualities' of a worker (*see* above). As a result, from a formal point of view discrimination against disabled persons is also prohibited. A direct statement in law that such practices are discriminatory would have a practical impact by informing employers and employees about their existing rights and obligations in this respect.

Much more important for Russian law and practice is another requirement of international law prohibiting discrimination against people with disabilities. The provision of the ESC quoted above requires employers to arrange 'specialised placing services, facilities for sheltered employment and measures to encourage employers to admit disabled persons to employment' (Article 15, para. 2 of the ESC). According to the approach of the ECSR,[31] this means that employers are under an obligation to provide what is called *reasonable accommodation* for persons with disabilities at workplaces. This reasonable accommodation is usually understood as the employer's obligation to introduce certain technical facilities that enable a disabled person to work, study, and use the facilities of the social infrastructure along with other people.[32] An employer's failure to apply measures that amount to reasonable accommodation is usually treated in economically and socially developed countries as indirect discrimination against the disabled.[33] The CEACR also holds that reasonable accommodation is an integral part of disabled persons' right to work.[34] The criteria and requirements for measures that amount to reasonable accommodation are listed in the special ILO Code of Practice adopted in 2002.[35] Russia is also a party to the UN Convention on the Rights of Persons with Disabilities of 2006 that is based on the reasonable accommodation principle and directly mentions the refusal to provide reasonable accommodation as discrimination in employment.[36] 'Reasonable accommodation' means, according to

---

and 35 of the Constitution). General Survey on the reports on the Vocational Rehabilitation and Employment (Disabled Persons) Convention (No. 159) and Recommendation (No. 168), 1983, 28. (ILO, Geneva, 1998).

30. *See* Art. 3 of the RF Labour Code.
31. Council of Europe. *Conclusions of the European Committee of Social Rights, 2007, Statement of Interpretation on Article 15§2, §10, 12,* ECSR Database.
32. *See* more about the reasonable accommodation concept at: Lisa Waddington and Aart Hendriks, *The Expanding Concept of Employment Discrimination in Europe: From Direct and Indirect Discrimination to Reasonable Accommodation Discrimination,* 18(4) The International Journal of Comparative Labour Law and Industrial Relations 403–428 (2002); Lisa Waddington, *Reasonable Accommodation* in Dagmar Schiek, Lisa Waddington and Mark Bell (eds.), *Cases, Materials and Text on National, Supranational and International Non-discrimination Law* 740–745 (Hart, Oxford, 2007); Mark Bell, *Advancing EU Anti-discrimination Law: The European Commission's 2008 Proposal for a New Directive,* 3 The Equal Rights Review, 7–18, at 10 ff. (2009).
33. Lisa Waddington, Aart Hendriks, *supra* at, 405.
34. International Labour Conference, 100th Session, 2011. *Report of the Committee of Experts on the Application of Conventions and Recommendations (CEACR).* Report III (Part 1A), 624, Normlex Database.
35. ILO Code of Practice. Managing disability in the workplace, 1ff (ILO, Geneva, 2002).
36. Article 2, UN Convention on the Rights of Persons with Disabilities (2006).

the Convention, 'necessary and appropriate modification and adjustments not imposing a disproportionate or undue burden, where needed in a particular case, to ensure to persons with disabilities the enjoyment or exercise on an equal basis with others of all human rights and fundamental freedoms'.[37]

The federal legislation contains the concept that 'disabled persons employed at any company irrespective of their legal form of organization and form of ownership shall be afforded with the necessary working conditions according to their individual program of rehabilitation'.[38] Theoretically, this provision is supposed to establish an obligation to apply the reasonable accommodation principle. But neither this nor any other norm of Russian domestic legislation gives an explanation of who (the employer or the state) is under this obligation and who is required to pay for fulfilling it. The 'individual program of rehabilitation' of a person with disabilities is specified in a form approved by the Government[39] and is designed in such a way that an officer of the medical rehabilitation authority is free to choose among different forms of rehabilitation for disabled persons. These forms include: adaptation at the previous workplace; adaptation at the previous workplace with changes in working conditions; search for an appropriate workplace; creation of a special workplace; and others. There are no provisions in law concerning the priority of inclusive measures that would promote the integration of the disabled people into normal work and social activity.[40]

As a result, even at a formal level the principle of reasonable accommodation is not applied in Russia at this time. Therefore there is no known case law on the employment discrimination of disabled persons from the point of view of reasonable accommodation.[41] However, large-budget programmes that are aimed at including

---

37. *Ibid.*
38. Article. 23, para. 1, Federal'nyi Zakon *O sotsial'noi zashchite invalidov v Rossiiskoi Federatsii* (Federal Law *On Social protection of the disabled*).
39. Prikaz Minzdravsotsrazvitiia (Order of the Ministry of economic Development (4 Aug. 2008) No. 379n, *RG* (2008), No. 4747.
40. *See* Ekaterina R. Voronkova, *Otkaz rabotodatelia ot ispolneniia obiazannosti po obespecheniiu razumnogo prisposobleniia kak forma kosvennoi diskriminatsii po priznaku invalidnosti (The refusal of the employer from the obligation to ensure reasonable accommodation as a form of indirect discrimination on grounds of disability)*, 3, Trudovoie pravo v Rossii i za rubezhom (Labour Law in Russia and abroad), 45-48 (2013).
41. However, there is some case law associated with the employer's obligation to create special workplaces for disabled people (without reference to discrimination). *See* Opredelenie Verkhovnogo Suda Rossiiskoi Federatsii 'Ob otmene resheniia Verkhovnogo Suda Respubliki Tyva ot 03.03.2011 i priznanii nedeistvuiushchimi punktov 1, 5 - 14, 16 - 21 Prilozheniia k postanovleniiu Pravitel'stva Respubliki Tyva ot 01.11.2010 No. 464 "Ob ustanovlenii organizatsiiam Respubliki Tyva mimimal'nogo kolichestva spetsial'nykh rabochikh mest dlia trudoustroistva invalidov"' (The statement of the Russian Federation Supreme Court about cancellation of the decision of the Supreme Court of Republic of Tyva dated 03 Mar. 2011 and the invalidation of the paras 1, 5–14, 16–21 of the Annex to the Decree of the Government of the Republic of Tyva dated 01 Nov. 2010 No. 464 'On the establishment of organizations of the Republic of Tyva of the minimum quantity of special workplaces for employment of the disabled') (11 May 2011), Consultant Database. Available at <http://base.consultant.ru/cons/cgi/online.cgi?req=doc;base=ARB;n=199796/>, *Opredelenie Plenuma Verkhovnogo Suda Rossiiskoi Federatsii* (25 Nov. 2011), No. 19-V11-19, Consultant Database. Available at <http://base.consultant.ru/cons/cgi/online.cgi?req=doc;base=ARB;n=242241>, Opredelenie Vysshego Arbitrazhnogo Suda Rossiiskoi Federatsii (The definition of the Russian Federation Supreme Arbitration Court)

disabled people in normal life are currently in progress in Russia.[42] Until recently most of the public infrastructure (buildings, public transport) was almost completely lacking in any special facilities for people with disabilities. After the start of the governmental Accessible Environment project[43] special facilities including accommodations at the entrances to buildings and on public transport as well as special parking places have become available in large numbers. Although the situation of people with disabilities still seems far from ideal, it is apparently changing for the better.[44]

The UN Committee on Economic, Social and Cultural Rights (which is responsible for application of the UN Covenant on Economic, Social and Cultural Rights of 1966) has made proposals concerning the need to strengthen the integration of disabled persons into the labour market.[45] However, these proposals were aimed at a more stringent application of the older system of setting aside a quota of workplaces for disabled persons and at sanctions for employers who refuse to employ people with disabilities. This system is important, but currently it is less comprehensive than the reasonable accommodation principle because the Covenant of 1966 tends to segregate disabled persons into a 'special labour market for the disabled' rather than include them in normal life. At the international level, Russia has not yet been criticized for failure to apply reasonable accommodation measures.

§3.05 AGE DISCRIMINATION

In addition to the gaps in regulation that are described above and that lead to shortcomings in the application of anti-discrimination employment law, some legislative norms in Russia (at least arguably) contain discriminatory provisions.

One such example is *age discrimination*. The Labour Code contains a provision that the employer and the employee may conclude a fixed-term employment contract only in cases directly listed in the law.[46] This limited list of grounds is aimed at protecting employees from an employer's abuse of its right to conclude fixed-term contracts. Without such a list of permissible grounds, it is probable that the great majority of employment contracts would be fixed-term ones, and protection from unfair dismissal would be inapplicable in practice. Therefore, inclusion of a particular

(19 Mar. 2013), No.VAS-2824/13 po delu No. 19-2250/2012, Consultant Database. Available at <http://base.consultant.ru/cons/cgi/online.cgi?req=doc;base=ARB;n=323878>, et al.

42. *See* the information about the 'Dostupnaia sreda' Project website. Available at <http://zhit-vmeste.ru/>.
43. *See supra* note.
44. *See* more details about protection of disabled persons in employment and social security in: Roman N. Zhavoronkov *Pravovoe regulirovanie truda i sotsial'nogo obespecheniia invalidov v Rossiiskoi Federatsii (Legal regulation of labour and social security of the disabled in the Russian Federation)* 1-318 (Fond NIPI, Moscow, 2014).
45. United Nations Committee on Economic, Social and Cultural Rights, Report on the thirtieth and thirty-first sessions (5-23 May 2003, 10-28 Nov. 2003), Economic and Social Council Official Records, 2004. Supplement No. 2. UN Doc. No. E/2004/22, E/C.12/2003/14. paras 486, 69.
46. The list of grounds is given in Art. 59 of the RF Labour Code.

category of workers in this list puts those workers in an inferior position compared to all other workers, and this disadvantageous status may be justified only by the 'inherent requirements of the job' (according to ILO Convention No. 111, *see* above), as is the case with chief executive officers, their deputies, and chief financial officers.[47] Those who are entitled to a retirement pension are listed,[48] among other groups of workers, with whom fixed-term employment contracts are permissible with the agreement of both parties. Taking into account that older workers have a weaker position in the labour market[49] and that age seems to be the most 'popular' justification for discrimination,[50] it is not difficult to understand that in the majority of cases such workers have no other choice than to agree to employment on a temporary basis. In 1992 the Constitutional Court found that the norm of the previous Code of Laws on Labour of Russia[51] mentioning the retirement age as grounds for dismissal on the employer's initiative[52] was discriminatory and incompatible with ILO Convention No. 111.

Although special grounds for dismissal and the permissibility of concluding a fixed-term employment contract are not strictly identical, there is a clear parallel between these two provisions. The provision of the current Labour Code concerning fixed-term contracts was criticized in some academic publications[53] and was also

47. Article 59, para. 2 of the RF Labour Code.
48. The applicable age is 60 years for men and 55 for women, according to Art. 7, Federal'nyi Zakon *O trudovykh pensiiakh* (Federal Law *On labour pensions*) (17 Dec. 2001) No. 173-FZ, *SZ RF* (2001) No. 52 (Part 1) item 4920.
49. *See* more on the topic: 5th Annual Legal Seminar of the European Labour Law Network (ELLN) *Labour Law in a Greying Labour Market: Challenges of Active Ageing*. Seminar Report (The Hague, 11–12 Oct. 2012). Available at the ELLN site <http://adapt.it/adapt-indice-a-z/wp-content/uploads/2013/08/seminar-report_ELLN_2012.pdf>. For the Russian situation *see*: Tatiana A. Vasilieva, *Spetsifika diskriminatsii po priznaku vozrasta i pravovykh mekhanizmov ee predotvrashcheniia* (*The Specifics of Age Discrimination and of the Legal Mechanisms Aimed at its Prevention*) in Tatiana A. Vasilieva (ed.) *Zashchita lichnosti ot diskriminatsii po priznaku vozrasta: sbornik dokumentov* (*Protection of Persons from the Age Discrimination: A Collection of Documents*), (Iuriks, Moscow, 2010), 7–12.
50. *See* Viacheslav A. Biziukov, Sotsiologicheskoie issledovaniie *Diskriminatsiia v sfere truda: rasprostranennost', formy i prichiny sushchestvovaniia* (Tsentr sotsial'no-trudovykh prav,) (Sociological study *Discrimination in Employment: Prevalence, Forms and Causes of Existence*, Centre of social and labour rights) Moscow (2008) Available at <http://trudprava.ru/expert/research/discriminsurv/565>.
51. Article 33, para. 1.1, Kodeks zakonov o trude Rossiiskoi Federatsii. Vedomosti Verkhovnogo Soveta RSFSR (Code of Labour Law in the Russian Federation) (1971) No. 50 item 1007.This paragraph was rescinded by the Federal Law (12 Mar. 1992) No. 2502-1 adopted after this Constitutional Court Ruling (*see* next footnote).
52. Postanovlenie Konstitutsionnogo Suda RSFSR 'Po delu o proverke konstitutsionnosti pravoprimenitel'noi praktiki rastorzheniia trudovogo dogovora po osnovaniiu, predusmotrennomu punktom 1.1 stat'i 33 KZoT RSFSR' (Ruling of the Russian Federation Constitutional Court on the case about the verification of constitutionality of the law enforcement practice of terminating an employment contract on grounds envisaged by item 1.1 of Art. 33 of the Labour code of the RSFSR) (4 Feb. 1992) No. 2-P-Z, Vedomosti Soveta Narodnykh Deputatov i Verkhovnogo Soveta RSFSR (1992) No. 13 item 669.
53. Kantemir N. Gusov, *supra*, 31–36 et al.

challenged in the Constitutional Court. However, contrary to its own position in 1992, the Constitutional Court in this case refused to consider the current norm discriminatory.[54] The main reasoning of the Constitutional Court on this matter was that this exclusion from permanent employment is made not for all workers, but only for those who receive pensions; therefore, the ground of 'differentiation' is not age but an additional source of income. It is difficult to agree with these arguments not only because the retirement pension level is very low in Russia, but mainly because any other sources of income that a person may have are not considered as legitimate grounds for differentiation in law. Therefore it is not surprising that the Constitutional Court judge specializing in labour law (Olga S. Khokhriakova) has expressed her separate opinion, which is contrary to this decision.[55]

Problems of this kind are not confined to Russia. For example, the Court of Justice of the European Union has found the German law waiving the requirement that employers justify concluding fixed-term employment contracts with employees older than 52 years as contradicting the fundamental principle of non-discrimination established in the EU Directives.[56] It seems that a similar conclusion could be reached concerning this provision of the Russian Labour Code as being in contradiction with the Constitution, ILO Convention No. 111, the ESC, and other basic international treaties on the matter.

§3.06 CONCLUSION

The main conclusion that can be drawn after this analysis of the law and practice concerning age and disability discrimination in employment in Russia compared to the international labour standards is that gaps and shortcomings in the legislation and case law are significant. Some of them are associated with the transformation from a planned to a market economy and to a lack of clear understanding of the notion of discrimination by judges, employers, employees, and trade unions. Others are grounded in weak mechanisms of protection from discrimination.

What is obvious is that a 'copy-and-paste' adoption of the anti-discrimination legislation of 'Western' industrial economies in the Russian system would not eliminate the problem. This is so both because of the general problem of transposing foreign

54. Opredelenie Konstitutsionnogo Suda Rossiiskoi Federatsii '*Ob otkaze v priniatii k rassmotreniiu zaprosa Amurskogo gorodskogo suda Khabarovskogo kraia o proverke konstitutsionnosti polozheniia stat'i 59 Trudovogo Kodeksa Rossiiskoi Federatsii*' (The *statement of the Russian Federation Constitutional Court about refusal in acceptance to consideration of inquiry of the Amur city court of the Khabarovsk region about check of constitutionality of provisions of article 59 of the Labour Code of the Russian Federation* (15 May 2007), No. 378-O-P., Vestnik Verkhovnogo Suda RF (2007) No. 6.
55. *Ibid.*
56. *Werner Mangold v. Rüdiger Helm*, ECJ (Grand Chamber) Judgment (22 Nov. 2005) Application No. I-9981. (Case-144/04). For more details *see*: Catherine Barnard, *EC Employment Law*, 3rd ed. 320 (Oxford University Press, Oxford, 2006).

law into any country's national legal system[57] and also because this Western system of protection against discrimination is itself not perfect.[58]

One measure that might improve the situation with employment discrimination would be the adoption of the complex of anti-discrimination law that has been discussed among human rights activists for several years.[59] The UN Committee on Economic, Social and Cultural Rights recommended enacting such laws,[60] and there is a draft law of this kind submitted to the State Duma for consideration,[61] although without any indication of practical steps towards its adoption.

Among the legal norms that could be changed in order to make Russian labour law meet international anti-discrimination standards, one could suggest a substantial alleviation of standards of proof of discrimination, including the option to use statistical data, situational testing, and less stringent requirements for the sources of evidence. A shift of the burden of proof may be an improvement only in certain specific areas, such as the protection of employees from retaliation by employers. In cases in which an employee has filed a complaint against his or her employer, it seems logical that any disciplinary sanction that has been imposed on the employee after the complaint

57. *See*, on this issue, Otto Kahn-Freund, *On Uses and Misuses of Comparative Law*, The Modern Law Review 1-27 (1974). The limits of adaptation of international and foreign labour law in the Russian context are more specifically discussed by professors Lushnikov and Lushnikova. *See* Andrei M. Lushnikov and Marina V. Lushnikova, *Predely zaimstvovaniia mezhdunarodnogo i zarubezhnogo opyta pravovogo regulirovaniia trudovykh otnoshenii v Rossiiskoi Federatsii: teoreticheskie i prikladnye problemy*, (*The limits of borrowing of international and foreign experience of labour relations legal regulation in the Russian Federation: theoretical and applied issues*) 11(66) Evraziiskii iuridicheskii zhurnal (Eurasian Law Journal) 124–126 (2013).
58. For some criticism of the US anti-discrimination law *see*, for example: Terry Smith, *Everyday Indignities: Race, Retaliation and the Promise of Title VII*, 34(3) Columbia Human Rights Law Review 531-574 (2003); D. Wendy Greene, *Categorically Black, White, or Wrong: Misperception Discrimination and the State of Title VII Protection*, 47(1) University of Michigan Journal of Law Reform 87-166 (2013); Trina Jones, *Family-Friendly for Whom? Low-Wage Workers and Workplace Benefits in the U.S.*, presentation at XIV Marco Biagi Conference 2016 (Modena, 17–18 Mar. 2016, *see* this volume). For Russian perspective on the Western concepts of discrimination *see*: Andrei M. Lushnikov, Marina V. Lushnikova and Nadezhda N. Tarusina, *Gender v zakone (Gender in Law)* 23–35 ((Prospekt, Moscow, 2015); Nikita L. Lyutov, *Diskriminatsiia v sfere truda i zaniatii: problemy opredeleniia*, 4 Trudovoe pravo v Rossii i za rubezhom, (*Discrimination in Employment and Occupation: Problems of Definition*) Labour Law in Russia and abroad, 20–24ff. (2011).
59. Alexander G. Osipov, *Antidiskriminatsionnoie zakonodatel'stvo i praktika v Rossii i zarubezhnykh stranakh (rasovaia i etnicheskaia diskriminatsiia)* (*Anti-discrimination Legislation and Practice in Russia and Foreign Countries (Racial and Ethnic Discrimination)*) 87 (Iuriks, Moscow, 2009).
60. United Nations Committee on Economic, Social and Cultural Rights, Report on the forty-sixth and forty-seventh sessions (2–20 May 2011, 14 Nov.–2 Dec. 2011), *Economic and Social Council Official Records*, 2012. Supplement No. 2. UN Doc. No. E/2012/22, E/C.12/2011/3, 35.
61. Draft Law *O vnesenii izmenenii v Zakon Rossiiskoi Federatsii 'O zaniatosti naseleniia v Rossiiskoi Federatsii' i otdel'nie zakonodatel'nie akty Rossiiskoi Federatsii (o dopolnitel'nykh merakh po sodeistiiu zaniatosti lits, nakhodiashchikhsia v sotsial'no uiazvimom polozhenii, i zaprete na rasprostraneniie diskiminatsionnoi informatsii o vakansiiakh) ('On amendments to the Law of the Russian Federation "On employment in the Russian Federation"' and certain legislative acts of the Russian Federation (on additional measures for promotion of employment of persons in a socially vulnerable position, and prohibition on the dissemination of discriminatory information about the job)* (2013) No. 236214-6, available at < http://asozd2.duma.gov.ru /main.nsf/%28Spravka%29?OpenAgent&RN = 236214-6&02 > .

should be treated as retaliation, unless the employer could prove otherwise. The same approach could be applied to any disciplinary actions that target trade union activists.

The alleviation of burden of proof is closely linked with the necessity to change the state attitude towards the implementation of the anti-discrimination law including the already existing administrative and penal sanctions for its infringement. Anti-discrimination law enforcement may also become much more effective if labour inspections were to acquire the right to interfere in situations of discrimination. However, this change of approach would work only if the competence and resources allocated to the inspections themselves were to be harmonized with the international labour standards on the matter.

There are discriminatory provisions in Russian law that should be abrogated. These include the permissibility of concluding temporary employment contracts with workers who have reached retired age, as well as several others.

CHAPTER 4

Psychosocial Risk of Harassment at Work: Comparative Research of French and Italian Experience and Possible Implications for Russia

Elena Sychenko[*]

§4.01 INTRODUCTION

This chapter explores the employee's protection from the psychosocial risk of harassment in France and Italy. France has adopted legal provisions on this matter and explicitly acknowledged psychological risk as an occupational risk, while in Italy protection was developed through judicial interpretation of the employer's obligation to protect the employee's physical integrity and moral personality. Having identified the differences in the two national approaches to the risk of harassment, this chapter investigates which of these approaches could serve as vector for the development of protection from harassment in Russia, where psychological risk is not yet acknowledged.

Psychosocial risks are acknowledged to be one of the key challenges for occupational health and safety specialists and policymakers in Europe. Measures include European Directives establishing the possibility to treat harassment as discrimination, soft law instruments on stress and harassment, national legislation and case law. In Russia, however, the notions of psychosocial risk and moral harassment at work are

* Associate Professor at State Institute of Economics, Finance, Law and Technology (Leningrad region, Russia).

unfamiliar to labour law, and scholars point to the need to adopt special provisions on these matters.[1]

European experience could help to determine an appropriate way to develop employee protection from moral harassment at work in Russia. This chapter aims to consider the most appropriate way for Russia to introduce such protection through the comparative research of French and Italian experience. These countries were chosen for the comparison as they represent different approaches to protection from moral harassment.[2] Italy has developed protection from mobbing on the basis of jurisprudence and the judicial interpretation of the employer's duty to protect the employee's personality. In the last ten years France has adopted special provisions, laying down the notion of moral harassment in the legislation and stipulating special duties of the employer in this regard.

This chapter begins with a general reflection on the notion and the place of human dignity in labour law, acknowledging its fundamental status for protection from harassment. The analysis of French and Italian experience, presented in the following sections of this chapter, focuses on such points as the notion of moral harassment (mobbing), the duties of the employer, and the allocation of the burden of proof. The last part investigates Russian legislation and case law relevant to protection from moral harassment at work and considers whether either French or Italian experience might be followed for the advancement of employee protection.

§4.02 HUMAN DIGNITY AS A BASIS OF ANTI-HARASSMENT PROTECTION

The problem of the protection of employee dignity is fairly new in the context of labour law. Although already at the beginning of the twentieth century the founder of German labour law Prof. Hugo Sinzheimer stated that the dignity of employee is one of the three basic values of labour law,[3] the legislative acknowledgment of this principle was rather long in coming.

The history of this acknowledgement can be dated from the Universal Declaration of Human Rights (1948) that enshrined a human right to dignity[4] and the Declaration of Philadelphia (1944) that proclaimed human dignity as a universal value of the International Labour Organization (ILO).[5] Despite the fact that these documents have a universal character, the perception of human dignity as a value has noticeably influenced the European legal system much more than the American one. The

1. Alexander Lushnikov, *Pravo rabotnika na ohranu truda: novye podhody* (The right of the worker to occupational health and safety: New Approaches), 52 Sotsial'noye i pensionnoye parvo (2009) 1.
2. This chapter only covers moral harassment not covered by anti-discrimination legislation.
3. *See* Manfred Weiss, *Re-Inventing Labour Law*, 47 (Guy Davidov & Brian Langille eds., *The Idea of Labour Law*, Oxford, OUP, 2011).
4. The Universal Declaration of Human Rights (UDHR) adopted by the United Nations General Assembly on 10 Dec. 1948. Text available at: http://www.un.org/en/documents/udhr/ (accessed 20 Oct. 2015).
5. ILO Declaration of Philadelphia, 10 May 1944.

European Union is proclaimed to be founded on the indivisible, universal values of human dignity, freedom, equality and solidarity and this priority applies equally to labour law.[6] Over the last thirty years the right to dignity has been mentioned and protected by various branches of law in European countries implementing regulations on occupational health and safety.

The Italian Constitution (1947) stipulated that, 'private economic enterprise may not be carried out [...] in such a manner that could damage safety, liberty and human dignity'.[7] The French Constitution, in contrast, does not mention human dignity, though it was acknowledged to be a 'constitutional principle' by the Constitutional Court in 1994.[8] In Russia the need to protect human dignity was recognized by the post-Soviet Constitution, adopted in 1993.[9]

The penetration of the principle of human dignity protection into labour law was rather slow. In Italy it was first mentioned in the first section of the Italian *Statuto dei lavoratori*, adopted in 1970, and was intended to protect employee privacy and the freedom of expression. In 1996 the French *Conseil d'Etat* acknowledged the principle of human dignity of employees, prohibiting the practice of 'dwarf-throwing'.[10] This principle was further developed in 2002 when the French Labour Code was complemented by Article L1152-1, prohibiting acts of psychological harassment that may violate employee's rights and dignity. In Russia the need for the protection of employee dignity was stipulated as one of the fundamental principles of labour law in the Labour Code adopted in 2001, though this principle has so far not been implemented in practice. The doctrine of labour law already in the Soviet period acknowledged the necessity to draw the attention of the legislator to this aspect of working conditions.[11] Nowadays scholars often refer to foreign experience and urge the authorities to adopt suitable provisions, providing the right of employees to a favourable psychological working environment and laying down the prohibition of moral harassment[12] in order to ensure the protection of employee dignity.

In the following sections the French, Italian and Russian approaches to the protection of the dignity of employees in the case of moral harassment will be

6. The Charter of Fundamental Rights of the European Union (2000/C 364/01).
7. *See* Art. 47 of Italian Constitution, the text in English is available at: https://www.senato.it/documenti/repository/istituzione/costituzione_inglese.pdf (accessed 20 Nov. 2015).
8. The decision is available at: http://www.conseil-constitutionnel.fr/conseil-constitutionnel/francais/les-decisions/depuis-1958/decisions-par-date/1994/94-343/344-dc/decision-n-94-343-344-dc-du-27-juillet-1994.10566.html (accessed 20 Nov. 2015).
9. *See* Art. 21 of the Russian Constitution, available at: http://www.constitution.ru/10003000/10003000-4.htm (accessed 20 Nov. 2015).
10. *See* Susan Millns, *Dwarf-Throwing and Human Dignity: A French Perspective*, 375–391, 18(3) Journal of Social Welfare and Family Law (1996). *See also* the decision of the UN Human Rights Committee in the case Manuel Wackenheim *v.* France, Communication No 854/1999, U.N. Doc. CCPR/C/75/D/854/1999 (2002).
11. Sergey Ivanov, *Trudovoye pravo i nauchno-tekhnicheskiy progress* (Labour law and scientific and technological progress), 329 (Moscow, 1974).
12. Alexander Lushnikov, *Pravo rabotnika na ohranu truda: novye podhody* (The right of the worker to occupational health and safety: New Approaches), 52 Sotsial'noye i pensionnoye parvo (2009) 1; Alla Zherukova, *Obespecheniye prava rabotnikov na zashchitu svoyego dostoinstva v period trudovoy deyatel'nosti* (Ensuring the right of workers to protection of their dignity at work), 7 (Abstract of thesis, Moscow, 2011).

examined in order to suggest the most appropriate way to fill the gaps in Russian labour legislation.

§4.03 PROTECTION FROM MORAL HARASSMENT AT WORK IN FRANCE

The French experience of combating harassment dates back at least to 2002 when the Social Modernization Act was enacted[13] introducing changes to the French Labour Code. It must be noted that some case law rulings on the protection of employees from harassment preceded these innovations. For example, in 1973, the French Supreme Court found in favour of a manager whose employer took his secretary and telephone away and demoted him to sweeping a warehouse floor in order to force him to resign.[14] Another important case was heard in 2000 when the Social Security Court of Vosges recognized that an accident caused by moral harassment would qualify as a 'work accident' for the purposes of collecting benefits from the regional health insurance agency.[15]

Summing up the most important traits of the new legal provisions I will consequently explain the meaning of each innovation. The distinguishing traits are as follows.

[A] Legal Definition of Harassment

The new Article L. 1152-1 of the French Labour Code[16] states: 'that no employee may be subjected to repeated deeds of moral harassment aimed at or leading to a deterioration of working conditions likely to detract from the rights of employees and their dignity, to undermine their physical or mental health or to compromise their professional future'.[17]

It is worth noting that these notions contain a wide variety of actions which could be treated as harassment. According to this definition harassment is present in cases where degrading treatment was intentional and also in cases where it was non-intentional but still led to the undermining of health or/and dignity.

French scholars note that in judicial practice the wide-ranging legal definition is subject to a more concrete and practicable interpretation. In the court's interpretation the scope of application of the Social Modernization Act goes beyond the strict concept

13. Loi n° 2002-73 du 17 janvier 2002 de modernisation sociale, available at: http://www.legifrance.gouv.fr/affichTexte.do?cidTexte=JORFTEXT000000408905&dateTexte=&categorieLien=id (accessed 30 Sept. 2013).
14. Maria Isabel S. Guerrero, *The Development of Moral Harassment (or Mobbing) Law in Sweden and France as a Step Towards EU Legislation*, 27 (2) Boston College International & Comparative Law Review 489 (2004).
15. *Id.*, 490.
16. Code du travaille available at: http://www.legifrance.gouv.fr/affichCode.do?cidTexte=LEGITEXT000006072050&dateTexte=vig (accessed 23 Aug. 2015).
17. *Ibid.*

of moral harassment to include 'suffering at work' and the courts go even further in recognizing the right to the protection of mental health at work.[18]

French case law confirms that harassment exists even in the absence of malicious intent and sometimes attributes it to certain organizational factors of work.[19] Some French scholars underline the fact that organizational factors have a great impact on harassment at work. It is supposed that prevention of workplace psychological harassment can be achieved by analyzing and eliminating organizational factors in the workplace (such as intensification of the work, weakness of management authority, precariousness of the ties to employment, incivility) and cultural aspects that constitute a fertile breeding ground for the emergence of violent behaviour between members of the work organization.[20]

[B] Obligations of Employer and Employees for Prevention and Investigation of Acts of Harassment

The director of the enterprise has an obligation to prevent moral harassment at work by making 'all the necessary provisions for preventing activities constituting moral harassment'.[21] His duty to display the text of Article 222-33-2 of the Penal Code (concerning criminal responsibility for harassment at work) in the workplace may be seen as one possible measure of prevention.

When the act of harassment has occurred the employer has to investigate the case immediately and take the necessary steps to remedy the situation.[22] According to the new legislation workers also have obligations in this respect: they have to take care of their own health and safety and that of other people affected by their actions or omissions at work.[23] This obligation is supported by the possibility to take disciplinary action in relation to an employee carrying out acts of harassment.[24]

[C] Trade Union Rights in the Sphere of Anti-harassment Protection

This provision can be estimated as enforcing protection from harassment as representative trade unions of the enterprise are entitled to take legal action on behalf of an employee who considers himself to be the victim of harassment.[25] As a result, the employee who suffers from harassment can count on support and legal advice free of

18. Loic Lerouge, *Moral Harassment in the Workplace: French Law and European Perspectives*, 32 Comparative Labour Law & Policy Journal 110, 112 (2010).
19. *Id.*, 110.
20. Michel Vézina, Julie Dussault, *Au-delà de la relation «bourreau-victime» dans l'analyse d'une situation de harcèlement psychologique au travail* (Perspectives Interdisciplinaires sur le Travail et la Santé, 2005, 7(3)). Available at: http://pistes.revues.org/3155 (accessed 20 Jun. 2013).
21. French Labour Code, Art. L1152-4.
22. *Id.*, Art. L2313-2.
23. *Id.*, Art. L4122-1.
24. *Id.*, Art. L1154-2.
25. *Id.*, Art. L1154-2.

charge. The written consent of the employee is sufficient to start the proceedings that can be stopped at any moment at his request.

[D] Possibility of Mediation at the Enterprise Level

Mediation is the best way to reconcile the parties of conflict where the victim and the perpetrator of harassment work together. This is why the French Labour Code provides a framework for mediation at work in the case of harassment. According to its provisions the mediation process may be initiated by the person who believes being harassed or the person accused of harassment. The mediator is appointed by agreement between the parties. The aim is to search for compromise and stop the harassment. If the mediator fails to obtain this goal, he/she has to inform the parties of possible penalties and procedural safeguards granted to the victim of harassment.

The French Labour Code ensures the proper functioning of the mediator's activities and lays down responsibility for acts aimed at undermining the exercise of his functions.[26] Although the provisions on the process of mediation play down the possibility to resolve the conflict with minimal costs and time, most scholars note that this procedure is little known and rarely used in France.[27] However, the mere opportunity to use mediation process instead of suing the offender is one of the most important advantages of the French system of protection from harassment.

[E] Reverse Burden of Proof

Reverse burden of proof means that the employee has to demonstrate the facts which support the presumption that harassment has occurred. It is then up to the defendant to prove that the actions that led to the complaint did not constitute harassment and that his actions were grounded on the reasons not connected with harassment. As a result, this is a crucial point for the effectiveness of anti-harassment protection. Taking into account the peculiar nature of acts of harassment, it is almost impossible for the employee to gather evidence that would demonstrate the facts of humiliation beyond reasonable doubt.

[F] Protection of Harassment Victim

The French Labour Code lays down the methods of protection of employees who suffered harassment (witnessed or reported it) due to the illegal conduct of the employer. It is prohibited to penalize, dismiss, or subject to discrimination, direct or indirect, employees for being subjected to or for refusal to be subjected to repeated acts

26. *Id.*, Art. L. 1152-6, according to Art. L1155-1 of the Labour Code such behaviour may be punishable with imprisonment for one year and a fine of EUR 3,750.
27. Loic Lerouge, *Workplace Bullying and Harassment in France and Few Comparisons with Belgium: A Legal Perspective*, 46 (JILPT Report n° 12/2013 – Workplace Bullying and Harassment – 2013 JILPT Seminar on Workplace Bullying and Harassment, 2013).

of moral harassment, or for witnessing or reporting such conduct.[28] Article L1152-3 states that any termination of the employment contract in breach of the above-mentioned rules is void.

This provision cannot be overestimated as it prohibits the measures that can be used by the employer to influence the employee and to make him tolerate harassment.

[G] Possibility of Criminal Liability for Harassment at Work

Criminal liability for the acts of harassment was also introduced in 2002. The *corpus delicti,* according to Article 222-33-2 of the French Penal Code[29] is the following: repeated acts of harassment that had as their aim or effect to deteriorate working conditions that may undermine employee's rights and dignity, to alter his physical or mental health or to compromise his professional future. The sanction is rather severe as it includes both imprisonment (up to two years) and a fine of EUR 30,000. It must be noted that initially the sum of the fine was EUR 15,000, that was changed in 2012.

The courts may also issue an order to publish the decision in the press at the offender's expense.[30] Presumably this measure could contribute to the raising of social awareness of the problem.

[H] Developed Jurisprudence on Harassment

Judicial practice on harassment at work is rather curious and demonstrates that this type of legislation takes time to raise social awareness of new rules. It must penetrate to the social conscience, and allow employees, trade unions and the courts to apply new provisions. The first harassment case was heard by the French courts only four years after the adoption of new rules (*Propara* case heard by the Court of Cassation on 21 June 2006).[31]

With regard to early judicial practice on harassment at work, scholars noted that the French courts were reluctant to hear appeals on workplace harassment, since the concept was not clearly defined by law.[32]

Concluding this overview of French anti-harassment legislation it is worth emphasizing that the French approach to this problem provides answers to a wide range of questions and is evidently able to ensure effective protection for the employee. The main traits of this approach as listed above are at the same time the advantages of French regulations.

---

28. French Labour Code, Arts L1152-2.
29. Code pénal available at: http://www.legifrance.gouv.fr/affichCode.do?cidTexte=LEGITEXT000006070719 (accessed 20 Oct. 2015).
30. *See* Loic Lerouge, *supra* note 18, 115.
31. *Id.*, 126.
32. Julie Bourgault, *Le harcèlement moral en France: un concept juridique subjectif- objectif,* 116 (Santé, Société et Solidarité, 2006, 5.2).

Since the adoption of these provisions the quantity of harassment claims has been rising from year to year.[33] Scholars note that the French courts are reluctant to receive appeals on workplace harassment, since the concept has not been clearly defined by law.[34] They consider that the possibility of various interpretations opens the door to abuses and urge the necessity to develop social dialogue in this sphere.[35]

§4.04 THE PROTECTION FROM MOBBING AT WORK IN ITALY

The Italian approach to the protection of employees from moral harassment, known in Italian case law as mobbing, was developed by the courts on the basis of wide interpretation of Article 2087 of the Italian Civil Code.[36] This Article lays down the employees' right to dignity and obliges the employer to protect the physical integrity and personality of an employee. Italian courts refer to this Article in cases of employees' protection from offensive or humiliating conduct if anti-discrimination mechanism is not applicable.

It must be noted that historically this approach derives from the acknowledged principle of the protection of human dignity. Even if the Constitution of Italy[37] does not mention the dignity of the employee directly, interpretation of several articles provides a notion of the protection of human dignity.[38] The Constitutional Court of Italy widely uses the concept of employee dignity: in consideration of the cases relating to fair remuneration,[39] commensuration of disciplinary penalty[40] or unfair

33. The search for judicial documents containing words "harcèlement moral" was carried out on the site of the official French jurisprudence database. It demonstrated the following quantity of documents per year were found: 199 in 2009, 195 in 2010, 370 in 2011, 372 in 2012, 279 in 2013 and 404 in 2014. The search was carried out on. http://www.legifrance.gouv.fr/rechJuriJudi.do?reprise=true&page=1, (accessed 21 Aug. 2015).
34. Julie Bourgault, 115.
35. *See* C. Manaouil, M. Graser, A. Verrier, E. Castel-Turbant, C. Doutrellot-Philippon, O. Jardé, *Le harcèlement moral au travail: rapports de la loi du 17 janvier 2002,* 15 Médecine & Droit 73 (2005).
36. *See* Ilaria Valenzi, *Le trasformazioni del lavoro e l'insorgenza di nuovi rischi: mobbing e stress lavoro-correlato,* 9–10 Lavoro e previdenza oggi, 979–980 (2011); Nadia Girelli, *La protezione del benessere psicofisico dei lavoratori: mobbing, molestie sessuali, straining,* 5 Lavoro nella giurisprudenza, 466–472 (2012).
37. Italian scholars identify a dual constitutional interpretation of dignity: as a necessity in material terms, which is suitable for guaranteeing a dignified existence; and as a wider notion, which obviously implies the first, but which 'takes into consideration all the other social conditions which make the individual "a fully participating member of society"' (*see* Veronica Papa, *Dignity as the foundational paradigm of Labour law,* 36 European Journal of Social Law, 1 (2012); Maria Rosaria Marella, *Il fondamento sociale della dignita umana. Un modello costituzionale per il diritto europeo dei contratti,* Rivista Critica di Diritto Privato, 81 (2007).
38. *See* Art. 3 (proclaiming equal social dignity of people), Art. 35 (protecting all forms of labour), Art. 36 (protecting wages that must be sufficient for 'free and dignified existence'), Art. 41 (limiting economic freedom by 'safety, liberty, and human dignity'). Italian scholars consider that idea of protection of human dignity is implicitly present in many other Constitutional provisions. (*see* Daniela Bifulco, *Inviolabilita dei diritti sociali,* 124 (Napoli 2003), cit. from Iolanda Piccinini, *Sulla dignità del lavoratore,* 3 Argomenti di diritto del lavoro 743 (2005).
39. Sentenza della Corte Costituzionale 11 ottobre 2012, n. 223.
40. *Sentenza della Corte costituzionale 01 giugno 1995 n. 220.*

dismissal[41] or equality of rights of employees in the probation period.[42] The possibility of limitation of employer's power by the dignity of the employee was ruled by the Italian Court to be fundamental in 1989.[43]

Article 2087 of the Italian Civil Code implements the employees' right to dignity and obliges the employer to protect the physical integrity and personality of the employee. Judicial practice in Italy gives a wide-ranging interpretation of this norm, using it for protecting employees from offensive or humiliating conduct in the cases when an anti-discrimination provision is not applicable.

An Italian employee in such cases can claim that the employer failed to ensure the protection of the employee's personality. As stated in the decision of Italian Court of Cassation the plaintiff suing his employer for harassment/mobbing has to prove: 'the existence of such damage, as well as the harmful effects of the working environment and the relationship between the one and the other.'[44]

In the absence of a legal definition of mobbing the concept was developed by case law influenced by psychology.[45] The Italian Court of Cassation defined this notion[46] and introduced seven parameters for the recognition of mobbing: the working environment; the duration of acts constituting mobbing, their frequency, the type of hostile actions, inequality of the employee's and employer's positions, the trend according to the later stages, the persecutory intent.[47]

It is important to note that the implied obligation to protect the employee from mobbing is also relevant in cases when the acts of harassment were committed by another employee, giving rise to vicarious liability.[48]

The traditional allocation of the burden of proof when the plaintiff has to prove facts to justify his or her claim is another peculiarity of this legal method. From one point of view, the combination of these special traits makes the employee's defence more difficult but from the other point of view it contributes to the prevention of abuses of rights and ensures a balance of rights at the workplace.

The Italian approach to anti-harassment protection has, in my opinion, the following shortcomings in comparison with the French legislation: (1) legal provisions do not contain the means of prevention of harassment at work; (2) in the case of harassment the worker cannot count on mediation within the enterprise or legal aid of special bodies; (3) protection (immunity) of employees from dismissal and changing of contractual terms of the employee filing a harassment claim is not provided in the

41. *Sentenza della Corte costituzionale 14 gennaio 1986 n. 2 or Sentenza della Corte costituzionale 10 marzo 1983 n. 46.*
42. *Sentenza della Corte costituzionale 22 dicembre 1980 n. 189.*
43. *Corrado Guglielmucci, Potere imprenditoriale,dignità dell'uomo lavoratore e parità di trattamento (Diritto del lavoro, 1997, 1–2).*
44. Sentenza Cassazione civile sez. Lav. n. 2038, 2013.
45. Mariangela Cistaro, *Il mobbing nella dottrina e in giurisprudenza*, 940 (Diritto & Pratica Del Lavoro, 2009, 16).
46. Corte di Cassazione, Sez. lav. 17 febbraio 2009 N 3785 *see also* Corte di Cassazione, Sez. lav., sentenza 31 maggio 2011, N12048; Cassazione Civile, Sez. Lav., 28 agosto 2013, N19814; Cass., sez. lav., 25 settembre 2014, N 20230.
47. Cassazione Civile, Sez. Lav., 15 maggio 2015, N 10037.
48. Cassazione Civile, sez. lavoro, 25 luglio 2013, N 18093.

legislation; (4) the plaintiff has to bear the burden of proof; (5) the employer can be held responsible only in the case of proven intention of hostile behaviour, its focus on humiliation of employee, and damages to mental or physical health, that without doubt makes the protection less effective.

§4.05 PREREQUISITES FOR THE ELABORATION OF ANTI-HARASSMENT PROTECTION IN RUSSIA

There is an evident lack in the provisions regulating the employee's right to dignity and protection from mobbing in Russia and very little jurisprudence on this matter. Scholars point out that the cases dealing with these issues relate to either discrimination, unfair dismissal, or both, but do not aim at tackling harassment or mobbing per se.[49] However, Russian employees like Italian workers often experience mobbing at the workplace. In recent years many research papers investigating this problem have been published, both from a psychological and legal point of view.[50] It has been noted that 5%–20% of Russian employees have been victims of mobbing.[51]

In my opinion Russian employment legislation contains certain norms which could be used as a basis for the judicial acknowledgment of the employer's duty to protect employees from mobbing.[52] First it is possible to refer to the fundamental principles of labour law, laid down in Article 2 of the Russian Labour Code which stipulates the right of employees to protection of their dignity. This principle is not developed further and the legal provisions do not lay down any corresponding duty of the employer. However, reference to this Article might be used in the way that the Italian courts apply Article 2087 of the Italian Civil Code, deducing from it the obligation of employer to protect employees from mobbing.

In one case a Russian court has referred to the principle of protection of the employee's dignity and interpreted it as laying down the obligation of employer to compensate non-pecuniary damage in the case of degrading treatment of an employee.[53] In other cases concerning, for example, the situations in which employees were sanctioned for unethical behaviour and harassment of their colleagues, the courts did not refer to the principle of protection of employee dignity and were reluctant to find employees who were harassing their colleagues guilty of a disciplinary offence.[54] Regretfully, the principle of protection of the employee's dignity is referred to by the

49. Daria Chernyaeva, *The Regulation of Mobbing and Harassment in Russia: Current Challenges and Future Prospect, 14–31 (* E-Journal of International and Comparative Labour Studies, 2014, 3 (2)).
50. *See*, for example, Natalia Plastinina, Kak zashchishchat'sya ot mobbing (How to ensure the protection from mobbing?) (Trudovoye pravo, 2012, 2); Daria Chernyaeva, *supra* note 49.
51. Galina Bryntseva, *Mobbing Dik* (Rossiyskaya gazeta, 24 Mar. 2010). Available at: http://www.rg.ru/2010/03/24/mobbing.html (access 14 Apr. 2015).
52. Certain protection might be obtained through the application of provisions of Criminal and Administrative law. *See* more in: Daria Chernyaeva, *supra* note 49, 19.
53. The appeal decision of the Tomsk Regional Court N 33-4101/2011, adopted 30 Dec. 2011.
54. The appeal decision of the St-Petersburg City Court N33-5330, adopted 08 Apr. 2013; Decision of Cherkessk City Court N2-634/2011, adopted 22 Mar. 2011; The appeal decision of the St-Petersburg City Court N33-6119/2012, adopted 17 May 2012.

Russian courts only rarely, and it is not mentioned in the jurisprudence of higher courts.

Another prerequisite for the elaboration of the implied duty of the employer to protect employees from mobbing might be found in Article 237 of the Russian Labour Code. It provides the obligation of the employer to compensate non-pecuniary damage in case of illegal action or in the absence of due action in respect of the employee. If the jurisprudence of the Supreme Court of the Russian Federation were to deduce from the principle of protection of the employee's dignity the corresponding duties of the employer, Article 237 could provide the necessary framework for the compensation of damages.

An additional basis for the protection from mobbing is provided by the jurisprudence of the Supreme Court of the Russian Federation. The Supreme Court pointed out that in the cases in which the employee alleges that he was forced to resign, the lower courts have to investigate whether the resignation was voluntary.[55] The burden of proof is imposed on the employee.

Decisions in favour of the applicant with the court finding that the employee was forced to resign as a result of moral harassment at the workplace are almost absent. However, in one case the court decided that the employee was forced to resign as the employer created a hostile environment, and the applicant's resignation was the result of negative emotional factors.[56] In the majority of cases the applicants suffering from a hostile work environment failed to win their cases as they did not manage to prove coercion.[57]

In my opinion the elaboration of the implied duty of employer to protect the dignity of the employee might provide additional legal support to the claims for reintegration or compensation of damages in case of forced resignation. The courts might consider the hostile work environment as a main factor of cohesion and decide in favour of the employee on this basis.

According to the Italian and French experience the employer can be held liable for the creation of a hostile environment in case of numerous disciplinary sanctions imposed on an employee without sufficient grounds,[58] or in cases of sanctions imposed with the intent to harass.[59] The Russian courts, however, are reluctant to conclude that unfair disciplinary sanction forced the applicant to resign from work and do not uphold these claims for the compensation of damages.[60]

These examples demonstrate that foreign experience could serve as a vector of development of Russian employment law. The French understanding of harassment as a psychological risk which should be prevented is also an important point. It might be developed in Russia through the wide interpretation of the notion of health, as

55. Decision of the Plenary Session of the Supreme Court 'On Application of the Labour Code of the Russian Federation by the Courts of the RF' (adopted 17 Mar. 2004).
56. Decision of the Central District Court of Chita region N 2-1055-07, adopted on 3 May 2007.
57. Cassation ruling № 33–4995 of the Perm Regional Court, adopted on 23 May 2011.
58. Cass. soc., 22 Mar. 2007, N 04-48308.
59. Cassazione Sezione Lavoro N 6907 del 20 marzo 2009.
60. Decision of the Irkutsk Regional Court N 33-7469-10, adopted 27 Oct. 2010.

contained in ILO Convention No. 155,[61] which indicates not merely the absence of disease or infirmity but also the physical and mental elements affecting well-being which are directly related to health and safety at work.

§4.06 CONCLUSIONS

The research into the Russian legislation and case law supports the view that the Italian experience might serve as an example for the elaboration of an analogous duty in Russia. The French provisions demonstrate the need to widen the notion of health and acknowledge the protection of mental health of employee, which should be ensured through the organization of healthy psychosocial conditions at work. As a result both the Italian and French experience could significantly contribute to the development of anti-harassment protection if followed by the Russian authorities.

Russian labour legislation is very conservative and the adoption of new provisions, such as the prohibition of discrimination, introduced in 2001, is often an half-hearted measure, as the relevant provisions lack precision, and effective implementation is often long in coming. The anti-harassment provisions, if adopted, might have the same destiny and remain for years 'a paper tiger'. This is why the Italian way of employee protection seems more appropriate for Russia in the near future, in particular, considering that the Russian courts have already acknowledged on a few occasions the employee's right to dignity. The attention of the Russian Supreme Court to this problem and the adoption of a relevant explanatory resolution in respect of the practical realization of employees' right to dignity in employment relations might form the basis for further case law. Provided with such interpretative support, the lower courts would be able to find the acts of moral harassment on the part of the employer to be in breach of labour legislation and oblige the employer to pay non-pecuniary damages under Article 237 of the Russian Labour Code.

61. ILO Occupational Safety and Health Convention, 1981 (No. 155), ratified by Russia 2 Jul. 1998.

CHAPTER 5

Low-Wage Workers and Employment Benefits in the United States: A Bleak Forecast*

Trina Jones

§5.01 INTRODUCTION

Compensation is a key element of workplace happiness. Receiving a decent wage for one's labor is essential both to caring for one's family and self, as well as to one's sense of self-respect and dignity. In recent years, low-wage workers in the United States have undertaken a herculean struggle to garner a living wage through efforts like the Fight for $15. As explained on its website, the Fight for $15 began with "a few hundred fast food workers in New York City striking for USD 15 an hour and union rights. Today, [it's] an international movement in over three hundred cities on six continents of fast-food workers, home health aides, child care teachers, airport workers, adjunct professors, retail employees—and underpaid workers everywhere."[1] Due in large part to the Fight for $15, and against all odds, several states and cities in the United States have agreed to increase their minimum wage incrementally to USD 15 an hour.[2]

While the struggle for a living wage is receiving some attention in the United States, the dearth of workplace benefits (e.g., flextime, leaves, healthcare and retirement benefits) available to low-wage workers has garnered less consideration. This is unfortunate for a number of reasons. First, low-wage workers experience illness and the daily demands of attending to dependents, and require accommodation for these life events and obligations. Second, modest wage increases are unlikely to procure, for

* A longer version of this chapter appears under the title: *A Different Class of Care: The Benefits Crisis and Low-Wage Workers*, 66(3) AM. U. L. REV. 691-760 (2017).

1. Fight for $15, About Us, http://fightfor15.org/about-us/ (last visited Aug. 27, 2016).
2. *Id.*

low-wage workers, the sort of group benefits that employers accord high-wage workers, as the costs of these benefits will in most instances exceed the increase in wages. Third, benefits have been shown to improve parenting outcomes and to reduce gender inequality. In light of the above, careful analysis of the availability of employment benefits to low-wage workers is warranted.

This chapter undertakes such analysis and explains why the outlook for low-wage workers in the United States is grim. The examination proceeds as follows. Sections 5.02 and 5.03 demonstrate the vulnerability of low-wage workers by first describing salient characteristics of these workers in the United States, and then comparing benefits that are generally available to high- and low-wage workers. Section 5.04 explains that while employees, employers, and the larger society gain from having benefit policies in place, employers are less likely to perceive a need to adopt these policies for low-wage workers because of the surplus of low-wage workers in the labor market. Section 5.04 also demonstrates the ways in which class bias and negative views about the skill and value of low-wage labor may influence employer decision-making. Section 5.05 explains why the outlook for change is bleak.

§5.02 DEMOGRAPHIC CHARACTERISTICS OF LOW-WAGE WORKERS

In the United States, definitions of low-wage workers vary. Some researchers define low-wage workers as those who cannot support a family of four, above the official poverty threshold, after working forty hours a week for fifty-two weeks in a year.[3] Others define low-wage workers as those who earn less than 150% of the federal minimum wage.[4] Employing either definition, in 2015, with a poverty threshold of USD 24,036,[5] and with a federal minimum wage of USD 7.25 an hour,[6] low-wage workers earned less than USD 12 per hour.[7] Approximately 25-35% of the US workforce fell into this category.[8]

---

3. Office of the Assistant Sec'y for Planning and Evaluation, US Dep't of Health & Human Serv., *Who Are Low-Wage Workers?* 1 (2009), http://aspe.hhs.gov/hsp/09/lowwageworkers/rb.pdf (defining low-wage workers as "workers age[d] 16 to 64 whose hourly wage rate is such that even if they worked full-time, full-year their annual earnings would fall below the poverty line for a family of four").
4. Gregory Acs & Austin Nichols, Low-Income Workers and Their Employers: Characteristics and Challenges 3 (2007), http://www.urban.org/sites/default/files/alfresco/publication-pdfs/411532-Low-Income-Workers-and-Their-Employers.PDF.
5. US Census Bureau, https://www.census.gov/topics/income-poverty/poverty.html (last visited Aug. 16, 2016). This number is for a family of four.
6. US Dep't of Labor, *Minimum Wage*, https://www.dol.gov/general/topic/wages/minimumwage (last visited Aug. 16, 2016).
7. Regardless of methodology, most researchers use "a range of $10-11/hour in current dollars as a good cut-off point for those considered lower-wage." Anna Danziger & Shelley Waters Boots, Urban Institute, *Lower-Wage Workers and Flexible Work Arrangements* at 3 fn. 5 (2008), http://scholarship.law.georgetown.edu/cgi/viewcontent.cgi?article=1000&context=legal [hereinafter *Lower-Wage Workers*].
8. Importantly, estimates regarding the size of the low-wage workforce vary depending upon how low-wage employment is defined. See Randy Albelda & Michael Carr, *Low-Wage and Low-Income Workers in the U.S.*, 1979-2009, 6-7 (Ctr. for Soc. Policy, Working Paper No. 2012-1, 2012), http://scholarworks.umb.edu/cgi/viewcontent.cgi?article=1059&amp=&context=csp_pubs&

In addition to earning less by definition, low-wage workers share the following demographic characteristics when compared to high-wage workers. They are younger on average,[9] and a higher percentage is female.[10] They are mostly White, but a larger percentage of low-wage workers is of color when compared to high-wage workers.[11] Low-wage workers have less formal education than high-wage workers, but most have at least a high school diploma or its equivalent.[12] Although a majority of low-wage workers are married or partnered, they are less likely to be married/partnered than high-wage workers.[13] Low-wage workers are almost as likely as high-wage workers to have parental responsibilities.[14]

A typical image of low-wage workers in the United States is that of the fast-food or restaurant worker.[15] Low-wage workers, however, are located throughout the US

---

sei-redir = 1 (concluding that the number of low-wage workers remained constant from the 1990s to 2009 at about 28%); James T. Bond & Ellen Galinsky, Families & Work Inst., *Workplace Flexibility and Low-Wage Employees* 2 (2011) [hereinafter *Workplace Flexibility*], http://familiesandwork.org/downloads/WorkFlexandLowWageEmployees.pdf (estimating that about one-third, or 35%, of the US workforce was low-wage in 2008); Heather Boushey et al., Ctr. for Econ. Policy & Research, *Understanding Low-Wage Work in the United States* 5 (2007) (finding that approximately 44 million workers, or 33% of workers, held low-wage jobs earning USD 11 or less); David Cooper, Econ. Policy Inst., *Raising the Minimum Wage to $12 by 2020 Would Lift Wages for 35 Million American Workers* 2 (2015), http://www.epi.org/files/2015/raising-the-minimum-wage-to-12-dollars-by-2020-would-lift-wages-for-35-million-american-workers.pdf (finding that raising the minimum wage to USD 12 by 2020 would "directly or indirectly lift wages for 35.1 million workers," or 25% of US workers); Pamela Loprest et al., Office of the Assistant Sec'y for Planning & Evaluation, US Dep't of Health & Human Servs., *Who are Low-wage Workers?* 2 (2009), http://aspe.hhs.gov/hsp/09/lowwageworkers/rb.pdf (finding that 31% of US workers were low-wage based on 2001 data); John Schmitt, *Low-Wage Lessons*, Ctr. For Econ. & Policy Research (Jan. 2012), http://cepr.net/documents/publications/low-wage-2012-01.pdf (finding that about 24.8% of the US workforce was low-wage using data from 2009); Rebecca Thiess, *The Future of Work: Trends and Challenges for Low-Wage Workers*, EPI 7 (Apr. 27, 2012), http://www.epi.org/files/2012/bp341-future-of-work.pdf (finding 26% of US workers were low-wage using 2010 data).

9. Ellen Galinsky, James T. Bond & Eve Tahmincioglu, *Not Just "Jobs" . . . "Good Jobs": The Low-Income Workforce Challenge* 5 (2012) [hereinafter *Not Just Jobs*] (stating that approximately 38% of low-wage workers are under 25 years old, compared with 8% of middle-income and 3% of high-income workers).
10. Bond & Galinsky, *Workplace Flexibility*, *supra* note 8, at 5.
11. Danziger & Boots, *Lower-Wage Workers*, *supra* note 7, at 2.
12. About 35% of low-wage workers have a high school diploma, while 45.5% have at least some postsecondary education. Gregory Acs & Austin Nichols, *Low-Income Workers and Their Employers: Characteristics and Challenges* 5 (2007), http://www.urban.org/sites/default/files/alfresco/publication-pdfs/411532-Low-Income-Workers-and-Their-Employers.PDF. About 10% of low-wage workers have a four-year college degree. John Schmitt & Janelle Jones, Ctr. For Econ. & Policy Research, *Low-Wage Workers are Older and Better Educated Than Ever* 2 (2012), https://cepr.net/documents/publications/min-wage3-2012-04.pdf.
13. Bond & Galinsky, *Workplace Flexibility*, supra note 8, at 5 (finding that 54% of low-wage workers are living with a spouse or partner while 73% of high-wage workers are living with a spouse or partner).
14. Bond & Galinsky, *Workplace Flexibility*, *supra* note 8, at 3.
15. This image is unsurprising given that food workers constitute the second largest category of low-wage employees, behind cashiers. US Dep't of Labor, Bureau of Labor Statistics, *Employment and Wages for the Highest and Lowest Paying Occupations*, May 2012, http://www.bls.gov/oes/2012/may/high_low_paying.htm (listing occupations with the lowest median wage in May 2012).

economy. In addition to food preparers and restaurant workers, they serve as healthcare aides, childcare workers, housekeepers, porters, meat processers, agricultural workers, laundry operators, hairdressers, and manicurists, among other things.[16] Because they tend to be located in sectors of the economy that lack opportunities for the development of skills that may lead to middle-class lives, low-wage workers are generally locked into low-wage jobs.

Importantly, the number of low-wage positions in the United States has increased in recent decades due to globalization and the outsourcing of middle-class manufacturing jobs.[17] Economic instability has augmented this trend. Following the great recession of 2007–2009, the low-wage workforce in the United States grew faster than other sectors of the labor market. According to the National Employment Law Project, although most employment losses in the recession occurred in mid-wage occupations, during the recovery, gains were concentrated in low-wage occupations, which increased 2.7 times as fast as high-wage occupations.[18] Thus, while the US unemployment rate is down with numbers approximating pre-recession figures,[19] wages among US workers have decreased or become stagnant and the number of low-wage positions has increased.[20]

Despite the many ways in which high- and low-wage workers differ demographically, it bears remembering that these workers are almost equally likely to have childcare responsibilities at home.[21] However, with fewer financial resources (even after working multiple jobs to make ends meet), low-wage workers are less able to purchase childcare services that might reduce the time demands of providing care. In addition, they are less likely to have partners with whom to share childcare responsibilities.[22] Thus, low-wage workers are likely to value and to need workplace flexibility and benefits as much as, and perhaps more than, their high-wage counterparts.[23]

§5.03 THE BENEFITS GAP

Employment benefits in the United States generally fall within three categories: (1) flexible work arrangements (FWAs); (2) leave time; and (3) healthcare and retirement benefits. FWAs include, among other things, flexible daily start and stop times, compressed work weeks, part-time work, schedule swaps, job sharing, and

16. Beth Shulman, The Betrayal of Work: How Low-Wage Jobs Fail 30 Million Americans and Their Families 45 (2003); OXFAM America, Working Poor in America 3 (2014); US Dep't of Labor, Bureau of Labor Statistics, *Employment and Wages for the Highest and Lowest Paying Occupations,* May 2012, http://www.bls.gov/oes/2012/may/high_low_paying.htm.
17. Katherine Peralta, *Outsourcing to China Cost U.S. 3.2 Million Jobs Since 2001*, US News World Rep. (Dec. 11, 2014), http://www.usnews.com/news/blogs/data-mine/2014/12/11/outsourcing-to-china-cost-us-32-million-jobs-since-2001.
18. National Employment Law Project, *The Low-Wage Recovery and Growing Inequality* 1, 4 (2012).
19. US Dep't of Labor, Bureau of Labor Statistics, http://data.bls.gov/timeseries/LNS14000000 (showing unemployment rates from January 2006 - July 2016).
20. National Employment Law Project, *supra* note 18, at 1, 4.
21. Danziger & Boots, *supra* note 7, at 2.
22. *Id.* at 2, 6.
23. *Id.* at 6, 7.

telecommuting.[24] Leave time includes maternity and paternity leave, sick leave to care for an employee or her family member, short-term disability leave, and authorized leave under statutes like the Family and Medical Leave Act.[25] Healthcare and retirement benefits include access to employer-sponsored health-insurance programs and pensions (including both defined-contribution and defined-benefit plans).[26] At times, family-friendly benefits are embodied in formal policies (e.g., maternity and paternity leaves), and at other times they are merely informal practices (e.g., a supervisor's exercise of discretion in deciding whether to grant a schedule adjustment).

Before delving into the benefits gap between high- and low-wage workers in the United States, it is important to keep the larger picture in mind. Among developed nations, the United States has some of the least favorable employment benefits. For example, in Europe, women generally receive fourteen to twenty weeks of paid maternity leave and both parents have access to additional paid and unpaid parental leave,[27] usually amounting to one year of paid leave when combined.[28] The United States, by contrast, is one of only two economically developed democracies that does not guarantee basic benefits like paid family leave.[29] Even the unpaid leave that is available under statutes like the Family and Medical Leave Act[30] is much lower when compared to the unpaid leave offered in other countries.[31] Not surprisingly, researchers have found that, among developed nations, the United States has the largest happiness gap between parents and non-parents, and that this gap can be entirely explained by the lack of better family-friendly policies.[32] As the US Secretary of Labor stated in a recent report, the United States has stood still "while family policy in the rest of the

24. Mary Secret, *Identifying the Family, Job, and Workplace Characteristics of Employees Who Use Work-Family Benefits*, 49 FAM. REL. 217, 217 (2000).
25. *Id.*
26. A defined benefit plan is an account in which the employer supplies all of the funds and promises the employee a set payout upon retirement. A defined contribution plan, e.g., 401(k) and 403(b) accounts, require employees to put in their own money. *What is the Difference Between a Defined Benefit Plan and a Defined Contribution Plan?* Time.com, http://time.com/money/2791222/difference-between-defined-benefit-plan-and-defined-contribution-plan/.
27. Christopher J. Ruhm, *Policies to Assist Parents with Young Children*, FUTURE CHILD., Fall 2011, at 37, 41-42; Glassdoor Economic Research & Llewellyn Consulting, *Which Countries in Europe Offer the Fairest Paid Leave and Unemployment Benefits?* 3, 6-9 (2016), https://research-content.glassdoor.com/app/uploads/sites/2/2016/02/GD_FairestPaidLeave_Final.pdf.
28. Rebecca Ray et al., Center for Economic and Policy Research, *Parental Leave Policies in 21 Countries* (2008), http://cepr.net/documents/publications/parental_2008_09.pdf.
29. Only Australia and the United States provide no paid leave. The next lowest is Switzerland, which guarantees 11 weeks of paid leave. Ray, *supra* note 28, at 21 (finding that "the United States has the least generous parental leave policies among the 21 high-income countries we studied."); *see also* Int'l Lab. Org., *Maternity and Paternity at Work: Law and Practice Across the World* (2014), http://www.ilo.org/wcmsp5/groups/public/---dgreports/---dcomm/---publ/documents/publication/wcms_242615.pdf.
30. *See infra* notes 45-47 for discussion of the Family and Medical Leave Act.
31. Ray, *supra* note 28.
32. Jennifer Glass, Robin Simon & Matthew Andersson, CCF Brief: Parenting and Happiness in 22 Countries, Council on Contemp. Families (June 15, 2016), https://contemporaryfamilies.org/brief-parenting-happiness ("The negative effects of parenthood on happiness were *entirely* explained by the presence or absence of social policies allowing parents to better combine paid work with family obligations.").

world passes us by."[33] The situation is thus grim for all workers with familial obligations in the United States, and as this section shows, it is even more so for low-wage workers.

[A] Flexible Work Arrangements and Part-Time Work

In the United States, low-wage workers are less likely than high-wage workers to be offered flextime,[34] which includes a broad range of practices designed to afford employees flexibility in determining their work schedules.[35] Even when they have access to flextime, researchers report that low-wage workers are more likely than high-wage workers to report that using it will negatively impact their job advancement.[36]

While low-wage employees are less likely than high-wage employees to be afforded flextime, they are more likely to be over-represented in part-time positions.[37] Generally speaking, part-time work can be something of a mixed blessing. On the one hand, it allows employees to pursue other life goals (e.g., to go to school, care for family members, travel, engage in personal hobbies, or phase into retirement). On the other hand, part-time employment tends to be associated with lower-paying occupations and industries, often resulting in fewer workplace benefits, limited statutory protections,[38] and less financial stability.[39] Thus, unlike in high-wage employment, where part-time work may sometimes be desired and affordable, in low-wage work,

33. US Dep't of Labor, *The Cost of Doing Nothing: The Price We All Pay Without Paid Leave to Support America's 21st Century Working Families* i (Sept. 4, 2015) [hereinafter *The Cost of Doing Nothing*].
34. James T. Bond & Ellen Galinsky, *What Workplace Flexibility is Available to Entry-Level, Hourly Employees?* 4 (2006) [hereinafter *Hourly Employees*]. *See also* Office of Disability Emp't Policy, Women's Bureau, US Dep't of Labor, *Advancing Workplace Flexibility Policy and Practices* 1 (2011), available at http://www.dol.gov/odep/pdf/WBForum.pdf [hereinafter *Advancing Workplace Flexibility*].
35. As noted earlier, flexible work arrangements include, among other things, flexible arrival and departure times, flexible scheduling of breaks, the use of lunch in exchange for early departures, banking time to secure future time off, and voluntary scheduling swaps. *See supra* text accompanying note 24.
36. *See* Amy Richam, Arlene Johnson, and Lisa Buxbaum, *Workplace Flexibility for Lower-Wage Workers*, Corp. Voices for Working Families 16 (Oct. 2006).
37. BOND & GALINSKY, *Hourly Employees*, *supra* note 34, at 5–6. *See also* BOND & GALINSKY, WORKPLACE FLEXIBILITY, *supra* note 8, at 3 (noting that low-wage workers are much more likely than high-wage workers to have part-time jobs (32% *v.* 9%)).
38. For example, to be covered under the Family and Medical Leave Act, an employee must have worked at least 1,250 hours for her employer in the previous twelve months. *See infra* notes 45–47 and accompanying text for a discussion of the FMLA's eligibility requirements. Under the Affordable Care Act, employers are only required to provide health insurance to their full-time employees. US Treasury Dep't, Fact Sheet, *Final Regulations Implementing Employer Shared Responsibility Under the Affordable Care Act* (ACA) for 2015, https://www.treasury.gov/press-center/press-releases/Documents/Fact%20Sheet%20021014.pdf (last visited Aug. 18, 2016).
39. *See* SUSAN BISOM-RAPP & MALCOLM SARGEANT, LIFETIME DISADVANTAGE, DISCRIMINATION AND THE GENDERED WORKFORCE 7 (2016) (noting that "[b]y one estimate, the wage penalty for working part-time increased in the United States 'from 30 to 46 percent' between 1979 and 2012"). Importantly, some employers have hired part-time workers to avoid paying benefits. *See, e.g.*, Laura Heller, *Obamacare Is Turning Walmart Workers into Temps*, FORBES (June 14, 2013, 6:47

full-time employment is often preferred. Indeed, in the past decade, the number of workers who worked part-time because they could not get full-time employment nearly doubled, and low-wage workers were disproportionately represented within this group.[40]

[B] Leave

In addition to fewer flexible work arrangements, low-wage workers are less likely than high-wage workers to have access to paid family leave, paid sick leave, or short-term disability leave. Family leave covers maternity and paternity leave for parents following the birth, adoption, or foster placement of a child as well as time off for an employee to care for herself, her child, or an adult family member with a serious health condition.[41] Sick leave, by contrast, grants workers time off for more temporary and less serious illnesses (e.g., migraines, stomach aches, short-term absences due to viruses). Short-term disability leave plans generally cover temporary leaves due to disability. When one disaggregates the various forms of leave, data show that 22% of high-wage workers in the United States have access to paid family leave,[42] while 5% of low-wage workers have such access; 62% of high-wage workers have access to short-term disability leave, while 16% of low-wage workers have such access;[43] and high-wage workers are almost twice as likely as low-wage workers to receive paid sick leave.[44]

To be sure, many low-wage workers in the United States are eligible to take leave to care for themselves, or for the worker's parent, child, or spouse under the federal Family and Medical Leave Act (FMLA).[45] The FMLA, however, only applies to employers with fifty or more employees and these employees must have worked for their employer at least 1250 hours in the twelve-month period prior to requesting leave. Because many low-wage workers are employed in small firms, and are engaged in part-time work, their employers may not be covered by the FMLA or the workers

PM), http://www.forbes.com/sites/lauraheller/2013/06/14/obamacare-is-turning-walmart-workers-into-temps (describing Wal-Mart's efforts to avoid providing health-care coverage to its workers by moving more of its workforce to part-time status).

40. Galinsky, Bond & Tahmincioglu, *Not Just Jobs*, *supra* note 9, at 1.
41. A serious health condition would include an illness, injury, impairment, or physical or mental condition requiring inpatient care in a hospital or other residential medical facility, or continuing medical treatment or supervision by a health care provider.
42. *The Cost of Doing Nothing*, *supra* note 33, at 8 (using 2014 data for private sector employees). Overall, only 12% of all private sector workers had access to paid family leave. *Id.*
43. *Id.* Overall, only 40% of all private sector workers had access to paid short-term disability leave in 2014.
44. Bond & Galinsky, *Hourly Employees*, *supra* note 34, at 3. Researchers found that only 39% of low-wage workers had paid sick leave and 61% of these workers had none. *Id.* By contrast, 79% of high-wage workers had at least some paid time off for personal illness, while only 21% did not. *Id.* In addition, only one-quarter (24%) of low-wage employed parents were allowed time off to care for a sick child without losing pay, while three-quarters (76%) were not allowed any paid time off for this purpose. *Id.* By contrast, more than half (54%) of high-wage employed parents were allowed a few days off to care for sick children without losing pay or having to use vacations days. *Id.*
45. 29 U.S.C. §2612(a)(1)(C), (D) (2012).

themselves may be unable to meet the eligibility requirements. In addition, it is important to note that the floor provided by the FMLA is for *unpaid* leave,[46] and workers compensated at or near the minimum wage generally cannot afford the loss of income required to use it.[47]

[C] Healthcare and Retirement Benefits

In addition to flexible work arrangements and leave time, low-wage workers are less well off than high-wage workers with regard to healthcare and retirement benefits. For example, low-wage workers are more likely to work for companies that offer no health care coverage.[48] In 2010, only 18% of workers in small firms earning less than USD 15 an hour were covered by their employers' health plans, while more than half (53%) of high-wage workers in small firms had such coverage.[49] In larger firms, only 47% of workers with wages under USD 15 an hour had health benefits through their jobs, compared with 81% of those with higher wages.[50] Even when low-income workers have employer-sponsored health insurance, they often have difficulty paying their share of the costs.[51] Early evidence suggests that the Affordable Care Act has not greatly changed this state of affairs.[52]

---

46. 29 U.S.C. §2612(c). Employers are, of course, allowed to provide paid leave if they so choose.
47. *See* Council of Economic Advisors, *The Economics of Paid and Unpaid Leave* 3 (Jun. 2014) (noting "even if workers are covered, many cannot afford to take advantage of the FMLA's guarantees ... given the large loss of income it entails"); *The Cost of Doing Nothing, supra* note 33, at 12–13 (same).
48. Ruth Robertson et al., The Commonwealth Fund, *Realizing Health Reform's Potential: Jobs Without Benefits: The Health Insurance Crisis Faced by Small Businesses and Their Workers* 4 (2012), *available at* http://www.commonwealthfund.org/~/media/files/publications/issue-brief/2012/oct/1640_robertson_jobs_without_benefits_small_businesses.pdf ("Low-wage workers in small and large firms were the least likely of all employees to have health benefits through their jobs"); Sherry Glied & Bisundev Mahato, The Commonwealth Fund, *The Widening Health Care Gap Between High- and Low-Wage Workers* 2 (2008), *available at* http://www.commonwealthfund.org/~/media/Files/Publications/Issue%20Brief/2008/May/The%20Widening%20Health%20Care%20Gap%20Between%20High%20%20and%20Low%20Wage%20Workers/Glied_wideninggapbetweenhighlow%20wageworkers_1129_ib%20pdf.pdf (noting that low-wage workers are less likely than high-wage workers to work for companies offering health coverage).
49. Robertson et al., *supra* note 48, at 4.
50. *Id.*
51. Sara R. Collins et al., The Commonwealth Fund, *On the Edge: Low-Wage Workers and Their Health Insurance Coverage* 4 (2003), *available at* http://www.commonwealthfund.org/~/media/files/publications/issue-brief/2003/mar/on-the-edge--low-wage-workers-and-their-health-insurance-coverage/collins_ontheedge_ib_626-pdf.pdf.
52. The Affordable Care Act, also known as Obamacare, requires that employers with more than fifty workers provide their full-time employees (defined as those working thirty or more hours per week) with employer-sponsored healthcare plans or pay a penalty for noncompliance. If an employer offers health-insurance plans, workers are ineligible to buy insurance through healthcare exchanges, even if their income level would have rendered them eligible in the absence of their employer's plan. Thus, some low-wage workers (those who are not offered coverage through their employers) have been able to secure previously unaffordable insurance through healthcare exchanges by using subsidies and expanded Medicaid benefits. However, data show that low-wage workers who receive coverage through their employers have been reluctant to use employer-sponsored plans. Stacy Cowley, *Many Low-Income Workers Say "No"*

Similar findings have been reported with regard to retirement benefits. Among all civilian workers in the United States, 42% in the lowest 25% wage category have access to retirement benefits, while 89% in the highest wage category have such access.[53] Twenty-two percent of workers in the lowest 25% actually participate in their employer-sponsored plans, while 79% of employees in the highest 25% do so.[54]

In summary, this section has demonstrated that, across the board, low-wage workers enjoy fewer employment benefits than their high-wage counterparts. Although this section focuses heavily on empirical data, it is important to remember that the lives of real people lie behind the numbers. For example, consider:

> ***Meghan Brachle.*** *Meghan makes USD 11 per hour working at Whole Foods, which is one of her three part-time jobs. She can only get 29 hours a week at Whole Foods. She notes that while Whole Foods wants more availability from her, the company will not promise her more hours.*[55]

> ***Paola Angel.*** *Before New York City enacted paid sick leave in 2013, Paola worked as a security guard. "She typically had to leave one of her two school-age sons at home when they got sick because she could not afford to forgo a day of pay or to put her job at risk. [Feeling horrible, she would have her sons] take some medicine before [she] left the house and crossed [her] fingers that they [would not] get worse."*[56]

> ***Myrna de los Santos.*** *For more than ten years, Myrna worked at fast-food restaurants in the U.S., including 4.5 years at McDonalds. She was a hard worker, and walked through rain and snow when she couldn't afford transportation. Myrna struggled with health issues for years, but with wages of USD 9 an hour, she could not afford to go to the doctor, nor could she afford health insurance. On August 27, 2016, she died at the age of 49 due to complications from diabetes.*[57]

---

to Health Insurance, N.Y. Times (Oct. 19, 2015) http://www.nytimes.com/2015/10/20/business/many-low-income-workers-say-no-to-health-insurance.html?_r=0.

53. US Dep't of Labor, Bureau of Labor Statistics, Table 2. *Retirement Benefits: Access, Participation, and Take-Up Rates, Civilian Workers, National Compensation Survey*, March 2015, http://www.bls.gov/ncs/ebs/benefits/2015/ownership/civilian/table02a.pdf. For defined benefit programs, the numbers are 8% for those in the lowest 25%, and 50% for those in the highest 25% of wage earners. *Id.* For defined contribution plans, the numbers are 37% for those in the lowest 25%, and 71% for those in the highest 25% of wage earners. *Id.*
54. *Id.* "Take rate" (i.e., the percentage of employees who use benefits when they have access to them) differences suggest that not only must policy-makers be attentive to the issue of who gets benefits, they must also consider the accessibility of these benefits, in terms of costs, when they are provided.
55. Patrick Gillespie, *Part-time Jobs Put Millions in Poverty or Close to It*, Money.CNN.Com (Nov. 20, 2014), http://money.cnn.com/2014/11/20/news/economy/america-part-time-jobs-poverty/ (last visited Oct. 7, 2016).
56. Noam Scheiber, *U.S. Will Require its Contractors to Provide Paid Sick Leave*, N.Y. Times (Sept. 29, 2016), http://www.nytimes.com/2016/09/30/business/economy/paid-sick-leave-government-contractors.html?_r=0 (last visited Oct. 3, 2016).
57. At http://fightfor15.org/hear-many-stories-like-myrnas/; Bryce Covert, *Two of the Biggest Movements in the U.S. Just Teamed Up to Demand Economic and Racial Justice*, Think Progress (Sept. 12, 2016), https://thinkprogress.org/fight-for-15-moral-mondays-7779bb959a50#.eowiasr3k (last visited Oct. 3, 2016).

§5.04 EMPLOYER INCENTIVES

As section 5.03 demonstrates, significant disparities exist in the United States between low- and high-wage workers with regard to flextime, leaves, healthcare, and retirement benefits. This section explains that while employment benefits in general advance the interests of employers, employees, and the larger society, employers may be loath to extend these benefits to low-wage workers because of market forces and class bias.

[A] *Advantages v. Disadvantages of Extending Employment Benefits*

Many employers argue that extending employment benefits to low-wage workers would be too expensive and disruptive.[58] For example, it is claimed that offering FWAs to low-wage workers would be administratively challenging because it would require the hiring and training of temporary replacements for absent employees, or the rearrangement of schedules and the reassignment of projects in order to avoid hiring new workers. The extension of other benefits (e.g., health insurance coverage and retirement benefits) to low-wage workers is also objectionable to some because, it is argued, this extension would not only involve tedious administrative paperwork (e.g., checking eligibility requirements), but would also require more out-of-pocket expenses for employers due to a larger number of covered employees. And finally, some have argued that the provision of additional benefits, and the ensuing costs, will lead employers to discriminate against low-wage workers and women.[59]

Costs, however, must always be balanced against benefits. Too frequently proponents of the cost argument overlook, or too readily dismiss, the numerous studies showing that the provision of employment benefits produces positive returns for employees, employers, and the general public. For example, researchers have found that when employers enable employees to balance their work-life needs more effectively, employees report greater satisfaction with their jobs.[60] They are also physically

58. *See The Cost of Doing Nothing*, *supra* note 33, at 16 (stating that the most common objection to paid family leave is costs). Five explanations are frequently offered for the benefits gap: (1) costs; (2) the surplus of low-wage worker; (3) the comparative skill and value of low- and high-wage labor; (4) bias; and (5) structural limitations of low-wage workplaces. For detailed analysis of the merits of each of these explanations, *see* Trina Jones, *A Different Class of Care: The Benefits Crisis and Low-Wage Workers*, 66 AM. U. L. REV. 691, 717-46 (2017).
59. *See, e.g.*, Mary Ann Case, *How High the Apple Pie? A Few Troubling Questions About Where, Why, and How the Burden of Care for Children Should Be Shifted*, 76 CHI.-KENT L. REV. 1753, 1760-61 (2001); Naomi Cahn & June Carbone, *Lifting the Floor: Sex, Class, and Education*, 39 UNIV. OF BALT. L. F. 57, 73 (2008); Veronique de Rugy, *Women vs. the State*, REASON MAG. (Mar. 8, 2012), https://reason.com/archives/2012/03/08/women-vs-the-state. To be sure, the concern about a reduction in available jobs would seem to apply to both high- and low-wage positions. However, employers may be more willing to assume these costs when dealing with scarce labor.
60. Ellen Ernst Kossek & Cynthia Osseki, *Bridging the Work-Family Policy and Productivity Gap: A Literature Review*, 2 COMMUNITY, WORK AND FAM. 7, 14 (1999); Galinsky, Bond & Tahmincioglu, *Not Just Jobs*, *supra* note 9, at 5-6.

and mentally healthier,[61] and are less distracted and stressed by the demands of life outside of the workplace.[62]

Increasing employee satisfaction is good for employers. Happier employees are more likely to want to remain with their current employers, which decreases high turnover costs and enables employers to retain experienced talent and to minimize the loss of firm-specific skills.[63] When workers are less stressed and distracted by family responsibilities to which they cannot attend, they are more focused and engaged on the job, which increases productivity. Furthermore, having a reputation for being a healthy workplace has proven to be a powerful draw for prospective employees.[64] These gains in recruitment, retention, and productivity should not be ignored.

Beyond benefitting employees and employers, reducing the benefits gap helps the broader society. FWAs and paid leave allow more workers to keep their jobs. This in turn decreases the need for public assistance[65] and makes more money available for injection into local economies. The provision of employment benefits also promotes gender equality. For example, access to paid maternity leave positively affects women's labor force participation rates and earnings.[66] Employment benefits can also

61. Galinsky, Bond & Tahmincioglu, *supra* note 9, at 5; Lucy A. Peipins, Ashwini Soman, Zahava Berkowitz & Mary C. White, *The Lack of Paid Sick Leave as a Barrier to Cancer Screening in Medical Care-Seeking*, 12 BMC PUBLIC HEALTH 520 (2012).
62. Galinsky, Bond & Tahmincioglu, *Not Just Jobs, supra* note 9, at 5; Sharon Lerner & Eileen Appelbaum, *Business as Usual? New Jersey Employers' Experiences with Family Leave Insurance*, Center for Economic and Policy Research 16 (2014), http://www.cepr.net/index.php/publications/reports/business-as-usual-new-jersey-employers-experiences-with-family-leave-insurance.
63. Galinsky, Bond & Tahmincioglu, *Not Just Jobs, supra* note 9, at 5–6 (noting that "having more generous benefits is strongly related to employees' plan to stay with their employers"); *see also* EY (Formerly Ernst and Young), *Global Generations: A Global Study on Work-Life Challenges Across Generations: Detailed Findings* 20 (2015), http://www.ey.com/Publication/vwLUAssets/EY-global-generations-a-global-study-on-work-life-challenges-across-generations/$FILE/EY-global-generations-a-global-study-on-work-life-challenges-across-generations.pdf (finding that 86% of millennial workers reported that they would be less likely to leave an employer who offered paid parental leave and increased flexibility); Eileen Appelbaum & Ruth Milkman, *Leaves that Pay: Employer and Worker Experiences with Paid Family Leave in California*. Center for Economic and Policy Research Working Paper (2011) (reporting that low-wage workers who used California's paid leave benefits were more likely to return to their same employer than those who did not use leave benefits).
64. Bond & Galinsky, *Workplace Flexibility, supra* note 8, at 2; *see also* Brad Harrington et al., *The New Dad: Take Your Leave*, Boston College Center for Work and Family (2014), http://www.bc.edu/content/dam/files/centers/cwf/news/pdf/BCCWF%20Executive%20Summary%20The%20New%20Dad%202014.pdf (reporting that nine out of ten professional fathers stated that whether an employer provided paid paternity leave would be important when looking for a new job).
65. *The Cost of Doing Nothing, supra* note 33, at 15–16 (noting that 15% of workers in the Department of Labor's FMLA survey who received partial or no pay during their leave reported going on public assistance); LINDA Houser & Thomas P. Vartanian, *Pay Matters: The Positive Economic Impacts of Paid Family Leave for Families, Businesses and the Public*, Center for Women and Work (2012) (noting that women with access to paid parental leave were 39% less likely to receive public assistance in the year following their child's birth).
66. *See* Michael Baker & Kevin Milligan, *How Does Job-Protected Maternity Leave Affect Mothers' Employment?*, 26 J. LAB. ECON. 655–91 (2008); Jane Waldfogel, Yoshio Higuchi & Masahiro Abe, *Maternity Leave Policies and Women's Employment After Childbirth* (Center for Analysis of Social Exclusion, London School of Economics, CASE Paper 3, 1998), http://sticerd.lse.ac.uk/

advance gender equality by increasing men's engagement in childcare,[67] which has the potential to: (1) challenge stereotypes of men as "breadwinners, largely uninterested in childrearing;" (2) facilitate a more equitable division of labor in the home;[68] and (3) increase the ability of women to engage in paid work. Finally, employment benefits are good for children. For example, maternity leave has been linked to decreases in infant mortality and premature birth rates, as well as increases in birth weights.[69]

While understating the benefits that accrue from family-friendly workplace policies, employers tend to overstate the costs. For example, in the past, dire predictions of financial doom and gloom have not come to pass either because fewer employees than anticipated chose to take advantage of flexible work arrangements and leaves, or the administrative costs were lower than expected.[70] In a comprehensive survey prepared for the Department of Labor in 2012, researchers found that three-quarters of worksites covered by the FMLA said that administering the law was easy,[71] and very few covered worksites reported experiencing negative effects on business profitability and on "employee productivity, absenteeism, turnover, career advancement, and morale."[72] Only 2.5% said they suspected employees had misused the FMLA.[73] To be sure, FMLA usage rates may be affected by the fact that FMLA leave is unpaid. However, early data from states with mandatory paid leave statutes indicate that employers have had "positive or neutral experiences and few negative effects" as a result of these statutes.[74]

In summary, employment benefits exact some costs on employers, and these costs will likely increase with a larger number of covered employees and potential requests. The essential question, however, is whether these costs are outweighed by the resulting benefits. While one cannot answer this question definitively for all

---

dps/case/cp/Paper3.pdf; Heather Boushey, *Family-Friendly Policies: Helping Mothers Make Ends Meet*, 66 Rev. Soc. Econ. 51–70 (2008).

67. For example, studies show that men who took two weeks or more of paternity leave were "much more likely to be actively involved in their child's care nine months after birth, including feeding, changing diapers, and getting up at night." Lenna Nepomnyaschy & Jane Waldfogel, *Paternity Leave and Fathers' Involvement with their Young Children: Evidence from the American Ecls-B*, 10 Community, Work & Fam. 427, 442–45 (2007).
68. *The Cost of Doing Nothing*, *supra* note 33, at 24 (noting that "[w]hen men increase their use of paternity leave, the amount of housework fathers and mothers perform may become more gender balanced over time, with men spending longer amounts of time per day on household chores and childcare").
69. *The Cost of Doing Nothing*, *supra* note 33, at 5.
70. *See* Jacob Alex Klerman et al., Abt Associates, Inc., Family and Medical Leave in 2012: Technical Report, at 48, 162 (2013), *available at* http://www.dol.gov/asp/evaluation/fmla/FMLA-2012-Technical-Report.pdf (finding that a majority of worksites covered by the FMLA found administering the Act was easy and had either a positive effect or no noticeable effect on employers and their businesses). These factors are related. It could be that administrative costs are lower than expected because fewer employees than expected have taken FMLA leave.
71. *Id.* Large employers report higher administrative costs than smaller employers, with only 68% of the former saying that complying with the FMLA was somewhat easy, very easy, or had no noticeable effect. *Id.*
72. *Id.* at 162. Again, a higher percentage of large employers reported adverse effects.
73. *Id.* at 156; *see also* D. Cantor et al., *Balancing the Needs of Families and Employers: Family and Medical Leave Surveys* (2000), *available at* http://www.dol.gov/whd/fmla/toc.pdf (reporting similar findings from a 2000 survey).
74. *The Cost of Doing Nothing*, *supra* note 33, at 29.

employers, research suggests that as a general matter the upsides are considerable, and in many cases exceed the costs. Importantly, the data show that employment benefits have the same or greater positive effects for low-wage employees as for high-wage employees.[75] Given these results, the extension of greater benefits to low-wage workers should not be rejected out of hand. These benefit policies need not be viewed automatically as a net loss for employers. Instead, as researchers at the Family and Work Institute found, they should be seen as "strategic management tool[s] that can produce positive business results."[76]

[B] Competition (The Law of Supply and Demand)

Although benefit policies help employers, employees, and the larger society, employers may not be incentivized to extend these benefits to low-wage workers due to the law of supply and demand. Put simply, some argue that the limited supply of high-wage workers requires that employers compete aggressively for their services by offering greater benefits. The flip side of this argument is that low-wage workers are plentiful, indeed a dime a dozen, and their services are considered more fungible. Thus, employers will perceive less of a need to offer incentives to attract and retain these workers, particularly when unemployment is high and labor markets are soft.[77]

The competition argument may indeed explain, at least in part, the dearth of benefits to low-wage workers. Some indicators suggest that the current supply of low-wage workers in the United States exceeds the demand for their labor. For example, the unemployment gap between high- and low-income families is higher than ever. In 2013, unemployment for the lowest-income families (those making under USD 20,000 a year) was over 21%.[78] By contrast, the unemployment rate for the wealthiest households was 3.2%, which is "traditionally defined as full employment."[79] Furthermore, in 2014, unemployment rates for workers with a high school diploma or less tripled that of workers with an advanced degree.[80] These disparities in employment

75. Danziger & Boots, *Lower-Wage Workers*, *supra* note 7, at 7–8; *see also* David Villano, *Work-Life Balance Benefits Low-Wage Workers, Employers*, PAC. STANDARD (Sept. 7, 2011), http://www.psmag.com/business-economics/work-life-balance-benefits-low-wage-workers-employers-35733 (detailing how a good work-life balance benefits low-wage workers and employers); Joan Williams & Penelope Huang, *Improving Work-Life Fit in Hourly Jobs: An Underutilized Cost-Cutting Strategy in a Globalized World*, Center for Work Life Law 3-4 (2011), http://www.worklifelaw.org/pubs/ImprovingWork-LifeFit.pdf.
76. Bond & Galinsky, *Hourly Employees*, *supra* note 34, at 7.
77. Bond & Galinsky, *Workplace Flexibility*, *supra* note 8, at 1.
78. *Gap in U.S. Unemployment Rates Between Rich and Poor Continues to Widen*, ASSOCIATED PRESS (Sept. 16, 2013), http://www.nj.com/business/index.ssf/2013/09/gaps_in_us_unemployment_rates.html.
79. *Id.*
80. Heidi Shierholz, Economic Policy Institute, *Is There Really a Shortage of Skilled Workers?* (2014), http://www.epi.org/publication/shortage-skilled-workers/; US Dep't of Labor, Bureau of Labor Statistics, *Employment Projections, Earnings and Unemployment Rates by Educational Attainment*, 2015 (last modified Mar. 15, 2016), http://www.bls.gov/emp/ep_chart_001.htm.

rates exist despite the fact that the number of low-wage jobs in the United States has increased over the past two decades.[81]

These data tend to support that employers may not be motivated to offer low-wage workers benefits in order to secure or retain their services. In short, if the supply of low-wage laborers exceeds the demand for their labor, then employers will not be incentivized to provide low-wage workers benefits. The data, however, also underscore the vulnerability of low-wage workers as these same market forces deprive low-wage workers of bargaining power (i.e., the excess supply of low-wage labor has decreased the ability of low-wage workers to advocate effectively for themselves). These employees cannot realistically pushback against employment packages or negotiate for better terms because they risk either not being hired or being terminated[82] as, with a glut of available laborers, employers will have ready access to less demanding (or more desperate) alternative or replacement workers. The declining power of unions has only aggravated the situation.[83] In effect, low-wage workers have little real choice or power as the labor market is currently structured. When one considers that these workers face greater financial and familial pressures than their high-wage counterparts, the need for some form of structural intervention to disrupt the status quo is apparent.

[C] Skills, Value, and Class Bias

In addition to market forces, views about the value of low-wage work, and the skill level and class status of low-wage workers, may influence employer decision-making. For example, some seek to justify the benefits gap by arguing that workers are paid commensurate with their talent levels and the overall value of their contributions. Thus, because low-wage work is presumably less skilled and less socially valuable than high-wage work, it is compensated at a lower rate; conversely, because high-wage work is presumably more skilled and more socially valuable, it is compensated at a higher rate. Inherent in this explanation is the idea that if a worker invests in higher

81. In 1996 and 1999, the percentage of the US workforce considered low-wage was twenty-five and twenty-eight, respectively. Office of the Assistant Sec'y for Planning & Evaluation, US Dep't of Health & Human Servs., *Who Are Low-Wage Workers?* (2009), https://aspe.hhs.gov/basic-report/who-are-low-wageworkers. By 2001, that number had increased to 31%. *Id.; see also* David Autor, Ctr. For Am. Progress, The Polarization of Job Opportunities in the US Labor Market 2 (2010), http://economics.mit.edu/files/5554 ("Employment growth is polarizing, with job opportunities concentrated in relatively high-skill, high-wage jobs and low-skill, low-wage jobs."); Paul Beaudry et al., The Great Reversal in the Demand for Skill and Cognitive Tasks 22 (Nat'l Bureau of Econ. Research, Working Paper No. 18,909, 2013), http://www.nber.org/papers/w18901.pdf ("The relative growth of the lowest percentile occupations becomes very strong after 2000.").
82. In addition to termination, employees who press for greater benefits may encounter other risks (e.g., less favorable shifts, a decreased likelihood of being promoted, fewer pay increases). *See* Deborah Maranville, *Workplace Mythologies and Unemployment Insurance: Exit, Voice and Exhausting All Reasonable Alternatives to Quitting*, 31 Hofstra L. Rev. 459, 493 (2002).
83. For a discussion of the decline of unions in the United States, *see* infra section 5.05[A].

education or the acquisition of advanced skills, then she should receive a commensurate return on her investment with better employment terms (i.e., higher wages, greater benefits, and better employment conditions).[84]

In addition to perceptions about the skill of low-wage workers and the value of low-wage work, negative stereotypes related to the economic class of low-wage workers may also shape the allocation of employment benefits. It is fairly common knowledge that economic inequality in the United States has increased in recent decades.[85] To be sure, some politicians, policy-makers, and advocacy groups have expressed concern about this development.[86] Yet, their attention has focused largely on the "middle-class;" low-wage workers have received little air time.[87] It could be that by concentrating on the middle-class, politicians and advocacy organizations are attempting to appeal to the broadest array of citizens, or to swing voters. But it could also be that low-wage workers receive little attention because they are viewed as somehow having failed, in a land of plenty, to develop skills or to seize opportunities that would lead to a better life. In other words, they are blamed for their plights. This blame game likely affects any evaluation of their needs for accommodation and assistance in the workplace. In short, if low-wage workers are deemed insufficiently ambitious, insufficiently responsible, and undeserving,[88] then they become the targets of disdain,

---

84. In short, the argument is that if low-wage workers roll up their sleeves, get busy, and acquire more skills, they too will have more to offer society and will receive greater benefits. For analysis of the weaknesses of the skill/value argument, *see* Jones, *supra* note 58, at 732-35.
85. There is more space between those at the top and those at the bottom of the US economic hierarchy, and people at the top tend to improve their economic positions at a faster rate, and with greater success, than those at the bottom. *See generally* Estelle Sommeiller & Mark Price, The Increasingly Unequal States of America: Income Inequality by State, 1917 TO 2012, at 12-14 (2015), http://www.thenation.com/wp-content/uploads/2015/04/IncreasinglyUnequalStatesofAmerica1917to2012.pdf. Consequently, income distribution today is highly concentrated at the top, with the top 1% of the population earning more than 20% of all income and the top 10% earning almost half of all income. Annie Lowrey, *The Rich Get Richer Through the Recovery*, N.Y. TIMES (Sept. 10, 2013), http://economix.blogs.nytimes.com/2013/09/10/the-rich-get-richer-through-the-recovery/?_r = 1.
86. President Barack Obama, for example, gave a speech in 2013 in which he decried the "dangerous and growing inequality and lack of upward mobility that has jeopardized middle-class America's basic bargain." *Remarks by the President on Economic Mobility*, https://www.whitehouse.gov/the-press-office/2013/12/04/remarks-president-economic-mobility. In addition, Hillary Clinton made income inequality an issue in her 2016 presidential campaign, *see* https://www.hillaryclinton.com/issues/plan-raise-american-incomes/ (recognizing that "[i]nequality is a drag on the economy"), as did Senator Bernie Sanders during the Democratic primary. Margaret Talbot, *The Populist Prophet*, NEW YORKER (Oct. 12, 2015), http://www.newyorker.com/magazine/2015/10/12/the-populist-prophet (describing the importance of the issue of income inequality to Senator Sanders's campaign).
87. Binyamin Appelbaum, *The Millions of Americans Donald Trump and Hillary Clinton Barely Mention: The Poor*, N.Y. TIMES (Aug. 11, 2016), http://www.nytimes.com/2016/08/12/us/politics/trump-clinton-poverty.html?smid = fb-share&_r = 1 (observing that the 2016 presidential nominees both tended to focus on the middle-class and largely to ignore the "47 million Americans who yearn to reach the middle class").
88. For discussion of stereotypes to which poor people are subject, *see* Trina Jones, *Foreword, Race and Socioeconomic Class: Examining an Increasingly Complex Tapestry*, 72 L. & CONTEMP. PROBS. v–viii (2009).

instead of a system—including an employment system—that denies them access to decent benefits and the flexibility to care for themselves and their families.[89]

Analysis of class bias brings into sharper focus a paradoxical aspect of family-friendly benefits. Proponents of family-friendly policies frequently argue that because parenting is socially valuable, society (including employers) should better equip parents to parent well. Indeed, because the welfare of children is at stake, some maintain that there is a moral imperative that society does so. In addition, it is argued that family-friendly policies are a critical component of efforts to increase gender equity. Because most women work and women continue to bear the bulk of responsibility for childrearing in the United States, it is important not only for the well-being of children, but for women's economic success, to create workplaces in which women can balance their work and family obligations. Yet, as this chapter shows, the necessary support structures are less likely to be offered to those women who are most vulnerable in the labor market (e.g., poor women) and to those parents most needing assistance (i.e., poor parents). This raises questions about the justifications that are offered for family-friendly benefits and the efficacy of programs designed to secure the stated objectives. Does US society care about all women and all children, or only upper-middle class women and their children? As presently distributed, family-friendly programs appear to suggest an affirmative answer only with regard to the latter.

In summary, class bias likely fuels the benefits gap. It prevents employers and the larger society from appreciating the skill that low-wage workers bring to their jobs and the tremendous value that low-wage work brings to the US economy. Class bias, however, does more than this. It also deflects attention from structural barriers to economic mobility, and instead blames those who are harmed most by these structural impediments (i.e., low-wage workers). Between this "blame game" and the competition argument discussed earlier, the future looks grim.

§5.05 A BLEAK FUTURE FORECAST

A primary purpose of this chapter has been to highlight the fact that low-wage workers in the United States not only experience substandard wages, but their other terms and conditions of employment are also woefully inadequate. Consequently, these workers struggle to provide for themselves and for their families. A huge problem for low-wage workers is that employers have few incentives to act on their own initiative. The situation is aggravated, as demonstrated below, by the decline of organized labor and limited legislative action.

[A] The Decline of Organized Labor

Since at least 1935 and passage of the National Labor Relations Act, unions have played a significant role in advancing employment terms and conditions for millions of

89. For consideration of the interplay of class, race, and gender in the allocation of employment benefits, *see* Jones, *supra* note 58, at 735-43.

workers in the United States.[90] In the 1950s and 1960s, unions helped to elevate autoworkers, steelworkers, machinists, truck drivers, carpenters, and some apparel workers into the middle class.[91] In recent years, unions like the Service Employees International Union (SEIU) have advocated successfully for the rights of janitors, hotel housekeepers, home-care aides, and other low-wage workers.[92] As a result, today unionized workers in major US cities have higher earnings and better benefits than their non-unionized counterparts.[93] This applies across demographic groups, as data indicate "a substantial boost in wages[94] and benefits[95] for union workers [in general,] and a particularly large union advantage for workers in low-wage jobs and occupations."[96]

Despite the strong connection between unions and economic mobility, over the last five decades unions have been under sustained attack in the United States,[97] and

90. *See* Jonathan Fox Harris, *Worker Unity and the Law: A Comparative Analysis of the National Labor Relations Act and the Fair Labor Standards Act, and the Hope for the NLRA's Future*, 13 N.Y. City L. Rev. 107, 110–14 (2009) (describing the impetus behind passage of the NLRB as a desire to alter the balance of power in favor of workers over management); Chris Tilly, *Trade Unions, Inequality, and Democracy in the US and Mexico*, 2 Rethinking Dev. & Ineq. 68 (2013, Special Issue), http://www.irle.ucla.edu/publications/documents/Tilly-Unions-inequality-democracy-inUS_MX-13-45-1-PB-RethinkingInequality_Devel-2013.pdf (reviewing the history of unions and inequality in the United States and Mexico, and acknowledging the potential of recent waves of unions to become a "powerful equalizing and democratizing force"); Craig Becker, *The Pattern of Union Decline, Economic and Political Consequences*, 98 Minn. L. Rev. 1637, 1639–40 (2014) (noting that from the rise of unions until union membership began to decline, wages and productivity in the US were closely linked).
91. *See, e.g.*, Becker, *supra* note 90, at 1638–40 (discussing the historic role of unions in the growth of the middle class); Steven Greenhouse, *How to Get Low-Wage Workers into the Middle Class*, Atlantic (Aug. 19, 2015), http://www.theatlantic.com/business/archive/2015/08/fifteen-dollars-minimum-wage/401540/ (same).
92. Notably, in the Fight for $15, SEIU has convinced major cities like Los Angeles, Seattle, San Francisco, and New York to incrementally increase the wages of food service workers to USD 15 an hour. Bruce Kennedy, *Fast-Food Workers Plan to Strike in 190 U.S. Cities*, CBS MoneyWatch (Dec. 3, 2014, 8:00 AM), http://www.cbsnews.com/news/food-fight-work-stoppages-planned-at-many-fast-food-restaurants (noting that "Seattle and San Francisco passed laws raising wages to $15 over the next couple years—and cities from New York to Los Angeles are pushing for higher wages too."). SEIU has convinced Chicago and Kansas City to adopt a USD 13 wage and has obtained more modest increases in Alaska, Arkansas, Nebraska and other states and localities. Greenhouse, *supra* note 91.
93. See Econ. Policy Inst., Fact Sheet, Collective Bargaining's Erosion Has Undercut Wage Growth and Fueled Inequality (Mar. 17, 2015), http://www.epi.org/files/2015/factsheet_80229.pdf.
94. *Id.* at 1 (noting the union wage premium to be 13.6%).
95. *Id.* at 2 ("Unionized workers are 28.2% more likely to be covered by employer-provided health insurance and 53.9% more likely to have employer-provided pensions, and also enjoy more paid time off with their families.").
96. John Schmitt, *The Union Wage Advantage for Low-Wage Workers*, Center for Economic and Policy Research 2 (2008), http://cepr.net/documents/publications/quantile_2008_05.pdf (showing that unionization raises wages for low-wage workers by about 21%); Heidi Shierholz, *Low Wages and Few Benefits Mean Many Restaurant Workers Can't Make Ends Meet*, Economic Policy Institute 4 (Aug. 21, 2014), http://www.epi.org/publication/restaurant-workers/ (highlighting how workers in the restaurant industry receive few benefits, but noting that unionized restaurant workers are better off than the average worker).
97. *See* Harold Meyerson, *The State of the American Unions* 3-4 (2012), http://library.fes.de/pdf-files/id-moe/08922-20120302.pdf (describing forces that, over the last three decades, have led to the decline of unions in the United States). Hostility to unions has ramped up in recent years. For

the number of unions and union members has steadily declined. In 1950, about 33% of US workers belonged to unions; in 2014, that number had shrunk to about 10% (with only about 6.6% in the private sector).[98] Union membership has declined despite the fact that more workers "want collective bargaining than are able to benefit from it and the desire for collective bargaining has increased significantly since the 1980s."[99]

The demise of organized labor in the United States is attributable, in part, to intensification in employer opposition.[100] In addition, the US workforce has changed with more workers occupying nontraditional jobs (e.g., temps, freelancers, part-time workers, independent contractors, on-call workers, employees in franchises). This structural change makes it more difficult to organize workers as they are dispersed and do not stay in one workplace for long periods of time. In addition, many low-wage workers, whose economic status is already perilous, are frightened of losing their jobs and are reluctant to join any entity that their employers may view as threatening.[101]

With the sustained attack on unions, the vulnerabilities of low-wage workers, and the decline in unionization, it is hard to imagine organized labor as a force for change in the near future. As David Role, the Vice President of the Service Employees International Union (SEIU) has noted "any model that shrinks for 50 years in a row in all 50 states is probably not a part of the future."[102]

---

example, in 2011, Wisconsin Governor Scott Walker signed a law that denies public-sector employees (with the exception of police officers and fire fighters) the right to collective bargaining. *Id.* at 5–6.

98. Ben Bergman, *Unions Have Pushed the $15 Minimum Wage, But Few Members Will Benefit*, NPR Broadcast (Feb. 10, 2015), http://www.npr.org/2015/02/10/384980527/unions-have-pushed-the-15-minimum-wage-but-few-members-will-benefit.
99. Richard Freeman, *Do Workers Still Want Unions? More Than Ever*, Economic Policy Institute 2 (2007) (finding that in 2005 a "majority of nonunion nonmanagerial workers would vote for union representation if they could," compared with only about 30% of such workers in 1980). Approval ratings for labor unions are also on the rise. *See* Lydia Saad, *Americans' Support for Labor Unions Continues to Recover*, Gallup.com (Aug. 17, 2015), http://www.gallup.com/poll/184622/americans-support-labor-unions-continues-recover.aspx (chronicling approval rates over time and indicating that approval rates had jumped five points in 2015, from 53% to 58%).
100. Keith J. Gross, *Separate to Unite: Will* Change to Win *Strengthen Organized Labor in America*, 24 Buff. Pub. Int. L. J. 75, 122–23 (2006) (describing aggressive union-busting activities of employers and noting that in cases "where employees do seek union representation and file an election petition…, employers manage to avoid unionization more than 50% of the time"): Economic Policy Institute, The Benefits of Collective Bargaining, Fact Sheet (Apr. 14, 2015), http://www.epi.org/publication/benefits-of-collective-bargaining/ (noting a greater employer focus today on "more coercive and punitive tactics designed to intensely monitor and punish union activity" than in the 1990s).
101. This is particularly true of undocumented workers, who are disproportionately located in low-wage work. *See* Randy Capps et al., Immigrant Families and Workers, Urb. Inst., A Profile of the Low-Wage Immigrant Workforce 1 (2003), http://www.urban.org/sites/default/files/alfresco/publication-pdfs/310880-A-Profile-of-the-Low-Wage-Immigrant-Workforce.PDF (finding that "[i]mmigrants are 11 percent of all U.S. residents, but 14 percent of all workers and 20 percent of low-wage workers").
102. Bergman, *supra* note 98.

[B] Legislative Action and Inaction

Governmental action to address the benefits gap has been limited. The void left by organized labor has been filled by powerful corporate lobbyists, and others, who have argued forcefully against governmental intervention. For example, Carly Fiorina, a former Republican candidate for the US Presidency and a former CEO of Hewlett-Packard,[103] stated in 2015, in response to calls for paid maternity leave: "I don't think it's the role of government to dictate to the private sector how to manage their businesses, especially when it's pretty clear that the private sector ... is doing the right thing because they know it helps them attract the right talent."[104]

Ms. Fiorina's statement is wrong: the private sector has failed to address the absence of paid leave in the United States.[105] In 2012, only 11% of all private sector workers in the US had paid family leave,[106] and only 61% of private sector workers had paid sick leave.[107] As the data set forth in section 5.03 show, the numbers for low-wage workers are even worse.[108] Moreover, the absence of governmental regulation has left a lot of discretion with employers, rendering the provision of benefits both tenuous and inconsistent across workplaces.

A federal statute mandating *paid* family leave and *paid* sick leave would make it much more feasible for all workers, not just those who are well off, to attend to themselves and to their families. Although Democrats in the US Congress have proposed legislation that would provide for paid family leave,[109] this legislation has not

103. Ashley Parker, *Carly Fiorina Drops Out of Republication Presidential Race*, N.Y. TIMES (Feb. 10, 2016).

104. Bryce Covert, *Carly Fiorina Thinks Corporations Should Be Able to Deny Paid Leave to New Mothers*, THINKPROGRESS (Aug. 10, 2015), http://thinkprogress.org/economy/2015/08/10/3689780/fiorina-paid-family-leave/.

105. Government employees tend to fare better in terms of paid leave than workers in the private sector. For instance, federal government employees are entitled to up to six weeks of paid leave after the birth of a child. Andy Medici, *Obama Gives Federal Employees Paid Family Leave*, FED. TIMES (Jan. 15, 2015), http://www.federaltimes.com/story/government/management/compensation/2015/01/15/paid-family-leave/21802251/.

106. US Dep't of Labor, Bureau of Labor Statistics, *Paid Leave in Private Industry Over the Past 20 Years, Table 1. Access to Paid Holidays, Vacations, Sick Leave Benefits, and Other Paid Leave Benefits for Private Industry Workers*, 1992–1993 AND 2012 (Aug. 2013), http://www.bls.gov/opub/btn/volume-2/paid-leave-in-private-industry-over-the-past-20-years.htm.

107. *Id.*

108. *See supra* text accompanying notes 41–47; *see also* Emily Crockett, *New York Just Passed the Most Generous Paid Family Leave Law in the Country*, VOX POLICY & POLITICS (Apr. 1, 2016), http://www.vox.com/2016/4/1/11347192/new-york-paid-family-leave-yuge ("noting that 5 percent of workers in the lowest-paid 25 percent of the workforce have paid leave, while 22 percent of the top 10 percent of earners do").

109. Senator Kirsten Gillibrand (D-NY) and Representative Rosa DeLauro (D-Conn) have proposed the FAMILY Act (the Family and Medical Insurance Leave Act), which would provide for universal paid leave. *See* S. 786, 114th Cong. (as introduced to Senate Mar. 18, 2015). The American Opportunity Agenda: Expand Paid Family and Medical Leave, http://www.gillibrand.senate.gov/issues/paid-family-medical-leave (summarizing the legislation) [hereinafter *Expand Paid Leave*]. More specifically, the FAMILY Act would provide eligible employees with up to twelve weeks of paid leave, with two-third's wage replacement (capped at USD 4,000), to care for a newborn or adopted child or to attend to the employee's or her family member's medical emergency. *Expand Paid Leave, supra*. The Act would be funded through "employee and employer contributions of two-tenths of 1% of a worker's wages—about $2.00

been put to a vote in Congress—nor is it likely to be as long as Republicans continue to control both legislative chambers. To be sure, during the final months of his Presidential campaign, Donald Trump put forth a child-care policy that included six weeks of paid maternity leave for working women whose employers did not offer such leave.[110] Commentators, however, have criticized the Trump plan because it does not extend to fathers.[111] This omission may negatively affect women's labor force participation rates and aggravate the gender pay gap.[112] In addition, considerable doubt exists about whether Mr. Trump will be able to get his proposal through Congress, should he decide to proceed with it, given traditional Republican hostility to social welfare legislation.[113]

Thus, at the federal level, the main statute granting workplace benefits continues to be the 1993 Family and Medical Leave Act. As noted earlier, because the FMLA mandates only unpaid leave, its benefits are of limited use to workers who cannot afford a loss in wages.

There has been more action at the individual state level. In recent years, four states (New York, California, Rhode Island, and New Jersey) have enacted paid family leave,[114] and five states (California, Connecticut, Massachusetts, Oregon, and

per week for a typical worker." *Id.* Importantly, the Act is more expansive than the FMLA as it would cover all workers, regardless of their age, marital status, gender, or full-time or part-time employment status. *Id.* It also would cover all employers, regardless of their size. *Id.* Hillary Clinton, the 2016 Democratic Presidential nominee, also set forth a proposal that would have in effect extended the FMLA to provide for paid leave. *See* Hillary for America, Paid Family and Medical Leave, https://www.hillaryclinton.com/issues/paid-leave/ (last visited Aug. 14, 2016). Clinton proposed to pay for her plan by raising taxes on wealthy Americans and corporations. *Id.* Importantly, neither the Clinton proposal nor the FAMILY Act provide for accrued sick leave.

110. Donald J. Trump For President, Child Care Reforms That Will Make America Great Again 4–5, https://assets.donaldjtrump.com/Childcare_Reform.pdf (last visited Feb. 5, 2017). The proposed Trump plan would also offer an income tax deduction for childcare costs, create a dependent care savings account (funded with pre-tax income) for childcare expenses, and offer a tax credit to incentivize employers to provide childcare at work. *Id.* at 1–4. Mr. Trump stated that he would fund the plan with savings gained from eliminating fraud in the unemployment insurance program. *Id.* at 5.

111. *See, e.g.*, Lisa Petrillo, *President-Elect Trump's Paid Parental Leave Is Only for Mothers After Childbirth*, Soc'y for Hum. Resource Mgmt. (Nov. 10, 2016), https://www.shrm.org/resourcesandtools/hr-topics/employee-relations/pages/trump-paid-parental-leave-.aspx.

112. *See* Sean Sullivan & Robert Costa, *Donald Trump Unveils Child-Care Policy Influenced by Ivanka Trump*, WASH. POST (Sept. 13, 2016), https://www.washingtonpost.com/news/post-politics/wp/2016/09/13/donaldtrump-joined-by-ivanka-trump-to-outline-child-care-policy (quoting a Clinton senior advisor who noted that "by focusing solely on leave policies that benefit women, Trump may actually be hurting their cause, contributing to the attrition of women from the workplace after childbirth and the gender pay gap").

113. *Id.*; Allen Smith, *Trump's Maternity Leave Proposal May Not Be Popular on Capitol Hill*, Soc'y for Hum. Resource Mgmt. (Nov. 16, 2016), https://www.shrm.org/resourcesandtools/legal-and-compliance/employment-law/pages/trump-maternity-leave-proposal.aspx.

114. An overview of each state's law is available at National Conference of State Legislatures, State Family and Medical Leave Laws, http://www.ncsl.org/research/labor-and-employment/state-family-and-medical-leave-laws.aspx (last visited Aug. 15, 2016). Links to each state's law can be found at National Conference of State Legislatures, Paid Family Leave, http://www.ncsl.org/research/labor-and-employment/paid-family-leave-resources.aspx (last visited Aug. 14, 2016).

Vermont) have enacted paid sick leave.[115] For example, New York's paid family leave law, which was passed in April 2016, provides all employees with three months of partially paid time off to care for a new child or a seriously ill family member.[116] Connecticut, which was the first state to adopt paid sick leave for private employees in 2012, allows employees to accrue paid sick leave at a rate of one hour of leave for each forty hours worked, up to a maximum of forty hours per calendar year.[117] Importantly, in adopting these laws, legislators have been sensitive to employer cost concerns and have developed mechanisms to minimize the financial burden on employers.[118]

115. Links to each state's law are available at National Conference of State Legislatures, Paid Sick Leave, http://www.ncsl.org/research/labor-and-employment/paid-sick-leave.aspx (last visited Aug. 14, 2016).

116. New York's law has been characterized as the most comprehensive in the United States. *See* Crockett, *supra* note 108. California's paid family leave program "provide[s] up to six weeks of [partial] wage replacement benefits to workers who take time off work to care for a seriously ill child, [or other family member,] or to bond with a minor child" following birth, adoption, or foster care placement. California Paid Family Leave, Unemployment Insurance Code §§3301–3303, http://leginfo.legislature.ca.gov/faces/codes_displaySection.xhtml. New Jersey and Rhode Island's plans are similar, with New Jersey offering six weeks of paid family leave, and Rhode Island offering four. State of New Jersey, Department of Labor and Workforce Development, *Family Leave Insurance,* http://lwd.dol.state.nj.us/labor/fli/fliindex.html; State of Rhode Island, *Temporary Disability Insurance,* §§28–41–35(d)(1), http://webserver.rilin.state.ri.us/Statutes/TITLE28/28-41/28-41-35.HTM. Under their respective disability benefits laws, these states also provide similar or longer coverage, at partial pay, for employees needing time off to care for their own serious illnesses.

117. Connecticut Department of Labor, Connecticut Gen. Stat. §§31–57s, *Paid Sick Leave,* http://www.ctdol.state.ct.us/wgwkstnd/SickLeaveLaw.htm. California, which enacted its paid sick leave statute in 2014, allows one hour for every thirty hours worked, up to a maximum of forty-eight hours or six days. California Healthy Workplaces, *Healthy Families Act* of 2014, Assembly Bill No. 1522, §246(B), (I), http://leginfo.legislature.ca.gov/faces/billNavClient.xhtml?bill_id=201320140AB1522&search_keywords=. Oregon and Massachusetts similarly provide for one hour of paid leave for every thirty hours, but unlike California, these states allow for up to forty hours (or five days) of sick leave to accrue per year. *Earned Sick Time for Employees,* 149 Mass. Gen. L. §148C (d), http://www.mass.gov/ago/docs/government/earned-sick-time-law.pdf; Mandatory Provision of Sick Time for Employees, Oregon Gen. L. §653.606, https://www.oregonlegislature.gov/bills_laws/ors/ors653.html. Vermont's law, which goes into effect on Jan. 1, 2017, allows employees to accrue one hour for every fifty-two hours worked, up to a maximum of twenty-four hours a year until Dec. 31, 2018, and up to forty hours per year after that date. *See* http://legislature.vermont.gov/assets/Documents/2016/Docs/ACTS/ACT069/ACT069%20As%20Enacted.pdf. In addition to these state policies, a number of cities across the country have also adopted paid sick leave policies in recent years. For a summary of these laws, *see* Council of Economic Advisors, *supra* note 47, at 20–21.

118. To alleviate employer cost concerns, states have funded their paid leave programs by having employees make payroll contributions to a government fund. For example, California's law states that its paid family leave program "shall be a component of the state's unemployment compensation disability insurance program, shall be funded through employee contributions, and shall be administered in accordance with the policies of the state disability insurance program." California Paid Family Leave Act, Unemployment Insurance Code §3300(G), http://www.leginfo.ca.gov/cgi-bin/displaycode?section=uic&group=03001-04000&file=3300-3306 (last visited Aug. 15, 2016). New Jersey states that its "family leave program is financed 100% by worker payroll deductions. Employers do not contribute to the program." State of New Jersey, Department of Labor and Workforce Development, *Cost to the Worker,* http://lwd.dol.state.nj.us/labor/fli/content/cost.html (last visited Aug. 15, 2016). Rhode Island and New York's plans are similarly financed through employee contributions. RI Department of Labor and Training, Temporary Disability Insurance, http://www.dlt.ri.gov/tdi/pdf/TCIBrochure.pdf (stating that Rhode Island's temporary caregiver insurance "is financed entirely by

Moreover, early evidence suggests that costs are not nearly as high as employers feared they would be.[119]

The good news from the foregoing analysis is that models for successful legislation exist. The bad news is that the nine states to act are among the more socially progressive and liberal states in the United States. Convincing other, more conservative, states to follow will be no easy feat, given a strong employer lobby and declining unionization.

In closing, federal legislation is necessary in order to maximize the possibility that all workers will have access to some minimum level of benefits. While such legislation would be a substantial improvement, it would not be sufficient to bridge the benefits gap as there are certain benefits, like FWAs, that lie uniquely within the province of employers and require consideration of particular workplace circumstances. The problem is that few structural mechanisms exist to encourage employers to move beyond their current mindsets. And workers, in a context where the supply of workers exceeds the demand for their labor, are ill-equipped to advocate individually on their own behalves.

§5.06 CONCLUSION

The benefits gap in the United States is alarming. Low-wage workers face the same (or more) work-life challenges as high-wage workers, but they receive less workplace flexibility and fewer employment benefits than high-wage workers. As section 5.04 demonstrates, these benefits produce positive returns for employees, employers, and the general society. Yet, employers may be loath to extend them to low-wage workers because of a surplus of low-wage workers in the labor market. In addition to market forces, negative class stereotypes and bias concerning the skill and value of low-wage labor may affect employer decision-making and the willingness of other interveners to act.

This chapter suggests that overcoming these hurdles is a near impossible task in the current political and economic climate in the United States, particularly with the decline of organized labor and the arrival of the Trump era. With Republicans in control of the Presidency, both houses of the US Congress, and many state legislatures, very little pro-labor legislative action is likely to occur. Absent such legislation, employers will not be pressed to reconsider their treatment of low-wage workers. Thus,

---

employee payroll deductions"); Crockett, *supra* note 108 (stating that New York's law will be funded solely by employee payroll contributions, with no contributions from employers or taxpayers). Costs have also been reduced in others ways. For example, costs associated with paid *family* leave have been decreased by only partially reimbursing wages for missed days at work, and by requiring that employees use accrued vacation and personal sick leave before using family leave. The costs of paid *sick* leave have been reduced by, for example, implementing an accrual system and by limiting the total number of hours of available paid sick leave. With both paid family leave and paid sick leave, states mandate that paid leave operate concurrently with leave under the FMLA, thereby minimizing the length of an employee's absence from the workplace.

119. *See* The *Cost of Doing Nothing*, *supra* note 33, at 29 (summarizing studies); Council of Economic Advisors, *supra* note 47, at 16–18 (same).

25–35% of the US labor market will continue to work without workplace flexibility and without basic benefits like paid family leave and paid sick leave. The fact that other developed nations, and several US states, have been able to provide greater benefits for workers across the board suggests that the benefits gap reflects a lack of social and political will, and not structural impossibility. The United States can do better.

Part II Company Welfare and Work-Life Balance

CHAPTER 6

The Use of Paternity Leave in the Private Sector: The Role of Company-Level Welfare Provisions

Maddalena Cannito[*]

§6.01 INTRODUCTION

The issue of work-life balance has become increasingly important in recent years, also in Italy. This is because of changes in the demographic composition of the population, in the labour market, in the position of women in the family and in the public sphere and the world of work.[1] To deal with these new social needs many measures and policies have been implemented both at national level – including provisions on parental leave[2] – and at company level. In particular, as a counterweight to cuts in public expenditure on social policies, Corporate Social Responsibility and company-level welfare are becoming increasingly important.[3]

* Ph.D. candidate at Department of Cultures, Politics and Society of University of Turin, Italy.

1. *See* Rosemary Crompton, *Employment and the Family. The Reconfiguration of Work and Family Life in Contemporary Societies* (Cambridge: Cambridge University Press, 2006); Eurostat, *Reconciliation between work, private and family life in the European Union* (Luxembourg: Office for Official Publications of the European Communities, 2009); Istat, *La conciliazione tra lavoro e famiglia* (Rome: Istat, 2011); Manuela Naldini & Chiara Saraceno, *Conciliare famiglia e lavoro. Vecchi e nuovi patti tra sessi e generazioni* (Bologna: Il Mulino, 2011); European Commission, *Gender equality in the workforce: Reconciling work, private and family life in Europe* (Brussels: RAND Europe, 2014).
2. In Italy parental leave was introduced with Act no. 53/2000, in G.U. 13 Mar. 2000, no. 60.
3. European Commission, *Renewed EU Strategy 2011–14 for Corporate Social Responsibility* (Brussels, 2011); Franca Maino, *Il secondo welfare: contorni teorici ed esperienze esemplificative*, 4 Rivista Politiche Sociali, 167–182 (2012); Sara Mazzucchelli, *Conciliazione famiglia e lavoro. Buone pratiche di welfare aziendale in Lombardia, Piemonte, Friuli Venezia Giulia, Marche*, 43–74 (Pierpaolo Donati ed. Rome: Carocci, 2012); Nuria Chinchilla & Marc Grau, *Corporate Family Responsibility e ambienti flessibili: un 'must' per le aziende del XXI secolo*, 16 Sociologia e

This paper aims to investigate the relationship between company-level welfare measures for work-life balance and the national policy on parental leave, with a focus on paternity leave. In fact, the role of fathers in work-life balance and care duties is an issue that has only recently attracted the attention of Italian policy-makers. However, if we look at the use of parental leave by fathers in the private sector, it becomes apparent that the policy on paternity leave is not always effective in encouraging men to take time off work in favour of time spent with their children.

For these reasons, empirical research was carried out, focused on Piedmont, on the use of parental leave by male employees in the private sector and on the influence exerted by the work environment in family-friendly firms. The main finding is that the sole presence of company-level welfare policies for work-life balance is insufficient to encourage fathers to take parental leave since management attitudes and the organizational culture also play a key role. Moreover, the gender neutrality of company-level welfare policies does not produce a sense of entitlement in fathers, neither in taking advantage of these measures nor in taking parental leave. Based on interviews with Human Resources Managers in a sample of family-friendly firms and with the fathers who took parental leave in the same companies, the research aimed to test these hypotheses.

This approach is interesting because most studies on this topic[4] focus on the influence that national policies have on the implementation of company-level welfare measures. In this paper, we also explore how firms can have a countervailing effect on parental leave policy and on the demand that this policy is intended to generate.

§6.02 DECENTRALIZED OR COMPANY-LEVEL WELFARE

An important initial step is to clarify what is meant when talking about company-level welfare, and the policies implemented by firms for the work-life balance of their employees. It is necessary to frame the question of the company-level welfare within the debate on decentralized or company-level welfare. What is this form of welfare and how is it different from tradition forms? Moreover, why do we need it? In order to address these questions we need to look at the austerity and budget constraint policies adopted by the European countries. Moreover, we need to take into account how public social expenditure is allocated in Italy: it is heavily weighted towards retirement pensions to the detriment of expenditure on new forms of welfare (disability, unemployment, family, housing and social exclusion benefits represent less than the 2% of

Politiche Sociali, 43–66 (2013); Tiziano Treu, *Welfare aziendale. Migliorare la produttività e il benessere dei dipendenti* (Roma: Ipsoa, 2013); Ylenia Curzi & Iacopo Senatori, *Welfare aziendale, competitività e relazioni industriali: luci e ombre di un connubio possibile*, 1 QFMB Saggi, 1–32 (2015); EIGE, *Reconciliation of work, family and private life in the European Union. Policy review* (Vilnius: European Institute for Gender Equality, 2015).

4. Among others Berit Brandth & Elin Kvande, *Reflexive Fathers: Negotiating Parental Leave and Working Life*, 9 Gender, Work and Organization, 186–203 (2002); Linda Haas L. & Philip Hwang, *Is Fatherhood Becoming More Visible at Work? Trends in Corporate Support for Fathers Taking Parental Leave in Sweden*, 7 Fathering, 303–321 (2009); EIGE, *supra* n. 3.

public social expenditure).[5] Moreover, in the Italian case, the attempts to rebalance public welfare investments seem to remain ineffective and obstructed by the vested interests defending existing entitlement programmes.[6]

Finally, since the 1980s the gradual decentralization of social protection has been taking place with a partial shift from the welfare state to the welfare regions,[7] often promoted by central government in order to reduce the expenditure on social policies without losing electoral support, based on a strategy of blame avoidance.[8]

As a result, the idea of decentralized welfare derives from changes in the traditional forms of welfare in the past thirty years and from the recognition of shortcomings in the measures provided by the public actor.

The main features of company-level welfare are: the involvement of private actors in the provision of social policies; the construction of multi-stakeholder networks and of partnerships between public authorities and banking institutions, voluntary organizations, companies and so on, strongly rooted in the local territory; the search for innovative and efficient responses to social needs both old and new.[9]

There is no need to discuss the pros and cons of this model here, though it seems important to clarify that recognizing the need for complementary welfare systems does not mean advocating the replacement of public expenditure with private schemes, nor does it mean justifying the replacement of the public actor in safeguarding universal rights for citizens.[10] As pointed out by Caselli,[11] the neoliberal model of welfare gives rise to risks such as the commodification of social welfare programmes while granting a leading role to private for-profit actors in the planning of social policies.

§6.03 CORPORATE SOCIAL RESPONSIBILITY, COMPANY-LEVEL WELFARE AND WORK-LIFE BALANCE

In this scenario, private companies could play a key role in providing company-level welfare or, in the words of Titmuss,[12] occupational welfare. It seems useful to frame the topic of company-level welfare in the broader picture of Corporate Social Responsibility (CSR), a concept that has become increasingly important in recent years in Europe. In this connection mention should be made of the launch of the European Business Network for Social Cohesion (EBNSC) in 1996; the Lisbon Strategy 2010 adopted in 2000; the European Commission Green Paper on Promoting a European Framework on Corporate Social Responsibility published in 2001; the report issued by the European

5. Maino, *supra* n. 3, at 168–170.
6. Maurizio Ferrera, *Secondo welfare: perché? Una introduzione*, 7–16 (Franca Maino & Maurizio Ferrera eds. Turin: Centro di Ricerca e Documentazione Luigi Einaudi, 2013).
7. Maurizio Ferrera, *Dal welfare state alle welfare regions: la riconfigurazione spaziale della protezione sociale in Europa*, 3 Rivista Politiche Sociali, 23–46 (2008).
8. Emmanuele Pavolini, Ugo Ascoli U. & Maria Luisa Mirabile, *Tempi moderni. Il welfare nelle aziende in Italia*, 20–28 (Bologna: Il Mulino, 2013).
9. Maino, *supra* n. 3, at 170–176.
10. Ferrera, *supra* n. 6, at 8.
11. Davide Caselli, *Comunità, impresa, responsabilità. Processi di neoliberalizzazione nel welfare italiano*, 111–128 (Giulio Moini ed., Rome: Ediesse, 2015).
12. Richard Titmuss, *Essays on the Welfare State* (London: Allen and Unwin, 1958).

Commission in 2006, Implementing the Partnership for Growth and Jobs: Making Europe a Pole of Excellence on Corporate Social Responsibility; the Strategy, launched in 2010 by the European Commission; Europe 2020: A European Strategy for Smart, Sustainable and Inclusive Growth, the Renewed EU Strategy 2011–14 for Corporate Social Responsibility published in 2011.

For present purposes we can use the definition of CSR in the *Green Paper: Promoting a European Framework on Corporate Social Responsibility* in which Corporate Social Responsibility is defined as 'a concept whereby companies integrate social and environmental concerns in their business operations and in their interaction with their stakeholders on a voluntary basis'.[13] This definition was expanded in 2011 with the Renewed EU Strategy 2011–14 for Corporate Social Responsibility in which the importance of the CSR in promoting social and economic growth of the European Union is recognized. In these reports, the main features of CSR are outlined, such as the voluntary nature of the social and environmental commitment of the firms, the construction of networks with other stakeholders, and the synergy of this commitment with company values and core business. Moreover, in these reports we find the distinction between external CSR, which concerns relationships with clients, suppliers, local communities, political institutions, voluntary organizations and so on, and internal corporate social responsibility intended to benefit employees. This internal CSR, that includes investment in human capital, and employee health and safety, constitutes company-level welfare.

However, the concept of company-level welfare is fuzzy. It is a catch-all category generically defined as 'all the benefits and non-monetary measures supplied by companies in order to improve and sustain the economic and social life of the employees and their families'.[14] According to this definition, it includes both traditional welfare schemes, related to pensions and health, and measures intended to address emerging social needs such as work-life balance.[15] Another problem in discussing company-level welfare is that a clear institutional and regulatory framework on this matter is lacking in Italy.[16]

Despite the fuzzy definitions, both theoretical and juridical, the importance that company-level welfare is acquiring in Western welfare systems is undeniable: in Italy, in the last decade, it represented 0.6% of GDP, lower than in other European countries, but in continuous expansion.[17] Moreover, this topic is interesting because it is closely

13. European Commission, *Green Paper: Promoting a European Framework on Corporate Social Responsibility*, 7 (Brussels, 2001).
14. CERGAS, *Il welfare aziendale contrattuale in Italia*, 6 (Milan: CNEL/Ministero del Lavoro Università Bocconi, 2014).
15. Curzi & Senatori, *supra* n. 3, at 3.
16. The main laws containing references to company-level welfare in Italy are Legislative Decree 252/2005, G.U. 13 Dec. 2005, no. 289; Art. 9 Legislative Decree 502/1992, G.U. 30 Dec. 1992, no. 305; D.M. 27/10/2009, G.U. 16 Jan. 2010, n. 12; Art. 9 Act no. 53/2000, in G.U. 13 Mar. 2000, no. 60.
17. Pavolini et al., *supra* n. 8, at 11–13.

connected with changes in the national welfare state, *in primis* the decentralization of certain functions from the state to regional and local actors.[18]

Examining the role of firms in the provision of welfare programmes makes it possible to go beyond the more traditional theories depicting employers as a homogeneous group, firmly opposed to the extension of the social rights and protections. In addition, it allows us to assume a more dynamic vision of the relationship between companies and welfare programmes, both national and local.[19]

Investment in human capital includes measures intended to rebalance work, family and life.[20] The issue of work-life balance is becoming important especially in Italy because of the well-known family-based configuration of the Italian welfare state, with limited childcare services and an implicit expectation that women will be the primary caregivers.[21]

Employers can help their employees to deal with their care duties and to balance life and work adopting a policy of Corporate Family Responsibility (CFR) that may be defined as:

> the commitment of a company in promoting a culture, a leadership, and flexible measures meant to facilitate the integration of work, family and personal life of the employees. As a fundamental part of the Corporate Social Responsibility, the CFR, should contribute to the construction of a society focused on people, in which men and women can have the same opportunities and can contribute to create a fairer and more sustainable world.[22]

Clearly, this commitment on the part of companies is not an act of philanthropy, but an efficient and innovative approach to human resource management, in line with their status as for-profit organizations.[23] The commitment of firms in supporting the work-life balance of their employees also has strong economic justifications. This kind of measure can engender loyalty and satisfaction on the part of employees, a reduction

18. *See* Maurizio Ferrera, *Le politiche sociali* (Bologna: Il Mulino, 2006); Yuri Kazepov & Domenico Carbone, *Che cos'è il welfare state* (Rome: Carocci 2007).
19. Gøsta Esping Andersen, *The Three Worlds of Welfare Capitalism* (Princeton: Princeton University Press, 1990).
20. In Italy, three laws make explicit reference to company-level welfare promoting work-life balance: Art. 1 of Act no. 125/1991, in G.U. 15 Apr. 1991, no. 88 (Azioni positive per la parità uomo-donna nel lavoro); Legislative Decree 198/2006, in G.U. 31 maggio 2006, no. 125 (Codice delle pari opportunità tra uomo e donna, a norma dell'articolo 6 della legge 28 novembre 2005, no. 246); and Art. 9 of Act no. 53/2000, in G.U. 13 Mar. 2000, n. 60 (Disposizioni per il sostegno della maternità e della paternità, per il diritto alla cura e alla formazione e per il coordinamento dei tempi delle città). *See* Isabella Quadrelli, *Promuovere la conciliazione tra responsabilità familiari e impegno lavorativo nei luoghi di lavoro*, 37–40 (Rome: Osservatorio Nazionale sulla famiglia, 2012).
21. *See* Naldini & Saraceno, *supra* n. 1; Chiara Saraceno C. & William Keck, *Towards an integrated approach for the analysis of gender equity in policies supporting paid work and care responsibilities*, 25 Demographic Research, 371–406 (2011); Rossella Ciccia & Inge Bleijenbergh, *After the Male Breadwinner Model? Childcare Services and the Division of Labor in European Countries*, 21 Social Politics, 50–79 (2014).
22. Chinchilla & Grau, *supra* n. 3, at 45–46.
23. Mazzucchelli, *supra* n. 3, at 46–47.

in staff turnover, enhanced productivity, a stronger attractiveness of the firm for new talents, and a return in terms of the image of the company.[24]

In conclusion, company-level welfare seems to have the potential to be a useful instrument to enable the state to keep public spending under control, while benefiting the workers and their employers, with a positive impact on GDP and a reduction of inequality between men and women.[25] However, it is important to highlight possible risks: first, these kinds of welfare benefits are available only in large firms, while in Italy the majority of companies are small or medium-sized. The second risk, related to the first, is the potential worsening of inequalities between insiders and outsiders, increasing labour market segmentation. Finally, in view of the strong regional differences and of the varied nature of the services provided by the public welfare state in Italy, this sort of privatization in the provision of social services can exacerbate these inequalities, slowing down the process of homogenization.[26]

[A] Main Initiatives of Company-Level Welfare for Work-Life Balance in Italy

Based on the analysis of Thompson[27] and Ghislieri & Colombo[28] it is possible to distinguish between formal solutions, i.e. policies provided by the organization to facilitate work-life balance, and informal solutions, i.e. a family-friendly organizational culture and work environment, sensitive to employees' needs for reconciliation of work and life.

The main initiatives are summarized in Table 6.1.

Table 6.1 Main Initiatives of Company-Level Welfare for Work-Life Balance (Adapted from Ghislieri & Colombo)[29]

Strategies	*Programmes*
Time-based strategies	Flextime Job sharing Part-time work Telecommuting Leave for new parents Unpaid leave for personal needs

24. *Ibid.*
25. Ferrera, *supra* n. 6.
26. *Ibid.*
27. Cynthia A. Thompson, *Managing the Work-Life Balancing Act: An Introductory Exercise*, 26 Journal Management Education, 210 (2002).
28. Chiara Ghislieri & Laura Colombo (eds.), *Psicologia della conciliazione tra famiglia e lavoro. Teoria e ricerche in organizzazione*, 48 (Milan: Raffaello Cortina, 2014).
29. *Ibid.*

Strategies	*Programmes*
Information-based strategies	Intranet work-life website Resource and referral service Work-life brochures Support for the career
Money-based strategies	Vouchers/agreements for child care Vouchers/agreements for travel, gym membership Health insurance Support in the form of loans Vouchers for textbooks and/or periods of study abroad for the children of employees Summer camps for the children of employees Improving the replacement rate of the wage of parental leave
Direct services	On-site child care On-site gyms Concierge services and time-saving services Shuttle services Social and health assistance services
Culture-change strategies	Training for managers and supervisors about work-life reconciliation Linking managerial pay to employee satisfaction Focus on employees' actual performance, not 'face time' Monitoring of employees' needs Monitoring of effectiveness of policies

In the Italian case, it is evident that the implementation of company-level welfare policies for work-life balance is still at an early stage, both from the point of view of the number of firms providing these measures, and in terms of the number of policies implemented.

As pointed out by Den Dulk et al.[30] and Ponzellini,[31] the reasons for this slow development are various. First, the structure of the national welfare state: its family-based conception, combined with traditional gender roles, the unequal distribution of care duties inside the family and a high rate of female unemployment, means that there is insufficient pressure on firms to implement these measures. Second, small and

30. Laura Den Dulk, Pascale Peters & Erik Poutsma, *Variations in adoption of workplace work-family arrangements in Europe: the influence of welfare-state regime and organizational characteristics*, 23 International Journal Human Resource Management», 2785–2808 (2012).
31. Anna M. Ponzellini, *Work-life balance and industrial relations in Italy*, 8 European Societies, 273–294 (2006).

medium-sized firms dominate the Italian economy and in most cases they are not interested in or do not have the resources to introduce these policies.

One important factor could be the proportion of women employed in a firm, but in Italy low-skilled women workers are segregated in low-productivity service sectors with insecure jobs, while highly qualified women are employed in male-dominated sectors. In both cases, though for different reasons, no pressure is exerted on employers to implement these policies. Moreover, trade unions have traditionally paid scant attention to work-life balance though in recent times they have they started to raise the issue in collective and decentralized bargaining.

The amount of research in Italy into company welfare policies on work-life balance is limited. The following is an overview of the findings of different studies.[32] The scenario that emerges from this analysis is not encouraging, although it is in evolution. Out of 1,300 cases considered at national level, we find 130 measures for the reconciliation of work and life in just 184 companies. All these studies underline the fact that the initiatives adopted are traditional and in most cases time-based strategies: flextime, part-time work, parental leave, telecommuting. Also from this point of view, Italy is far behind other European countries. If we look at other initiatives for work-life balance, such as direct services, we find that they are not widespread at all and they are implemented only by large companies.

Another interesting matter is the number of firms applying for funding through Article 9 of Act no. 53/2000 (Parental Leave Act).[33] The number of applications submitted is growing, but still many projects are rejected, a fact that shows the limited ability of firms to present projects focused on the topic of work-life balance.[34]

Moreover, the Istat data show that most family-friendly companies are located in the north of Italy. Almost all the companies that applied for funding for projects are in Emilia-Romagna, Piedmont, Lombardy, Veneto and Tuscany.[35]

[B] Company-Level Welfare in Piedmont

The starting point for the empirical research was to contact family-friendly companies. The Piedmont region was chosen because it has a long history of innovative firms sensitive to the issue of Corporate Social Responsibility (the best known example is Olivetti, that was well known for measures in support of the company workforce)

32. *See* Anna M. Ponzellini & Anna Tempia, *Quando il lavoro è amico. Aziende e famiglie: un incontro possibile* (Roma: Edizioni Lavoro, 2003); Anna M. Ponzellini, *Work-life balance and industrial relations in Italy*, 8 European Societies, 273–294 (2006); Arnold Riedmann, Harald Bielenski, Teresa Szczurowska & Alexandra Wagner, *Working time and work-life balance in European companies* (Luxembourg: European Foundation for the Improvement of Living and Working Conditions, Office for Official Publications of the European Communities, 2006); Monica Boni & Alessandra Vultaggio, *La via italiana al welfare aziendale: scenari attuali e prospettive future*, 16 Sociologia e Politiche Sociali, 93–107 (2013); Istat, *La situazione del Paese* (Rome: Istat, 2015).
33. Act no. 53/2000, in G.U. 13 Mar. 2000, no. 60.
34. Quadrelli, *supra* n. 20, at 45.
35. Istat, *La situazione del Paese*, 172–174 (Rome: Istat, 2015).

though there are not many studies on this topic. As a result, many good practices remain in obscurity and are not even recognized and shared by the companies adopting them.[36] For these reasons, in the last few years the Piedmont Region has been promoting 'opportunities and initiatives to encourage changes in society and in the labour market, with particular attention to the issue of work-life balance and gender differences connected to it'.[37]

One of the most important steps was the introduction of Regional Law no. 34/2008 *Norme per la promozione dell'occupazione, della qualità, della sicurezza e regolarità del lavoro.*[38] The aim was to encourage the spread of practices of corporate social responsibility among firms through the integration on a voluntary basis of social and environmental concerns into their business operations and in their interaction with stakeholders and the local community.

Moreover, since 2009, together with the employers' association Unioncamere, the Regional Authority launched the project *La responsabilità sociale d'impresa in Piemonte- CSRPiemonte*, funded by the European Social Fund. The aim of the project was to map the firms with a higher level of awareness of CSR and company-level welfare practices, in order to disseminate these practices to other companies. In the first five years of its implementation (2009–2013), the aim of the project was to promote good practices of Corporate Social Responsibility through constant monitoring, promotion and training on this topic.[39]

Finally, in 2010 the Piedmont Region presented a series of initiatives intended to facilitate the reconciliation of work and life, funded by the Department for Equal Opportunities in Rome.

This project was intended to implement measures to support work-life balance, both in the private and the public sector, such as the setting up of on-site kindergartens, the adoption of flextime strategies, a phased return to work following childbirth for women, and training provision for employees on maternity and parental leave.

Three reports provide an overview of company-level welfare in Piedmont: the two reports *È-Quality – viaggio nelle imprese dove parità è qualità*, produced in 2010 and 2011 by the Regional Department for Equal Opportunities of Piedmont and the Regional Observatory of the Labour Market, and the report *Politiche di conciliazione in azienda: Rapporto Piemonte 2014* produced for the Regional Authority by Unioncamere Piemonte. This paper will focus on the findings of the most recent of these reports[40] that is entirely focused on company welfare.

The scenario that emerges is consistent with the national picture. In the 1,009 firms covered by the research project, the most common company-level welfare policies are time-based strategies: part-time work is the most common with 46.6% of

36. Unioncamere Piemonte, *L'importanza delle risorse umane: focus sul welfare aziendale* (Regione Piemonte e Unioncamere Piemonte, 2012).
37. *Id.*, 22.
38. Regional Act no. 34/2008, in B.U. 24 Dec. 2008, no. 52.
39. *Ibid.*
40. Unioncamere Piemonte, *Politiche di conciliazione in azienda: rapporto Piemonte 2014. Monitoraggio e best practices delle imprese piemontesi* (Regione Piemonte e Unioncamere Piemonte, 2014).

companies adopting vertical part-time (in the sense of a few days a week for a full day's work), and 21% adopting horizontal part-time (a few hours a day) followed by flextime, adopted by the 36% of firms.

Policies explicitly focused on work-life balance are unusual: 12% of companies adopted initiatives for involving families in the work of employees (such as giving Christmas gifts, organizing visits to the companies), 3.4% had on-site childcare services, and just 0.2% had agreements for the care of older members of the family.

Considering strategies for changing the company culture, only 16% of the companies conducted internal surveys on their employees' work-life balance needs, 15.9% implemented measures to promote equal opportunities at work, and 14% involved trade unions in decisions concerning human resources management.

It is significant that the 56% of small firms, 46% of medium-sized firms and 20% of large firms admitted they are not interested or are not able to implement policies to support the work-life balance of employees. However, 77% of the sample recognized the positive effects of these measures on the attachment of the employees to the firm, and 72% acknowledged the benefits in terms of the working environment.

§6.04 PARENTAL LEAVE IN ITALY

[A] The Legislation

With reference to the Italian case, the first important step in terms of social policies for work-life balance was the approval of the law on parental leave (Act no. 53/2000 *Disposizioni per il sostegno della maternità e della paternità, per il diritto alla cura e alla formazione e per il coordinamento dei tempi delle città*),[41,42] the provisions of which were carried over into the Consolidated Legislative Decree or *Testo Unico*, no. 151/2001).[43] This law was still based on a traditional understanding of care duties and of the relationship between maternity/paternity and work, far removed from the more equal sharing of care duties between mothers and fathers promoted by the European directives.

However, for the first time in Italy, the law reduced the insistence on maternity, recognizing and expanding the rights of the father and acknowledging the duty/right to

41. For an in-depth analysis on parental leave, inside and outside Europe, *see*: Peter Moss (ed.), *International Review of Leave Policies and Related Research 2015* (London: International Network on Leave Policies and Research, Institute of Education), *http://www.leavenetwork.org /lp_and_r_reports/ (accessed 5 Sept. 2016)*.
42. Act no. 53/2000, in G.U. 13 Mar. 2000, n. 60. A series of European Community's directives strongly influenced the enactment of this law. The most important is the Council Directive on the Framework agreement on Parental leave 96/34/EC, followed by: the Equal Treatment in Employment Directive 2002/73/EC and by Directive 2010/18/EU. However, the law on parental leave in Italy is also the arrival point of a long revision of the constitutional normative started in the 1970s. On this point *see*: Roberta Nunin, *Dalla conciliazione alla condivisione. La regolamentazione normativa dei diritti dei padri lavoratori tra diritto comunitario e diritto interno*, 173–200 (Annalisa Murgia & Barbara Poggio eds. Florence: ETS, 2011).
43. Legislative Decree 151/2001, in G.U. 26 Apr. 2001, no. 96.

care of both working parents.[44] The legislation granted the right to additional parental leave to the working mother after statutory maternity leave for a maximum period of a further six months;[45] and to the working father for a maximum period of six months, that could be extended to seven months in cases in which the father chooses to take leave for at least three months.[46] Either parent could take leave until the child reaches the age of eight, whereas the replacement rate of the wage is 30% for a maximum of six months until the child reaches the age of three, and none after that.[47]

The legislation not only recognized fathers as autonomously entitled to the right to parental leave, but also provides an extra month of benefit to encourage fathers to use it. However, paternity leave is not provided in this law. Moreover, the low replacement rate results in a bias in the use of leave: due to the gender pay gap (i.e., lower in Italy than the average of the EU, but still significant at around 7%) it is more likely for the mother to take leave as the father usually earns more.[48]

In this scenario an important, though symbolic, shift is represented by Article 4 of Act no. 92/2012 *Disposizioni in materia di riforma del mercato del lavoro in una prospettiva di crescita* (the Fornero Act).[49] This Act provides that the father who is a salaried worker, in the first five months after the child birth, is obliged to take one day off work [as an experimental measure for 2013–2015]. During the same period, he can also take two more days off to replace the mother in her period of maternity leave', with a replacement rate of 100% of the wage.[50] Despite the fact that this introduces paternity leave with a high replacement rate of the wage, the measure is still far below the fifteen days of paternity leave recommended by the European Parliament in 2010.[51]

44. *Ibid.*
45. Women workers have the right to maternity leave (statutory) of five months during pregnancy and after the birth of the child (or the adoption of a child). Italian maternity leave is one of the longest and economically most generous maternity leave schemes compared to other countries in the European Union and the OECD. In Italy, it is not only a statutory entitlement, but it is also paid for the entire period at a high flat rate (*see* Moss *supra* n. 42, at 14). *Post-partum* maternity leave is granted also to the father but just in case of death or serious illness of the mother, abandonment of the child by her or when exclusive custody is granted to the father.
46. The law granted the right to parental leave for mothers who are self-employed workers (but not for fathers). They can use the leave during the first year of the child for a maximum of three months, with a 30% replacement rate of the regular earnings.
47. For public employees, instead, the collective agreement provides a replacement rate of 100% for the first thirty days of leave.
48. European Commission, *Tackling the gender pay gap in the European Union* (Brussels: RAND Europe, 2014).
49. Act no. 92/2012, in G.U. 3 Mar. 2012, no. 153. Another interesting measure introduced by this law for the mothers is the baby-sitting voucher: at the end of maternity leave, during the following eleven months, working mothers can ask their employers to provide vouchers for baby-sitting services or for private or public childcare services and nurseries.
50. *Ibid.*
51. I am referring here to the legislative resolution of the 20 Oct. 2010 of the European Parliament. It contained the proposal for a directive of the European Parliament and of the Council amending the Council Directive 92/85/EEC, on the introduction of measures to encourage improvements in the safety and health at work of pregnant workers and workers who have recently given birth or are breastfeeding *and on the introduction of measures to support workers in balancing work and family life* (COM(2008)0637 - C6-0340/2008 - 2008/0193(COD)). In Article 8a, *paternity leave* is explicitly mentioned: 'Member States shall take the necessary measures to ensure that workers whose life partner has recently given birth are entitled to a continuous period of

Other changes to the legislation were introduced by Legislative Decree no. 80/2015[52] and the Stability Act for 2016 approved in November 2015.[53] This Legislative Decree raises the age of the child for which the parents can take leave from eight to twelve years; paid leave is extended from the age of three to the age of six, while unpaid leave can be taken until the child reaches the age of twelve years. The total amount of leave remains unchanged. Paternity leave is extended to all the kind of workers (both employees and self-employees).

The law also contains an innovative measure concerning telework, providing benefits for private employers introducing telecommuting as part of company-level welfare in order to promote work-life balance. However, the law considers the mother as the target of the policy and so the only one responsible for care duties. This is evident from the title of the law that refers to 'protection of maternity' and not protection of paternity and maternity or protection of parenthood. Moreover, the word father is rarely used in the text and fathers are mentioned only in those articles focused on the replacement of mothers who they are absent, or in cases in which they have abandoned the child, are seriously ill or have died.

The Stability Act for 2016[54] extends compulsory paternity leave from one to two days to be taken by fathers during the five months after the childbirth with a replacement rate of 100%. Again, it is evident that mothers continue to be considered the primary caregivers and that the legislation is far from recognizing an equal share of care duties between mothers and fathers.

[B] Some Data on the Use of Parental Leave in Italy

In Italy the most recent research on the use of parental leave is that of De Pasquale[55] for 2009. With regard to the public sector, only 4.9% of public employees (76% of whom were women) took parental leave. In terms of the gender composition of the employees, 6.2% of female salaried workers took parental leave compared to just 2.9% of male salaried workers.

In the private sector, in 2009 only 1.9% of workers took parental leave: 3.9% of female workers and 0.3% of male workers. The difference between the public and private sector is evident and for the most part can be attributed to the different replacement rate of the wage.

---

non-transferable paid paternity leave of *at least two weeks*, granted on an equivalent basis – except with regard to its duration – to maternity leave, to be taken after the confinement of the worker's spouse or partner during the period of the maternity leave.'

52. Legislative Decree 80/2015, in G.U. 24 Jun. 2015, n. 144 (Misure per la conciliazione delle esigenze di cura, di vita e di lavoro, in attuazione dell'articolo 1, commi 8 e 9, L. 183/2014).
53. Act no. 208/2015, in G.U. 30 Dec. 2015, no. 302.
54. *Ibid.*
55. Annalisa De Pasquale, *L'uso dei congedi genitoriali in Italia*, 169–205 (Pierpaolo Donati ed. Roma: Carocci, 2012).

Considering the most recent data available on the INPS database, for employees in the private sector, we find that in 2013 only 2.1% of employees took parental leave: 4.6% of female workers and just 0.4% of male workers.[56]

§6.05 PARENTAL LEAVE AND WORK-LIFE BALANCE MEASURES: FOCUS ON MALE WORKERS

[A] Company-Level Welfare Provisions and Male Workers

The changing conditions of work – such as a more fragmented and insecure labour market, more service-oriented and customer-focused work, and the reconfiguration of working time – are undermining the traditional male breadwinner model with an impact on the male experience of work and the role of work in the construction of male identity.[57] However, empirical evidence shows that the use of company-level welfare provisions by male workers is still minimal in general and in particular in terms of measures focused on work-life balance.[58] Clearly, the reasons for such low rates of use of these measures by male workers are multiple: some are rooted in the unequal treatment of men and women in the labour market, others in a more general problem of gender culture and roles. Especially in Italy, gender arrangements for the care of children and older people are still quite traditional with women presumed to be the primary caregivers. Other reasons can be found in the work environment. Despite the limited amount of research on this topic, it may be argued that one of the constraints on the use of these measures by male workers is the *female bias in work-life balance*. This may be defined as 'the perception held by managers of organizations and fellow-workers that the need for reconciling, and the family-work conflict, are questions specifically relating to women and not so much to men'.[59]

Even when policies are gender-neutral, they are implicitly addressed to women and men are only rarely targeted as potential users.[60] In general, firms with a high proportion of women in the workforce are the one that most often implement company-level welfare policies, and in particular the most effective work-life balance policies. Moreover, it is often the case that the implementation of these measures is the result of the increase of the female workforce in the company.[61] As a result, men feel

56. Data available at: *http://www.inps.it/portale/default.aspx?itemdir=10083* (accessed 20 Aug. 2016). Only the figures for private employees are considered here because the figures for employees in the public sector are not available in the INPS database.
57. Øystein Gullvåg Holter, *Men's Work and Family Reconciliation in Europe*, 9 Men & Masculinities, 425–456 (2007).
58. *See* European Foundation for the Improvement of Living and Working Conditions, *Parental Leave in European Companies* (Luxembourg: Office for Official Publications of the European Communities, 2007a); Øystein Gullvåg Holter, *supra* n. 57, 425–456 (2007); Lorenzo Escot L., José-Andrés Fernandez-Cornejo, Carmen Lafuente & Carlos Poza, *Willingness of Spanish Men to Take Maternity Leave. Do Firms' Strategies for Reconciliation Impinge on This?*, 67 Sex Role, 29–42 (2012).
59. Escot et al., *supra* n. 58, at 32.
60. Holter, *supra* n. 57, at 431.
61. *See* Den Dulk et al., *supra* n. 30; Mazzucchelli, *supra* n. 3.

less entitled to use company-level welfare measures, while on the other hand, the less they feel entitled, the less they use them and the less often the management perceive work-life balance to be a male problem.[62]

Lewis highlights the question of the sense of entitlement and the fact that beliefs and perceptions about one's own right affect positively or negatively the use of policies, public or private, for reconciliation of work, family and private life.[63] In this connection, other important factors affecting the use of company-level welfare measures by men are the company culture and awareness on the part of management of the issue of work-life balance for fathers. Clearly, company-level welfare provisions matter, but what is crucial is the perception of an organizational culture favourable towards the issues of reconciliation, gender and of paternity. The sole presence of certain policies does not enable fathers to feel entitled to use company-level welfare measures.[64] Most firms still have a company culture with a gender subtext that tends to reproduce male domination at work and the traditional characteristics of the male breadwinner.[65] Connected to that is the image of the ideal worker, who has unlimited time for work and no distractions at home, and this is still dominant within organizations.[66] This image is implicitly masculine since women remain the primary caregivers and the ones who either leave work or set aside their career aspirations after the birth of a child.

With regard to managerial attitudes, we can say that they contribute to the promotion of the company culture and to the construction of the sense of entitlement perceived by both fathers and mothers in respect of the use of company-level welfare measures. The expression 'management lottery'[67] perfectly illustrates the variable and discretionary powers of managers in facilitating – or failing to facilitate – employees' work-life balance. Den Dulk & De Rujiter[68] show that managers are more positive towards requests submitted by female employees to take advantage of work-life policies, especially in the case of parental leave or short-term leave to take care of sick children. To sum up, care duties are more often associated with women than men. The authors also underline that managers are more positive towards requests to take advantage of types of work-life policies that are less disruptive to the conduct of work and that do not affect the achievement of short-term goals. So far, it seems that they fail to perceive the long-term advantages associated with the use of company-level welfare provisions.[69]

---

62. Escot et al., *supra* n. 58.
63. Janet Lewis, *The Decline of the Male Breadwinner Model: Implications for Work and Care*, 8 Social Politics, 152–169 (2001).
64. Haas & Hwang, *supra* n. 4.
65. *Ibid.*
66. *See* Linda Haas & Philip Hwang, *Company Culture and Men's Usage of Family Leave Benefits in Sweden*, 44 Family Relations, 28–36 (1995); Escot et al., *supra* n. 58; Margaret W. Sallee, *The Ideal Worker or the Ideal Father: Organizational Structures and Culture in the Gendered University*, 53 Research in Higher Education, 782–802 (2012).
67. Laura Den Dulk L. & Judith De Rujiter, *Managing work-life policies: disruption versus dependency arguments. Explaining managerial attitudes towards employee utilization of work-life policies*, 19 International Journal Human Resource Management, 1223 (2008).
68. *Ibid.*
69. *Ibid.*

Finally, the role of information and training. Company-level welfare measures are very often not publicised and employees are not well informed: in this case too, managers play a central role.[70]

[B] Acceptance of the Use of Parental Leave by Men in Private Firms

As shown above, in Italy the use of paternity leave in private companies is minimal. The reasons for this failure to take leave are multiple and linked to gender stereotypes, the structure of the welfare state, the design of the policy on parental leave and other factors, but here we focus on the constraints exerted by the work environment.[71] Some authors[72] have identified important variables linked to working conditions such as: type of sector (public or private), productive sector of the firm, type of employment contract, type of position, percentage of female employees. Among these variables, organizational culture and managerial attitudes play a key role also in this case.[73] Organizational culture is understood here as 'the company's commitment to caring [and work-life balance] values, the company's level of father friendliness, the company's support for women's equal employment opportunity, fathers' perceptions of support from top managers, and fathers' perceptions of work group norms that reward task performance vs. long hours at work.'[74]

As for company-level welfare provisions, the use of parental leave is affected not only by the presence of these measures, but also by a family-friendly work environment, sensitive work-life balance.

Following the study of Haas et al.[75] and Haas and Hwang,[76] it is possible to indicate five central dimensions of the organizational culture affecting the use of parental leave by fathers. The first three are related to the family-friendliness of the company, while the other two are connected to the father-friendliness of the firm. It is important to distinguish between these two cultural features because they have a different impact on men in terms of taking parental leave. The dimensions are:

---

70. Holter, *supra* n. 57.
71. For a detailed study on opportunities and constraints on the use of parental leave by fathers in Italy *see* Maddalena Cannito, *Quando il congedo è maschile? Vincoli e opportunità nell'uso dei congedi parentali da parte dei padri in Italia*, 2 Autonomie Locali e Servizi Sociali, 323–339 (2015).
72. *See* Brandth & Kvande, *supra* n. 4; Linda Haas, Karin Allard & Philip Hwang, *The impact of organizational culture on men's use of parental leave in Sweden*, 5 Community, Work & Family, 319–342 (2002); Magnus Bygren M. & Ann-Zofie Duvander, *Parents' Workplace situation and Fathers' Parental Leave use*, in 68 Journal of Marriage and Family, 363–372 (2006); Haas & Hwang, *supra* n. 4; Egidio Riva, *Quel che resta della conciliazione. Lavoro, famiglia, vita privata tra resistenze di genere e culture organizzative* (Milan: Vita e Pensiero, 2009); Annalisa Murgia & Barbara Poggio, *Svelare la maschilità egemonica nelle organizzazioni. L'esperienza dei congedi parentali raccontata dagli uomini*, 201–232 (Annalisa Murgia & Poggio B. eds. Florence: ETS, 2011b).
73. *See* Haas et al., *supra* n. 72; Haas & Hwang, *supra* n. 4; Escot et al., *supra* n. 58; Trude Lappegard, *Couples' Parental Leave Practices: The Role of the Workplace Situation*, 33 Journal Family and Economic Issues, 298–305 (2012).
74. Haas et al., *supra* n. 72, at 1.
75. *Ibid.*
76. Haas & Hwang, *supra* n. 4.

- Caring ethic. This concerns the extent to which organizations stress the relational dimensions of life, such as empathy, helpfulness and caring.
- Equal employment opportunity ethic. They are understood as the commitment of the firm to pursuing equal treatment of men and women.
- Masculine ethic. This refers to the gender subtext in the organization concerning traditional markers of masculinity: competitiveness, commitment to work and to the organization.
- The father-friendliness of the firm. This can be evaluated by the presence of formal policies and support for fathers taking parental leave, by means of positive informal support from managers and co-workers for fathers taking parental leave, with a significant proportion of fathers taking leave, thus helping to establish a workplace norm.[77]
- Top management's attitudes toward the participation of men in childcare.

§6.06 OBJECTIVES AND METHODS

The main aim of the present study is to understand whether and how company initiatives for reconciliation create a family-friendly environment encouraging fathers to take parental leave. In addition, it was decided to use this research to map the best practices of a number of large firms in Piedmont and to investigate the relationship between traditional and company-level welfare policies. The focus was both on the influence of the national policy on parental leave on company-level welfare and on the ways in which these schemes affect the implementation of the law. The research was designed as a qualitative study, consisting of interviews in private firms, belonging to different productive sectors, in different provinces of Piedmont, with at least 350 employees and recognized (by certification or self-definition) as sensitive to the issue of work-life balance. Thirty-nine companies were selected that presented all the features mentioned above, consulting different sources:

- the 'Great place to work Italy' website (http://www.greatplacetowork.it/);
- the '*È-quality*' reports of the 2010 and 2011 produced by the Piedmont Region in 2010 and 2011;
- the CSR Piemonte website (http://www.csrpiemonte.it/);
- the list of firms implementing projects through the '*Fondo Conciliazione dei Tempi di Vita e di Lavoro*' ('Fund for Reconciliation between work and life time') of the Piedmont Region; (http://www.regione.piemonte.it/pariopportunita/cms/index.php/lavoro/conciliazione/422-repertorioprogetticoncilizionebandi2011).

77. *Id.*, 308–309.

The recruitment phase was a long and difficult process taking almost four months.[78] As pointed out by Von Alemann et al.,[79] the process of gaining insights into work organization is itself an important source of knowledge because of the enormous effort it requires on the part of the researcher.

In the end, ten firms confirmed their willingness to take part in the research,[80] and it was decided to conduct interviews not only with Human Resources managers but also with fathers. The HR managers also provided the contact details of fathers working in their firms because, for reasons of privacy, they could not provide me their names without their consent. As a result, the interviews with the managers were conducted first, and then fifteen interviews with fathers who took parental leave (two/three per company) were conducted. The characteristics of the sample were as follows:

- HR managers: six men and four women aged between 38 and 59 years of age; eight of them have a master's degree and two have a high-school diploma; eight out of ten have children but just one of them (one of the women) took parental leave.
- Fathers: aged between 31 and 45 years of age; three have a middle-school qualification, five have a high-school diploma, seven have a master's degree; they all have open-ended contracts; twelve are employed full-time, three part-time. Their partners are all employed: one is a shopkeeper; three are freelance workers; eight are employed on open-ended full-time contracts; three are employed on open-ended part-time contracts. With regard to the amount of leave taken, except for one who took leave for just seven days, the others fourteen fathers took parental leave for a period from one to eight months.

The data analysis was conducted by means of thematic analysis, based on numerous readings of the empirical material.[81] In examining the HR managers' interviews, an attempt was made to grasp the main features of the 'official' organizational culture, the values of the firm and the company-level welfare policies, their vision of the reconciliation of work and family, and of the use of parental leave, with specific attention to working fathers. In examining the interviews with the fathers, on the other hand, an attempt was made to understand how organizational culture is constructed and disseminated, the experience of fatherhood and of balancing work and family duties. In particular, they were asked to describe the practical problems they

78. The channels used were multiple: Job Placement Office of the University of Turin; contacts with four professors at the University of Turin; contacts with the research group '*Secondo Welfare*' of Milan; participation in two meetings of the Department for Equal Opportunities of Region Piedmont; participation to the conference '*Riconciliare Lavoro e Famiglia*' organized by IRES Piedmont; participation at a summer school at the International Training Center of the International Labour Organization; mail and/or phone calls with the firms.
79. Annette Von Alemann, Sandra Beaufaÿs & Thordis Reimer, *Gaining Access to the Field of Work Organizations with the Issue of "Work-Family Life Balance" for Fathers*, 7 SFB 882, 1–40 (2012).
80. Only six companies out of ten (Enaip, Iren, Michelin, Reale Mutua, Solvay, UnipolSai) gave their consent to be cited in the study. For this reason, the others will remain anonymous.
81. Daniela Della Porta, *L'intervista qualitativa* (Rome-Bari: GLF Editori Laterza, 2010).

faced with reconciling family duties and work and their personal experience of taking leave such as requesting the leave, the reaction of colleagues and management and so on. Moreover, an attempt was made to find out if they were aware of the company-level welfare policies of their firms and their impact on their choice to take parental leave.

§6.07 THE USE OF PARENTAL LEAVE BY FATHERS IN FAMILY-FRIENDLY COMPANIES IN PIEDMONT

[A] Company-Level Welfare Policies and Parental Leave: The Management Point of View

This section examines the management point of view about the issue of work-life balance and parental leave. First, the main initiatives implemented by the firms in this study are considered, with a focus on the motivation and factors behind their implementation, while attempting to ascertain whether paternal leave is included in these policies. Second, an attempt is made to cast light on the connections between national policy on parental leave and company-level welfare measures for work-life balance.

Policies and motivations

The empirical findings seem consistent with the literature. The most common measures of company-level welfare are time-based initiatives. Part-time working is definitively the most common and the most flexible: every firm adopts this measure and has many types of part-time working schedules. Flexibility in working time arrangements is the other most common measure, even if it varies considerably according to the productive sector and the role of the employee in the firm. Companies where production takes place on assembly lines offer flexibility measures only for white-collar workers. The others, especially in insurance and banking, provide flextime for all employees at all levels.

Telecommuting presents the same characteristics but is less common. Six firms had experience of telework, but only one firm adopted it in response to childcare needs, whereas the other four firms adopt personalized measures for employees with serious illnesses. In any case, three other firms are evaluating the possibility of introducing telecommuting. All the companies provide many types of leave, paid and/or unpaid, for personal, family or childcare needs.

With regard to the provision of services, three companies have on-site nurseries and summer camps for the children of their employees. Moreover, the same companies provide financial support in the form of vouchers for the purchase textbooks, and special agreements for study holidays for the older children of their employees. This shows an attention to family needs of the employees also in the later stages of the child's development and not only in the early years of childhood. Three other companies have agreements with private nurseries where the children of their employees have priority access and reduced fees. Three firms provide a shuttle service for their employees, due to their location in peripheral areas and to meet the needs of employees living in surrounding towns. Finally, six firms implement culture-change strategies and training for managers and supervisors relating to work-life balance, and six others regularly monitor employees' needs and the effectiveness of their company-level welfare policies.

The driving forces behind the implementation of these policies are related to economic and productive factors: six managers reported that the main advantage of family-friendly policies is related to productivity and the reduction in absenteeism. Four managers pointed out the positive influence of family-friendly policies on loyalty to the firm and reduction in staff turnover, while one underlined the positive impact of these measures on the attractiveness of the firm for the recruitment of highly skilled staff. It is evident that the decision to adopt these policies is not due to philanthropy, but to the competitive advantage they can bring to the company.

The influence of Act no. 53/2000 on parental leave

The national law on parental leave does not seem to have had a strong impact on company-level welfare provisions, nor on the understanding that firms have of work-life balance.[82] All the companies had already implemented policies of work-life balance before the new law was enacted, and had acquired an awareness of the needs of their employees for family-friendly policies. All the managers interviewed pointed out that the policies of their firms stem from a family-friendly organizational culture that was already in existence before the law was adopted. All the managers stated that the most recent expansion and adjustment of the policies was the result of the autonomous recognition by the firms of the family needs of employees. Four managers reported that their companies simply implemented the rights laid down by the law, but the legislation did not affect their understanding of the issue of work-life balance, nor their policies. It seems that the law has failed to promote a cultural change towards a reduction of the time fathers spend at work in favour of time spent with their children. The statement of one manager is emblematic in this respect:

> I would say that we simply apply the law: the law provides these initiatives and we put them to work. But I would answer no to the question as to whether the law has changed our view about the inclusion of men in childcare duties. We apply the law, and if it provides measures that are more advanced we implement them, but I do not think it is necessary to discuss the role of men (HR Manager 1, male, 56 years old).

Four companies added some new measures to their company-level welfare provisions by extending some of the rights laid down in the national law on parental leave. Four of them already provided one day of paternity leave and three of these companies extended this leave to two or three days with the introduction of Act no. 92/2012.[83] Three firms increased the replacement rate of wages during parental leave: one paid 70% of the wage during the first thirty days of leave for mothers and fathers, another one paid 10% of the wage only for fathers for each day of parental leave.

82. Act no. 53/2000, in G.U. 13 Mar. 2000, no. 60.
83. Act no. 92/2012, in G.U. 3 Mar. 2012, no. 153.

Finally, one manager reported that after the new law was approved they decided to 'make an inventory' of their company-level welfare policies on work-life balance. This enabled them to gain a better understanding of the issues and to improve the internal communication with employees about their rights and the measures available to them. However, only one firm applied for funds under Article 9 of Act no. 53/2000. The other managers justified their policies by saying that their welfare measures were already more advanced and that the issue of work-life balance was already part of their practices and the culture of the organization.

Gender-neutral or gendered policies?

One of the most interesting aspects in the interviews with managers is the adoption of a gender perspective in implementing policies. Although in three firms internal polices changed in some way after the introduction of the law on parental leave, the theme of the role of fathers in care duties never emerged, not even in those firms where men account for the majority of the workforce.

As noted above, two measures are aimed specifically at fathers: one-day's leave at the birth of the child, extended to two days after the approval of Act no. 92/2012,[84] implemented by three firms, with an increase in the replacement rate for paternity leave implemented by two companies. All the managers insisted that the rationale of their company-level welfare measures for work-life balance is to support the family in general and that these measures are intended for *parents*:

> We did not think about the fact of supporting the fathers, we went beyond that, I mean, we want to support the family, all kind of families, [...] we are not interested in the gender identity of the person [...] Designing projects specifically for fathers would be misleading because it would miss the point which is sustaining the family. (HR manager 3, male, 43 years old).
>
> The initiatives, alternative or integrative with respect to parental care that (name of the firm) implement, [...] are not aimed at fathers or mothers: they are aimed at parents. (HR manager 4, woman, 59 years old).

One firm that is particularly aware of the interrelations between work and family adopts measures to support employees in the transition to parenthood, with a gender-neutral perspective:

> No, projects addressed to fathers no, but we decided to call the project '*Genitori-alità*'[85] and not 'maternity'. '*Genitorialità*' means both mothers and fathers. (HR manager 8, female, 53 years old).

As this manager admits, only female workers becoming mothers take part in this scheme. As a result, it seems that gender-neutral policies reinforce traditional parental and gender roles according to which women are the primary caregivers and the only ones affected by the problems of work-life balance. As noted by one manager:

84. *Ibid.*
85. 'Parenthood' in English.

> All the measures are available to men, too. I don't see the need to push men, because they are all aware of what they can or cannot do. It would be a discrimination against women, I mean, I support fathers and not mothers. No, everyone is at the same level, equal duties, equal rights. Maybe women have more problems because they have to manage a family and everyone recognizes that. (HR manager 1, male, 56 years old).

In fact, there is a marked gender segregation in the use of these schemes in all the firms: while both men and women use flextime, part-time work is a female prerogative.

One interesting finding consistent with these observations is the fact that in one of the firms, with a 90% male workforce, no one has ever used or requested part-time. In all the firms men use measures for balancing work and private life more often than measures for childcare, *in primis* flextime. Except for some personalized or experimental schemes, companies tend not to deal with work-life balance, parental leave and company-level welfare. As a result, gender segregation is reproduced at the management level, while on the other hand, not all managers are aware of the company-level welfare measures or the legislation on parental leave.

The justification that one manager put forward for this shortcoming is the fact that all the companies list their policies on the Intranet website, so that all workers are potentially aware of their rights. It seems that managers do not consider the company to be responsible for promoting cultural change and the involvement of men in childcare duties:

> It is not the culture, even among young men, to take parental leave in the place of women. In the case of employees making this choice it was normally someone with a self-employed partner who does not have the right to maternity leave or who has just started a career [...]. As a result, it is more a cultural problem for men than for firms. [...] I believe it is more a process of growth of men than women or managers who should be granting certain rights. (HR manager 2, female, 56 years old).

We find the same patterns also with regard to parental leave. As reported by all the managers, only a few men take parental leave for work-life balance purposes. Not all the companies were able to provide quantitative data but it was stated that, over the past five years, in one firm not one man took parental leave, while in the others over the same period no more than ten men took leave. The only firm in which a significant number of men took parental leave is rather atypical as it is a publicly owned company. The other firm with quite a high rate of men taking parental leave is a company whose core business is training which has a flexible working schedule and a goal-oriented approach to work.

The lowest rates of men taking leave are in companies in more 'traditional' productive sectors, with a rigid organization of work and a high percentage of men in the workforce. As pointed out by one manager, the productive sector has an impact:

> Bear in mind that this is an engineering company so most of employees are men. Let's say, they are not keen to take paternity leave, or anything of that kind. (HR manager 4, woman, 59 years old).

Six managers, though, maintain that the low rates of men taking leave are due to cultural and economic factors:

> In my opinion, I believe that men in Italy fail to take parental leave due to a cultural problem. In other countries childcare duties are shared in a completely different way, but also because of an economic problem because men earn more than women. Giving up 70% of the man's wage is more problematic [...]. (HR manager 7, male, 55 years old).

Concerning the use of parental leave by managers, all the interviewees confirmed that employees in different roles and positions of power took parental leave, but normally women. Arguably this gender segregation in the use of leave also among managers affects men's sense of entitlement and their perception of the legitimacy of their using this measure:

> HRM: Family-friendly measures cut across all positions and levels, but they do not cut across gender, because they are mainly – above all (strong emphasis) – used by women.
>
> I: And in respect of parental leave?
>
> HRM: Same thing (laughing). Same thing. (HR manager 8, female, 53 years old).

Finally, with regard to the use of leave we find a gender-neutral approach that neither discourages nor encourages men in the use of leave. As reported by one manager:

> We are not bothered whether [the leave] is taken by a men or a woman. Really, if a woman takes the leave or her male colleague in any case I have a problem of work organization. It's the position of the worker that is problematic, not the gender of the person in that position. (HR manager 2, female, 56 years old).

[B] Parental Leave and the Work Environment: The Point of View of Fathers

The second research question was whether and to what extent company-level welfare creates a more family-friendly and father-friendly environment that encourages employees to take paternity leave. To answer this question we used the interviews with male employees who took parental leave.[86] As noted in the previous section, the quantitative data on the use of leave by men in the firms taking part in the research do not seem to support the hypothesis that company-level welfare measures per se have a positive effect on employees taking paternity leave.

The reasons that led the interviewees to take parental leave are linked to practical problems, for example when their partners were not entitled to take leave, or due to a personal decision to be actively involved as fathers:

86. In order to respect the privacy of the interviewees the names have been changed and in quoting them the firm they work for will not be specified due to the limited number of fathers interviewed in each company.

> I decided to take leave from the very beginning. Your priorities change, so that is the priority. It is unusual, I know. I know this is unusual, but I had no doubts anyway. I would have changed my job, I would have looked for another job if they had not allowed me to take leave. (Luca, 42 years old, master's degree).

> Let's say that I didn't meet any resistance at work. Of course I created some problems, but I had already made my decision and I would have never negotiated. (Adriano, 43 years old, high-school diploma).

However, all the fifteen fathers expressed a positive opinion of the work environment and of the possibilities of work-life balance implemented by their companies. Although none of them mentioned the work environment as a factor encouraging them to take leave, every interviewee described his firm as family-friendly:

> Well, with respect to other firms, I consider it to be a good working environment compared to other sectors or other companies. (Gilberto, 34 years old, high-school diploma)

> My brother-in-law thought about taking parental leave, but he didn't even dare ask for it because he knew it was impossible. That's why I feel lucky working here, because I never had any problems. I feel my rights are recognized from that point of view. (Michele, 44 years old, master's degree)

> I can't complain about the measures implemented by the company [...]. I feel lucky with respect to other firms and work environments. (Federico, 41 years old, high-school diploma)

However, only half of the interviewees were well informed about company-level welfare measures implemented by their firms. It seems that the positive evaluation of their work environment derives more from the perception of an organizational culture that includes an awareness of the employee's work-life balance needs. This supports the hypothesis that company-level welfare policies per se are not necessarily effective if they are not sustained by a family-friendly organizational culture.

One interviewee made the interesting point that working in a family-friendly company risks making the worker see the firm as a family and the request of parental leave as a sort of betrayal:

> It is very difficult to take paternity leave because it is like a betrayal, there is this theme of the company as a second family. (Simone, 37 years old, master's degree).

Even if all the fathers showed an awareness of their entitlement in respect of parental leave, three of them reported that they took leave while trying to avoid being disruptive to the conduct of work both for managers and colleagues. As a result, it seems that men perceive parental leave as a legitimate right, but the exercise of this right is subordinated - or at least strongly conditioned - by production needs:

> It was something linked to my sense of duty, so I was bothered by the fact that my colleagues had to do my job because I was on parental leave, so I tried to make it right, to find solutions (Luca, 42 years old, master's degree).

> If you are close to your boss then you know you create organizational problems in that period, so you try to postpone the leave, and try to find an agreement when you can (Gilberto, 34 years old, high-school diploma).

These attitudes bring to mind the ideal worker whose work duties take priority over family responsibilities. Since taking parental leave, all the interviewees reported that they had put their career ambitions on hold. As a result, it can be argued that there is a strong perception of the impossibility of reconciling their career with the decision to take paternity leave. As stressed by one interviewee:

> The system is expected to reward those who are devoted to work, those who are like monks dedicated to work and that's a problem because, speaking about leave, we have managers who choose managers who are just like them [...]. We continue to reward people with the same characteristics: workaholic, super focused, super alone sometimes, that's the trend. (Simone, 37 years old, master's degree).

As shown by the literature on this topic, management plays a decisive role in the choice of fathers to take parental leave. A significant variable is what is sometimes known as the management lottery. The sole presence of family-friendly policies is not enough to encourage the use of leave by fathers because the implementation of such policies is mediated by managers and their opinion on work and the use of parental leave. Three of the interviewees reported that they faced some problems when they applied for parental leave, but they all stated that this was related to the manager's attitudes and not to the company culture:

> Anyway, I didn't feel supported, these are things that they do not say explicitly: they give you to understand. I had the feeling that my decision was not entirely accepted and approved. However, parental leave is my right...But I think it was a problem of the office where I used to work, I would not say it involves the entire company [...] (Luca, 42 years old, master's degree).

> As workers of this company, we don't have big problems with managers. Of course, they are not supportive when you apply for parental leave because they have to give up a worker, they have to deal with your absence and they are thrown into crisis. [As managers], they are always upset when someone is absent from work. (Gilberto, 34 years old, high-school diploma).

Some other fathers reported that their managers were sensitive to their work-life balance needs and that they were supportive when they asked to take parental leave:

> I believe I'm lucky because I work in this company. Not everywhere is like that, so probably I was lucky because I have always had managers who are sensitive to my choice, they never stood in my way. (Michele, 44 years old, master's degree)

> My supervisor, who is a woman, was very proud of me and my boss did not try to interfere with my decision and did not express any form of judgment. (Federico, 41 years old, high-school diploma).

Another factor positively affecting the choice of fathers to take leave and the attitudes of managers is the 'contagion effect' mentioned by two interviewees. It seems easier for a father to take parental leave in firms where a number of men have taken it in the past because managers are more used to dealing with possible organizational problems and they have internalized the legitimacy of this choice for fathers:

> They [the managers] didn't say anything about the leave because in my company a number of fathers take parental leave. (Fabrizio, 37 years old, high-school diploma).

The findings from these interviews seem to support the existence of the 'management lottery' theorized by Den Dulk & De Rujiter.[87]

In order to measure the degree of legitimacy accorded to the choice of a father to take parental leave and to measure the family-friendliness of the firms, the interviewees were also asked about the reactions of colleagues. Only two of them perceived real support on the part of colleagues and other workers:

> It's paternal solidarity. They [the colleagues] know the difficulties of being a father, the difficulties are always the same, so they are sympathetic. If you take parental leave, they say "If you can take it, do it, because it's time that you can spend with your children". (Gilberto, 34 years old, high-school diploma)

> I mean, as a man who made certain kind of choices, sometimes I feel like my colleagues admire me, this [the use of leave] helped a lot in my relationship with them. (Michele, 44 years, master degree)

All the other interviewees reported reactions of surprise because the decision of a male employee to take parental leave is still seen as a 'brave' choice:

> At the time I asked to take parental leave, I was responsible for a group of 200 people, so I had an important position, I was not one among the others and the idea that at a certain point of you career you make a choice like that, well, some people were surprised [...] positively surprised, but surprised. I would like you to mention that because it's not a decision that you take just like that, without thinking. (Adriano, 43 years old, high-school diploma).

Five of the interviewees underlined that sometimes they had to deal with jokes and subtle forms of mobbing on the part of their colleagues:

> Going back to the theme of work, with my colleagues it's hard [...]. I do not tolerate some jokes, like: "Tomorrow you are again on parental leave, are you? Luckily we are here working in your place". (Simone, 37 years old, master degree)

> Going back to the theme of work, with my colleagues it's hard [...]. I do not tolerate some jokes, like: "Tomorrow you are again on parental leave, are you? Luckily we are here working in your place". (Simone, 37 years old, master degree)

> It's clear that we are a big firm, also unionized, so certain things cannot be said explicitly, but it is evident that this is a choice [to go on leave] that generates surprise. I heard many comments, for example at the bar, one of my colleagues, a woman recently promoted to manager, made a comment like "They sent me to a

87. Den Dulk & De Rujiter, *supra* n. 67.

workplace in which I have to deal with a '*mammo*'[88] who decided to stay home for three months". (Adriano, 43 years old, high-school diploma).

§6.08 CONCLUSIONS

The aim of the study was to investigate the influence of the work environment in family-friendly firms in the private sector on the use of parental leave by fathers. The main idea was to understand the interrelations between company-level welfare measures of work-life balance and the national policy on parental leave. An attempt was made to answer this question by intersecting the point of view of managers and of fathers taking parental leave.

First, even if the companies in the study are committed to sustaining the work-life balance of their employees, the measures implemented are still fairly traditional and principally time-based strategies. In particular, what emerges is the lack of attention to the importance of culture-change strategies and of training in respect of the new social needs such as the reconciliation of work and family life. Since the implementation of company-level welfare policies is mediated by managers, this weakness in training can undermine the effectiveness of the measures.

Second, a gender-neutral approach emerged from the interviews. Policies are addressed to parents and/or meant to support the family. This neutrality produces a clear gender segregation in the use of these measures and, as a result, men tend not to use them because of the female bias in reconciliation. Since childcare duties have always been a female prerogative, this lack of attention to the gender dimension does not encourage men to feel entitled to reconcile work and family or responsible for childcare. Companies do not feel accountable for the promotion of a cultural change and the only reasons for the implementation of company-level welfare initiatives are of an economic nature. As a result, when we talk about company-level welfare and the involvement of private actors in providing welfare, it is important to remember that firms are for-profit subjects and their interventions are not philanthropic. This could lead to new inequalities and to indifference in relation to non-remunerative social interventions.

This is evident in the case of parental leave. Even if the companies in the study are firms where we might expect resistance to the use of paternity leave to be the weakest, the picture that emerges is different. As reported by all the managers, they simply implemented the law without taking measures to promote the use of leave among fathers. The companies did not adopt a formal policy to support fathers taking leave, they did not implement special programmes to encourage fathers to take leave and they did not designate anyone to encourage fathers to take leave. In fact, also in these family-friendly firms the use of leave by fathers is rare. However, we have to acknowledge that all the fathers who took leave recognize the family-friendliness of the

88. The expression '*mammo*' is sometimes used to refer in a disparaging manner to a stay-at-home father. It is derived from the word '*mamma*' (mother), and it is generally used with a negative connotation.

work environment and only three of them encountered some resistance at the time they requested the leave. In this sense, a family-friendly organizational culture and the support of managers and co-workers can play a more important role in encouraging or discouraging fathers from taking parental leave than the presence of policies per se.

As a result, we can conclude that company-level welfare provisions matter, but what is essential is the perception of an organizational culture favourable towards the issues of work-life balance and of paternity. The sole presence of family-friendly policies does not grant the freedom to take parental leave without consequences for the father's reputation as a worker and as a man.

Finally, the findings allows us to express some considerations and critiques of the policy of parental leave, casting light on its ineffectiveness for fathers working in the private sector due to the inadequate support given to them both from an economic point of view and from the point of view of legitimacy. This policy does not seem to have had an impact on how companies perceive the issue of work-life balance, and it does not appear to have given paternity greater visibility at work.

CHAPTER 7

Flexibility Tools For Part-Time Work: The Italian Jobs Act

Carla Spinelli[*]

§7.01 THE DEFINITION OF PART-TIME EMPLOYMENT AND THE REGULATION OF WORKING CONDITIONS

One of the most important factors contributing to well-being at work concerns working hours, including the transfer from full-time to part-time work, and vice versa, in an attempt to achieve a life-work balance. The far-reaching and wide-ranging reform of non-standard employment contracts in Italy pursuant to Act No. 134/2015 (known as the Jobs Act) introduced significant changes also for part-time work. The regulation laid down in Legislative Decree No. 61/2000, was repealed[1] with the new provisions now laid down in Articles 4–12 of Legislative Decree No. 81/2015.

First, it should be pointed out that the new definition of part-time work, introduced by Article 4 of Legislative Decree No. 81/2015, makes no more reference to the diversification of its forms, namely horizontal, vertical and mixed part-time.[2]

The legal definition of part-time work now takes 'normal' full-time working hours – as adopted in the Italian legislation on working time – as the frame of reference. As a result, part-time work includes all those activities performed for less than a forty-hour week or less than the working week as laid down in collective agreements.

The most important effect of eliminating the diversification of part-time arrangements in the three types of part-time work mentioned above concerns the regulation of

* Associate Professor of Labour Law, University of Bari Aldo Moro, Italy.

1. Article 55, para. 1, *a)*, Legislative Decree No. 81/2015.
2. Part-time work may be performed according to three different patterns, known in Italy as: horizontal, with working time corresponding to a portion of the standard working week; vertical, with full- time work for a limited period of the week, month or year; and mixed, combining the first two configurations.

the flexibility tools of part-time working, since this measure – as argued in the following (*infra*, section 7.02) – implies the elimination of the regulatory differences characterizing the previous legislation on supplementary work, overtime and 'flexibility clauses'.

However, the new legal provision does not preclude a distinction between the forms of part-time – horizontal (a few hours a day), vertical (a few days a week) and mixed – in collective agreements, existing or to be negotiated. Maintaining the distinction between the various models of part-time working would also be useful to ensure a more adequate implementation of the principle of proportionality, that is safeguarded in Legislative Decree No. 81/2015, albeit with major changes in terms of content.[3]

The new provision concerning the principle of proportionality (Article 7) is much more concise than the previous one, stipulating that part-time workers should not receive less favourable treatment than full-time employees of the same establishment with the same type of employment contract or relationship, engaged in the same or a similar work or occupation. It also provides that part-time workers have the same rights as comparable full-time workers, even though the economic and legal treatment has to be pro rata because of the reduced duration of the working hours.[4]

The current legal regulation provides for the application of the principle of *pro-rata temporis* to all working conditions, due to reduced working hours. However, this does not exclude the norm to be interpreted so that, in the application of this principle, a clear distinction should be made between economic rights and those pertaining to the protection of the person.[5]

From this perspective, the concerns expressed by some authors with reference to the provisions of Article 7 (2) of the Legislative Decree No. 81/2015 are easily understood. According to the above-mentioned Article, collective agreements can apply the principle of proportionality to the duration of the trial period, the period of continuity of employment in the case of sickness and accident and the length of the notice period in the case of dismissal and resignation.

In the light of the distinction between economic and personal rights, the lawfulness of applying the principle of proportionality to the notice period is dubious, considering the protection against the loss of employment that characterizes this measure. In the same perspective, even the possibility of negotiating the reduction of the duration of the trial period and the period of continuity of employment in the case of illness and (now also) injury, originally foreseen only for vertical part-time work, appears difficult to justify with reference to the other forms of reduced working hours.[6]

3. *See* Art. 3, Legislative Decree No. 61/2000 and now Art. 6, Legislative Decree No. 81/2015.
4. Article 7, para. 2, Legislative Decree No. 81/2015.
5. Stefano Bellomo, *Il lavoro a tempo parziale tra semplificazione e unificazione*, in *Speciale Lex 24*, luglio 2015, 35; Vincenzo Bavaro, *Il lavoro part-time dopo il d.lgs. n. 81/2015*, in Edoardo Ghera, Domenico Garofalo (eds.), *Contratti di lavoro, mansioni e misure di conciliazione vita-lavoro nel Jobs Act 2*, Bari, Cacucci, 222 (2015).
6. Vincenzo Bavaro, *supra*, 222; Roberto Voza, *Il 'riordino' del contratto di lavoro a tempo parziale*, in LG, n. 12, 1118–19 (2015).

As a result, it seems clear that the reintroduction of the forms of part-time working through collective agreements could result in a considerable advantage for the consistent interpretation of the new regulation of part-time work, even for the implementation of the legal provision on the competence of the collective bargaining to apply the principle of proportionality.

The peculiarity of the part-time regulation, evident also in Legislative Decree No. 81/2015, is to foresee flexibility tools for working hours in the interest of both the employers and the workers, with different results in terms of how to balance those interests.

The following analysis focuses on the most significant provisions concerning the flexibility tools for part-time work provided by the new legal regulation.

§7.02 PART-TIME WORK FLEXIBILITY IN THE EMPLOYER'S INTEREST

With respect to part-time work flexibility in the interest of the employer, significant changes are to be seen in the regulation of supplementary work, overtime and 'flexibility clauses' (Article 6), also as a result of the decision to eliminate the distinction between the different forms of part-time, as noted above (*supra*, section 7.01).

[A] Supplementary Work and Overtime

According to the previous regulation, the employer is allowed to request the employee to work in excess of the hours agreed between the parties in the part-time contract, and falling within the normal working-time limits only in the case of horizontal part-time working.[7] At present, supplementary work is allowed whatever the distribution of working hours with reference to the day, week, month and year,[8] as determined by the parties pursuant to Article 5 (2) of Legislative Decree No. 81/2015.

Similarly in the past, the possibility for the employer to require working hours exceeding the normal working hours was limited to the vertical and mixed forms of part-time working,[9] while the current regulation generally allows for overtime in part-time employment.[10] The legal and contractual rules concerning overtime in full-time employment, as laid down in Article 5, Legislative Decree No. 66/2003, will apply to part-time workers, though this is not expressly provided for in Legislative Decree No. 81/2015, as was previously the case, in Legislative Decree No. 61/2000.[11]

As a result, the new regulatory framework makes it possible not only to perform supplementary work and overtime for any type of part-time employment, but also to combine supplementary work and overtime.

7. Article 3, para. 1, Legislative Decree No. 61/2000.
8. Article 6, para. 1, Legislative Decree No. 81/2015.
9. Article 3 (5), Legislative Decree No. 61/2000.
10. Article 6 (3), Legislative Decree No. 81/2015.
11. *See* Art. 3 (5), Legislative Decree No. 61/2000.

Another significant change relates to the role of collective bargaining, since the limit to the imposition of supplementary work is covered in general terms by compliance with the provisions of the collective agreement,[12] while Articles 3 (2) and (4) of Legislative Decree No. 61/2000 laid down detailed powers for collective agreements.[13]

In order to promote the use of supplementary work, the legislator has adopted a specific regulation, to be applied when 'the collective agreement applied to the employment relationship does not regulate supplementary work' (Article 6 (2) Legislative Decree No. 81/2015).

The legal regulation is supplementary and, as a result, does not apply if there are norms governing supplementary work laid down in collective agreements, meaning, for all flexible employment contracts pursuant to Article 51 of Legislative Decree No. 81/2015, collective agreements signed at national, local or company level by the negotiating agents indicated by the norm.[14]

According to the current legal regulation, the employer may require the worker to perform supplementary work to an extent not exceeding 25% of the agreed weekly working hours, and in this case is required to remunerate the supplementary work with a rate of pay increased by 15%, including the application of the increased rate of pay to indirect and deferred wage components.

Another important aspect of the new supplementary legal regulation, which introduces an entirely new principle, concerns the strengthening of the employer's unilateral power to require supplementary work.[15] The worker is entitled to turn down the employer's request to work extra hours – avoiding any disciplinary consequence, including dismissal – only on the basis of the justified requirements listed in the legal provision, which are 'work, health, family, or vocational training'.[16]

If the employee cannot appeal to any of the above-mentioned circumstances, he/she will have to perform hours of work in excess of those agreed between the parties in the part-time contract and within the normal working-hour limit as required by the employer.

On the contrary, according to the previous regulation, in the absence of regulation by collective agreement, it was always necessary to obtain the worker's consent to carry out supplementary work, pursuant to Article 3 (3) of the Legislative Decree No. 61/2000, which also provided that the employee's refusal to perform supplementary work could not in any case constitute justified grounds for dismissal.

---

12. *See* Art. 6 (1) Legislative Decree No. 81/2015.
13. These competences concerned: the determination of the maximum number of supplementary work hours allowed and the reasons for their lawful use; the consequences of failing to comply with the limit on supplementary working hours; the possibility to foresee a pay increase for supplementary work and to establish its implications for wages, including its indirect and deferred components.
14. The negotiating parties on the workers' side can be the comparatively most representative trade unions at the national level and their representatives at company level (RSA) or the elected unitary representative body at company level (RSU).
15. As far as overtime is concerned, the employer has to apply to part-time workers the same rules pertaining to full-timers. As a result, the same principles of mutual consent apply, except when the obligation to work overtime is prescribed by the collective agreement or established by law in particular cases (Art. 5 (2–4), Legislative Decree No. 66/2003).
16. Article 6 (2) Legislative Decree No. 81/2015.

[B] 'Flexibility Clauses'

Other key flexibility tools in organizing part-time work provided in the interest of the employer, are the 'flexibility clauses' (*clausole elastiche*), which, if included in the part-time contract of employment, allow the employer to increase working hours.

As in the case of supplementary work, the current regulation of flexibility clauses refers only in general terms to compliance with the provisions of collective agreements, thus dealing with the issues arising from Article 3 (7), Legislative Decree No. 61/2000.[17] However, there is still a specific competence in collective bargaining concerning the determination of compensatory measures for workers who accept these clauses in part-time contracts; as before, these measures are not necessarily of an economic nature.

This competence granted to collective agreements is laid down in Article 6 (7), Legislative Decree No. 81/2015, which appears to be ambiguous, and have thus attracted the attention of scholars. While the related provision in the previous regulations established that the worker's right to compensatory measures arose in the case of the exercise of the employer's power to modify the timing or duration of part-time work, the new provision can be interpreted as upholding the right to compensatory measures merely on the basis of the stipulation of flexibility clauses.

According to Article 6 (5), 'in the cases referred to in section 4, the employee is entitled to a notice period of two working days, subject to any other arrangement between the parties, as well as to specific compensatory measures, to the extent and in the forms prescribed by collective agreements' (Article 6 (5), Legislative Decree No. 81/2015). In fact, the cases dealt with in section 4 consist of the stipulation of flexibility clauses.[18]

This interpretation has attracted criticism considering that even the worker's right to the notice period relates to the cases mentioned in section 4, but such a right can be established only when the employer effectively exercises the power to modify the timing or the duration of the part-time work. A further criticism relates to Article 6 (6) of Legislative Decree No. 81/2015, according to which a wage premium has to be paid when real changes are made to working time.[19]

As already seen in the case of supplementary work, the new legal regulation of flexibility clauses plays only a supplementary role, since it applies only in the absence of collective agreement provisions on this matter at any level.

First and foremost, it is laid down that the extension of the duration of the part-time work, agreed with the inclusion of the flexibility clauses in the contract of employment, may not exceed 25% of the normal annual working hours specified in the

17. These competences concerned the determination of: the conditions that the employer had to respect to use the two types of flexibility clauses; the maximum limit on extending the duration of working hours; the conditions that gave the worker the possibility to ask for the elimination or the modification of the flexibility clauses.
18. Stefano Bellomo, *supra*, 32.
19. Vito Leccese, *Il lavoro a tempo parziale nel d.lgs. n. 81/2015*, in L. Fiorillo, A. Perulli (eds), *Tipologie contrattuali e la nuova disciplina delle mansioni*, vol. III de *Il nuovo diritto del lavoro*, directed by L. Fiorillo, A. Perulli, Torino, Giappichelli, 2015, 55–56.

part-time contract. Moreover, the wage increase to be granted when the originally agreed working time is modified is set at 15% of the overall wage, including the application of the extra pay to indirect and deferred wage components.

Unlike the legal regulation of supplementary work, with regard to flexibility clauses, the necessity of the worker's consent was not only maintained, but also assisted by a system of safeguards. Under Article 6 (6) of Legislative Decree No. 81/2015, in the event that the collective agreement applied to the employment contract does not regulate flexibility clauses, these clauses may be agreed in writing by the parties before a certification panel, and the worker has the right to be assisted either by a representative of the union, a lawyer or an employment specialist.

In this regard, it is true that, as repeatedly pointed out, Legislative Decree No. 81/2015 finally sets aside the need for a double consensus, individual and collective, as a necessary means for the adoption of flexibility clauses. On the other hand, the new provision provides reinforced protection for workers,[20] since it not only establishes that the clauses agreed in the individual contract of employment are null and void when they do not respect the prescribed conditions of employment, but it also provides for a minimum legislative framework, which limits the autonomy of the parties to the employment relationship in determining the terms of the contract.

[1] The Worker's Right to 'Reconsider'

To complete the analysis of the flexibility clauses, it has to be stressed that the legislator has also reshaped the regulation concerning the worker's right to revoke the previously expressed consent to perform part-time work in a flexible way (Article 6 (7), Legislative Decree No. 81/2015).

The right to 'reconsider', clearly aimed at protecting the worker's needs referred to in the Constitutional Court judgment No. 210/1992,[21] was foreseen in Legislative Decree No. 61/2000, but suppressed by Legislative Decree No. 276/2003, and finally reinstated by Act No. 92/2012.

According to the Fornero reform (2012), the employee who found himself/herself 'under the circumstances referred to in Article 12-*bis* of this Decree or in those referred to in Article 10, first paragraph, Act No 300, 20 May 1970'[22] was granted the right to

20. For a different opinion, *see* Rosario Santucci, *Il contratto di lavoro* part-time *all'epoca del* jobs act*: un agguato gattopardesco?*, in Studi in onore di De Luca Tamajo, forthcoming.
21. In the well-known ruling No. 210/1992, the Italian Constitutional Court established that the working hours of a part-time worker should be organized so that he or she has the possibility to perform another part-time job in order to earn a sufficient wage and an adequate retirement provision (Arts. 36 and 38 of the Italian Constitution) or to balance work with personal life.
22. The circumstances referred to in Article 12-*bis* of Legislative Decree No. 61/2000 and in Art. 10, (1) of Act No 300, 20 May 1970, concern: workers affected by oncological disease, with a reduced working capacity, also caused by invalidating treatment; workers whose spouse, children or parents are affected by oncological disease; workers who live and take care of a person with total and permanent inability to work; workers who live with children who are below the age of 13 years or disabled; student-workers attending courses of primary or secondary school courses or in vocational training.

withdraw his/her consent to perform part-time work under flexible arrangements.[23] The Fornero reform also assigned a significant role to collective bargaining with respect to the determination of additional cases or forms of worker protection.[24] However, while some collective agreements simply confirmed the conditions required by the law to allow the worker to exercise the right to reconsider, other collective agreements introduced specific limits to the exercise of that right, such as any procedural requirements to be subject to observation or a maximum percentage of entitled employees to be met.[25]

The legal regulation of the right to reconsider was reinstated in Legislative Decree No. 81/2015 and even extended in scope to include workers affected by chronical degenerative disease or whose spouse, children or parents are affected by such a condition (*infra*, section 7.03). On the contrary, any reference to collective agreements on this matter was deleted, meaning that the limitations to the exercise of the right to reconsider provided in the collective agreements still in force can no longer be applied in the circumstances regulated by the Legislative Decree.[26]

§7.03 TOOLS OF FLEXIBILITY PROVIDED IN THE INTEREST OF THE PART-TIME WORKER: TRANSFERRING FROM FULL-TIME TO PART-TIME AND VICE VERSA

As far as the flexibility instruments adopted in the interest of the worker are concerned, due attention has to be given to the legal regulation on transferring from full-time employment to part-time (and vice versa), which is dealt with in Article 8, Legislative Decree No. 81/2015.

First, the new legal regulation foresees an extension of the cases in which the employee's request to transform his/her employment from full-time to part-time cannot be refused by the employer. This right is granted not only to workers in the public and private sectors affected by oncological diseases, already covered by Article 12-*bis* (1), Legislative Decree No. 61/2000, but also to those who are suffering from 'serious chronic degenerative and deteriorating diseases, entailing a loss of working capacity'.[27] This provision has certainly extended the scope of the right to transfer from full-time to part-time, although it cannot be denied that having considered, among the serious diseases, only those involving a progressive deterioration constitutes a restriction on the exercise of that right.[28] If the employee so requests, the employee has to be transferred back to full-time.

23. Article 3, para. 9, Legislative Decree No. 61/2000, as amended by Act No. 92/2012.
24. Article 3, para. 7, n. 3-*bis*, Legislative Decree No. 61/2000.
25. *See*, for example, the following collective agreements: Alimentaristi (Confindustria) 27 Oct. 2012 and Laterizi (Confindustria) 24 Jun. 2013.
26. *See* Leccese, *supra*, ss. 62.
27. Article 8 (3), Legislative Decree No. 81/2015.
28. *See*, on the draft decree, Silvia Fernández Martínez e Fabiola Silvaggi, *Jobs Act e part-time: l'estensione di un diritto per i malati cronici*, in *Bollettino Adapt*, 2 Mar. 2015, *www.bollettino-adapt.it*.

The legislator also introduced the right to opt for part-time work instead of taking parental leave, but setting some limits. In fact, the provision imposes a cap on working-time reduction, which cannot exceed 50% of normal working hours; moreover, this right has to be exercised within the period of parental leave and, finally, the request to transfer to part-time work instead of taking parental leave can be made to the employer 'only once'.[29] With reference to this latter provision, a less rigid interpretation of the prescription has been proposed. Since the norm establishes that the period of part-time work does not necessary coincide with the entire period of parental leave, but can be chosen 'within the limits of the still available period of parental leave', in the case in which the worker has chosen to transfer his from full-time to part-time for a shorter period than those time limits, then he/she cannot exercise this right for 'the second time' *for the same child*. However, he/she will still be able to exercise the right to transfer to part-time work instead of taking parental leave in the future, for another child.[30]

There is another possibility in which part-time is an option, which has been introduced, however, by Legislative Decree No. 80/2015, Article 24, which regulates leave for women victims of domestic violence, establishing, among other things, that these workers 'are entitled to transfer from full-time employment to part-time, vertical or horizontal,[31] if there is a suitable vacancy in the workplace' (Article 24 (6), Legislative Decree No. 80/2015). Also in this case, as in the case of workers suffering from oncological diseases or serious chronic degenerative and deteriorating diseases, at the request of the worker, the part-time position must be reconverted into full-time (Article 24 paragraph 6).

Other modifications in the legal regulation affect the situations in which the worker has not a right but only a priority to transform his/her employment relationship from full-time to part-time.[32] On the one hand, this priority is now given to the workers whose children (or parents) are suffering from serious degenerative conditions. As for the cases in which the worker assists a cohabitant with total and permanent incapacity for work, considered to be severe under Article 3 (3) Act No. 104/1992, it is no longer necessary for the partner's degree of disability to be recognized as equal to 100%, but this person should be in need of 'continuous care due to the fact of not being able to carry out daily tasks of life'.

Finally, there has been an amendment of the rules relating to the worker's right to priority for the transfer from part-time to full-time,[33] in order to adapt the existing regulation to the amendment of Article 2103 of the Civil Code.[34] The new provision foresees that an employee who has been transferred from full-time to part-time has priority in applying for employment on a full-time contract, not only to carry out the

29. Article 8 (7), Legislative Decree No. 81/2015.
30. Leccese, *supra*, 70–71, Bavaro, *supra*, 230–31.
31. Referring to different forms of part-time work, this provision does not appear to be consistent with the modification of the definition of part-time work introduced by Art. 4, Legislative Decree No. 81/2015 (*supra*, para. 1).
32. Article 8 (4–5), Legislative Decree No. 81/2015.
33. The previous regulation was provided in Art. 12-*ter*, Legislative Decree No. 61/2000.
34. Article 2103 of the Civil Code was amended by Art. 3, Legislative Decree No. 81/2015.

same tasks, but also all the 'tasks of the same level and legal category'.[35] The previous text made reference to all the tasks 'equivalent' to those performed under part-time employment. As a result, if can be argued that, based on the new wording of Article 2103 of the Civil Code,[36] the employer's unilateral power to modify the worker's tasks has been extended. It should be pointed out that the right to a priority for the transfer from part-time to full-time employment has been extended as well, as a result of the legislative change.

§7.04 CONCLUDING REMARKS

As for the aim to rationalize and simplify the regulatory framework stratified over the years, common to the entire project of reorganization of non-standard employment contracts implemented by the present Government, the result can be said to be achieved for part-time contracts as well. The same conclusion cannot be reached, however, with regard to overcoming the ambiguous multipurpose value of part-time work.[37]

The overall result of the 2015 regulatory intervention, with particular reference to the tools of the temporal variability of part-time work, can be acknowledged as allowing an increased use of supplementary work, overtime and flexibility clauses, that confirms the legislative tendency to adapt part-time contracts mainly to the organizational requirements of the employers, rather than enhance the work-life balance needs of the workers, which have been only slightly strengthened.

On the other hand, taking into account the incentives for collective agreements based on the concept of 'expansive solidarity', signed at company level pursuant to Article 41, Legislative Decree No. 148/2015, which provides for a reduction in working hours for the workers already employed by a company to enable the employer to hire new workers, and the regulation of part-time work for older workers close to retirement introduced by the 2016 Stability Law (Article 1 (284) Act No. 208/2015), it may be argued that, ultimately, part-time work is increasingly attracting the interest of the legislator as a means to combat unemployment.

35. Article 8 (6), Legislative Decree No. 81/2015.
36. Article 2103 of the Civil Code was amended by Art. 3, Legislative Decree No. 81/2015.
37. Laura Calafà, *Il lavoro a tempo parziale (artt. 4–12)*, in Franco Carinci (ed.), *Commento al d.lgs. 15 giugno 2015, n. 81: le tipologie contrattuali e lo jus variandi*, Adapt Labour Studies e-Book series n. 48/2015, ss 98 (2015).

CHAPTER 8

Well-Being at and Through Digital Work?

Marco Tufo[*]

§8.01 INTRODUCTION

The exponential increase of the use of Information and Communication Technology in the workplace since the 1980s has given rise to new questions for labour law. In this discussion, telework has been one of the most debated topics, attracting the attention of sociologists, economists and labour lawyers[1] due to its potential to modify the concepts of place, time and work in traditional work performance.[2]

In particular, the positive and negative aspects of telework have been underlined so many times over the past forty years[3] that they have 'made scholars sick'.[4] Among

* Ph.D. candidate, Marco Biagi Foundation, University of Modena and Reggio Emilia, marcotufo88@gmail.com.

1. The discussion on telework as a legal topic emerged later than in economics and sociology because of the slowness of law in qualifying new social phenomena, like the introduction of Information and Communication Technology in production processes (Marco Biagi & Tiziano Treu, *Lavoro e Information Technology: riflessioni sul caso italiano*, 1 Diritto delle Relazioni Industriali, 5 (2002); Pietro Ichino, *I problemi giuridici del telelavoro*, 75 Notiziario del lavoro, 47–52 (1995). The first research into telework and labour law dates back to the mid-1980s (Lorenzo Gaeta, *Prime osservazioni sulla qualificazione giuridica del (telelavoro)*, *Lavoro 80*, 344 et seq. (1986), whereas this concept came into use around a decade earlier (*see* Jack M. Nilles, F. Roy Carlson Jr., Paul Gray, Gerhard J. Hanneman, *The telecommunications-Transportation Tradeoff. Options for tomorrow*, John Wiley & Sons, New York, London, Sidney, Toronto (1976). During the 1990s, more research into telework was carried out (e.g., Lorenzo Gaeta, *Il telelavoro: legge e contrattazione*, 4 Giornale di Diritto del lavoro e di Relazioni Industriali, 547–581 (1995) and Gino Giugni, *È necessario, subito un altro (tele-)statuto*, 2 *Telèma*, 46 et seq. (1995).
2. Lorenzo Gaeta, *Il telelavoro: legge e contrattazione*, *supra*, 547.
3. An important contribution was made by Jack M. Nilles, F. Roy Carlson Jr., Paul Gray, Gerhard J. Hanneman, *supra*, who, seeking a solution to reduce transport costs and commuting, after the 1973 oil crisis, proposed replacing commuting with working from home using ICT. The idea of 'telecommuting', or, as it was later called, 'telework', came into being.
4. Patrizio Di Nicola, *Impiegati in pantofole*, 6 Liberetà, 56–57 (1996).

the advantages for society in general, we can mention: the reduction of pollution;[5] the reduction of transport costs; the potential for rural[6] and depressed areas,[7] in addition to the advantages for employers and workers. First of all, ICT makes work performance more flexible and enables employers to save on workplace costs.[8] Second, workers enjoy greater flexibility, achieving a better work-life balance and avoiding commuting.[9] Moreover, disadvantaged categories such as people with disabilities,[10] women, older workers[11] and ex-detainees[12] could benefit from more opportunities for inclusion. Among the disadvantages, the most significant concerns working conditions. Working away from the employer's premises does not mean not working at all, spending time on family duties. Conversely, the risk of becoming a workaholic is high, as well as that of not observing good practices to protect the health and safety of the worker, due to the difficulty for teleworkers to manage their work outside the firm without the direct supervision of the employer.[13] Another risk of telework is isolation. Distance from work makes it more difficult to socialise with colleagues and take part in trade union activities, while also tending to reduce the prospects of promotion.[14]

In spite of the ongoing debate on these issues, the legal and theoretical framework still seems vague and confusing. Taking into account the advantages of telework mentioned above, the use of ICT is frequently regarded as something positive and able to create more and better jobs. However, it appears that the protection of digital workers is often missing in institutional discussions, overlooking the risk that ICT can make labour law ineffective in some cases.

This paper provides an overview of the legal framework on telework in the European Union, to assess whether the current regulation offers suitable responses to problems emerging from digital work. First of all the evolution of telework in the EU debate will be outlined; second, an assessment will be made of the effectiveness of the European telework rules, namely the European Framework Agreement of 2002 (EFA on Telework), in the Member States; finally, some solutions will be proposed to regulate the digital labour market.

5. Alan Denbigh, *The Teleworking handbook. The essential guide to working from where you want*, A & C Black, London, 4th ed., 4 (2003); Patrizio Di Nicola, *Contrattare il telelavoro*, 3 Lavoro e Diritto, 494 (1997); *id.*, *Impiegati in pantofole*.
6. Alan Denbigh, *supra*, 12; Vittorio Di Martino & Linda Wirth, *Telework: a new way of working and living*, 129 (5) International Labour Review, 532–533 (1990).
7. Patrizio Di Nicola, *Impiegati in pantofole*, *supra*.
8. Alan Denbigh, *supra*; Patrizio Di Nicola, *Contrattare il telelavoro*, *supra*; *ibid.*, *Impiegati in pantofole*; Ursula Huws, Werner B. Korte & Simon Robinson, *Telework. Towards the Elusive Office*, John Wiley & Sons, Chichester, (1990); Vittorio Di Martino & Linda Wirth, *supra*.
9. Alan Denbigh, *supra*; Ursula Huws, Werner B. Korte & Simon Robinson, *supra*.
10. Vittorio Di Martino & Linda Wirth, *supra*, 532.
11. Alan Denbigh, *supra*, 12–13.
12. Giuseppe Cassano & Stefania Lopatriello, *Il telelavoro: profili giuridici e sociologici*, 2 Il Diritto dell'Informazione e dell'Informatica, 2, 398 (1998).
13. Giuseppe Cassano & Stefania Lopatriello, *supra*, 399; Patrizio Di Nicola, *Contrattare il telelavoro*, *supra*, 494–495; *id.*, *Impiegati in pantofole*.
14. Alan Denbigh, *supra*; Giuseppe Cassano & Stefania Lopatriello, *supra*; Ursula Huws, Werner B. Korte & Simon Robinson, *supra*.

§8.02 FROM THE SOCIAL TO THE LEGAL DIMENSION OF TELEWORK

Starting from sociological theories, the European Community began to pay attention to telework in the first half of the 1990s, due to the increasing importance of telework as a social phenomenon[15]. The first European documents on telework focused, on the one hand, on encouraging the spread of Information Technologies and teleworking with the aim of making Europe more competitive in the global market.[16] In this perspective, the positive economic aspects of telework such as productivity gains, increased flexibility and cost savings for companies and public administrations were emphasised. On the other hand, the advantages for employees were stressed, such as 'more flexible working arrangements for all those tied to the home, and for people living in remote locations', as well as the benefits for the general public, namely the reduction of pollution levels, traffic congestion and energy consumption.[17] However, the negative aspects of telework were downplayed and generally identified in terms of the isolation and privacy of workers[18] and the impact of ICT on labour legislation and social security provisions.[19] This optimistic vision of telework led the members of the High Level Group on the Information Society, which presented the Bangemann report on 24–25 June 1994 at the meeting in Corfu to set the following objectives: 'Create pilot teleworking centres in 20 cities by end 1995 involving at least 20,000 workers. The aim is for 2 % of white-collar workers to be teleworkers by 1996; 10 million teleworking jobs by the year 2000'.[20]

The idea of promoting Information and Communication Technology and telework in Europe, while downplaying the negative aspects, was adopted by the Commission of European Communities, which adopted an official position with a Communication to the Council, the European Parliament, the Economic and Social Committee and the Committee of Regions.[21] This Communication was conceived as an action plan to develop policies promoting the spread of the information society in the Member States.[22]

---

15. Commission of the European Communities, *Growth, competitiveness, employment. The challenges and ways forward into the 21st century. White paper*, 6 Bulletin of the European Communities, 93 (1993). The Commission of European Communities had already highlighted 'the potential of telework "to reduce the social and economic gap between urban and rural, central and peripheral regions"' in the report on 'Opportunities for applications of information and communication technologies in rural areas', published in 1989, as discussed by Vittorio Di Martino & Linda Wirth, *supra*, 532–533.
16. *See* Martin Bangemann et al., *Bangemann Report, Europe and the Global Information Society. Recommendations to the European Council*, Brussels (1994); Commission of the European Communities, *supra*, 92 et seq.
17. Martin Bangemann et al., *supra*, 29.
18. Commission of the European Communities, *supra*, 93.
19. Martin Bangemann et al., *supra*, 29.
20. *Ibid.* This project was not entirely successful, considering that in 1997 just 1% of EU workers were teleworkers (Antonio Lo Faro, *Politiche comunitarie e diritto internazionale*, in Lorenzo Gaeta & Paolo Pascucci (eds.), *Telelavoro e diritto*, Giappichelli, Turin, 221, fn 10 (1998).
21. Commission of the European Communities, *Europe's way to the information society: an action plan. Communication from the Commission to the Council and the European Parliament and to the Economic and Social Committee and the Committee of Regions*, Brussels (1994).
22. Commission of the European Communities, *supra*, 3.

This Communication can be taken as the starting point of the discussion of telework from a legal point of view. The European Parliament responded to the document with a Resolution in 1996,[23] outlining its point of view on the Information Society and criticising the optimistic vision of the Commission.[24] In particular, the European Parliament stressed the lack of a legal framework providing protection from the negative aspects of new technologies and the need to adopt common policies to avoid the marginalisation of vulnerable groups such as low-paid and unskilled workers, migrants, older workers, persons with disabilities, peripheral and ultra-peripheral regions, women and young women.[25] Furthermore, the European Parliament was aware of the possible increase in social dumping and deregulation, flexibilisation and individualisation due to the globalising and decentralising effects of Information and Communication Technology.[26] A legal framework concerning the information society was intended to be adopted at supranational level to deal with a phenomenon that was evidently global.[27] Turning its attention to telework, the European Parliament underlined the need for research on the effects of video display units on the health of teleworkers, with the aim of establishing a code of practice for their protection, and the need to give teleworkers a legal employment status, with a European Directive to ensure that they would enjoy the same rights as other employees.[28] Moreover, the Directive on telework was to address the effects of telework on housing, child-care, and privacy, with particular attention to the 'apparently' self-employed and employees with insufficient social insurance.[29] The proposals put forward by the European Parliament resulted in the extension of the debate on the information society and telework to Member States and social actors.

Also significant is the Green Paper of 1996 in which the Commission pointed to the need to further develop the political dialogue with European Institutions and Member States and to stimulate social dialogue on these themes.[30] The trade unions began to take note of the pressure from the Commission. The ETUC proposed basing the regulation of telework on certain pillars such as: its reversible and voluntary character; the classification of teleworkers as employees; the conservation of the economic and normative status in the transfer to telework; health protection for

23. European Parliament, *Resolution on 'Europe and the global information society — Recommendations to the European Council' and on a communication from the Commission of the European Communities: 'Europe's way to the information society: an action plan'*, 39 Official journal of the European Communities, 164–176 (1996).
24. 'The Commission's policy with regard to the information society has for too long had an economic slant, with technological developments given prominence; [...] there has been no questioning of who such developments serve, what they signify for the citizens and [...] there has been no dialogue on developments which will radically alter all our lives, although an in-depth dialogue is taking place with industry' (Commission of the European Communities, *Green paper. Living and working in the Information Society: people first*, Brussels, 165, H (1996).
25. European Parliament, *supra*, 164.
26. European Parliament, *supra*, 165.
27. *Ibid.*
28. European Parliament, *supra*, 171, points 57–58, 72.
29. European Parliament, *supra*, 172, point 72.
30. Commission of the European Communities, *Green paper. Living and working in the Information Society: people first*, *supra*, 7.

teleworkers; negotiation with the trade unions on the introduction of telework in enterprises; the ratification of the ILO Convention on Homework, no. 177/1996, by the Member States.[31] As a result, the debate about telework was now more focused on the legal consequences, even though the social dimension was still prevalent.[32]

§8.03 THE GUIDELINES FROM SECTORAL SOCIAL DIALOGUE

The intention of stimulating the social parties to discuss the information society as indicated in the Green Paper was reinforced by the European Employment Strategy adopted in Luxembourg in November 1997,[33] as a continuation of the first Guidelines on Employment adopted at the Essen meeting in 1994, extended at the Lisbon European Council in March 2000.[34] The idea was to deal with the 'knowledge-driven economy' and its consequences in terms of globalisation through the modernisation of the labour market towards flexicurity,[35] promoting job quality with 'more and better jobs' to combat social exclusion.[36] This objective, reflecting the need to close the technology gap between Europe and other global competitors (especially the US),[37] was pursued through the 'open method of coordination' (OMC), laid down as the general method of regulation for employment policies by Article 128 of the EC Treaty and for all the main social policy areas after the Lisbon European Council.[38] The role of social parties was considered fundamental both to modernise the labour market through collective agreements and to collaborate with the Member States to adapt the existing legislation to changes in the economy.[39]

In the European Employment Strategy, telework was seen to be an important flexicurity tool, due to its potential to modernise work organisation, to reconcile work and social life, and to facilitate the integration of disadvantaged workers into the labour market. On this basis, in July 1997 the Commission stated that a consultation with the social partners on whether and to what extent Community action on the protection of teleworkers was advisable, starting in 1998.[40] As a result, action was taken through sectoral social dialogue. In 1998 the Commission established the Sectoral Dialogue

31. Antonio Lo Faro, *Politiche comunitarie e diritto internazionale, supra*, 224.
32. European Commission, *Building the European Information Society for us all. Final policy report of the high-level expert group*, Luxembourg (1997); European Commission, *Partnership for a new organization of work*, 4 Bulletin of the European Union, 21 (1997).
33. Marco Biagi & Tiziano Treu, *supra*, 6.
34. Massimo Roccella & Tiziano Treu, *Diritto del lavoro dell'Unione Europea*, Cedam, Padua, 23–24 (2012).
35. European Council, *Lisbon European Council 23 and 24 March. Presidency conclusions*, Lisbon (2000).
36. European Council, *supra*; Michele Faioli, *Telelavoro, Postilla di aggiornamento*, in *Enciclopedia giuridica Treccani*, Rome, 2 (2002).
37. Massimo Roccella & Tiziano Treu, *supra*, 30.
38. Massimo Roccella & Tiziano Treu, *supra*, 24.
39. European Council, *Council Decision of 19 January 2001 on Guidelines for Member States' employment policies for the year 2001*, Brussels, points 13–14 (2001).
40. Commission of the European Communities, *Communication from the Commission on The social and global market dimension of the Information Society. People first - The next steps*, Brussels (1997).

Committees to promote social dialogue pursuant to Articles 138 and 139 of the EC Treaty.[41] Particularly, in 2000[42] the Sectoral Dialogue Committee on Telecommunications Services replaced the Joint Committee set up in 1990.[43] At the Lisbon European Council in March 1990, the objective of drawing up guidelines on telework was set for the Committee.[44] After a brief negotiation,[45] the Guidelines for Telework in Europe were released in February 2001.[46] These Guidelines laid down a series of principles aimed at the protection of teleworkers, such as the voluntary nature of telework and equal treatment between teleworkers and employees working on the company premises.[47] However, as a soft law tool, the Guidelines were not binding, thus it was 'recommended' that they be adopted by the telecommunications companies in Europe by the end of 2001, 'on a voluntary basis and according to each country's laws and collective bargaining practices'.[48] In addition, they asked for the conclusion of collective agreements 'at the appropriate level (e.g., industrial, company) in order to provide a framework for the introduction of individual telework arrangements'.[49]

§8.04 THE EFA ON TELEWORK: VOLUNTARY...

A second action was taken within the cross-industry Social Dialogue. The European Commission, in the second stage of consultations with the social partners on modernising and improving employment relations, invited the social partners to start negotiations on telework, following the mechanism of Article 138 of the EC Treaty. On 20 September 2001, the ETUC, UNICE/UEAPME and CEEP announced their intention to start negotiations, pursuant to Article 139(1) EC Treaty.[50] In December 2001 they presented a joint contribution to the Laeken European Council, held on 14–15 December, clarifying their intention to develop 'a spectrum of diversified instruments (various types of European framework agreement, opinions, recommendations, statements, exchanges of experience, awareness-raising campaigns, open debates, etc.)'[51]

---

41. *See* Commission Decision no. 98/500/EC.
42. Buatier de Mongeot, *Le linee guida sul telelavoro*, 1 Diritto delle Relazioni Industriali, 19 (2002).
43. *See* Art. 7, Commission Decision no. 98/500/EC. The Joint Committee on Telecommunications Services was established with Commission Decision no. 90/450/EEC. According to Art. 3 of the Decision, its duties, concerning telecommunications services, were: (a) to issue opinions and submit reports to the Commission, either at the latter's request or on its own initiative; (b) to promote dialogue and cooperation between the employers and employees associations; (c) to arrange for studies to be carried out, participate in discussions and seminars.
44. Buatier de Mongeot, *supra*, 20.
45. *See* Buatier de Mongeot, *supra*, 21.
46. On 21 Apr. 2001 Eurocommerce and Uni-Europa signed an agreement on Guidelines for telework, as commented on by Massimo Roccella & Tiziano Treu, *supra*, 273.
47. Sectoral Dialogue Committee on Telecommunications Services, *Guidelines for telework in Europe*, Brussels, 2–3 (2001).
48. Sectoral Dialogue Committee on Telecommunications Services, *supra*, 3.
49. Sectoral Dialogue Committee on Telecommunications Services, *supra*, 2.
50. European Framework Agreement on Telework, Art. 1.
51. ETUC, UNICE, CEEP, Joint contribution by the social partners to the Laeken European Council, 3 (2001).

and a 'more autonomous social dialogue'[52]. Finally, the European Framework Agreement on Telework (EFA on Telework) was signed on 16 July 2002.

The contents of that Agreement replicate and extend the principles of the Guidelines. The voluntary nature of telework and equal treatment between teleworkers and comparable workers at the employers premises are confirmed, both at a collective and an individual level, even if the possibility to carry out specific complementary collective and/or individual agreements is presented, 'in order to take into account the particularities of telework'.[53] In addition, privacy, equipment, organisational, health and safety and training rules are laid down, with a view to protecting teleworkers.[54]

Although the legal regulation of telework is undoubtedly a significant part of the Agreement, two further aspects are worth underlining. The first concerns the definition of telework. The Agreement considers telework as 'a form of organising and/or performing work, using information technology, in the context of an employment contract/relationship, where work, which could also be performed at the employers premises, is carried out away from those premises on a regular basis'.[55] In this sense, the EFA on Telework applies only 'in the framework of an employment contract or an employment relationship and on a regular basis', so that 'the framework agreement does not cover self-employed teleworkers and occasional telework' but 'if there is no formal employment contract but an employment relationship, the agreement applies anyhow'.[56] This means that, as argued by most scholars,[57] telework can take any juridical form, even self-employment, as it is a form of work organisation. Thus, a correct legal definition of the relationship in the specific case is fundamental because only telework employment is covered by the EFA protections.

The second and more significant aspect is related to the nature of the Agreement which is defined as 'voluntary'[58] and 'autonomous'.

The first adjective refers to the fact that the EFA on Telework was the first agreement to use the 'first or voluntary route' of implementation in Article 139(2) EC Treaty (now Article 155(2), TFEU),[59] according to which the agreement 'shall be implemented in accordance with the procedures and practices specific to management and labour and the Member States'[60] (emphasis added). The meaning of this formula was debated at length because of the use of the auxiliary verb 'shall'.[61] According to the

52. *Supra*, 2.
53. EFA on Telework, Article Art. 4.
54. *See* EFA on Telework, Arts 6-10.
55. EFA on Telework, Article Art. 2.
56. ETUC, *Voluntary agreement on telework*, Brussels, 10 (2003). According to Massimo Roccella & Tiziano Treu, *supra*, 274, the Agreement conceives of the teleworker as a 'normal employee'.
57. Lorenzo Gaeta, *La qualificazione del rapporto*, in Lorenzo Gaeta, Paolo Pascucci (eds.), *Telelavoro e diritto*, Giappichelli, Turin, 1-22 (1998).
58. *See* EFA on Telework, Art. 1.
59. The other Framework Agreements implemented by the Social Partners are: the Agreement on Work-related Stress, signed on 8 Oct. 2004; the Agreement on Harassment and Violence at Work, signed on 21 Apr. 2007; the Agreement on Inclusive Labour Markets, signed on the 25 Mar. 2010.
60. It is intended to be implemented by the members of the signatory parties in the Member States but also in the countries of the European Economic Area, as provided in Art. 1 of the Agreement.
61. Marco Peruzzi, *Autonomy in European Social Dialogue*, 27 (1) International Journal of Comparative Labour Law and Industrial Relations, 14 (2011); Christina Niforou, *The role of trade*

Commission, this gives rise to a legal obligation to implement the agreement and 'for the signatory parties to exercise influence on their members in order to implement the European agreement'.[62] As Weiss points out,[63] some scholars have gone beyond this view, arguing that the voluntary agreements are not only binding between the concluding parties, but also for third parties, in particular the national social actors. In this perspective, implementation through collective agreements without *erga omnes* effects at national level would not be sufficient, and as a result extension mechanisms should be used or established where not available. Furthermore, in the specific case of the EFA on Telework, this view could be strengthened by the provision of a term (three years after the signature) for its implementation.[64] This opinion is firmly rejected by most scholars as it is rooted in the outdated and unrealistic idea of building a European collective bargaining system[65] by abolishing the differences among the Member State industrial relations systems.[66]

On the contrary, a number of factors can be invoked to claim the non-legally binding nature of these voluntary agreements.

First, 'European peak associations have no power or authority to enforce compliance of their national member organisations',[67] thus they cannot guarantee binding implementation by their affiliates also because of the lack of binding sanctions on non-compliant negotiation partners.[68]

Second, even if the European social partners could enforce on their affiliates the implementation of the voluntary agreement, a homogeneous transposition would be unlikely, due to the differences among Member State industrial relations traditions, and a legal binding effect at national level, because some Member States have neither high union densities nor legal *erga omnes* clauses.[69]

Third, when social dialogue was carried out for the Social Agreement annexed to the Maastricht Treaty, the Member States attached a Declaration[70] stating that 'the first of the arrangements for application of the agreements between management and

---

unions in the implementation of autonomous framework agreements, 87 Warwick Papers in Industrial Relations, Coventry, University of Warwick, 9 (2008).

62. Commission of the European Communities, *Communication from the Commission. Partnership for change in an enlarged Europe - Enhancing the contribution of European social dialogue*, Brussels, 16 (2004); *see also* Paul Verbruggen, *Does Co-Regulation Strengthen EU Legitimacy?*, 15 (4) European Law Journal, 440 (2009).
63. Manfred Weiss, *European Labour Law in Transition from 1985 to 2010*, 26 (1) International Journal of Comparative Labour Law and Industrial Relations, 13–14 (2010).
64. EFA on Telework, Art. 12.
65. European Social Dialogue is different from collective bargaining because 'wages and salaries, the focal issue of collective bargaining, as well as strikes and lock-outs, the threats of industrial action, are explicitly excluded from the procedural arrangements for social dialogue', according to Art. 137 EC Treaty (now Art. 153 TFEU), Berndt Keller, *Social Dialogue – The Specific Case of the European Union*, 24 (2) International Journal of Comparative Labour Law and Industrial Relations, 220 (2008).
66. Manfred Weiss, *supra*, 13–14.
67. Berndt Keller, *Social dialogues — the state of the art a decade after Maastricht*, 34 (5) Industrial Relations Journal, 415 (2003).
68. *Ibid.*
69. *Ibid.*
70. As stated in Art. 4(2).

labour at Community level [...] will consist in developing, by collective bargaining according to the rules of each Member State, the content of the agreements, and that consequently *this arrangement implies no obligation on the Member States to apply the agreements directly or to work out rules for their transposition, nor any obligation to amend national legislation in force to facilitate their implementation*' (emphasis added).

Fourth, the binding nature of the voluntary agreements could be seen as a violation of the principle of self-government of British industrial relations, according to which collective agreements enjoy the status of mere 'gentlemen's agreements'.[71]

Finally, management and labour have different conceptions about the nature of voluntary agreements. While UNICE[72] defined the EFA on Telework as a non-legally binding agreement,[73] the ETUC stated that 'In all cases the agreement should have a binding character'.[74] These different views reflect the imbalance of power between European management and labour. The employers have no interest in European regulation on social issues, seeking to dilute the impact of social policy measures.[75] On the other hand, labour has insufficient bargaining power to negotiate on important social issues due to the divergent interests of labour organisations across Europe and to the difficulties in developing traditional forms of industrial action, such as strikes.[76] As a result, UNICE prefers non-binding and soft law norms[77] and is hostile to legally binding regulation,[78] whereas the ETUC is more interested in strict and binding norms, such as Directives.[79] For these reasons, it is claimed that UNICE adopts a 'wait-and-see position' because its position on taking part in negotiations depends on the will of the Commission.[80] If the Commission threatens to take legislative action on a social issue,

71. Marco Peruzzi, *supra*, 14; Alan C. Neal, *The United Kingdom*, in Roger Blanpain (ed.), *European Framework Agreements and Telework. Law and Practice, A European and Comparative Study*, Kluwer Law International, Alphen aan den Rijn, 237–238 (2007).
72. UNICE, *UNICE offers negotiations on telework*, UNICE Press release, Brussels (2001).
73. This position was apparently motivated by UNICE, *supra* stating that telework would be 'a way of working, not a legal status', so that it could not be 'a theme for regulation at EU level' but only for 'voluntary negotiations [which] could [have] help[ed] develop telework in Europe'.
74. ETUC, *supra*, 8.
75. Ann Branch, *The Evolution of the European Social Dialogue Towards Greater Autonomy: Challenges and Potential Benefits*, 21 (2) International Journal of Comparative Labour Law and Industrial Relations, 335.
76. Stijn Smismans, *The European Social Dialogue in the Shadow of the Hierarchy*, 28 (1) Journal of Public Policy, 165 (2008).
77. Berndt Keller, *Social dialogues – the state of the art a decade after Maastricht, supra*, 423.
78. Christina Niforou, *supra*, 10.
79. Berndt Keller, *Social dialogues – the state of the art a decade after Maastricht, supra*, 423. These positions of management and labour emerged also during the negotiations for the EFA on Telework. According to Trine P. Larsen & Søren Kaj Andersen, *A new mode of European Regulation? The Implementation of the Autonomous Framework Agreement on Telework in Five Countries*, 13 (2) European Journal of Industrial Relations, 184 (2007) at first UNICE, reflecting the views of their British affiliate (the Confederation of British Industry), opposed any form of regulation, whereas CEEP was in favour of an autonomous agreement and the ETUC was divided (the Nordic affiliates shared the CEEP position, while the British Trades Union Congress and some continental unions preferred a directive). Thus, an important reason for the conclusion of a voluntary agreement in this case was that CEEP and UNICE would have accepted only a non-legal binding regulation.
80. Berndt Keller, *Social dialogues – the state of the art a decade after Maastricht, supra*, 423.

the employers enter into negotiations to avoid the risk of binding provisions; if not, negotiation is unlikely to start.[81]

§8.05 ...AND 'AUTONOMOUS' AGREEMENTS

Due to the controversy over the interpretation of 'voluntary',[82] since 2004 the Commission has started to define the agreements adopted through Article 139(2), EC Treaty as 'autonomous'.[83] This reflects the absence of the public authorities and legal mechanisms in the process of endorsement of and compliance with these agreements.[84] 'The Commission fully recognises the negotiating autonomy of the social partners on the topics falling within their competence',[85] namely bilateral negotiation between social partners without any interference by the Commission.[86] This kind of bargaining was an innovation when the EFA on Telework was signed, because until 2002 Social Dialogue had been developed 'in the shadow of the law',[87] that is under the threat of a legislative intervention by the Commission in case the social partners failed to conclude a voluntary agreement. In this sense, the Commission defined these agreements as 'new-generation texts',[88] to mark the difference compared to the previous agreements, implemented by Council Directives, according to the second route of implementation in Article 139(2) EC Treaty (now Article 155(2) TFEU). However, as Smismans points out,[89] the lack of the 'shadow of the law' in concluding this new kind of agreements does not mean that the 'shadow of hierarchy' is absent. Although the European social partners set their own agenda for Social Dialogue through their multiyear work programmes, the new-generation texts emerged only after Commission consultation or after the Commission made clear its intention to regulate a certain field. The Commission has played a more or less direct role even in the adoption of autonomous agreements. This is the case of the EFA on Telework where, as noted above, the Commission invited the social partners to start negotiations on telework.[90]

Taking these developments into account, autonomous agreements, and in particular the EFA on Telework, are considered 'soft law' tools with a 'recommendatory character',[91] or as codes of conduct that have only '"moral consequences" for the

81. Stijn Smismans, *supra*, 165.
82. Christina Niforou, *supra*, 9; Ann Branch, *supra*, 321, fn 1.
83. Commission of the European Communities, *supra*.
84. Christina Niforou, *supra*, 9.
85. Commission of the European Communities, *supra*, 10.
86. Berndt Keller, *Social Dialogue – The Specific Case of the European Union*, *supra*, 202.
87. This expression was used for the first time by Brian Bercusson, *The Dynamic of European Labour Law After Maastricht*, 1 *Industrial Law Journal*, 20 (1994) and it has been adopted by several authors since then (e.g., Berndt Keller, *Social Dialogue – The Specific Case of the European Union*, *supra*, 208; *id.*, *Social dialogues — – the state of the art a decade after Maastricht*, 414).
88. Commission of the European Communities, *supra*.
89. Stijn Smismans, *supra*, 164, 172.
90. Stijn Smismans, *supra*, 173.
91. Christina Niforou, *supra*, 10.

parties involved', also because they are not enforceable in the courts.[92] As a result they depend 'completely on the goodwill of the member organizations, who may implement the agreement at their will'.[93] After all, soft law has been seen as appropriate for subjects such as telework, which regard the development of new practices and tools at company level than protecting basic employee rights.[94] As Weiss claims,[95] autonomous agreements 'are nothing but an outline for the actors on national scale to give them some guidance and to enrich their imagination'. In other words, they are 'a European input promoting better coordination of collective bargaining on a national scale by offering ideas on how to cope with specific problems. The national social actors are supposed to reflect on the basis of the framework agreement'.[96] Thus, establishing a connection between the European social partners and the national social actors is crucial to reach that coordination of levels. The 'reporting system' at the end of EFA on Telework should be read in this sense. As a result, the provision according to which the European social partners should monitor the implementation of the agreement, entrusting an ad hoc group to prepare a joint report on the actions of implementation to be taken within four years of the date of the signature,[97] can be regarded as 'an institutionalised link between the national member organisations and the European social partner confederation to ensure follow-up'.[98]

In conclusion, the EFA on Telework has proposed a more autonomous social dialogue than was the case prior to 2002, even if the autonomy of the European social partners has been more concentrated in the phase of implementation (*see* next section), due to their commitment to implementing the agreement and monitoring follow-up by their affiliates, than in the phase of negotiations, where the shadow of the Commission was perceptible. On the other hand, the EFA on Telework reflects the gradual shift from hard law to soft law, as a result of the difficulty of legislating in the social field, considering the heterogeneous interests of the Member States.[99]

§8.06 THE IMPLEMENTATION OF THE EFA ON TELEWORK

Mention should be made of one further factor demonstrating the non-legal binding character of the EFA on Telework, in addition to those mentioned above: the effective implementation of the Agreement in the Member States after 2002. As noted in the previous section, Article 12 of the EFA on Telework laid down a period of three years

92. Roger Blanpain, *The European Social Dialogue And Voluntary Framework Agreements*, in Roger Blanpain (ed.), *European Framework Agreements and Telework. Law and Practice, A European and Comparative Study*, Kluwer Law International, Alphen aan den Rijn, 33 (2007); *id.*, *Belgium: Some Belgian and European aspects*, 24 Comparative Labor Law & Policy Journal, 47 et seq. (2002).
93. Roger Blanpain, *The European Social Dialogue And Voluntary Framework Agreements*, *supra*, 33.
94. Trine P. Larsen & Søren Kaj Andersen, *supra*, 184.
95. Manfred Weiss, *supra*, 14.
96. *Ibid.*
97. *See* EFA on Telework, Art. 12.
98. Stijn Smismans, *supra*, 175.
99. Manfred Weiss, *supra*, 15.

from 16 July 2002 for its implementation and a 'reporting system' to assess the follow-up in the four years after signature. On 28 June 2006 the Social Dialogue Committee adopted the report on the implementation of the EFA on Telework. The final assessment was generally positive but some issues emerged. It is worth discussing two of them here. First, only a small number of Member States (Italy, Hungary, the Netherlands, Spain and the UK) met the deadline.[100] Second, there was a considerable variety in the forms of implementation across Member States, so that the social partners identified 'two broad categories of implementation: collective agreements or other bilateral social partners' agreements on the one hand, and legislation or other types of tripartite activities on the other hand'.[101]

These two issues, namely the partial implementation of EFA on Telework and the variety of ways to follow-up the Agreement, can be considered still unresolved. Taking a general view of the current situation, the forms of implementation in the EU can be classified in four clusters:[102] countries that have implemented the Agreement through legislation (Bulgaria, the Czech Republic, Hungary, Lithuania, Poland, Portugal, Slovakia and Slovenia); countries that have adopted collective agreements (Austria, Belgium, Denmark, Germany, Greece, France, Italy, Luxembourg and Spain); countries that preferred soft law tools, such as joint guidelines, codes and recommendations (Croatia, Finland, Ireland, Latvia, the Netherlands, Sweden, the UK, Iceland and Norway);[103] and countries that have still not implemented the Agreement (Cyprus, Estonia, Malta and Romania). However, this classification shows only the main trend in each country because in some cases more than one type of measure was used during implementation and in other cases the method of implementation is different in the private and public sectors.[104]

[A] The 'Legislation Cluster'

Looking more closely at the countries in the 'legislation cluster', it may be said that they have all implemented the EFA on Telework through a reform of their Labour Codes or Laws on Labour Relations. However, a distinction should be made. Some countries,

100. Stefan Clauwaert, Wiebke Düvel & Isabelle Schömann, *Report on the implementation of the ETUC/UNICE-UEAPME/CEEP Framework agreement On TELEWORK. Executive Summary*, ETUI-REHS, Brussels, 4 et seq. (2005).

When the EFA on Telework was concluded the Member States were fifteen. In 2004 the new ten Member States, and then Romania and Bulgaria, which joined the European Union in 2007, were invited to implement the Agreement (ETUC, UNICE, CEEP, UEAPME, Implementation of the European Framework Agreement on Telework. Report by the European Social Partners, Brussels, 4 (2006)). This may partially explain the delays in the implementation in some Member States.

101. ETUC, UNICE, CEEP, UEAPME, *supra*, 7.
102. Nuria Ramos Martín & Jelle Visser, *A More 'Autonomous' European Social Dialogue: The Implementation of the Framework Agreement on Telework*, 24 (4) International Journal of Comparative Labour Law and Industrial Relations, 524 (2008).
103. This chapter will analyse the implementation process also in Iceland and Norway, as members of the European Economic Area.
104. Nuria Ramos Martín & Jelle Visser, *A More "Autonomous" European Social Dialogue: The Implementation of the Framework Agreement on Telework*, *supra*, 524.

such as the Czech Republic and Lithuania, do not provide a proper definition of telework because their regulations do not mention the use of Information Technology by workers. In this sense, the Czech Labour Code, approved in January 2007, states that its rules 'shall apply to the labour (employment) relationship of an employee who does not work at the employer's workplace (site) but who performs the agreed type of work under the laid down conditions within working time (working hours) which he organizes himself'.[105] Moreover, no information on possible definitions in company-level collective agreements is available about the Czech Republic.[106] Concerning Lithuania, Article 115 of the Labour Code provides that 'an employment contract may establish that an employee will perform the job functions agreed therein at home'.[107] Furthermore, due to the fact that, according to Article 115, 'The characteristics of employment contracts with homeworkers shall be established by the Government and collective agreements',[108] the Lithuanian Decree no. 1043 states that home working consists in 'work done by an individual at home for a wage agreed on with the employer'[109] and that 'Homeworkers shall be subjected to provisions laid down in the Labour Code and other legislation of the Republic of Lithuania together with exceptions set forth'[110] in the Decree. On the contrary, no collective agreements have been concluded by the social partners, because according to them 'there is no need for it'.[111] In other words, it may be said that in these two countries telework is considered to be a synonym of home working. Consequently, the EFA on Telework is deemed to be implemented through the rules governing home working.[112]

Other countries consider telework as a particular type of home working.

An amendment of 1 September 2007 introduced in Article 52 of the Slovak Labour Code on home working refers to telework. In fact, telework is subject to a specific regulation in this article, so that it can be seen as an autonomous form of working and not a type of home working in a strict sense. It is worth noting that, according to Article 52(2), 'An employee shall not be considered to perform home work or telework if he/she works at home or at another agreed workplace than usual only occasionally or in exceptional circumstances with the consent of employer or under an agreement with him/her subject to the condition that the type of work that the employee performs under the employment contract allows this'.[113] In other words, an employee who – with the approval of the employer – performs work at home or at other than usual places of work only exceptionally or under extraordinary circumstances is not considered to be a teleworker or homeworker.[114] In addition, the rules of the Labour Code on the allocation of weekly working time do not apply to teleworkers who are not entitled to wage compensation in cases of significant personal obstacles to work, with the

105. Czech Labour Code, s. 317.
106. Jaroslav Hála & Eurofound, *Telework in Czech Republic*, Eurofound, Dublin, 1 (2008).
107. Article 115, Lithuanian Labour Code.
108. *Supra*.
109. Inga Blažienė & Eurofound, Telework in Lithuania, Eurofound, Dublin, 2 (2008).
110. *Supra*, 3.
111. *Supra*, 2.
112. Jaroslav Hála & Eurofound, *supra*, 1; Inga Blažienė, Eurofound, *supra*, 2.
113. Article 52(2), Slovak Labour Code.
114. Miroslava Kordošová & Eurofound, *Telework in Slovakia*, Eurofound, Dublin, 1 (2007).

exception of the death of a family member. Furthermore, overtime wages and bonuses for night work, working at weekends or on public holidays are not paid to teleworkers. Thus, the equal treatment of teleworkers and other employees is questioned.[115] Also in the Slovenian legislation there is a specific reference to telework, although it cannot be said that there is a specific legislation on telework. Article 67(2) of the Employment Relationship Act states that 'Distance work performed by the worker by means of information technology shall also be deemed to be home work'.[116] In this sense, telework is considered a 'special category'[117] of home working strictly speaking.

In other countries in the 'legislation cluster' specific regulations on telework were laid down, even though some critical issues emerge. In May 2004 the Hungarian Labour Code and other employment-related acts were amended by Act XXVIII. As a result, now title 87, sections 196–197 of the Hungarian Labour Code is dedicated to telework. However, as Hárs and Neumann point out,[118] the regulation of telework concerns more the legal criteria of defining the teleworker than telework as an activity. According to title 87, section 196(2) of the Hungarian Labour Code, 'In the employment contract the parties shall agree on the worker's employment by means of teleworking' so that telework seems to be considered as an employment relationship, also due to the lack of any provision that allows the use of more flexible contracts for telework. However, some disagreement lies behind this legal definition. The idea of telework as an employment relationship is supported by the Ministry of Social Affair and Labour, while other ministries developing e-programmes to increase the spread of information technology, support a wider and more flexible idea of telework, not necessarily framed as a legal concept.[119] Moreover, the voluntary character, the reversibility of telework and the health and safety aspects, which were important issues in the EFA on Telework, are not mentioned.[120]

Finally, Bulgaria,[121] Portugal and Poland[122] provide specific regulations on telework in their Labour Codes.[123] As a result, these countries share the conception of telework as an autonomous form of work, without reference to home working but with the explicit idea of telework as an employment relationship. In addition, looking at the specific regulation of telework in these three countries, it may be said that their legislation comes close to the principles of the EFA on Telework.[124]

115. Miroslava Kordošová & Eurofound, *supra*, 2.
116. Article 67(2), Slovenian Employment Relationship Act.
117. Barbara Lužar, Aleksandra K. Mrčela & Eurofound, *Telework in Slovenia*, Eurofound, Dublin, 4 (2008).
118. Ágnes Hárs, László Neumann & Eurofound, *Telework in Hungary*, Eurofound, Dublin, 1 (2008).
119. Ágnes Hárs, László Neumann & Eurofound, *supra*, 1, 3–4.
120. Ágnes Hárs, László Neumann & Eurofound, *supra*, 3.
121. Violeta Kirova & Boyanov & Co., *Bulgaria*, in Charles Wynn-Evans, Georgina Rowley (eds.), *Employment & Labour Law*, Global Legal Group, London, 1st ed., 23–24 (2012).
122. On telework in Poland *see* Jan Czarzasty & Eurofound, *Telework in Poland*, Eurofound, Dublin (2007).
123. Article 107h, Bulgarian Labour Code; Arts 165–171, Portuguese Labour Code; Art. 67, Polish Labour Code.
124. Violeta Kirova & Boyanov & Co., *supra*, 23; Christian Welz, Felix Wolf & Eurofound, *Telework in the European Union*, Eurofound, Dublin, 11 (2010).

From an industrial relations point of view, it may be noted that the countries implementing the EFA on Telework through legislation are 'new' Member States, with the exception of Portugal and it seems that they preferred to implement the EFA on Telework by means of legislation due to the lack of strong traditions of collective bargaining.[125] Only a hard law instrument could ensure sufficient coverage and binding force for the regulation on telework in these countries.[126] Furthermore, telework regulation is an innovative concept in the Member States in question, because previous legislation made no reference to it.

[B] The 'Collective Agreements Cluster'

The 'collective agreements cluster' is the most significant in terms of the number of Member States. These countries can be classified in two groups, on the basis of the binding nature of the collective bargaining.[127]

The first group consists of Belgium, France and Luxembourg, which implemented the EFA on Telework through 'hard law collective agreements', namely collective agreements with *erga omnes* effects, after the intervention of the public authorities.

In Belgium the EFA agreement was implemented by the national collective agreement on telework, concluded in 2005, coming into force through the Royal Decree of 13 June 2006.[128] These provisions complement the 1996 Homeworkers Act, which aimed to cover all types of work at home, included teleworkers.[129] In that Act, telework was not considered an autonomous form of employment before 2005, and self-employed workers were not covered by the regulation.[130] The Royal Decree grants telework a specific regulation as an autonomous form of work. However, self-employed workers are still not covered by the new legislation, and its scope seems too narrow, considering that it does not apply to some important forms of telework such as occasional home working, telework in satellites and telecentres, and mobile work.[131]

In Luxembourg the Union of Luxembourg Enterprises (UEL), the Luxembourg Confederation of Independent Trade Unions (OGB-L) and the Luxembourg Confederation of Christian Trade Unions (LCGB) concluded a collective agreement on telework on 21 February 2006, that became generally applicable through the Grand Ducal

125. Christian Welz, Felix Wolf & Eurofound, *supra*, 10.
126. *Ibid.*
127. Christian Welz, Felix Wolf & Eurofound, *supra*, 11.
128. Roger Blanpain, *Belgium*, in Roger Blanpain (ed.), *European Framework Agreements and Telework. Law and Practice, A European and Comparative Study*, Kluwer Law International, Alphen aan den Rijn, 93–106 (2007); Chris Engels, *Belgium. A discussion on the Collective Bargaining Agreement No. 85 on Telework, Implementing the European Framework Agreement on Telework*, in Roger Blanpain (ed.), *European Framework Agreements and Telework. Law and Practice, A European and Comparative Study*, Kluwer Law International, Alphen aan den Rijn, 107–116 (2007).
129. Emmanuelle Perin & Eurofound, *Telework in Belgium*, Eurofound, Dublin (2007); Roger Blanpain, *Belgium*, *supra*, 98.
130. Roger Blanpain, *Belgium*, *supra*; *id.*, *Belgium: Some Belgian and European aspects.*
131. Roger Blanpain, *Belgium*, *supra*, 101, 106.

Regulation on 13 October 2006.[132] Applying to employees covered by the law of 24 May 1989 on employment contracts, with the exclusion of the public sector,[133] it can be said that this regulation is directed only at private-sector employees. The most important issue arising in Luxembourg concerns cross-border workers, accounting for around 40% of the labour force in Luxembourg. Considering that EU law requires employees who engage in telework to be registered with the social security system in their country of residence, even if the company that employs them is located in Luxembourg, if cross-border workers are employed part of the time on the employer's premises and part of the time at their home situated in the neighbouring country of residence, they will be registered in the country of residence for all of the work performed. As a result, since Luxembourg has lower social security contributions compared with neighbouring countries, the net salary will decrease and the cost to the employer will increase. Moreover, to avoid any risk of double taxation, cross-border teleworkers could be obliged to pay tax in the country of residence on the part of salary relating to time spent working from home, with further effects on their net income, due to the fact that Luxembourg has lower taxation rates than the neighbouring countries. As a result, telework could be less attractive for cross-border workers in Luxembourg.[134]

In the case of France, the social partners signed a national cross-sector collective agreement on 19 July 2005, that was granted *erga omnes* effect by a Ministerial Decree of 30 May 2006.[135] Moreover, company-level collective agreements, for instance at Renault, are fairly isolated cases.[136] In addition, some collective agreements on gender equality have introduced provisions for teleworking, but they have been selective and offer the option of telework for limited periods in the case of childbirth or adoption.[137] In 2012 a specific regulation on telework was laid down in the French Labour Code.[138] This measure reflects the national cross-sector agreement, although, according to the *Confédération Générale du Travail*–Force Ouvrière (CGT–FO), the provision in Article L1222-11 allowing an employer to impose teleworking on employees in exceptional circumstances[139] is in contrast with the principle that telework must be voluntary.[140] Furthermore, telework is seen as a form of work organisation, thus the lack of a definition of the teleworker's legal status could have a negative impact on the choice of

132. Odette Wlodarski & Eurofound, *Telework in Luxembourg*, Eurofound, Dublin, 1 (2008).
133. *Ibid.*
134. Odette Wlodarski & Eurofound, *supra*, 2.
135. Jean-Emmanuel Ray & Jacques Rojot, *France*, in Roger Blanpain (ed.), *European Framework Agreements and Telework. Law and Practice, A European and Comparative Study*, Kluwer Law International, Alphen aan den Rijn, 158 (2007).
136. Sandrine Jean & Eurofound, *Labour Code covers teleworking*, Eurofound, Dublin, 1 (2012); Nuria Ramos Martín & Jelle Visser, *Expert Report on the Implementation of the Social Partner's Framework Agreement on Telework*, Institute for advanced Labour Studies, Amsterdam, 44 (2008).
137. Sandrine Jean & Eurofound, *supra*, 1.
138. Articles L1222-9–L1222-11.
139. Article L1222-11: 'En cas de circonstances exceptionnelles, notamment de menace d'épidémie, ou en cas de force majeure, la mise en œuvre du télétravail peut être considérée comme un aménagement du poste de travail rendu nécessaire pour permettre la continuité de l'activité de l'entreprise et garantir la protection des salariés. Les conditions et les modalités d'application du présent article sont définies par décret en Conseil d'Etat'.
140. Sandrine Jean & Eurofound, *supra*, 1.

telework for both companies and employees in the view of the *Confédération française démocratique du travail* (CFDT).[141]

The second group consists of the remaining Member States of the 'collective agreements cluster', implementing the EFA on Telework through 'soft law collective agreements', namely through agreements that are binding only between the signatory parties, without extension clauses covering the entire workforce.

In Austria the EFA on Telework was implemented mainly through sectoral collective agreements[142] that included clauses on telework.[143] Moreover, in 2005, the main employer organisations (the Federation of Austrian Industry (WKO) and the Association of Public Enterprises (VÖWG)) presented a joint implementation guideline to help companies to implement the EFA on Telework, particularly those that are not covered by a collective agreement providing for telework.[144] However, some problems remain. One question is whether adopting a legal status for teleworkers is necessary. Home workers in Austria are not employees, and as a result it could be possible to treat teleworkers as home workers, due to the lack of a clear distinction between the two categories.[145]

In the case of Germany, the EFA on Telework was implemented mainly through company collective agreements,[146] concluded between the employer and the work council.[147] As a general trend, the agreements consider telework as 'rotating telework', that is when teleworkers are employed part of the time at the premises of the enterprise and part of the time elsewhere.[148] In addition, works councils play an important role in promoting and implementing telework in companies in order to promote employment.[149] In this sense, inequalities between teleworkers of companies with and without work councils could emerge, although a legislative intervention does not seem necessary at the moment due to the fact that telework is not seen as a widespread practice. As a result, collective company agreements seem to be a sufficient means of regulation.[150]

141. *Ibid.*
142. In the public sector, the 1979 Act on Service Regulations of Career Public Servants and the 1948 Act on Service Regulations of Contract Public Servants, both amended in 2004, allow public servants - under certain circumstances - to perform their work or part of their work outside of the employer's premises as teleworkers (Georg Adam & Eurofound, *Telework in Austria*, Eurofound, Dublin, 3 (2007).
143. Georg Adam & Eurofound, *supra*, 3.
144. Georg Adam & Eurofound, *supra*, 4.
145. Georg Adam & Eurofound, *supra*, 3.
146. Manfred Weiss, *Germany*, in Roger Blanpain (ed.), *European Framework Agreements and Telework. Law and Practice, A European and Comparative Study*, Kluwer Law International, Alphen aan den Rijn, 171-180 (2007). In Germany other means of implementation were carried out, such as joint declarations and guidelines (*see* Trine P. Larsen & Søren Kaj Andersen, *supra*, 188).
147. Nuria Ramos Martín & Jelle Visser, *A More 'Autonomous' European Social Dialogue: The Implementation of the Framework Agreement on Telework*, *supra*, 528.
148. Manfred Weiss, *Il telelavoro tra legge e contrattazione collettiva: il caso tedesco*, 3 Diritto delle Relazioni Industriali, 675 (2015); *id.*, *Germany*, 177.
149. Manfred Weiss, *supra*, 672; *id.*, *Germany*, 174.
150. Manfred Weiss, *supra*, 679; *id.*, *Germany*, 180.

In Denmark the EFA on telework has been implemented through collective agreements at confederal and sectoral levels, especially in manufacturing industry and commercial services.[151] In particular, the social partners have generally chosen to transpose the 2002 Agreement into their existing collective agreements on telework and home working.[152]

Regarding Spain, the EFA was included, at interconfederal level but without regulatory effect, in the Agreement on collective bargaining in 2003, in order to implement the European agreement.[153] Then, in 2012, due to the need to deal with the economic and financial crises, the Spanish Workers Statute was amended by the Royal Decree no. 3/2012, which modified Article 13 on homework to make it suitable also for telework.

In Italy an interconfederal national collective agreement, similar in its provisions to the EFA, was signed on 9 June 2005 by CGIL, CISL, UIL, the three major trade union confederations, and twenty employers' organisations.[154]

However, in both Italy and Spain telework is regulated at sectoral[155] and company level[156] and legislation has been enacted for the public sector.[157] As a result, there are various forms of regulation of telework in Spain and Italy. Telework in Italy is considered a form of work organisation rather than a specific employment relationship. In this sense, the teleworker could be regarded either as an employee (especially as a home worker) or as self-employed. On the other hand, the new regulation of telework, included with home working as *Trabajo a distancia* in Article 13 of the Spanish Workers Statute, could lead to the conclusion that in Spain telework and home working tend to be used as synonyms.

Finally, in Greece the EFA on Telework was implemented through the national collective agreement (EGSSE) for 2006–2007, covering all workers in each sector of the economy. However, the agreement has not been applied specifically. In addition, some

151. Trine P. Larsen & Søren Kaj Andersen, *supra*, 186–187.
152. Trine P. Larsen T.P. & Eurofound, *Telework in Denmark*, Eurofound, Dublin, 5 (2008).
153. Juan Arasanz Díaz & Eurofound, *Telework in Spain*, Eurofound, Dublin, 2 (2008).
154. On the implementation on the EFA on Telework in Italy *see* Diego Coletto & Eurofound, *Telework in Italy*, Eurofound, Dublin (2008); for an overview of telework in Italy *see* Michele Colucci, *Italy*, in Roger Blanpain (ed.), *European Framework Agreements and Telework. Law and Practice, A European and Comparative Study*, Kluwer Law International, Alphen aan den Rijn, 181–190 (2007) and Lorenzo Gaeta, *voce Telelavoro*, in *http://www.treccani.it/enciclopedia/telelavoro_(Diritto_on_line)/* (2015).
155. For Spain, for example, in the chemical and daily press sectors (Juan Arasanz Díaz & Eurofound, *supra*, 2); in Italy, for example, in the postal sector (Agreement on Telework signed on 4 Oct. 2007).
156. It must be underlined that collective bargaining at company level on telework in Italy may increase due to Art. 8 of Act no. 148/2011, which provides the possibility for company-level agreement to derogate from national collective agreements and even the law in some matters. Among these matters, the introduction of new technologies is indicated. Only a limited amount of data is available on company-level bargaining but it should be mentioned that the company-level agreement signed in InfoCert for the period 2013–2015 specifically regulates only "mobile telework" (Art. 7).
157. The reference is to a Spanish Royal Decree on Telework and to the Italian Presidential Decree no. 70/1999. On this point *see* Lorenzo Gaeta, *Il regolamento sul telelavoro nelle pubbliche amministrazioni*, 2 *Il Lavoro nelle Pubbliche Amministrazioni*, 311–326 (1999).

problems remain such as the lack of a legal definition of telework and the rather generic regulation.[158]

[C] The 'Soft Law Cluster' and the 'Incomplete Implementation Cluster'

The countries in the 'soft law' group all implemented the EFA on Telework through instruments such voluntary agreements, codes of conduct and guidelines.

In Finland and Iceland two voluntary framework agreements were concluded, respectively in 2005 and 2006.[159] In Ireland in 2010 the government updated the code of practice adopted in 2000 and some trade unions issued unilateral guidelines to be used for bargaining with employers.[160] In the Netherlands in September 2003[161] the European Agreement Labour Foundation (STAR) adopted a recommendation on telework, aiming to bring telework to the attention of employers and employees and to put in place agreements on that subject through decentralised negotiations.[162]

In Norway in February 2006 the leading social partners published a set of guidelines on telework, intended to be voluntary recommendations without any commitment for the company-level social partners. In addition, certain collective agreements regulate telework, but they generally state only that telework should be voluntary and based on an agreement between the employer and the employee.[163]

In Sweden[164] the social partners agreed on a set of joint guidelines on national implementation in 2003, while in the public sector the implementation took place through national and sectoral collective agreements starting in 2005. Also in the private sector the provisions of the EFA were included in sectoral collective agreements, but they are not adopted in some sectors, because telework does not exist there or a regulation is not required, or they are included in guidelines.[165]

In the UK[166] the Department of Trade Industry (DTI) published a guidance paper on telework as a result of an agreement between the Confederation of British Industry (CBI), the Trades Union Congress (TUC) and the Employers' Organisation for Local

158. Sofia Lampousaki & Eurofound, *Telework in Greece*, Eurofound, Dublin (2008).
159. Nuria Ramos Martín & Jelle Visser, *A More 'Autonomous' European Social Dialogue: The Implementation of the Framework Agreement on Telework*, *supra*, 531.
160. Christian Welz, Felix Wolf & Eurofound, *supra*, 13.
161. For an overview *see* Antoine Jacobs, *The Netherlands*, in Roger Blanpain (ed.), *European Framework Agreements and Telework. Law and Practice, A European and Comparative Study*, Kluwer Law International, Alphen aan den Rijn, 191–204 (2007).
162. Robbert van het Kaar & Eurofound, *Telework in the Netherlands*, Eurofound, Dublin, 2–3 (2008); Antoine Jacobs, *supra*, 200. In the public sector, there is a special regulation for civil servants: the Framework Decree on Telework (Antoine Jacobs, *supra*, 193).
163. Kristin Alsos, Kristine Nergaard, Håvard Lismoen & Eurofound, *Telework in Norway*, Eurofound, Dublin, 3 (2008).
164. *See* Birgitta Nyström, *Sweden*, in Roger Blanpain (ed.), *European Framework Agreements and Telework. Law and Practice, A European and Comparative Study*, Kluwer Law International, Alphen aan den Rijn, 217–228 (2007).
165. Paul Andersson & Eurofound, *Telework in Sweden*, Eurofound, Dublin, 2 (2007).
166. On telework in the UK *see* Jane Parker & Eurofound, *Telework in the United Kingdom*, Eurofound, Dublin (2008) and Alan C. Neal, *supra*.

Government (CEEP UK).[167] The guidelines faithfully adopted the principles of EFA, adapting it to the UK context. It is worth noting that the Government played a role in the negotiations, taking part in trilateral negotiations, while mediating between, funding and monitoring the social partners.[168] In addition, the Government delegated to the social partners the transposition of the guidelines, taking on an informing and facilitating role.[169]

In Latvia the implementation of the EFA was realised through a tripartite agreement, with the participation of the Ministry of Welfare and members of the Latvian Parliament, setting out non-binding guidelines on the introduction of telework, adopted on 12 April 2006.[170]

Finally, limited information is available in relation to Croatia, probably because it joined the EU only on 1 July 2013. However, it is reported that Croatia implemented the EFA on Telework through joint guidelines and recommendations, agreed by the national social partners, pending formal adoption and some clarifications on elements which depend on the public authorities.[171]

The 'incomplete implementation' cluster, as noted above, consists of four countries: Cyprus, Estonia, Malta and Romania.[172]

It seems that these countries have not implemented the EFA on Telework, either through hard law or soft law tools. As a result, the regulation of telework is left to the individual contract or informal agreements between employers and employees, as in the case of Malta[173] or Estonia,[174] without a minimum standard of protection for

167. *See* Department of Trade Industry, *Telework guidance* (2003).
168. Trine P. Larsen & Søren Kaj Andersen, *supra*, 193.
169. Nuria Ramos Martín & Jelle Visser, *A More 'Autonomous' European Social Dialogue: The Implementation of the Framework Agreement on Telework*, *supra*, 533.
170. Iveta Baltina, *Overview on European policies on TELEWORK*, Riga technical University, Riga, 10 (2012).
171. Patrick Itschert & Antonio Alfaiate, *Experts' Report. 'Promoting social dialogue and better implementation of EU social partners' autonomous framework agreements in selected countries'*, ETUC, BusinessEurope, CEEP, UEAPME, Brussels, 17 (2016). Moreover, Croatia amended the Labour Code in order to cover home working, but with no references to the ICT elements (*Ibid.*).
172. In Romania an amending bill of the Labour Code regarding telework is under debate (Patrick Itschert & Antonio Alfaiate, *supra*, 42).
173. Marvin Formosa & Eurofound, *Telework in Malta*, Eurofound, Dublin, 2 (2008). According to Patrick Itschert & Antonio Alfaiate, *supra*, 38, in Malta there has been a partial implementation of the EFA. For the public Sector a binding 'sectoral' collective agreement was concluded between the unions and the Government on 26 Oct. 2005. For the private sector, 'guidelines' were negotiated in the OSHA Board and Subsidiary Legislation 452.104 'The Telework National Standard Order' in 2008.
174. Kerly Espenberg, *Teleworking: a new way of working and living. Estonian case study*, University of Tartu, Tartu (2012).

The Estonian Employment Contracts Act provides that 'If an employer and employee agree that the employee does work, which is usually done in the employer's enterprise, outside the place of performance of the work, including at the employee's place of residence (teleworking), the employer shall […] notify the employee that the duties are performed by way of teleworking' (s. 6(4) Estonian Employment Contracts Act). In this country telework is ruled as a normal employment contract, where each aspect, according to s. 5 of the Employment Contracts Act, is left to the will of the parties. In this sense, it cannot be said that the EFA has been implemented in Estonia, due to the lack of any measures aiming to transpose

teleworkers. In particular, telework can be adapted to any type of contract, even of a commercial nature, so that the teleworker could be a self-employed person or an employee. In Estonia, as in Malta and Romania, it is argued that the home working rules are applicable to teleworkers but this is not the solution to the question of telework regulation due to the fact that in some countries, such as Malta, home workers are consider to be self-employed[175] and in others, such as Romania, home working is defined only as work carried out in the home,[176] so that an individual who works in different places away from the premises of the employer is not covered by the legislation.

§8.07 WHAT IS THE APPLICABLE LAW?

The legal framework outlined above leads to some observations. From an industrial relations point of view it should be noted that Article 155(2) TFEU, according to which autonomous agreements shall be implemented 'in accordance with the procedures and practices specific to management and labour and the Member States',[177] has never been applied. This is not only due to the incomplete implementation of the EFA on Telework in certain Member States, but also to the fact that in some countries implementation has taken place throughout procedures and practices that are relatively new in some national industrial relations frameworks.[178] This is the case, for instance, of the UK and Sweden, where tripartite negotiations, in the case of the UK, and negotiations between the social partners, in the case of Sweden, resulted in guidelines on telework.[179] Moreover, the EFA on Telework has had the effect of enhancing social dialogue in countries with weak collective bargaining traditions. This is the case, for example, of some central and eastern European Member States, such as the Czech Republic, Hungary and Slovakia, where the social partners have played a role in implementation through legislation.[180] Together with the fact that the agreement has been implemented in the majority of the Member States, this has led the European Commission to consider the implementation of the EFA on Telework a success, given the objectives and scope of autonomous agreements. Furthermore, the Commission regards the Agreement as a contribution 'to the Lisbon goals of

the EFA on Telework, setting a minimal regulation of this phenomenon, although, according to Espenberg, 2012, specific provisions could exist in company-level collective agreements.

175. Marvin Formosa & Eurofound, *supra*, 2.
176. Constantin Ciutacu & Eurofound, *Telework in Romania*, Eurofound, Dublin, 2 (2008); *see also* Dan Top & Lavinia Savu, *Need of regulation of the teleworking contract in Romanian legislation*, 1 Fiat Iustitia, 129–133 (2015).
177. Article 155(2), TFEU.
178. Trine P. Larsen & Søren Kaj Andersen, *supra*, 186.
179. Trine P. Larsen & Søren Kaj Andersen, *supra*, 190, 193.
180. Christian Welz, Felix Wolf & Eurofound, *supra*, 11.

modernising labour markets and achieving a more dynamic knowledge-based economy'.[181] Moreover, in some cases, as in Poland[182] and the Slovak Republic,[183] the regulation of telework was a novelty, given the lack of any regulation of this kind of work in the past. However, in other countries telework was already regulated especially through collective agreements at sectoral and company level,[184] thus, in these cases, the Framework Agreement did not appear to bring in any innovation.[185]

The most evident aspect of the implementation of the EFA on Telework is the diversity of implementation across the Member States. This obviously reflects the different industrial relations systems in each country but the result is that the legal framework has not been harmonised. It has been noted that the EFA on Telework does not aim 'to create a new employment status, but to fit [...] telework into the existing employment relationship in order to remove the obstacles for the expansion of this type of work'.[186] However, these differences in regulation could result in unequal treatment of European teleworkers at national and international level. On the one hand, in the Member States where the regulation on telework does not cover all the workers, such as the countries where the implementation was carried out through collective agreements without *erga omnes* effects, the unionised teleworkers would benefit from protection laid down in collective agreements transposing the EFA on Telework, whereas other teleworkers would not. On the other hand, the central point of the issues raised by telework should be taken into account. This is the means by which it is carried out, that is Information Technology, and particularly the Internet. On this basis, telework is 'transregional, transnational and transcontinental'[187] because the Internet allows work to be carried out for an employer established abroad without the need for the worker to move from the country of residence. In these situations, the inability of

181. European Commission, *Report on the implementation of the social partner's Framework Agreement on Telework*, Commission Staff Working Paper, SEC(2008) 2178, Brussels, 55 (2008).
182. Jan Czarzasty & Eurofound, *supra*, 2.
183. Miroslava Kordošová & Eurofound, *supra*, 2.
184. Take for example Italy, where in the mid-1990s some telework company-level agreements (in enterprises such as Saritel, Italtel, SEAT, Dun & Bradstreet, Telecom Italia, Digital and Zanussi) were in place, even if of experimental character (Di Nicola, 1997, 505 et seq.). Other cases include Denmark (Trine P. Larsen & Søren Kaj Andersen, *supra*, 188; Trine P. Larsen T.P. & Eurofound, *supra*, 5), the Deutsche Telekom agreement of 1996 in Germany, the mineral oils industry agreement of 1997 in Austria (August Gächter & Eurofound, 1997, *First collective agreement signed on teleworking*, Eurofound, Dublin (1997), the Renault agreement of 1997 in France mentioned above, and some company-level collective agreements in Spain such as those at Siemens Nixdorf Spain of 1997, BP Oil Spain of 2002, DHL International of 2003 and Telefónica of 2005 (Juan Arasanz Díaz & Eurofound, *supra*, 2).
185. Even if in some of these countries, such as Spain or Italy, the innovative aspects could be seen in the broader coverage stemming from the implementation of the Framework Agreement through legislation or interconfederal collective agreements.
186. Nuria Ramos Martín & Jelle Visser, *A More 'Autonomous' European Social Dialogue: The Implementation of the Framework Agreement on Telework*, *supra*, 547.
187. Antonio Lo Faro, *supra*, 213.

the EFA on Telework to ensure harmonisation of the Member State regulations is evident, because of its non-binding character and considering that the autonomous agreements are not enforceable in the courts.[188] As a result, in such cases, there is a need to clarify which national law should be applied to the teleworker involved. The answer is to be found in the EU Regulation on the law applicable to contractual obligations, known as Rome I.[189] Article 8, paragraph 2, of that Regulation states that where an individual employment contract exists and the applicable law has not been chosen by the parties, the relationship is 'governed by the law of the country in which or, failing that, from which the employee habitually carries out his work in performance of the contract'. According to this norm, some authors have claimed that the law applicable to the teleworker whose employer is established abroad should be that of the employer's country, assuming that the telework *locus laboris* should be where the benefit is derived.[190] This statement would be justified in that, as in Directive no. 96/71 on posting, the applicable law should be that of the country where the work is carried out on a continuous basis.[191] Moreover, for some scholars, the performance of telework could be split in two different phases: the fulfilment of the labour obligation and the realisation of the output. The labour takes place in the teleworker's country while the output is located in the employer's country, so that the whole obligation is fulfilled only when the data arrive at the undertaking.[192] However, other scholars do not agree with this interpretation.[193] It is worth noting that Article 8, paragraph 3, Regulation Rome I states that: 'Where the law applicable cannot be determined pursuant to paragraph 2, the contract shall be governed by the law of the country where the place of business through which the employee was engaged is situated.' Therefore, following the previous interpretation, this norm would not make sense, in the absence of any differences between paragraph 2 and paragraph 3.[194] It may be that Article 8, paragraph 4, could help to find a solution, as it states that: 'Where it appears from the circumstances as a whole that the contract is more closely connected with a country other than that indicated in paragraphs 2 or 3, the law of that other country shall apply.' However, this provision seems too vague.[195] In this sense, the telework *locus laboris* is

188. Roger Blanpain, *Belgium, supra*, 33; *id.*, *Belgium: Some Belgian and European aspects, supra*.
189. Regulation (EC) no. 593/2008 of the European Parliament and of the Council of 17 Jun. 2008 on the law applicable to contractual obligations (Rome I).
190. For this interpretation under the Rome Convention of 1980, *see* Antonio Lo Faro, *supra*, 232; with more doubts Lorenzo Gaeta, *voce Telelavoro, supra*.
191. Antonio Lo Faro, *supra*, 231.
192. Pietro Magno, *Il (luogo nel telelavoro)*, I Il Diritto del Lavoro, 550 et seq. (1996).
193. Franco Toffoletto, *Nuove tecnologie informatiche e tutela del lavoratore*, Giuffrè, Milan, 80 (2006).
194. Franco Toffoletto, *supra*, 81.
195. Franco Toffoletto, *supra*, 82. This general clause introduces flexibility in the criteria of the applicable law, leaving to judicial discretion the task of identifying the country most closely connected with the contract (Franco Mosconi & Cristina Campiglio, *Diritto internazionale privato e processuale. Parte generale e obbligazioni*, UTET, Turin, vol. 1, 5th ed., 189–191 (2011).

still unclear, although in the case of self-employed telework the coordinates may be more precise, according to Article 4, paragraph 1, (b), Regulation Rome I, which states that 'a contract for the provision of services shall be governed by the law of the country where the service provider has his habitual residence'. In any case, in the case in which the applicable law is specified as that of the employer, the problem would be not solved. It could not be the case that the regulation of the teleworker's country would be worse than that of the employer in terms of protection. By way of example, it is true that a Maltese or Estonian teleworker who works for a Polish employer might prefer Polish law, due to the fact that in the first two countries telework is not regulated whereas in Poland there is a specific legislation. However, if the employer was Maltese or Estonian and the teleworker Polish, the Polish worker would be unlikely to prefer the Maltese or Estonian legislation, due to the risk of being classified as self-employed.

In other words, the employment-related risk can easily be transferred to the teleworkers in transnational relationships. As mentioned above, the first criterion to identify the applicable law is the one chosen by the parties,[196] so it is likely that the law chosen will be the one that is more advantageous for the employer, due to the social and economic imbalance between the parties to the employment relationship. It should be noted that Article 8, paragraph 1, Rome I Regulation specifies that the choice 'shall not have the result of depriving the employee of the protection afforded to him by the mandatory rules of the law which would be applicable [...] in the absence of choice'. But this statement, known as 'the principle of the most favourable law' has a paradoxical effect. The employer knows that there is a need to apply the 'most favourable law', so that he 'loses all interest in a choice of law, for that would only cost him money'.[197] As a result, the employer might prefer to base the relationship on standard legal criteria, but the lack of a clear rule on telework in transnational relationships, would easily allow the employer to avoid granting the teleworker any protection.

The problem of the telework *locus laboris* concerns 'forum shopping' particularly in terms of wages. One of the main reasons for outsourcing the work to a teleworker in another country is the lower cost of labour.[198] In this sense, the labour costs for work performed using ICT could be reduced due to global competition, with consequences for teleworkers living in countries with higher living costs.[199]

---

196. Article 3, para. 1, Rome I Regulation.
197. Martin Franzen, *Conflicts of Laws in Employment Contracts and Industrial Relations*, in Roger Blanpain (ed.), *Comparative Labour Law and Industrial Relations in Indutrialize Market Economies*, Kluwer Law International, Alphen aan den Rijn, 260 (2014).
198. For this reason transnational telework is also called 'offshore telework'.
199. Obviously, these forum shopping issues are the same in relations between the Member States and the non-EU countries. It must be noted that according to Art. 2 of Rome I Regulation 'Any law specified by this Regulation shall be applied whether or not it is the law of a Member State'.

§8.08 THE EVOLUTION OF DIGITAL WORK: 'CROWDWORKING' AND 'WORKING ON DEMAND VIA APPS'

These effects described for telework, known as the 'demutualisation of risk'[200] have recently emerged from a relatively new phenomenon of the labour market that is crowdworking, crowdsourcing of labour or crowd employment.[201]

The term 'crowdworking' is often associated with the term 'working on demand via apps'. These two terms are the most widely recognised expressions of the 'gig economy' or 'on-demand' economy.[202] However, crowdworking and working on demand via apps may be seen as different phenomena. The first term refers to 'working activities that imply completing a series of tasks through online platforms' which 'put in contact an indefinite number of organisations and individuals through the Internet, potentially allowing connecting clients and workers on a global basis'.[203] The expression 'work on demand via apps', on the other hand, suggests 'a form of work in which the execution of traditional working activities such as transport, cleaning and running errands, but also forms of clerical work, is channelled through apps managed by firms

200. Mark Freedland & Nicola Countouris, *Introduction: the myths and realities of 'Social Europe'*, in Mark Freedland & Nicola Countouris (eds.), *Resocialising Europe in a Time of Crisis*, Cambridge University Press, Cambridge, 7 (2013); Mark Freedland & Nicola Countouris, *The Legal Construction of Personal Work Relations*, Oxford University Press, Oxford, 439–440 (2011). In their view: 'The idea of mutualisation and demutualisation of risks could be defined [as] the shifting of risks and bearing of costs of risks either away from individual workers so that the risks or risk-costs are borne by, or shared with, an entity or set of entities or a community (mutualisation) or back towards the individual worker (demutualisation)' (Mark Freedland & Nicola Countouris, *Introduction: the myths and realities of 'Social Europe'*, *supra*, 7).

201. Martin Risak & Johannes Warter, *Decent Crowdwork. Legal Strategies towards fair employment conditions in the virtual sweatshop*, Paper to be presented at the Regulating for Decent Work 2015 Conference Geneva, 8–10 Jul. 2015 (2015); Annamaria Donini, *Il lavoro digitale su piattaforma*, 1 (1) Labour & Law Issues, 49–71 (2015); Irene Mandl et al, *New forms of employment*, Eurofound, Publications Office of the European Union, Luxembourg (2015); Alek Felstiner, *Working the Crowd: Employment and Labor Law in the Crowdsourcing Industry*, in 32 (1) Berkeley Journal of Employment & Labor Law, 143–204 (2011). The word 'crowdsourcing' was proposed by Jeff Howe, *The rise of crowdsourcing*, in *http://www.wired.com/2006/06/crowds/*, 6 Jun. 2006 for the first time.

202. Valerio De Stefano, *The rise of the 'just-in-time workforce': on-demand work, crowdwork, and labor protection in the 'gig-economy'*, 37 (3) Comparative Labor Law & Policy Journal, 471 (2016).

As other authors (Antonio Aloisi, *Commoditized workers: case study research on labour law issues arising from a set of 'on demand/gig economy' platforms*, 37 (3) Comparative Labor Law & Policy Journal, 654 (2016) have claimed, it is possible to use these expressions, as well many others (e.g., 'sharing economy'; '1099 economy'; 'participatory economy'), indifferently in legal discourse, as a general umbrella concept. However, *see* Rachel Botsman, *The Sharing Economy Lacks A Shared Definition*, in *http://www.fastcoexist.com/3022028/the-sharing-economy-lacks-a-shared-definition* (2013) as an attempt to define some of these concepts.

203. Valerio De Stefano, *supra*, 471; *see also* Irene Mandl et al., *supra*, 107 et seq.; Alek Felstiner, *supra*; Jeff Howe, *Crowdsourcing. How the power of the crowd is driving the future of business*, Random House Business, London (2008); *id.*, *The rise of crowdsourcing.* The most famous and studied case of crowdworking is Amazon Mechanical Turk. Other platforms are, for example, Crowdflower and Clickworker.

that also intervene in setting minimum quality standards of service and in the selection and management of the workforce'.[204]

In this sense, the main differences between these phenomena is that in crowdworking the workplace is cyberspace, considering that tasks are performed on the platform from any part of the world, whereas in working on demand via apps the platform 'only matches online supply and demand of activities that are later executed locally'.[205]

These two methods present obvious advantages for employers and customers in terms of flexibility and cost saving, but at the same time many disadvantages for workers. First, using platforms and apps, with crowdworking, employers can contact an indefinite number of workers all over the world, whereas customers, contacting the service provider on demand via apps, can benefit from faster and more competitive local services.[206] The main point in terms of cost saving is that contracts are not concluded between employers/customers and crowdworkers/workers on demand via apps. In crowdworking, as in working on demand via apps, the only 'source' regulating the tripartite relationship (clients-platform-crowdworkers) is to be found in the terms and conditions to be accepted by both clients and workers in order to make use of the platform services. Consequently, neither the clients nor the platforms consider the workers to be employees. On the contrary, the terms and conditions are full of expressions, like 'tasks', 'gigs', 'favours', referring to the performance requested, indicating that platforms do not consider crowdworkers or workers via apps as workers in a proper sense.[207] In some cases, platforms claim explicitly that those individuals are 'workers' but also 'independent contractors', not excluding the possibility for them to be classified as employees in the case of repeated and frequent performance for the same client.[208] As a result, crowdworkers and workers on demand via apps are excluded from any kind of employment protection. In addition, their situation is made worse by the working conditions. First of all, the lack of employment protection is not offset by a good level of remuneration. Indeed, pay levels are generally low,[209] because crowdworking consists of micro and repetitive tasks,[210] whereas in the case of work on

204. Valerio De Stefano, *supra*, 471–472. The 'working on demand via apps' platforms became popular especially in the transport sector. Among these platforms, the best known are Uber and Lyft. Another important platform, for home services, is TaskRabbit.

205. Valerio De Stefano, *supra*, 473–474.

206. Miriam A. Cherry, *Beyond misclassification: the digital transformation of work*, 37 (3) Comparative Labor Law & Policy Journal, 580. This is the case of Uber as 'The app matches available drivers, who are using their privately-owned vehicles, with passengers nearby who need rides' (*Ibid.*).

207. Valerio De Stefano, *supra*, 477–478.

208. *See* s. 3, (a), Amazon Mechanical Turk Participation Agreement.

209. For Amazon Mechanical Turk (AMT) the average is USD 2 per hour (Antonio Aloisi, *supra*, 688). From the AMT website, it emerges that many tasks are paid USD 0.01, for a performance duration from five minutes to one hour (*see* the list of tasks in *https://www.mturk.com/mturk/findhits?match=false*).

210. These activities are called 'microtasks', which are 'extremely parcelled activities, often menial and monotonous, which still require some sort of judgment beyond the understanding of artificial intelligence (e.g., tagging photos, valuing emotions or the appropriateness of a site or text, completing surveys)' (Valerio De Stefano, *supra*, 474; *see also* Irene Mandl et al., *supra*, 107; Alek Felstiner, *supra*, 147–148).

demand via apps the worker is paid not directly by the customer but by the platform, which takes a percentage of the cost of the service.[211] In these jobs, the bargaining power for workers is non-existent because prices are determined by the platforms, and workers cannot negotiate but simply accept the terms and conditions. Thus, workers have to complete their tasks in the shortest possible time to earn as much as they can to get by. This can clearly have a negative impact on the workers' health, increasing stress levels[212] and, particularly in work on demand via apps, exposing workers to more frequent injuries and accidents.[213] Additionally, in crowdworking, some platforms allow clients the possibility to refuse to accept the completed tasks without giving a reason.[214] In these cases the critical issues are even more evident, because workers are obliged to perform more and more tasks in order to recover the lost money, in the absence of any guarantee that they will paid for their services. Not surprisingly, these practices have been taken as an evident example of 'commodification workers' or, in other words, as the idea of treating 'humans-as-a-service'.[215]

§8.09 SMART WORKING

Another practice is worth mentioning in order to come to some conclusions on digital jobs. The reference is to the debate taking place in Italy in recent years about the approval of a law on smart working (*lavoro agile* in Italian). Agreeing on a definition of smart working, from both a sociological and a legal point of view, is difficult. Arguably smart working is a more flexible form of teleworking, an employment practice according to which workers, together with their employers, decide when to work away from the firm using ICT. Such agreements also provide for face-to-face meetings with colleagues in the firm and performance pay systems.[216] Many collective agreements have been concluded on smart working in Italy in recent years in order to regulate it.[217]

211. *See* for example s. 4.4 of the Uber driver terms and conditions, updated on 11 Dec. 2015, at *http://ucustomersupport.com/wp-content/uploads/2016/01/Uber-Driver-Terms-and-Conditions .pdf*.
212. Manfred Weiss, *Digitalizzazione: sfide e prospettive per il diritto del lavoro*, 3 Diritto delle Relazioni Industriali, 659 (2016).
213. Taking into account transportation services, we could speculate that the worker would be forced to complete as many rides as possible, so that the risk of accidents would increase. Moreover, the lack of a regulation which obliges these drivers to have a rest after a certain number of hours makes the risk of accidents higher.
214. *See* for example s. 3 (a), Amazon Mechanical Turk Participation Agreement.
215. According to Valerio De Stefano, *supra*, 476–477, this expression was used by the CEO of Amazon Mechanical Turk. Also the CEO of CrowdFlower has expressed similar views, claiming that: 'Before the Internet, it would be really difficult to find someone, sit them down for ten minutes and get them to work for you, and then fire them after those ten minutes. But with technology, you can actually find them, pay them the tiny amount of money, and then get rid of them when you don't need them anymore' (quoted by Valerio De Stefano, *supra*, 476).
216. Gianluigi Chiaro, Giacomo Prati & Matteo Zocca, Smart working*: dal lavoro flessibile al lavoro agile*, 138 Sociologia del lavoro, 72 (2015).
217. For an overview of some smart working collective agreements *see* Emanuele Dagnino, Paolo Tomassetti, Clara Tourres & Michele Tiraboschi, *Il 'lavoro agile' nella contrattazione collettiva oggi. Analisi sui contenuti di 915 contratti della banca dati* www.farecontrattazione.it, 2 Working Paper, Adapt University Press (2016).

For the purposes of this chapter it may be useful to focus on the bill on smart working approved by the Italian Government on 28 January 2016.[218] The aim of the Government is to promote smart working as a flexicurity tool to improve productivity and, at the same time, to enable workers to achieve a good work/life balance.[219] The bill lays down a definition of smart working. According to Article 1, paragraph 1, smart working is an employment activity performed partially in the firm and partially away from the employer's premises, using ICT and without a fixed workspace during the periods away from the firm. The provisions of the bill are similar to the EFA on Telework: smart working is supposed to be voluntary; the equal treatment principle is extended to smart workers; organisational, privacy and health and safety provisions are laid down. However, the bill explicitly states that norms and collective agreements on telework are not applicable for smart working.[220] In this sense, smart working is considered to be different from telework, as shown by the provisions of the bill. After all, smart working is often said to be an evolution of telework, able to solve some of the problems raised by telework, and especially the issue of isolation, due to the fact that in smart working the performance never takes place entirely away from the firm.[221] On the contrary, some trade unions have expressed their concerns about smart working, claiming that it would increase the risk for the employee to be available at any time, with an evident erosion of the demarcation between normal working time and overtime,[222] and between working time and free time.

§8.10 CONCLUSION

After this overview of the most significant digital phenomena attracting the attention of labour law scholars in recent years, some conclusions may be drawn. One evident aspect of digital work is its complexity, that is the variety of phenomena stemming from it. As discussed above, after many years of discussion about telework, the legal debate shifted to new issues like crowdworking, working on demand via apps and smart working. Before these new forms of employment, various solutions were proposed to regulate digital jobs.

An initial solution, epitomised in the Italian bill on smart working, is to regulate each specific phenomenon with specific legislation. This approach does not appear to be practicable due to the complexity of the digital world mentioned above. If a regulation were to be made for each new digital job, we would see an endless proliferation of laws on the subject, taking into account the endless applications of

218. Tit. II, DDL no. 2233/2016 'Misure per la tutela del lavoro autonomo non imprenditoriale e misure volte a favorire l'articolazione flessibile nei tempi e nei luoghi del lavoro subordinato a tempo indeterminato'.
219. Article 1, Tit. II, para. 1, DDL no. 2233/2016.
220. Article 1, para. 2, DDL no. 2233/2016.
221. Gianluigi Chiaro, Giacomo Prati & Matteo Zocca, *supra*, 83.
222. FIOM-CGIL, *Smartworking. Cos'è? Che differenza c'è rispetto con il Telelavoro?*, in *http://www.fiom-cgil.it/web/aziende/settori/informatica/comunicati-di-settore/3008-smartworking-cos-e-che-differenza-c-e-con-il-telelavoro?utm_source=dlvr.it&utm_medium=facebook*, 2 Mar. 2016.

ICT.[223] In this sense, specific legislation would be ineffective considering the rapid evolution of digital technologies and jobs. Moreover, specific regulations could create a new status of workers thus exacerbating inequalities in labour law. Again with reference to the Italian case of smart working, it is worth noting that some commentators do not agree that smart working and telework are two different phenomena. For some authors smart working is nothing but a form of telework,[224] that may be described as 'telecommuting',[225] something that was intended to be included in the EFA on Telework concept of telework.[226] Consequently, if a law on smart working was approved, teleworkers would be excluded from that regulation, due to the narrower scope of application, and, furthermore, teleworkers not unionised would be without protection, due to the implementation of the EFA on Telework in Italy through collective agreements without *erga omnes* effect, but not through hard law instruments.

A second solution would be to rethink the principles of labour law, as repeatedly argued by many scholars for a long time, in order to deal with practices that fail to comply with the provisions for a regular employment relationship. In this sense, some authors have suggesting introducing an intermediate category between employment and self-employment.[227] This solution, aiming to apply to such workers only a 'percentage' of the employment provisions, reflects the difficulty of finding the traditional elements of subordination in digital jobs or, in other words, the erosion of the three '"Aristotelian rules of labour law" of pre-technological society: the unities of place and work (work performed on the premises of the firm), of time and work (work carried out in a single temporal sequence), and action and work (a mono-professional activity)'.[228] However, the solutions given for telework, crowdworking and work on demand via apps can be useful to assess the necessity of changing the principles of labour law. Some authors have tried to identify the factors that could be used to classify the 'digital relationship' as employment. In this perspective, it has been argued that the

223. For an overview of new forms of employment across the EU, including ICT-based work, *see* Irene Mandl et al., *supra.* For the most relevant ICT innovations in the workplace, *see* Gérard Valenduc, Patricia Vendramin & ETUI, *Working in the digital economy: sorting the old from the new*, Working Paper 2013.03, ETUI aisbl, Brussels (2016) and Ursula Holtgrewe, *New technologies: the future and the present of work in information and communication technology*, 29 (1) New Technology, Work and Employment (2014).
224. FIOM-CGIL, *supra*; Riccardo Pallotta, *Legge di Stabilità 2016: con il collegato nasce il 'lavoro agile'*, IPSOA Quotidiano, 31 Oct. 2015.
225. The word 'telecommuting', as noted at the beginning of this paper, was coined by Jack M. Nilles, F. Roy Carlson Jr., Paul Gray, Gerhard J. Hanneman, *supra*, and it has kept its proper meaning until today. Here the teleworker carries out tasks using ICT away from the firm and moving from place to place (*see* Giuseppe Cassano & Stefania Lopatriello, *supra*, 381–382; Vittorio Di Martino & Linda Wirth, *supra*, 530).
226. In this sense, ETUC, *supra*, 10, applies the EFA on Telework also to 'Nomadic, peripatetic or mobile telework [...]'.
227. This idea has had an application with parasubordinate or quasi subordinate employment, on which see the comparative report by Adalberto Perulli, *Economically dependent / quasi-subordinate (parasubordinate) employment: legal, social and economic aspects*, European Commission, Brussels (2003).
228. Bruno Veneziani, *New technologies and the contract of employment*, 2 (4) International Journal of Comparative Labour Law and Industrial Relations, 149 (1986).

employer's power of management is exercised in telework through the application software installed by the employer and used by the worker on the job. Actually, the worker cannot perform his work via telework without following the directives inserted in the application software, so he is indirectly managed by the employer.[229] This approach has been recently adopted for crowdworking and working on demand via apps. In particular, it has been noted that these activities are subject to some form of control by employers, for example, by platforms providing a rating system to assess the performance of each worker. Customers or clients can leave their evaluations on the platform after the performance of the work, so that the platform can evaluate their satisfaction. On this basis, the platforms can terminate the accounts of those workers who do not comply with company standards. Further, some platforms oblige workers to follow specific instructions about how to behave towards customers[230] or assess the eligibility of the worker to perform his or her tasks through a performance test.[231] Consequently, it has been proposed to apply the control test to these activities in order to classify the relationship as employment, when it is possible considering the specific case.[232]

This last approach seems to demonstrate that the principles of labour law are still valid even in the digital age. However, this solution could be fully applied only at national level, namely when digital performances take place within the borders of the same state, because national labour law, like legislation and jurisprudence, cannot be generally effective *proprio vigore* at transnational level. When the digital worker and the employer are located in different countries, as we have seen in the case of telework, there is a need to turn to private international law to find the applicable law. However, as already noted, those rules are difficult to apply to digital work, and as a result it is predictable that no employment protection will be made available. Moreover, the legal classification of the relationship would be determined only *ex post*, that is before the court in the specific case, with only limited beneficial effects for the conditions of digital workers in general. Not many cases on digital work have been reported so far[233] and this indicates the difficulty for workers to bring these situations before the courts.

Taking this into account, the adoption of the EFA on Telework leads to some significant findings. First of all, the issue of digital work needs to be addressed at supranational level. National legislation would be ineffective due to the transnational

229. Lorenzo Gaeta, *La qualificazione del rapporto*, *supra*, 19.
230. Lyft drivers are instructed to 'Greet every passenger with a big smile and fist bump'; 'Keep [the] car clean on the inside and outside'; 'Go above and beyond good service such as helping passengers with luggage or holding an umbrella for passengers when it is raining' (*see Cotter et al. v. Lyft Inc.*, Order Denying Cross-Motion for Summary Judgement, United States District Court, Northern District of Carolina, 6).
231. Uber, for instance, could require aspiring drivers to pass a 'city-knowledge test' in order to prove their ability to find destinations in their cities (Antonio Aloisi, *supra*, 672–673).
232. Valerio De Stefano, *supra*. In crowdworking and working on demand via apps it is unclear whether the employer is the platform or the client or both (Manfred Weiss, *Digitalizzazione: sfide e prospettive per il diritto del lavoro*, *supra*, 656). On this issue, *see* the functional approach by Jeremias Prassl, Martin Risak, *Uber, Taskrabbit, and co.: platforms as employers? Rethinking the legal analysis of crowdwork*, 37 (3) Comparative Labor Law & Policy Journal, 619–652 (2016).
233. For a number cases on digital work in the United States, *see* Miriam A. Cherry, *supra*.

relationships that are a key characteristic of digital work. In this sense, a study of the common elements and issues of digital jobs appears to be necessary, in order to understand the protections required by digital workers.[234] This minimum standard of protection could be the content, for example, of a European Regulation to be applied to digital relationships taking place across Member States. However, this solution would be applicable in relationships with platforms not based in the EU, and as a result an ILO Convention on digital work could in theory grant broader legal coverage.[235] Unfortunately, these 'obvious' proposals[236] are like a mirage in the desert of digital work regulation. In this connection, the limited practical effectiveness of the ILO Conventions must be considered.[237] In particular, it would be difficult for ILO Member States to agree on International Labour Standards for digital work, taking into account the function of digital work in reducing labour costs. Providing global protection could result in a reduction in competitiveness for countries where digital work is not regulated, with the effect of reducing the protections of 'protected' digital workers (such as teleworkers working in the EU Member States that have implemented the EFA on Telework through legislation) who perform work for employers situated in these third countries.

Considering these hurdles, the second conclusion to be drawn from the EFA on Telework is that social dialogue could be the way to follow to deal with digital work. The effective will of the social partners in addressing digital work has been lacking for a long time as is evident from the data on the dissemination of telework according to which this phenomenon still appears to be marginal in the labour market, despite national and European policies adopted in recent years.[238] In addition, it can be observed that national and supranational institutions often delegate the regulation of

234. According to Antonio Aloisi, *supra*, 686–687, specifically for crowdworking, 'An ideal roadmap for "decent crowdwork" should include, at least: (1) banning discrimination based on geographical preferences or rating charts; (2) avoiding and hindering potential risks of child labor or forced labor; (3) preventing "labor brokerage" from shifting into "social arbitrage"; (4) making ratings "portable" across platforms, leading to a comprehensive "digital identity"; (5) overcoming the exclusivity clause that ties workers to a given platform and keeping switching costs low; (6) promoting forms of collective engagement between workers, clients and platform'.
235. According to Martin Risak & Johannes Warter, *supra*, 14–15, at international level, it could be sufficient to complete the ratification of the ILO Home Work Convention no. 177 of 1996 which could serve as a guideline for decent working conditions for digital workers. Only ten Member States of the ILO have ratified this Convention (Albania, Argentina, Belgium, Bosnia and Herzegovina, Bulgaria, Finland, Ireland, Netherlands, Tajikistan, the former Yugoslav Republic of Macedonia).
236. Patrizia Tullini, *C'è lavoro sul web?*, 1 (1) Labour & Law Issues, 16 (2015).
237. Manfred Weiss, *International Labour Standards: A Complex Public-Private Policy Mix*, 29 (1) International Journal of Comparative Labour Law and Industrial Relations, 7–20 (2013).
238. Parent-Thirion et al., *Fourth European Working Conditions Survey*, Eurofound, Luxembourg (2007), claimed that, at the time of their research, slightly more than 8% of all EU workers did some form of telework, and less than 2% regularly worked from home with a PC. The proportion of people teleworking was highest in the Scandinavian countries, the Netherlands and the eastern European countries and lowest in the southern European countries. Moreover, telework was much more often carried out by self-employed persons than by employees. However, the real proportions of the dissemination of telework could be difficult to assess due to the different concepts of telework used by each Member State and research group.

digital work to the social partners, but neither the one nor the other consider it as a mass phenomenon worth regulating.[239] Moreover, the most significant advantage of digital work is its flexibility, both for workers and employees, and the low costs of the performance,[240] so that it could be argued that hard regulation would reduce the 'vitality' of digital work, limiting its organisational advantages. At the same time, it is sometimes claimed that employers do not like any kind of digital work because of the difficulty of physically supervising the workers.[241] With regard to the trade unions, although they have been the key players in the regulation of telework, they historically reject the dissemination of digital work on a large scale due to the fear that it could result in a reduction of social rights, also taking into account the difficulties in unionising workers who perform their tasks away from the employer's premises, where trade unions traditionally operate.[242]

In spite of the hurdles for social dialogue, industrial relations could be useful in seeking solutions for digital work. Trade unions can no longer postpone the action they need to take in relation to the digital age. Some trade unions have already taken steps, setting up platforms to bring together digital workers in order to organise them.[243] On this point, it is worth noting that digital collective action may soon be undertaken. In relation to telework, some cases of organising strikes at a distance, blocking telephone lines or obstructing the employer's server have been reported.[244] With regard to crowdworking and workers on demand via apps, it can be noted that platforms work because of the 'crowd' and in the end it is the crowd that has the power to determine the survival of the platform through its performance. In this sense, the coordination of crowdworkers/workers on demand via apps would improve exponentially their bargaining power. Moreover, also social responsibility instruments could be used to put

239. This is the case of Germany (Manfred Weiss, *Il telelavoro tra legge e contrattazione collettiva: il caso tedesco, supra*, 679). In addition, the European Union continues to promote the use of IT in employment without showing too much concern about the rights of e-workers. Towards this direction, Europe 2020 (*see* European Commission, *Communication from the Commission. EUROPE 2020. A strategy for smart, sustainable and inclusive growth*, Brussels (2010) has been the starting point to realise the European Digital Agenda and the Agenda for new skills and jobs. The first seems oriented to increase the use of IT in order to make the European market more competitive (*see* European Commission, *Communication from the Commission. EUROPE 2020. A strategy for smart, sustainable and inclusive growth, supra.*). The second aims to modernise the labour market following the flexicurity model and creating new jobs based on new skills, for social inclusion purposes (*http://ec.europa.eu/social/main.jsp?catId=958*). In this sense, IT could play a fundamental role in the development of new skills as it emerges from the EU campaign of skills certification called European e-Competence Framework: *http://www.ecompetences.eu/* (*see* Patrizia Tullini, *supra*, 18).

240. Christian Welz, Felix Wolf & Eurofound, *supra*, 19.

241. Manfred Weiss, *Il telelavoro tra legge e contrattazione collettiva: il caso tedesco, supra*, 668; Vittorio Di Martino & Linda Wirth, *supra*, 535.

242. Christian Welz, Felix Wolf & Eurofound, *supra*, 20; Vittorio Di Martino & Linda Wirth, *supra*, 535. As Manfred Weiss, *Il telelavoro tra legge e contrattazione collettiva: il caso tedesco, supra*, 667 reported, in 1983 the German metalworkers union asked for the formal abrogation of the use of telework.

243. As reported by Valerio De Stefano, *supra*, 501–502, an example is the platform FairCrowdWork (*see http://www.faircrowdwork.org/en*), created by the German union IG-Metall. Another example is the platform Turkopticon (*see https://turkopticon.ucsd.edu/*) designed to help Amazon Mechanical Turk workers.

244. Lorenzo Gaeta, *voce Telelavoro, supra*.

pressure on platforms.[245] In any case, employers' associations are participating in the debate on digital work, and as a result social dialogue on these topics could be possible.[246]

In conclusion coordinating the approaches proposed would probably be the best way to address digital work but, as a start, the commitment of trade unions seems to be crucial. Undoubtedly, the realisation of the European and international objectives of promoting decent work for all[247] should include digital work[248] in order to avoid the rise of 'digital labour as a commodity'.[249]

245. A first step in this direction could be the Code of Conduct. Paid Crowdsourcing for the Better. Guideline for a prosperous and fair cooperation between companies, clients and crowdworkers, in *http://crowdsourcing-code.com/*, signed by three platforms (Testbirds, Clickworker, Streetspotr) and supported by the German Crowdsourcing Association.
246. Valerio De Stefano, *supra*, 502.
247. *See* ILO, *Decent work for all in a global economy: An ILO perspective. Submission by Mr. Juan Somavia, Director General, International Labour Office To the Third WTO Ministerial Conference in Seattle (30th November to 3rd December)*, in *http://www.ilo.org/public/english/bureau/dgo/speeches/somavia/1999/seattle.htm* (1999) and Commission of the European Communities, *Communication from the Commission to the Council, the European Parliament, The European Economic and Social Committee and the Committee of the Regions. Promoting decent work for all. The EU contribution to the implementation of the decent work agenda in the world*, Brussels (2006) on its European implementation.
248. For telework conceived as specific decent work instrument *see* Vittorio Di Martino, *The high road to teleworking*, ILO, Geneva (2001).
249. Paraphrasing the principle 'labour is not a commodity' in the ILO Philadelphia Declaration (I, a).

Part III Health, Well-Being and Workers' Integration in the Labour Market

CHAPTER 9

Improving Return to Work and Disability Management in the Developing World: Pointers Emanating from International Instruments, Standards and Guidelines

*Marius Olivier & Avinash Govindjee**

§9.01 INTRODUCTION

Return to work of workers who suffer a disability as a result of an occupational injury or disease, and the management of their disabilities, is an area clearly in need of reform in the developing world. The paper considers salient aspects of key international instruments, standards and guidelines (specifically the UN Convention on the Rights of Persons with Disabilities (UNCRPD), relevant ILO Conventions, and the relatively recent 'Guidelines on Return to Work and Reintegration' of the International Social Security Association (ISSA Guidelines)) applicable to this area and their application to the developing world context. The paper matches these aspects against the approaches adopted / being adopted by two developing countries in particular, i.e., Malaysia and

* Marius Olivier, Adjunct-Professor, Faculty of Law, University of Western Australia; Extraordinary Professor, Faculty of Law, Northwest University, South Africa; Director: International Institute for Social Law and Policy, olivier@iislp.net.au; olivier@isl-p.org; Avinash Govindjee, Professor of Law and Head of Department, Department of Public Law, Faculty of Law, Nelson Mandela Metropolitan University (NMMU), South Africa; Consulting Attorney: Cliffe Dekker Hofmeyr; Senior Commissioner: CCMA (Commission for Conciliation, Mediation and Arbitration), Avinash.Govindjee@nmmu.ac.za.

South Africa. This methodology is designed to provide a comparative, context-specific sample of the application of selected issues emerging from the said instruments, standards and guidelines in order to provide some pointers for purposes of extrapolating how return to work and reintegration might be introduced and implemented in other (middle-to-high income) countries in the developing world.

§9.02 RATIONALE

The objective of a Return to Work (RTW) system is to return workers to employment at the earliest possible date following any injury or illness. It attempts to speed recovery from injury or illness and reduce compensation costs while ensuring that participation in a return to work plan will not, in itself, prejudice an injured employee. Employees who sustain an injury or illness should safely return to work at the earliest medically practical time [at least in a temporary (modified or alternate duty) assignment]. By allowing an employee to perform modified duties, the employee is allowed to remain a productive member of the workforce while he or she maintains their human dignity.[1]

Occupational rehabilitation requires accurate diagnosis and early and effective medical and occupational treatment, involving a seamless multi-skilled team approach, with clear objectives and milestones. It requires an assessment of the physical and mental capacities of the individual, and of the demands of the job, and the provision of counselling, training and selective work placement.[2] Principles underpinning successful Return to Work (RTW) and occupational rehabilitation include the fact that it:[3]

- is industry based (the employee's workplace and specific duties are the primary focus of the planned RTW activities) – the workplace can be an appropriate and effective place to rehabilitate injured employees;
- is function-orientated (i.e., aimed at minimising any disability rather than simply reducing/correcting the impairment);
- involves early intervention (rehabilitation and RTW processes should start as soon as possible after the injury or illness);

1. *See* Marius Olivier, Avinash Govindjee & Matthias Nyenti, '*Selected perspectives on return-to-work and disability management in two developing countries: Malaysia and South Africa*', 4 *International Journal of Social Security and Workers Compensation* 9–37 at 11 (2012/2013). For further remarks relating to addressing benefit dependence, exclusion among people with disability and the promotion of reintegration into employment, *see* OECD *Sickness, Disability and Work: Breaking the Barriers* (2010) 11.
2. Marius Olivier et al., *Reflections of developing an integrated comprehensive policy framework for rehabilitation, re-integration and return-to-work strategies in relation to workers who suffered occupational injuries or diseases* (Report prepared for the Compensation Fund of South Africa) 21 (2011).
3. *Ibid.*

- provides for individual programmes tailored to the needs of injured employees, since the rehabilitation process is different for everyone and depends upon the nature of injuries sustained or diseases contracted;
- uses a multidisciplinary team approach (RTW plans are tailored to the employee's needs, are well-coordinated, accountable and focus on results);
- involves shared responsibility (the employee must actively contribute to the RTW plan);
- usually makes the employer responsible for the close management and monitoring of RTW programmes in consultation with the health professionals and specialist rehabilitation providers involved;
- requires employers to take effective injury prevention action.

If properly introduced, it appears as if there are noteworthy benefits (from introducing a RTW framework) for employees, employers and the state, and that it is accordingly a worthwhile endeavour to strive to overcome the challenges that stand in the way of the introduction of a cohesive RTW system:

- Employees are able to remain in work or return to work in a timely manner.[4]
- For employers, a skilled workforce is important, and losing an employee unnecessarily due to workplace illness or injury must be avoided, also so that productivity can remain high.[5]
- For the state, RTW policies and programmes typically enable governments to reduce spending on social security and limiting the amount of benefit claimants. Incapacity or disability pensions are often long-term or permanent payments, with the claimant usually excluded from the job market.[6]

The need to introduce RTW in the developing world context is evident. As noted by Loewenson, with particular reference to Southern Africa, 'Unfortunately, the most creative social protection systems cannot confront a tidal wave of health problems from insecure, hazardous and low-quality jobs.'[9] Standard-setting in occupational health and safety is generally weak in developing countries. Loewenson remarks: 'In industrialised countries, standard setting in unclear situations may err on the side of controlling risks, but in poorer countries this often errs on the side of continued exposure'.[7] In many developing countries, including South Africa, the right to return to work, rehabilitation and retraining is also weakly developed.[8]

4. *See*, for example, E. Hagen, A. Grasdal and HR. Eriksen, *Does early intervention with a light mobilization program reduce long-term sick leave for low back pain: A 3-year follow-up study Spine* 9–16 as cited in Olivier 31 (2003).
5. Olivier, *Report prepared for the Compensation Fund of South Africa* 32. RTW and disability management can also include reducing insurance costs or assessments to be paid by employers, as well as reducing the costs of sick leave.
6. Olivier, *Report prepared for the Compensation Fund of South Africa* 33.
7. R. Loewenson, *Globalization and occupational health: A perspective from southern Africa*, 79(9) *Bulletin of the World Health Organization* 863--868 at 866 (2001).
8. *Id.*, 865.

§9.03 INTERNATIONAL LAW

[A] Background

International law is traditionally defined as that body of law which binds or regulates states in terms of their relationships with other states.[9,10] Most domestic systems automatically incorporate, or incorporate through a separate act of adoption, many rules of international law into their system of municipal law, the latter option being typical.[11] International law also influences the manner in which courts interpret domestic law. There are four sources of international law, which includes international conventions (otherwise known as treaties).[12] Treaties are international agreements entered into between states in terms of which states expressly agree to be bound by the terms of the treaty.[13] Treaties are multilateral where a number of states enter into the treaty. These treaties normally have the purpose of codifying international law with regard to the subject matter in question.[14]

[B] The Importance of International Law for RTW, also in Malaysia and South Africa

International law instruments are an important source in relation to the possible introduction of RTW in the developing world. One reason for this is that many developing world constitutions contain explicit reference to the role of international law and may be seen to adopt international-law friendly approaches. Countries in the developing world are increasingly persuaded to ratify international instruments and look towards international best practices in developing their own policies and legal frameworks, also in areas pertaining to labour law, occupational health and safety and return to work. In fact, in some cases, countries expressly promise in their constitutions to promote and maintain the welfare of their people by adopting, *inter alia*, policies aimed at membership of the International Labour Organisation (ILO) and, where possible, adherence to and action in accordance with the international Conventions and Recommendations of the ILO.[15]

9. *See*, in general, Marius Olivier, Avinash Govindjee and Matthias Nyenti, '*The role of international and regional standards in the development of an appropriate rehabilitation, reintegration and return-to-work policy framework in South Africa*' in Marius Olivier, O Ockert Dupper & Avinash Govindjee (eds.) *The role of standards in labour- and social security law: international, regional and national perspectives*, Ch. 13, 216–238 (Juta, 2013), from where this has been modified, expanded upon and developed.
10. H Waldock (ed.) *The Law of Nations* (6th Ed, 1963) 1.
11. H. Strydom and K. Hopkins, *International Law* in Woolman et al, 2 *Constitutional Law of South Africa* (2nd Ed), 30–2 (2008).
12. The other sources are customary international law, general principles of law recognised by civilised nations and judicial decisions and the writings of highly qualified publicists: Strydom and Hopkins, 30–3.
13. Strydom and Hopkins, 30–3.
14. *Ibid*.
15. *See*, for example, Art. 95(d) of the Namibian Constitution as well as Namibia's constitutional commitment to foster (general) respect for international law and treaty obligations, in Art. 96(d).

These are important considerations and intentions, even where these developing countries may not yet have formally ratified any of the ILO Conventions in relation to RTW. Of course, by ratifying and being a party to such instruments, provisions pertaining to, for example, workers' compensation and issues regarding workplace reintegration are binding upon these countries from the perspective of international law, and should find expression in domestic law.

International standards in relation to the status and treatment of persons with disabilities, including workers who have suffered an occupational injury or disease, provide crucial benchmarks for the development of appropriate RTW policies, also in the developing world. These standards have primarily been encapsulated by the United Nations (UN) and International Labour Organisation (ILO), although recent guidelines published by the International Social Security Association (ISSA) are also of relevance, as discussed below. By ratifying and being a party to instruments such as the UNCRPD, provisions pertaining to, for example, workers' compensation and issues regarding workplace reintegration are binding upon South Africa and Malaysia, from the perspective of international law and should find expression in these countries' domestic law.

South Africa ratified both the UNCRPD and the Optional Protocol in 2007.[16] Malaysia signed the Convention in April 2008 and ratified the same in 2010.[17] The UNCRPD contains several provisions which are of direct relevance and application to a RTW policy/programme and ILO instruments and the ISSA Guidelines also reflect key pointers for the operation of a successful RTW system in countries such as Malaysia and South Africa.[18] It is suggested elsewhere in this paper that the Malaysian SOCSO RTW model largely reflects standards and guidelines emanating from ILO, UNCRPD and ISSA instruments (e.g., in respect of governance and institutional arrangements, the role of case managers, reliance of public-private partnerships, the use of technology and emphasis of expert qualification and certification).[19] By contrast, South Africa has

16. The Convention and the Optional Protocol were ratified by South Africa on 30 Nov. 2007. Interestingly, from a regional (SADC) perspective, only Botswana and Tanzania have not yet ratified at least the UNCRPD: http://www.un.org/disabilities/countries.asp?id = 166.
17. From a regional (ASEAN) perspective, only Laos has not yet signed the UNCRPD; Brunei Darussalam has signed the Convention but not yet ratified it. While some may argue that the UNCRPD was the main impetus for the implementation of RTW in Malaysia, it must be noted that the Act which governs SOCSO, namely the Employees' Social Security Act, 1969 (ESSA) pre-dates the Convention: *see* Marius Olivier, Avinash Govindjee and Matthias Nyenti, *Selected perspectives on return-to-work and disability management in two developing countries: Malaysia and South Africa*, 4 *International Journal of Social Security and Workers Compensation* 9-37 at 15 (2012/2013).
18. Article 26, for example, specifies that member countries 'shall take effective and appropriate measures, including through peer support, to enable persons with disabilities to attain and maintain maximum independence, full physical, mental, social and vocational ability, and full inclusion and participation in all aspects of life ... [by organising, strengthening and extending] comprehensive habilitation and rehabilitation services and programmes, particularly in the areas of health, employment, education and social services ....
19. *See* Marius Olivier, Avinash Govindjee, Matthias Nyenti, Azman bin Dato Aziz Mohammed and Cheong Peck Huang, *E SOCSO Return-to-work Programme in Malaysia: A Handbook* 2012 (IISLP/SOCSO) 59 (2012) suggesting that by establishing the SOCSO Rehabilitation Centre, Malaysia is indirectly preparing to fulfil its international responsibilities in terms of the UNCRPD.

been criticised for failing to incorporate international instruments such as the UNCRPD adequately into its legal framework.

[C] UNCRPD

The UNCRPD contains several provisions which are of direct relevance and application to the establishment and functioning of a RTW policy/programme in developing countries. The core provision pertaining to the right to work and employment of persons with disabilities (PWDs) is Article 27, which obliges countries, also in the developing world, to 'safeguard and promote the realisation of the right to work, *including for those who acquire a disability during the course of employment,* by taking steps, including through legislation', to, *inter alia:*[20]

(a) Promote vocational and professional rehabilitation, job retention, and return to work programmes for persons with disabilities.[21]
(b) Enable persons with disabilities to have effective access to general technical and vocational guidance programmes, placement services and vocational and continuing training.[22]
(c) Prohibit disability discrimination in employment[23] – which includes a prohibition on the denial of reasonable accommodation.[24]
(d) Protect the rights of PWDs, for example with reference to equal opportunities and equal remuneration for work of equal value, and *safe and healthy working conditions.*[25]
(e) Promote employment opportunities and career advancement for PWDs in the labour market, as well as assistance in finding, obtaining, maintaining and returning to employment.[26]
(f) Promote employment opportunities for self-employment, entrepreneurship, the development of cooperatives and starting one's own business.[27]
(g) Ensure that reasonable accommodation is provided to PWDs in the workplace.[28]
(h) Promote the acquisition by PWDs of work experience in the open labour market.[29]

20. Article 27(1) – emphasis added.
21. Article 27(1)(k).
22. Article 27(1)(d).
23. Article 27(1)(a).
24. Article 27 (1)(i). *See* the definition of 'discrimination' in Art. 2 of the Convention.
25. Article 27(1)(b) – emphasis added.
26. Article 27(1)(e).
27. Article 27(1)(f).
28. Article 27(1)(i). 'Reasonable accommodation' means a necessary and appropriate modification and adjustments not imposing a disproportionate or undue burden, where needed in a particular case, to ensure to persons with disabilities the enjoyment or exercise on an equal basis with others of all human rights and fundamental freedoms – *see* Art. 2 of the Convention.
29. Article 27(1)(j).

The UNCRPD, furthermore, explicitly requires compliance with the following objectives, which are equally relevant to RTW programmes:

(i) Promotion of individual autonomy and independence.[30]
(ii) Involvement of those affected in (relevant) policy-making (i.e., at the macro-level)[31] and when developing individual rehabilitation plans (i.e., at the micro-level).[32]
(iii) Promotion of societal inclusion and participation.[33]
(iv) Promotion of the availability, knowledge and use of assistive devices and technologies, designed for PWDs, as they relate to habilitation and rehabilitation.[34]
(v) Introduction of appropriate training, for both –
 (a) Professionals and staff working in habilitation and rehabilitation services.[35]
 (b) PWDs.[36]

In particular, as far as rehabilitation is concerned, the UNCRPD requires State Parties to 'organize, strengthen and extend comprehensive habilitation and rehabilitation services and programmes, particularly in the areas of health, employment, education and social services...'[37] These multi-faceted rehabilitation services and programmes must:

- involve early intervention and a multidisciplinary assessment of individual needs and strengths;[38]
- support community and societal participation and inclusion;[39]
- be voluntary;[40]
- be available to PWDs as close as possible to their own communities, including in rural areas;[41]
- promote vocational and professional rehabilitation, job retention and return to work programmes for persons with disabilities;
- ensure that reasonable accommodation is provided to PWDs in the workplace;

30. Articles 3(a), 19 and 26(1).
31. Article 4(3) stipulates: 'In the development and implementation of legislation and policies to implement the present Convention, and in other decision-making processes concerning issues relating to persons with disabilities, States Parties shall closely consult with and actively involve persons with disabilities, including children with disabilities, through their representative organisations.'
32. *See* para. (o) of the Preamble: '*Considering* that persons with disabilities should have the opportunity to be actively involved in decision-making processes about policies and programmes, including those directly concerning them' (emphasis in original).
33. Articles 3(c) and 26(1)(b).
34. Article 26(3).
35. Articles 4(1)(i) and 26(2).
36. Article 27(1)(d).
37. Article 26(1).
38. Article 26(1)(a).
39. Article 26(1)(b).
40. *Ibid.*
41. *Ibid.*

- enable PWDs to have effective access to general technical and vocational guidance programmes, placement services and vocational and continuing training.

Article 32 of the Convention requires progressive realisation of the rights contained in the Convention through international cooperation and through State Parties taking appropriate measures such as development cooperation, exchange programmes, bilateral and trilateral agreements, domestication of international instruments, development of mainstreaming norms and standards in line with international laws. According to Article 33 of the Convention, states must establish national focal points for the implementation of the Convention, coordination mechanisms, implementation mechanisms and legal and administrative frameworks to promote and monitor implementation, as well as ensure the participation of civil society.

It is clear from these provisions that the Convention foresees rehabilitation and return to work arrangements that are multi-faceted and, to some extent, flexible, given the commitment to progressive realisation and the wide range of illustrations provided. This is particularly important for developing world contexts, given the realities of slow economic growth and the various competing demands on limited state resources. That the international framework would appear to support the measured, progressive introduction of RTW arrangements (e.g., through pilot studies and incremental increase of RTW-related expenditure) is significant. At the very least, it is clear that the Convention does not rigidly prescribe a fixed method for compliance with its provisos, enabling developing countries to push the boundaries of creativity and to introduce measures that are practically implementable in their own contexts. This approach might, in some countries, promote unexpected synergies between governmental departments as well as public-private partnerships that optimise the use of limited resources for RTW purposes.

[D] ILO

A number of prominent ILO instruments, of fairly recent origin, relate to the themes of injury benefits, health and safety, disability, injury prevention and vocational rehabilitation. These instruments include:

- ILO Employment Injury Benefit Convention, 1964 (No. 121).
- ILO Nursing Personnel Convention, 1977 (No. 149).
- ILO Occupational Safety and Health Convention, 1981 (No. 155).
- ILO Occupational Health Services Convention, 1985 (No. 161).
- ILO Prevention of Major Industrial Accidents Convention, 1993 (No. 174).
- ILO Promotional Framework for Occupational Safety and Health Convention, 2006 (No. 187).
- ILO Protocol to the Occupational Safety and Health Convention, 1981, 2002 (No. P 155).
- ILO Safety and Health in Agriculture Convention, 2001 (No. 184).
- ILO Safety and Health in Construction Convention, 1988 (No. 167).

- ILO Safety and Health in Mines Convention, 1995 (No. 176).
- ILO Social Security (Minimum Standards) Convention, 1952 (No. 102).
- ILO Vocational Rehabilitation and Employment (Disabled Persons) Convention 159 of 1983.
- ILO Vocational Rehabilitation and Employment (Disabled Persons) Recommendation 168 of 1983.
- ILO Vocational Rehabilitation (Disabled) Recommendation 99, 1955.

A number of developing countries have not yet ratified any of these instruments.[42] These ILO instruments nevertheless provide significant insight into the nature of vocational rehabilitation measures and standards required. Some of the ILO instruments mentioned above have particular relevance in the area of vocational rehabilitation services. These services should exist to contribute towards ensuring that injured or sick workers are prepared for returning to work as soon as possible (in appropriate circumstances and once a conducive enabling environment has been crafted). The objective of vocational rehabilitation services is to develop the working capacity of persons with disabilities, promote suitable employment opportunities and overcome discrimination against disabled persons in respect of their training and employment.[43] Vocational rehabilitation services should then be adapted consistently with the country's policy, abilities and conditions and should be developed progressively.[44]

To achieve effective implementation of vocational rehabilitation and integration programmes, cooperation between the competent authorities is imperative. Poor cooperation, coordination and evaluation can adversely affect successful implementation. According to the Vocational Rehabilitation Recommendation of 1955, administrative responsibility for the general development and application of vocational rehabilitation programmes can either be entrusted to one authority, or jointly to multiple competent authorities responsible for different activities in the programme (while entrusting one of the authorities with the primary responsibility of coordination).[45]

Vocational rehabilitation services should be developed with the assistance of representative advisory committees. The committees should include authorities

42. *See* http://www.ilo.org, accessed on 4 Jul. 2015.
43. Vocational Rehabilitation (Disabled) Recommendation of the ILO 'Application of the principles of vocational rehabilitation' (1955) 41.
44. Vocational Rehabilitation and Employment (Disabled Persons) Convention of the ILO (1983) Art. 2.
45. ILO *Vocational Rehabilitation* 'Administrative Organisation' para. 16(b). The intended cooperation should, for example, promote identification of persons in need of vocational rehabilitation and ensure early commencement of rehabilitation: ILO *Vocational Rehabilitation* 'Methods for enabling disabled persons to make use of vocational rehabilitation services' 26(2). The intended purpose of rehabilitation is to return the injured employee back to work as soon as possible upon recovery and ease the process of social and occupational integration. To fulfil the purpose of vocational rehabilitation and early return to work programmes, cooperation and understanding between the various authorities is of utmost importance. For example, Shrey and Lacerte note that insufficient cooperation and support between labour, management and disability managers may result in return to work initiatives faltering and causing friction between employers and their workers.

concerned with vocational rehabilitation,[46] employers' and employees' organisations,[47] specially qualified people with sufficient knowledge of (and concern about) the vocational rehabilitation of the disabled[48] and organisations of disabled persons.[49] The committees should function at the different spheres of government. At national level, they should advise on the development of vocational rehabilitation services policy. At regional and local level, focus would be better placed on adapting, coordinating and applying measures taken at national level.[50]

Appropriate financial assistance should also be made available to disabled persons. Financial assistance programmes should be designed to facilitate preparation and retention of suitable employment. Assistance should include, for example, free rehabilitation services, maintenance allowances, supply of necessary tools and equipment, prosthetics and necessary transportation. There is general acknowledgement that financial assistance programmes would have to be designed consistently with the country's abilities and conditions. Importantly, participation in vocational rehabilitation services should not disqualify or result in disabled persons losing available social security benefits that are unrelated to their participation in the rehabilitation programme.[51]

As illustrated above, a notable thrust of the instruments is on adaptability, cooperation, coordination and progressive realisation. The requisite assistance to be provided to injured/sick employees, including free rehabilitation services and work equipment is, significantly, dependent on a country's situation and resources. The significance of all of this for countries in the developing world is the notion that interventions need to be crafted in such a manner that there is proper synchronisation of return to work interventions in developing countries, notwithstanding the predictable resource and other constraints being experienced and that finances need to be utilised in an optimum manner, with meaningful collaboration on the part of the various stakeholders, as far as possible.

South Africa has ratified only two of the ILO instruments reflected above, namely the ILO Occupational Safety and Health Convention, 1981 (No. 155), and the ILO Safety and Health in Mines Convention, 1995 (No. 176).[52] Both of these (ratified) instruments fail to make a significant contribution towards advancing an RTW agenda.

Malaysia, on the other hand, has ratified only the ILO Promotional Framework for Occupational Safety and Health Convention, 2006 (No. 187) which, as the name suggests, focuses on occupational health and safety and the development of a national

46. Paragraph 18(2)(a).
47. Paragraph 18(2)(b).
48. Paragraph 18(2)(c).
49. Paragraph 18(2)(d).
50. Paragraph 18(3).
51. ILO *Vocational Rehabilitation* 23.
52. In 2003 and 2000 respectively – *see* http://www.ilo.org/dyn/normlex/en/f?p=1000:11200:0::NO:11200:P11200_COUNTRY_ID:102888, accessed on 30 Mar. 2017. *See also*, http://www.ilo.org/dyn/normlex/en/f?p=1000:12100:0::NO:12100:P12100_INSTRUMENT_ID:312300, http://www.ilo.org/dyn/normlex/en/f?p=NORMLEXPUB:12100:0::NO::P12100_ILO_CODE:C176.

preventative safety and health culture.[53] It has been argued that the involvement of the disability movement in rehabilitation and RTW would be bolstered by ratification of the ILO's Vocational Rehabilitation and Employment (Disabled Persons) Convention No. 159 of 1983.[54] Since ILO Conventions require a tripartite machinery to promote the implementation of international labour standards, this would automatically increase the involvement of other stakeholders and thereby facilitate greater involvement on the part of the disability movement in Malaysian rehabilitation and RTW.[55]

Given South Africa and Malaysia's signature and ratification of the UNCRPD, and their non-ratification of ILO instruments dealing directly with vocational rehabilitation, it is arguable that the UNCRPD provides a much better starting point than ILO standards for assessing these countries' conduct with respect to their reintegration and rehabilitation obligations.[56]

[E] ISSA (International Social Security Association)

In 2013 the International Social Security Association (ISSA) adopted important Guidelines on Return to Work and Reintegration (the Guidelines).[57] Although these Guidelines are non-binding, they are of particular relevance for the development of RTW in the context of the developing world, particularly in cases where a country is affiliated to ISSA. They are comprehensive in scope and content, and contain valuable and principles guidelines for countries and social security institutions intent on developing RTW frameworks. These principles and guidelines in essence:[58]

- set out the arguments in favour of RTW, highlighting general principles involved in RTW;
- stress the importance of a holistic process, entailing a comprehensive and integrated approach, which begins at the workplace, combines medical treatment and vocational treatment, and adopts a biopsychosocial approach;
- emphasise the need for early intervention, with reference to early identification and intervention, proactive reporting, beginning during acute medical treatment, and the role of facilitators;
- highlight an individualised approach, with case management, an individual (rehabilitation plan), workplace accommodation and quality control as core components;

53. *See* http://www.ilo.org/dyn/normlex/en/f?p=1000:11210:0::NO:11210:P11210_COUNTRY_ID:102960 (accessed on 14 Jan. 2016).
54. Olivier, Govindjee, Nyenti, Azman Bin Aziz Mohammed and Cheong Peck Huang, E *SOCSO Return-to-work Programme in Malaysia: A Handbook 2012* (IISLP/SOCSO) (2012) 50, *supra.*
55. *Ibid.*
56. *See* Govindjee et al., *The role of international and regional standards in the development of an appropriate rehabilitation, reintegration and return-to-work policy framework in South Africa* in Olivier, Dupper and Govindjee (eds.) *The role of standards in labour- and social security law: international, regional and national perspectives*, Ch. 13, at 225 (Juta, 2013).
57. ISSA, *ISSA Guidelines on Return to Work and Reintegration* (2013).
58. *See* in particular *Guidelines* 6–32.

- require the active participation of the employee concerned – with reference to engaging with employees, empowering the individual, confidence, motivation and self-determination, and confidentiality;
- set out principles for collaboration and dispute resolution, reflecting on communication, working with workplace actors, working with health-care professionals and service providers, and working with networks;
- consider the qualification of experts – by ensuring the high quality of RTW professionals, the education and continuing professional development of RTW professionals, and certification of RTW professionals;
- require monitoring and evaluation, comprehending policy evaluation, programme evaluation, individual outcomes and a formal audit.

In particular, the ISSA Guidelines emphasise the central role of employer involvement, with reference to employer duties and obligations; the enhanced use of employer and employee incentives; the introduction and enhancement of activating measures (i.e., moving away from over-reliance on disability benefit payments towards adjusted workplaces and alternative work and skilling arrangements); increased employment/job protection as a key component of successful RTW and DM (Disability Management) interventions; the enhancement of employee involvement in rehabilitation programmes through appropriate support; and introducing measures to build an adequate cadre of coordinated service providers.

These ISSA Guidelines chronicle good practice models, policies and procedures which have successfully been implemented by social security institutions in respect of return to work and reintegration. As such, they hold the potential to serve as a bridge between the implementation of RTW arrangements in the developed and developing world contexts and to ensure that lessons from various experiences worldwide may be used to inform future initiatives.

Models have specifically been developed by ISSA to identify approaches to enable decision-makers in social security institutions to benefit from global experience in this area. In particular, the Guidelines are designed to:

- outline strategic options for social security institutions in order to achieve these outcomes;
- stimulate discussion around good practice return to work programmes for social security institutions;
- identify critical success design elements;
- offer practical implementation tools.

While the ISSA Guidelines are non-binding in nature, it is evident that they hold important lessons for developing countries such as South Africa and Malaysia, having essentially served to distil internationally recognised good practice models (including policies, processes and procedures designed and implemented by social security institutions in various parts of the world). These models may serve to highlight approaches that will allow decision-makers in social security institutions in the developing world to tailor processes suitable for their own context.

[F] Analysis

Return to work of occupationally injured and diseased workers, and the management of their disabilities, is an area clearly in need of reform in the developing world, in particular given the tremendous challenges faced by developing countries in introducing and implementing return to work and reintegration arrangements. However, there appears to be no core reason to prevent state-of-the-art and internationally recognised RTW and disability management principles, practices and tools in the developing world. International law, particularly the recent ISSA Guidelines, but also the UNCRPD and ILO instruments, can be practically implementable and ought, therefore, to be carefully considered and analysed by countries seeking to introduce return to work and rehabilitation initiatives in a systematic fashion. Developing countries stand to gain by complying with their international obligations, including, for example, the submission of country reports in terms of the UNCRPD in cases where this Convention has been ratified. Yet, there is need to factor in the particular contexts of developing world realities and socio-economic contexts, to ensure appropriate and country-sensitive roll-out of RTW and DM. In fact, it may be argued that there is a (greater) need to develop unique, country-specific approaches in the developing world, bearing in mind the nature of the national labour market, and effective means to ensure stakeholder participation. Regional developments and the experience of Malaysia and South Africa, discussed below, provide further insights in this regard.

§9.04 REGIONAL DEVELOPMENTS

It should also be noted that developments are occurring at regional levels. From a developing world perspective, note could be taken of developments in the context of the Southern African Development Community (SADC). Various instruments largely reiterate the RTW and disability management (DM) principles that are embedded in the international instruments mentioned above.

The SADC Charter of Fundamental Social Rights (the Social Charter)[59] requires Member States to endeavour to create an enabling environment so that:

- every worker in the region has the right to health and safety at work and to a healthy and safe environment that sustains human development and access to adequate shelter;[60]
- workers have the right to services, that provide for the prevention, recognition, detection and compensation of work-related illness or injury, including emergency care, with *rehabilitation and reasonable job security after injury* and adequate inflation adjusted compensation;[61]

59. Adopted in 2003.
60. Social Charter, Art. 12(a).
61. *Id.*, Art. 12(h) (emphasis added).

- workplace-based health service for workers is accessible, affordable and equitable, and is provided on a professional ethical basis.[62]

Article 9 of the Charter, in relation to Persons with Disabilities (PWDs), stipulates that PWDs 'shall be entitled to additional concrete measures aimed at *improving their social and professional integration*.'[63] According to Article 9(2) these measures 'shall relate to, in particular, according to the capacities of beneficiaries, *vocational training, accessibility and mobility, means of transport and housing and appropriate organisation of work and workplaces to take into account their needs*.'[64]

The above provisions of the Social Charter are reinforced by similar and related provisions in the Code on Social Security in the SADC.[65] Article 12.6 of the Code, dealing with occupational injuries and diseases, provides that 'Social security systems should provide for *adequate rehabilitation and reintegration measures*. Member States should ensure that appropriate preventative measures are in place.'[66] Article 14.3 of the Code reiterates the Social Charter provision on the social and professional integration of PWDs, while Article 14.4 requires of SADC Member States to 'ensure that the *special needs (including the need for assistive devices) and circumstances* of persons with disabilities are provided for in national social insurance and social assistance instruments.'[67]

The most important provisions in this regard are contained in Article 19 of the Code, which deals with prevention and integration. This article stresses the importance of sufficient preventive and reintegrative measures instead of a primarily compensation-focused dispensation; emphasises both labour market and social integration; and requires effective rehabilitation and reintegration measures. Article 19 stipulates:

(19.1) Member States are encouraged to ensure that national social security systems adequately integrate sufficient preventative and reintegrative measures and are not primarily compensation-focused.

(19.2) Reintegrative measures should be aimed at ensuring that those persons affected by a risk-creating situation are meaningfully integrated, at least socially, and in the labour market, in order to encourage self-reliance and to support their human dignity.

(19.3) Member States should collectively and individually ensure that their social security systems adequately provide for the prevention of social risks that affect communities within and across the borders of Member States, and should also provide for effective measures of relief, rehabilitation, reconstruction, reintegration and revival for communities so affected.

62. *Id.*, Art. 12(j).
63. Article 9(1). Emphasis added.
64. Emphasis added.
65. Adopted in 2007.
66. Emphasis added.
67. Emphasis added.

More recently, in 2014, the SADC Protocol on Employment and Labour was adopted. Building on a right to a safe and healthy environment,[68] Article 12.3 of the Protocol stipulates that:[69]

> Member States shall adopt measures to ensure that workers have the right to services that provide for the prevention, recognition, detection and compensation of work-related illness or injury including emergency cases, with rehabilitation and reasonable job security after injury and adequate compensation appropriately adjusted from time to time.

Article 12.4(b) of the Protocol encourages Member States to ensure that 'A preventive safety and health culture based on a systems approach for the progressive improvement of Occupational Health and Safety performance is promoted'. Article 11.3(c) in turn provides that 'each Member State shall aim at developing an integrated and comprehensive social protection system which, among others, adequately integrates sufficient preventive and reintegrative measures, including measures aimed at integrating and reintegrating workers into the labour force.'

§9.05 CHALLENGES

There are some barriers to the establishment of a RTW system. Rehabilitation and RTW obligations are seen by many employers as another burden imposed by government. Where employees and/or trade unions are not properly informed and consulted on the establishment of a RTW system, they may not be supportive as the system could be perceived as depriving the employees of their entitlement to long-term occupational injury and disease compensation. Other barriers that have been identified as hindering rehabilitation and RTW systems include lack of knowledge on modified work and negative attitudes of employees; a longer period of time off work; the presence of psychological problems; a long period until settlement of a compensation claim; greater number of injuries and/or significant disability; the status of the employment market (high unemployment rate); the age of the injured worker; the level of skills/occupation in question; a longer period of actual or expected treatment; and the severity of (any) spinal injury. Further personal barriers include low morale and self-esteem; financial problems; family worries; unresolved anger or guilt; feelings of failure or anxiety; loss; depression; or insomnia.[70]

Apart from barriers that may impact negatively on policy formulation and development, there are also barriers which could hamper the successful

68. SADC Protocol on Employment and Labour (2014) (*see* http://www.ilo.org/wcmsp5/groups/public/---ed_protect/---protrav/---migrant/documents/genericdocument/wcms_379411.pdf, accessed on 30 Mar. 2017), Art. 12.1.
69. Emphasis added.
70. *See* also http://www.synergyinsurance.net/Handouts/ERTW.doc and http://www.iombudsman. org.nz/.

implementation and operation of RTW. An overview of the literature reveals several shortcomings, including:[71]

- the lack of appropriate applied work interventions and suitable adjustments to the working environment as a paramount consideration in significant cross-country differences in RTW;
- dysfunctions in organisational dynamics across RTW systems, relating to the workplace, health care, vocational rehabilitation and workers' compensation;
- inadequate health-care management acting as an impediment, as is the case with an inappropriately composed disability management team;
- limited knowledge of the claims process, and of beneficiary rights and responsibilities, against a background of treating beneficiaries with suspicion;
- a tendency to focus too much on ability;
- a lack of cooperation between the insurance sector, health-care providers, employers and occupational health-care providers, in terms of competence and cooperation;
- a lack of labour market activation/reintegration, though this may not be relevant to those who are not employable as a result of their injury or disease;
- a failure to construct a RTW system in compliance with the minimum compensation and human rights framework embedded in international standards: an overemphasis on returning workers to the labour market can infringe respect for their dignity, fairness and justice, and could increase their stigmatisation;
- inadequate protection of RTW beneficiaries against dismissal in the absence of a direct remedy of reinstatement, and as a result of delays as regards recourse to the (industrial or other) courts and complex litigation; overall, these deficiencies may lead to continuation of payments, thus rendering rehabilitation ineffective.

71. *See* J. Anema, A. Schellart, J. Cassidy, P. Loisel, T. Veerman and A. van der Beek, *Can cross country differences in return-to-work after chronic occupational back pan be explained? An exploratory analysis on disability policies in a six country cohort study*, 19(4) Journal of Occupational Rehabilitation, 419–426 419 (2006); E. MacEachen, A Kosny, S Ferrier & L Chambers, T*he 'Toxic Dose' of System Problems: Why Some Injured Workers Don't Return to Work as Expected*, 20(3) Journal of Occupational Rehabilitation 349 (2010); C. Ståhl, T. Svensson, G. Petersson & K Ekberg, *Swedish rehabilitation professionals' perspectives on work ability assessments in a changing sickness insurance system*, 33(15–16) Disability and Rehabilitation, 1373–1382 (2011); K. Lippel, *Preserving Workers' Dignity in Workers' Compensation Systems: An International Perspective*, 55 American Journal of Industrial Medicine 519–536 (2012); J. Eakin, *The Discourse of Abuse in Return to Work: A Hidden Epidemic of Suffering*, in Peterson, C & C Mayhew (eds.), *Occupational Health and Safety: International Influences and the 'New' Epidemics* 159–174 (Amityville, New York: Baywood, 2005); M. Ciccarelli and J. Dender *Contextual Factors Influencing Early Return to Work in the Rural and Remote Sector*, 2(1) International Journal of Social Security and Workers Compensation 17–28 (2010); R. Guthrie, *The Dismissal of Workers Covered by Return to Work Provisions Under Workers Compensation Laws*, 44(4) Journal of Industrial Relations, 545–561(2002).

Measures to address these shortcomings should be adopted. These include the need for improved, context-sensitive, workplace-oriented system design and implementation.[72] There is an evident need for RTW to be implemented with a focus on the individual worker, adjusting his/her work environment appropriately, accommodating his/her needs, health condition and personal circumstances, and ensuring that the individual's dignity is upheld.

§9.06 DEVELOPING WORLD EXPERIENCES

[A] Malaysia

Malaysia is generally regarded as the developing country with perhaps the most advanced system of RTW and Disability Management applicable to occupationally injured and diseased workers, among others.[73] The Return to Work Programme commenced under the auspices of the Malaysian Social Security Organisation (SOCSO) in 2005 by adopting an evidence-informed, multidisciplinary rehabilitation protocol-based system, borrowed from Finland, and relying on the assistance of the Commonwealth Rehabilitation Services (CRS) of Australia. The SOCSO system was clearly motivated by a variety of considerations, including the legal obligation of SOCSO (*see* below) as well as the high costs associated with the system prevailing in Malaysia at that time. Importantly, the actual roll-out of the programme was not done simultaneously across the country, but was first implemented by way of a pilot project. The positive results obtained in this pilot study, which were closely monitored (relating mainly to back pain cases) provided the impetus for the further roll-out of the programme.[74]

The primary legal basis is the Employees' Social Security Act of 1969 (ESSA).[75] This Act applies to all industries and formal sectors in Malaysia.[76] The Act contains a provision for the rehabilitation and return to work for disabled workers, including the utilisation of a case management approach.[77] Measures may include provision of artificial limbs and appliances, and opportunities for gainful employment under

72. E. MacEachen, A. Kosny, S. Ferrier and L. Chambers, *The 'Toxic Dose' of System Problems: Why Some Injured Workers Don't Return to Work as Expected*, 20(3) Journal of Occupational Rehabilitation, 349–366 350 (2010).
73. *See Selected perspectives on return-to-work and disability management in two developing countries: Malaysia and South Africa* (with Govindjee, and Nyenti), 4 International Journal of Social Security and Workers Compensation 9–37 (2012/13), on which this and the following parts have been largely based.
74. Olivier, Govindjee, Nyenti, Azman Bin Aziz Mohammed and Cheong Peck Huang, E *SOCSO Return-to-work Programme in Malaysia: A Handbook* 2012 (IISLP/SOCSO) 25 (2012).
75. Employees' Social Security Act, Act 4 of 1969.
76. Various other labour-related laws also apply in Malaysia, including the Employment Act, 1955, the Industrial Relations Act, 1967, the Trade Unions Act, 1959, the Occupational Safety and Health Act, 1994, the Social Security Act, 1969, the Employees' Provident Fund Act, 1991, and the Workmen's Compensation Act, 1952.
77. Some tax incentives for participation in return to work interventions may be found in sections of the Income Tax Act, 1967 (Act 53 of 1967).

suitable conditions.[78] In addition, the Employees' Social Security (General) Regulations, 1971 provide the basis for SOCSO to direct the Insured Persons to attend any course of physical or vocational rehabilitation provided by SOCSO.[79]

Apart from that, 'An Insured Person [under this Act] suffering from or claiming to suffer from invalidity or permanent disablement may be provided by the Organization, free of charge facilities for physical or vocational rehabilitation.'[80] The importance of return to work in the Malaysian context is also evident from jurisprudence emanating from the courts in Malaysia, which has seen workers' security of tenure in employment as synonymous with the notion of property rights.[81] Cases have also viewed the right to employment as a fundamental right which forms part of a person's right to livelihood, affording that notion a broad interpretation similar to that which is prevalent in India.[82]

Central to the success of the RTW programme in Malaysia is its well-developed case management system, which is supported by a country-wide state-of-the-art interactive web-based system. SOCSO adopted the case management approach to achieve the most optimal outcome. SOCSO Case Management is a collaborative process that facilitates recommended efficient treatment plans to assure that appropriate medical care is provided to disabled, ill or injured individuals to ensure that they return to employment. Proper planning and coordination of health-care services appropriate to achieve the goal of medical rehabilitation are designed by Disability Managers. Case management is focused on the affected client and the client's family. In so doing, the Malaysian RTW system is aligned with the ISSA Guidelines and ILO standards, which emphasises an individualised approach. Case management may also include examination of the workplace, in order to assess whether interventions in the working environment, or workplace modifications, might be appropriate.[83] In 2010, SOCSO

78. Section 40, Employees' Social Security Act 1969, Malaysia.
79. *See* Regulation 74(ii). This Regulation compels every claimant for and every beneficiary in receipt of disablement benefits to comply with every direction given to him/her by a competent office.
80. Section 57(1), Employees' Social Security Act 1969, Malaysia. In terms of s. 57(4), an insured person who has to undergo physical or vocational rehabilitation or who is to be fitted with prosthetic, orthotic or other appliances may be paid or reimbursed, as determined by the Organization, expenses reasonably incurred or to be incurred in respect of such measures.
81. *See*, for example, *Hong Leong Equipment SDN. BHD v. Liew Fook Chuan and Another* (1996) MLJ 481 at 509–510.
82. *See* Art. 5(1) of the Federal Constitution of Malaysia and the judgment of Eusoff Chin CJ in *R Rama Chandran v. The Industrial Court of Malaysia and Another* (1997) 1 MLJ 145 at 190. Also *see Kirloskar Brothers Ltd v. Employees' States Insurance Corp* (1996) LAD IC 1718 at 1721 (SC) and *Francis Coralie v. Union of India* (1981) AIR 746 (SC).
83. Stahl et al. have criticised sickness insurance reforms which have primarily targeted the compensation system in controlling in- and out flow from sickness benefits in countries, while the importance of involving the workplace arena has, according to the authors, been disregarded: Stahl, T. Svensson, G. Petersson and K. Ekberg, *Swedish rehabilitation professionals' perspectives on work ability assessments in a changing sickness insurance system* in 33 (15–16) *Disability and Rehabilitation*, 1380 (2011). Also *see* J.R. Anema, A.J.M. Schellart, J.D Cassidy, P Loisel, T.J. Veerman and A.J. van der Beek, *Can cross-country differences in return-to-work after chronic occupational back pain be explained? An exploratory analysis on disability policies in a six country cohort study* in 19 J Occup Rehabil 425 (2009). A focus on environment has, in

adopted the Canadian-based protocol from the National Institute of Disability Management and Research (NIDMAR) for the professional development of its case managers.

While Disability Management may not presently be a liability for employers, decentralisation is foreseen. SOCSO plans to offer the NIDMAR certification to employers. By doing this, SOCSO would be able to ensure that there exists a sufficient amount of generic disability management knowledge in the labour market needed for purposes of implementing a decentralised model in Malaysia. It is foreseen, for example, that larger companies may utilise part of their resources to manage their own cases in future (by employing or obtaining the service of a certified disability manager), while smaller companies may continue to rely on SOCSO Case Managers.[84] Furthermore, there are provisions in the ESSA to support a programme in terms of which employers are not allowed to dismiss or discharge an employee during a period of medical leave subsequent to an employment injury.[85] As noted earlier, employment protection is one of the core elements of successful RTW implementation and is specifically foreseen in the range of international standards and guidelines mentioned above. Enforcing this provision would itself encourage employee participation in the RTW Programme and would afford the case managers a proper timeframe to assist the injured worker to return to work. There are various tax incentives in the system which encourage employers to (continue to) employ persons with disabilities.[86]

Finally, while SOCSO has arrangements in place with numerous health and other service providers to help implement various aspects of disability management and RTW, it set up a multi-purpose and inter-disciplinary state-of-the-art rehabilitation centre in 2014.

In conclusion, it is evident that while there may be room for further improvement, the Malaysian SOCSO RTW model largely reflects standards and guidelines emanating from ILO, UNCRPD and ISSA instruments. This is in particular true of governance and institutional arrangements adopted by SOCSO (e.g., ensuring stakeholder buy-in via endorsement of RTW initiatives by the governing SOCSO tripartite Board); the rehabilitation and occupational health and safety advisory roles played by SOCSO case managers; reliance on public-private partnerships; use made of a state-of-the-art interactive, web-based system; and the emphasis of expert qualification and certification. In short, this is a clear reflection of what Guideline 6 of the ISSA Guidelines describes as a 'continuum':

---

addition, been considered to be significant for complex processes such as vocational rehabilitation that involve a variety of institutions and social actors: E. MacEachen, A. Kosny, S. Ferrier, K. Lippel, C. Neilson, R.L. Franche and D. Pugliese, *The 'ability' paradigm in vocational rehabilitation: Challenges in an Ontario injured worker retraining program*, 22 J Occup Rehabil 22: 105, 113, 115 (2012).

84. Olivier, M, Govindjee, A, Nyenti, M, Azman Bin Aziz Mohammed, M and Cheong Peck Huang, E *SOCSO Return-to-work Programme in Malaysia: A Handbook* 2012 (IISLP/SOCSO) 57 (2012).
85. Section 53, Employees' Social Security Act 1969, Malaysia.
86. Income Tax Act, 1967 (Act 53 of 1967). Such incentives include, for example, a double deduction in respect of remuneration paid to a disabled worker. Also *see* the provisions of the Disabilities Act, 2008 (Act 685 of 2008). In addition, it may be noted that the Employment Act, 1955, provides for penalties to be levied against employers who fail, for example, to allow employees to take sick leave, although such penalties do not apply as yet to (employers') conduct relating to return to work obligations.

A comprehensive and integrated approach operates on a continuum, from an emphasis on prevention to care, rehabilitation and a smooth transition back to work. It considers the full range of expectations and realities, especially in small and medium-sized enterprises. Preventive efforts focus particularly on occupational health and safety and promotion of health and well-being. Health-care and occupational rehabilitation measures aim at preserving the employability of the person concerned. The management uses the knowledge gained from return to work processes to enhance the institution's prevention policies and procedures, and vice versa.

[B] South Africa

Currently, RTW best practice models in South Africa are mostly in the form of Employee Assistance and/or Employee Wellness Programmes.[87] The majority of the South African companies operating related programmes focus on rehabilitation and functional assessment, through which an objective, specific instrument to match the capacity of an employee to the physical demands of a particular occupation is provided, thereby preventing premature injury or fatigue. The emphasis appears to be on work capacity evaluation.

Suitable RTW measures of a public nature[88] have not yet been introduced in South Africa, as the development of a policy and related framework for the country-wide introduction of a RTW system in relation to occupational injuries and diseases was only recently commenced with. The workers' compensation laws in South Africa lean, in a lopsided fashion, towards compensation, with little focus on rehabilitation and RTW. For example, there is little provision in the Compensation for Occupational Injuries and Diseases Act 130 of 1993 (COIDA), which specifically attempts to enforce reintegration measures such as compulsory rehabilitation or vocational training programmes. Measures aimed at remedying or repairing damage, such as reskilling or retraining, labour market and social integration need to be adopted as an integral part of the social security system, alongside compensatory measures.

This current (limited) statutory mandate includes the provision and funding of facilities to assist injured employees in returning to work.[89] The Director-General of Labour also has the discretion to apply unclaimed compensation for the general welfare of injured employees or employees suffering from occupational diseases, which will include the performance of any wider rehabilitation activities that the Compensation

87. The main goal of employee assistance programmes is to assist employees with current difficulties that affect their functioning at work and at home. On the other hand, an employee wellness programme refers to all strategies, action plans and methods used to promote the physical, emotional and mental health of employees, to ensure a productive workforce. The aim of such programmes is the prevention and/or early detection and treatment of identified health risks, as well as broader health programmes, focusing on the development of positive health practices by altering habits and behaviour.
88. However, certain sectors, in particular the mining sector in South Africa, have developed and implemented their particular versions of RTW.
89. Section 4(2)(b) COIDA.

Fund decides to support.[90] Nevertheless, various provisions currently contained in COIDA require expansion and amendment in order to clarify the Compensation Fund's role beyond medical rehabilitation matters alone. Reintegration into the labour market is currently not an express goal of COIDA.[91]

Based on a comprehensive study undertaken for the Compensation Fund of South Africa,[92] the Fund has prepared a comprehensive set of legal amendments and commenced with developing institutional arrangements to give effect to the introduction of RTW on a country-wide basis, to be preceded by pilot projects. As indicated in the ISSA Guidelines, institutional success with introducing RTW is often determined by the existence of an appropriate supportive and guiding legal framework.

It is envisaged that the Compensation Fund should play a three-pronged role in the new proposed system: firstly, by continuing to provide compensation for employees with an occupational injury or disease, while directing employers (and employees) to the obligations/recommendations of the new chapter proposed for introduction in COIDA. This includes the recommended new legal obligation to keep the position of an occupationally injured/diseased employee open for a particular period of time, subject to participation in an agreed rehabilitation plan) – as also advocated by international standards and guidelines referred to above, and of particular relevance, given the high unemployment rate in South Africa. Second, in the event that the employer is unable to reasonably accommodate and retain such employees, the Compensation Fund may itself carry out or contract out activities which will contribute towards the attainment of the broader (and new) objectives of that Act. Third, given the reality of the South African labour market, with specific reference to the large number of small- and medium-sized enterprises, and the perceived inability of these enterprises to provide rehabilitation, reskilling and reintegration services, it should only be expected of larger employers to roll-out RTW and Disability Management, and to provide rehabilitation and reskilling services.[93]

§9.07 IMPROVING EFFECTIVE IMPLEMENTATION: INTERNATIONAL STANDARDS AND GUIDELINES

It is suggested that there may be room for the adoption of further measures, informed by both international standards and guidelines and the experience of some developed world experiences, to improve effective implementation in developing countries such as Malaysia and South Africa:

---

90. Section 4(2)(d) COIDA.
91. Committee of Inquiry into a Comprehensive System of Social Security for South Africa *Transforming the Present Protecting the Future* 63 (2002).
92. *See* Marius Olivier, Avinash Govindjee, Matthias Nyenti & Adriaan Wolvaardt, *A Reflections on developing an integrated comprehensive policy framework for rehabilitation, re-integration and return-to-work strategies in relation to workers who suffered occupational injuries or diseases* (Final research report prepared for the Compensation Fund of South Africa)(April 2011).
93. On the problem of "passive employers" (i.e., employers who make no contribution to the rehabilitation / return to work process), *see* Stahl, T. Svensson, G. Petersson & K. Ekberg *Swedish rehabilitation professionals' perspectives on work ability assessments in a changing sickness insurance system* in 33 (15–16) Disability and Rehabilitation, 1379 (2011).

- Employer and workplace focus: Worldwide RTW legislation and policies are largely centred on the employer, and the duties and responsibilities of the employer. The employer has a number of responsibilities under the various RTW systems already in operation in the developed world. The focus on the responsibilities of the employer is important as it is in the workplace where the employee contracts occupational diseases, or picks up occupational injuries, and it is the employer who has control over the workplace. In Malaysia, direct employer obligations are currently limited, as the roll-out of the programme is at this stage a SOCSO-initiated activity. However, in both Malaysia and South Africa it is foreseen that larger employers in particular will bear more comprehensive obligations in future, as explained above.
- Incentives: Motivation is a crucial issue in RTW, and incentives are used in order to ensure that RTW is correctly implemented. These incentives can either be negative or positive, and may be applied to employees, employers and/or new employers of those recovering or recovered from occupational disease or injury. Some possible incentives are rebates on insurance premiums and experience rating (through safety measures and the development of an early return to work programme, employers may lower their experience rating, thereby reducing their premium costs). This is an area where both Malaysia and South Africa can innovatively invest in, to ensure greater participation by employers and employees in RTW programmes.
- Activating measures: Recently there has been a shift of focus by occupational injury and disease systems from passive compensation to active work reintegration.[94] As an alternative, countries could build more reskilling and alternative employment opportunities in addition to the existing compensation-focused frameworks. It is evident that in both Malaysia and South Africa much more can be done to support activating measures, regardless of the challenges involved – such as limited job opportunities in the labour market (*see also* the concluding remarks below).
- Employment protection: Ensuring that the injured or ill employee is not dismissed due to their occupational injury or disease is an integral part of RTW in a number of jurisdictions and supported by international standards. The employer has the responsibility not to dismiss the worker in the case of occupational disease or injury, at least for a specified time period; and also, in many jurisdictions, to provide the employee with suitable work while they are recovering.[95] Legislation therefore needs to be adopted or amended to ensure

94. *See* Stahl, Svensson, Petersson & Ekberg, *Swedish rehabilitation professionals' perspectives on work ability assessments in a changing sickness insurance system*, 1373 (2011).
95. This is the case in the Netherlands where the *Wet Verbetering Poortwachter* (Gatekeeper Improvement Act)_prohibits an employer from terminating the employment of an injured employee – *see* Organisation for Economic Co-operation and Development) *Sickness and Disability Schemes in the Netherlands – Country memo as a background paper for the OECD Disability Review – November 2007* (2007). This is also the case in New Zealand and in a number of Australian jurisdictions, such as New South Wales and Queensland, where the employer is guilty of an offence should they dismiss the injured worker within a specified time of the worker

that an injured or ill employee is not dismissed due to their occupational injury or disease. This will further ensure that space is made for return to work interventions, prior to employers being permitted to dismiss employees suffering from an occupational injury or disease or from another form of disability. In particular, provision would have to be made for protection of the job of the affected employee to allow him/her to participate in a multi-faceted rehabilitation programme without the fear of losing his/her position. It is suggested that dismissal protection in labour laws in both Malaysia and South Africa will need to be extended to include the remedies of reinstatement or re-employment of injured or diseased workers who are unfairly dismissed while undergoing RTW. Within the context of South Africa's Labour Relations Act, such protection will need to be extended to specifically protect occupationally injured/diseased employees from being dismissed or otherwise disadvantaged while they are engaged in an agreed rehabilitation activity. In the case of Malaysia, though there are provisions for securing employment during the course of temporary disablement (medical leave) due to employment injury,[96] there are no provisions in securing employment for those suffering from invalidity, apart from the basic but incomplete protection enjoyed under the Employment Act of 1955.

- Accreditation: In introducing an RTW programme, disability managers and return to work coordinators need to be accredited by the relevant disability insurance institutions or government department. In the case of South Africa, an accreditation system and standards have to be developed by the Compensation Fund, in consultation with professional bodies and relevant government departments (in particular the Department of Health). These standards have to be developed in relation to RTW and rehabilitation coordinators/disability managers, health and related services and also vocational rehabilitation providers and other service providers. As indicated above, in the case of Malaysia, health service providers contracted by SOCSO must be officially accredited and comply with criteria set by SOCSO.[97]

§9.08 CONCLUSION

While scientific advancements pertaining to RTW have increasingly been documented in the developed world, there is a comparative dearth of literature in respect of RTW in the developing world. In establishing RTW programmes in countries such as South Africa and Malaysia, international standards and best practices discerned from other

becoming injured - Commonwealth of Australia *Comparison of Workers Compensation Arrangements Australia and New Zealand 2009*, 211–212 (2010).

96. Section 53, Employees' Social Security Act 1969, Malaysia.
97. Olivier, Govindjee, Nyenti, Azman and Cheong *SOCSO Return-to-work Programme in Malaysia: A Handbook 2012*, 45 (2012).

countries must be properly contextualised to fit the workplace experiences of countries which are still emerging on the global landscape.

Both South Africa and Malaysia have committed (in terms of the UNCRPD) to safeguard and promote the realisation of the right to work, also for workers who acquire a disability during the course of employment. Various international obligations have been acknowledged by both countries, such as the promotion of vocational and professional rehabilitation and job retention for persons with disabilities and the promise to enable such persons to access technical and vocational guidance programmes and placement services effectively. The provisions of the UNCRPD indicate the core components of an effective rehabilitation and return to work programme, including that rehabilitation services must be multi-faceted and should involve early intervention, be voluntary and make use of assessments of individual needs and strengths. Such principles are particularly useful for developing countries which are on the cusp of introducing RTW mechanisms and approaches.

Given Malaysia's recent experiences with RTW, and South Africa's policy decision to embark on a path which will lead to the introduction of a publicly directed RTW and Disability Management system for occupationally injured and diseased workers, there exists a good basis for applying the available RTW literature to these countries' RTW-related initiatives. The literature review conducted suggests that there are numerous advantages (for employees, employers and the state / Compensation Fund) to the proper introduction of RTW mechanisms aimed at returning injured and ill workers back to the workplace. However, there are also serious barriers which might jeopardise the proper establishment of a RTW system in both the developed and developing world contexts. Such barriers (such as a lack of trust in the system and failure to construct RTW systems in a fashion compliant with the minimum compensation and human rights frameworks embedded in international standards), if not properly considered and overcome, could hamper the successful implementation and operation of RTW. Strategies for countering these hurdles are being implemented in various parts of the world and established techniques for countering the difficulties of RTW introduction and implementation should be adopted in countries which have recently initiated such interventions.

Although South Africa, in particular, is at an early stage in respect of developing and implementing RTW mechanisms, it has been criticised for failing to incorporate international instruments such as the UNCRPD adequately into its legal framework. Workers' compensation laws in South Africa have, until now, completely favoured compensation, with little attempt to enforce reintegration measures. The proposed establishment of a new, unified, health system in South Africa presents a fresh opportunity to correct the weaknesses of the past and the introduction of a proper RTW system for cases of occupational injury and disease (by way of a new chapter to be included in the main employment injury benefit law, the Compensation for Occupational Injuries and Diseases Act 130 of 1993 (COIDA)) should be prioritised in a manner which is synergised with the broader health-related policy and legal developments. The actual roll-out of this RTW programme is likely to occur gradually, and should include a pilot phase. Large enterprises are well placed to appoint DMs and the state should foster the development of capacity in this regard, educate and consult with the various stakeholders in a manner which encourages their participation in this initiative.

The results emanating from the Malaysian experience provide a benchmark for countries in the developing world. It is clear from the advancements in Malaysia that countries in the developing world should be encouraged to attempt to introduce RTW systems, just as South Africa has started to do. A critique of the Malaysian approach results in the conclusion that a proper legislative framework for the introduction of RTW is imperative. This needs to be coupled with appropriate incentives and disincentives targeted at both employers and employees. In addition, the Malaysian example illustrates that large employers should ideally be required to appoint their own Disability Managers as soon as possible (as already proposed in South Africa), so that they can demonstrate a hands-on approach to RTW and alleviate some of the pressure on the state in this regard.

Finally, there are a number of considerations which may be particularly relevant to the developing world context, also in South Africa, that need to be taken into account when shaping RTW systems in accordance with international standards and guidelines:

- The prevailing high un- and underemployment in most developing countries emphasises the importance of strengthening among others the job protection component of RTW and the continued payment of benefits while the worker is unable to work productively.
- It is necessary to deal with strong trade union perceptions of worker rights and job protection – addressing job protection and continued payment concerns, as well as enhanced communication with and involvement of trade unions are core elements of a RTW standardised framework.
- It is important to strengthen underdeveloped health system and weak labour market support frameworks. In the developing world context, this may have to be translated into the development of innovative and practical measures to deal with scarce resources – e.g., consolidated health-care service delivery to various disability streams (transcending the RTW context); and to invest in enhanced public employment support services.
- There is a need to invest as a priority in technological, infrastructural and institutional capacity-building and innovation, in the absence of which it may not be possible to introduce RTW effectively. Malaysia sets the example in this regard; countries such as South Africa could benefit from and follow the Malaysian example.

CHAPTER 10

Fit@work: The Comprehensive Health and Well-Being Programme of the European Commission

Ubaldo Macchitella & Giorgio Gallizioli[*]

§10.01 THE CONTEXT

The European Commission (EC) is a supranational organization with almost sixty years of activity. The employment of EC officials is governed by the Staff Regulations and Conditions of Employment of Other Servants (SR), adopted in 1962 and amended several times over the years in order to take into account the evolving goals of the organization due to the broadening of its competencies. The Staff Regulations specify the rights and duties of both the employer and the employees, whose skills and performances are required to keep pace with the changes in the objectives and the working environment.

The Staff Regulations were most recently amended in 2004 and 2014, in accordance with the pressing request from the budget contributors to trim running costs due to budgetary constraints imposed on them by the current economic downturn, and to increase efficiency. A cut in staff, an increase in working hours and a raising of the standard retirement age are only a few of the factors to be considered when examining the issue of well-being at work today with regard to EC personnel. Clearly, these changes do not affect only the EU Institutions. However, what is of particular interest here is the possibility for the EC to experiment with practices in a framework of

* Ubaldo Macchitella is a European Commission official working at the Directorate-General Human Resources and Security, Brussels. He contributed ss 2, 3, 4, 6 and 7. Giorgio Gallizioli is a former European Commission official, currently responsible for the Sports and Leisure Clubs Association within the European Commission. He contributed ss 1 and 5. The views expressed are those of the authors alone and do not necessarily represent the views of the European Commission.

Workplace Health Promotion (WHP) intended as the combined efforts of employers, employees and society to improve the health and well-being of people at work.

Another aspect to be taken into account is the requirement in the staffing procedure pursuant to which officials shall be recruited 'on the broadest possible geographical basis from among nationals of Member States of the Communities [now of the Union]'. As a result of this provision, the vast majority of those working for the Commission in Brussels and Luxembourg (the main locations) are expatriates originating from twenty-six States. Staff members joining the Commission therefore come from different cultural and educational backgrounds and professional experience. In this connection, it should be noted that officials normally spend their entire working life serving the EC and hence living far from their country of origin. Family members may also be expatriates, though it is not rare for the official to live alone as is increasingly the case in modern society. This situation results in a large number of officials who decide to stay on in Brussels after retirement and tend to keep links with their former colleagues. This is made easier by membership of one of the sports and leisure associations supported by the European Institutions.[1]

This particular context was taken into consideration when drafting the legislation relating to EC officials or other servants. This emerges in particular in Article 1 e)1 Staff Regulations which states that 'Officials in active employment shall have access to measures of a social nature, including specific measures to reconcile working life with family life, adopted by the institutions, and to services provided by the social welfare bodies referred to in Article 9'.[2] Interestingly, the provision goes further as it specifies that former officials may also have access to specific measures of a social nature.

This provision was approved in 2004, forty-two years after the adoption of the first Staff Regulations. As stated in recital n. 9 of Regulation EC/Euratom n.723/2004,[3] 'Express reference should be made to measures of a social nature and to working conditions which meet appropriate health and safety standards; such measures are intended to help reconcile work and private life, to promote equality of opportunity, as well as to protect the health and safety of the individual'.

In fact, this provision did not really introduce anything new, as for some time the European Commission had been adopting a series of health and safety measures aimed at improving the working conditions of its staff and at facilitating daily life, such as setting up canteens, kindergartens and schools, together with initiatives for financial support in special circumstances or aimed at encouraging the further education and training of EC officials.

1. The representation of interests of former staff towards the EU Institutions and national authorities is entrusted to an association called AIACE *(Association Internationale des Anciens de l'Union Européenne)*.
2. This provision refers to trade union and staff representatives (*see* SR, Ann. II). The Staff Regulations foresee joint committees made up of an equal number of representatives of the employer and the staff committees. One of these joint committees is responsible for social matters *(Comité paritaires des actions sociales: COPAS)*. Obviously, trade unions and staff representatives cannot be considered a body providing welfare directly, but they are rather entities with a responsibility to promote and monitor the welfare conditions of staff.
3. Official Journal of the European Union (OJ) L24, 27 Apr. 2004, 1.

It should be noted that the Commission pays particular attention to the health and safety of its staff. In fact, it was stated when the organization was established that an official may be appointed only on condition that he is physically fit to perform his duties (Article 28.e SR) and is under the obligation to undergo a medical check-up every year, either by the institution's medical officer or by a medical practitioner chosen by the official (Article 59.6 SR). Two reasons for this requirement may be cited: the first is that the official is required to discharge his duty in conditions that will ensure maximum efficiency;[4] the second is the need to curb, as far as possible, sickness costs incurred by the employer through preventive measures.

In addition to these provisions, the Commission adopts specific measures in order to comply with European labour law and in particular the requirements imposed on the employer by Directive 89/391,[5] implemented mainly through Commission Decision C(2006)1623, entitled: 'A harmonised policy on health and safety at work for all Commission staff'.

Paragraph 3 of the same Article 1e), is also relevant. It reads as follows: 'Measures of a social nature adopted in accordance with this Article shall be implemented by each institution in close cooperation with the Staff Committee, on the basis of multi-annual proposed actions. These proposed actions shall be transmitted each year to the budgetary authority in the framework of the budget procedure'.

Pursuant to this provision, the Commission is required to elaborate a specific multi-annual plan matched with financial support.

In this connection, in 2006 the Commission adopted the 'Wellbeing' multi-annual action plan (2006–2009),[6] followed by a second multi-annual plan, extended until 2014, that did not introduce any significant innovations. This plan was superseded by the '*Fit@work* programme' that will be presented in the following. This programme places special emphasis on the physical and mental health of staff.[7]

It is worth noting that the 2006–2009 well-being programme was adopted following a staff survey that highlighted some discontent and shortcomings, especially as regards the integration of the employee in the workplace and the need to balance professional and private life, including the specific needs of spouses and family members who have moved to the place of residence of the official. The scope of initiatives in the well-being domain was consequently broadened by placing an emphasis on the prevention of physical and psychological conditions. In this context, the promotion of physical fitness among staff was considered of particular importance.

The Commission's document noted also that many sports activities in Brussels and Luxembourg were organized by the staff themselves through the setting up of sports and leisure clubs. Moreover, it was envisaged that sports facilities would be set up and managed by the Commission in Brussels within easy reach of the workplace if adequate resources were available.

4. Regulation n. 31/1962, last recital (45 OJ, 14 Jun. 1962, 1385).
5. OJ L183, 29 Jun. 1989, 1.
6. European Commission, *Towards a strategy for well-being at work in the European Commission: multi annual action plan 2006–2009*, (SEC(2006)500).
7. The term health and safety relates also to sports and leisure activities: *see* R. Blanpain, *European Labour Law*, 14 ed., 809 (2014).

In the meantime, and in the same vein, the administration negotiated staff discounts for Commission staff with sports facilities, most of them located near the Commission. However, this measure did not have a significant impact on enhancing the feeling of belonging to the Institution (one of the main goals of the sports and leisure clubs, as described below), an outcome that can be achieved especially by officials practising sports or leisure activities together on a regular basis.

The opening up in 2014 of a complex of sport halls[8] in a Commission building conveniently located in Brussels made it possible to move a step further towards the goal of enhancing employees' physical well-being and facilitating better social interaction and inclusion. The availability of this new facility has helped to forge a new holistic well-being programme.

Those responsible for human resources have become aware of the findings of research reports proving the benefits of practising regular physical activity. It is commonly acknowledged that in modern life many individuals suffer from insufficient physical activity. This is conducive to the gaining of excess weight and related conditions, with negative consequences as regards work performance, absenteeism and an unnecessary burden on health insurance systems. Furthermore, quality of life is generally lower as a result of inadequate physical activity.

As 'excessive workload and work pace, job uncertainty, inflexible work schedules, irregular, unpredictable or unsocial work hours, poor interpersonal relationships, lack of participation, unclear role in the organization, poor communication, poor career development and conflicting demands of work and home'[9] impact negatively on individual health, it is the duty of and in the interest of the employer to reduce these risk factors.

The figures highlighting the increase in the number of persons affected by illnesses brought on by modern ways of living and working are alarming, as is the amount of money spent annually on national social security schemes.[10] This occurs in a context where the authorities are under pressure to cut public spending. The sickness insurance scheme of the European Union Institutions may well be facing a similar situation in the future because of work-related pathologies, the ageing of its active staff and the increasing number of retired officials covered by the health insurance scheme.

Conversely, 'Focusing on well-being at work presents a valuable opportunity to benefit societies by helping working individuals to feel happy, competent, and satisfied in their roles. The evidence also shows that people who achieve good standards of well-being at work are likely to be more creative, more loyal, more productive, and provide better customer satisfaction than individuals with poor standards of well-being at work'.[11]

8. In addition, where possible, facilities to practise physical activities have been made available in some Commission buildings.
9. EU-OSHA, *Calculating the costs of work-related stress and psychosocial risks – A literature review* (2014).
10. According to a recent study, inactivity causes economic costs exceeding EUR 80 billion per year across EU Member States: International Sport & Culture Association, *The economic cost of physical inactivity in Europe* (2015).
11. New Economics Foundation (NEF), *Well-being at work*, 6 (2014).

This new approach has brought about a shift from the mere implementation of basic standards aimed at protecting employee's health - mainly by means of provisions and measures concerning working environment and prevention of health problems - to a broader programme encompassing certain aspects relating to the private life of the employee now recognized as relevant for the organization. Staff policies tend nowadays to incorporate health targets into all other areas of the company. The encouragement to a healthy lifestyle emerges from this approach as a priority for the organization.

The Commission's proposal on promoting health-enhancing physical activity[12] (HEPA), converted into Council Recommendation 2013/C 354/01[13] addressed to the Member States, the first ever dedicated to sport, is one of the most significant expressions of this move. In this context, indicator n. 20 ('Existence of a national or sub-national (where relevant) incentive scheme for companies to promote physical activity at the work place, such as gyms, showers, walking stairs, etc.'[14]) is of particular relevance to evaluate the HEPA programmes.

The fact that the EU has acquired competences in the domain of sport by virtue of the Lisbon Treaty is central. As a result, the Commission became active by launching, *inter alia*, the first European Week of Sport across the EU (7–13 September 2015).[15] Considering that 'Available evidence supports the idea that the workplace should be the primary site in the adult daily life where a physically active lifestyle is supported and that this should be a matter of concern for employers and trade unions',[16] the Commission has elaborated the '*Fit@work*' programme, the objectives and the organizational adaptations of which are outlined below.

§10.02 OBJECTIVES, RATIONALE AND DESCRIPTION OF THE EC PROGRAMME *FIT@WORK*

Consistently with the body of legislation outlined above, on 20 May 2015 the Commission launched the multi-annual *Fit@work* programme, covering the period 2015–2019. In line with later trends of research into this topic, the new *Fit@work* programme encourages a healthy lifestyle, indicating a comprehensive health and well-being plan as a priority for the organization. The aim of the programme is to keep staff fit and healthy in a healthy work environment so that they can do their best at work throughout their career in ways which respect and accommodate the needs of each staff member.

The programme is tailored around the definition of 'health' provided by the World Health Organization (WHO) stating that 'health is a state of complete physical, mental and social well-being and not merely the absence of disease and infirmity'. As

12. European Commission, COM(2013)603.
13. OJ C354, 4 Dec. 2013, 1.
14. *See* the *EU Physical Activity Guidelines*, n. 33 and 34, adopted by EU Member States Sports Ministers, Biarritz, 27–28 Nov. 2008.
15. European Commission, Directorate General for Education and Culture (EAC). *See*: http://ec.europa.eu/sport/week/about-week-of-sport/highlights-2015_en.htm. The second edition of European week of sports ran from 10–18 Sept. 2016.
16. *EU Physical Activity Guidelines*, 30.

a result, *Fit@work* is based on two pillars: 'mental and physical health' and 'social well-being'. The first pillar 'Mental and physical health' proposes a strategy for developing awareness, increasing resilience and improving the mental and physical health of the Commission employees. It leverages on the existing in-house medical know-how to promote prevention and help staff make informed decisions about their lifestyle. Initiatives within this pillar fall into three different categories:

(i) Mental health – including prevention campaigns, training and counselling about the major psychological and psychiatric diseases (such as depression and burnout).
(ii) Physical health – including vaccination, pre-recruitment medical examinations, and annual medical check-ups.
(iii) Physical activity – including all the initiatives aimed at promoting physical fitness through a more active lifestyle such as sport, or generally health-enhancing physical activities (walking, cycling).

Consistently with the WHO definition of health, the second pillar 'social well-being' covers all other factors enabling employees to thrive at work. Initiatives within this pillar fall into four different categories:

(a) Work-life balance – including all measures aimed at favouring a balance between work and family life, which can be particularly challenging for a staff population significantly made up of expatriates. Example of these initiatives include welcoming newcomers, assistance in the purchase of property, flexible working conditions (e.g., flexitime, teleworking, part-time) but also childcare facilities run under the supervision of the European Commission.
(b) *Supportive working conditions* – including all the actions intended to create a positive work environment in terms of relations with other colleagues, managers and the hierarchy. Examples of these practices are a series of management guidelines aimed at managers to detect signs of psychological discomfort, prevent and manage sick leave, procedures for conflict resolution.
(c) *Working environment* – including all initiatives envisaged to create a healthy and pleasant working space, such as the maintenance and accommodation of offices and ergonomics.
(d) *Leisure activities* – including the support of the Administration for cultural activities, as an important opportunity for personal development and integration among colleagues.

Figure 10.1 The Fit@work Programme and the Areas It Covers

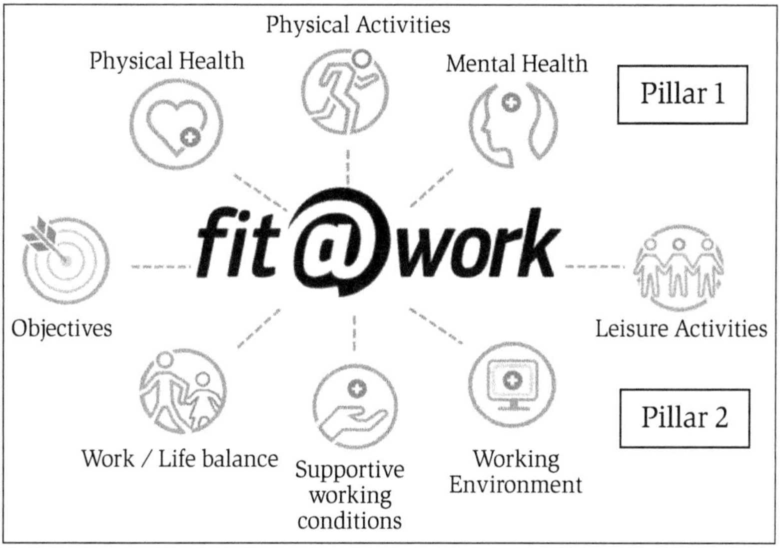

§10.03 *FIT@WORK*: THE FIRST YEAR OF LIFE

The programme was officially launched on 20 May 2015, in the presence of Vice-President Georgieva and the Director-General of Human Resources and Security. Since then, some major corporate initiatives have been undertaken as part of the *Fit@work* programme. More precisely:

- A communication campaign has been devised and implemented with the support of the Internal communication Unit of the Directorate-General for Human Resources and Security (DG HR). The first part of the campaign focused on raising awareness for the many initiatives that the European Commission has in place for the health and well-being of their staff. A consistent visual identity consisting of a common brand, posters, presentations, layout and website has been created and geared towards major *Fit@work* events.
- A number of flagship events have been proposed to all staff in order to draw attention to *Fit@work*. They include special fitness days, conferences and associations with major external events (e.g., European Sports Week).
- A series of discounts for joining sport clubs in Brussels and the surrounding area have been negotiated for all European Commission staff.
- A new decision on teleworking has been approved in order to enhance this arrangement, to improve uniformity of its implementation across different DGs and to favour work/life balance.

- A new option allowing for 95% part-time working has been added to the existing ones.

These initiatives, as well as all the other actions within the *Fit@work* framework, have been implemented with no additional funding. All the required resources were sourced from budgetary funds normally allocated to units and services.

§10.04 A COMPREHENSIVE PROGRAMME, SPANNING DIFFERENT ORGANIZATIONAL LEVELS

Aimed at covering a wide range of initiatives in a complex organizational setting, *Fit@work* involves several delivery partners distributed at three different organizational levels.

- *Political and corporate level*: Sponsored by the Vice-President of the European Commission Kristalina Georgieva and the Directorate-General for Human Resources and Security (DG HR) who designed and launched the new programme. More precisely, the initiatives included in *Fit@work* require the cooperation of different units and services of the DG HR family (namely DG HR itself, DG for budget, the Offices for Infrastructure in Brussels and Luxembourg, and the paymaster's office).
- A Steering Committee, consisting of representatives of the major delivery units and services, has been created to provide political steer and high-level coordination for the programme.
- *Managerial level*: as in most organizations, middle managers play a key role in implementing policies and practices defined at higher levels. *Fit@work* is no exception. In addition to correctly interpreting their role, as suggested by managerial guidelines, middle managers are important for putting 'healthy' work practices in place and allowing their co-workers to take advantage of the many initiatives proposed under the *Fit@work* framework. In order for this to happen, DG HR needs to carefully inform middle managers about the *Fit@work* programme, convince them about the importance of health and well-being, and offer the necessary tools to operate (e.g., training, formalized procedures, information desks). In this respect, a series of managerial guidelines has been envisaged. A first document containing indications on how to manage sick leave and a document containing guidelines on how to prevent psychosocial risk were circulated and promoted in 2015. Other guidelines aimed at providing support for middle managers are under preparation. The whole 'supportive working conditions' section of the programme focuses on the improvement of the working environment and deals with elements such as leadership and managerial style, communication, coordination. Managers are the primary targets for the actions in this field.
- *Individual level*: *Fit@work* is centred on the needs of the individual staff member. However, Commission staff are not only recipients but also active players in relation to their own health and well-being, individually or in

association with other colleagues. Individually, it is up to them to take part in the initiatives proposed. While many initiatives are envisaged, none of them are imposed while participation is left to the discretion of the staff member concerned. The communication strategy associated with *Fit@work* emphasizes this aspect. Staff members are also free to propose new initiatives in line with the aim of *Fit@work*. Clearly, proposals can also emerge from associations of staff members as is the case with the Sports and Leisure Club Association (SLCA) which, in a *Fit@work* context, certainly represents best practice.

Consistently, *Fit@work* has a relevant number of partners across the Commission, within and outside DG HR. Table 10.1 provides a non-exhaustive list of partners.

*Table 10.1 Major Partners, Fit@work. Units/Services with * Are Part of the Steering Committee*

Partners (As of Year 2015)	*Description*	*Main Role(s)*
At the corporate level		
Vice-President Georgieva	Vice-President and Commissioner responsible for personnel policy	Provides high-level political sponsorship
Within DG HR family		
Director-General	Director – General for Human Resources and Security	Ensures that HR policies and procedures help the organization meet its objectives. Keeps staff motivated, engaged, healthy and safe
Director HR.D*	Head of directorate responsible for Social Policy	Chairs the steering committee, is responsible for Social Policy
Unit HR D.1*	Unit working conditions and well-being	Coordinates the overall *Fit@work* programme
Unit HR D.3*	Medical Service Brussels	Responsible for pillar one and for medical activities in Brussels
Unit HR D.4,	Medical Service Luxembourg	Responsible for medical initiatives on the Luxembourg site
Unit HR D.5	Medical Service Ispra	Responsible for medical initiatives on the Ispra site
Adviser to Directorate D*	Adviser to Directorate D	Coordinates *Fit@work* for Ispra site

Partners (As of Year 2015)	*Description*	*Main Role(s)*
Unit HR A.4*	Internal Communication Unit	Follows promotional activities
Unit HR D.2*	Health and Safety unit	Unit responsible for health and safety at work
Unit HR B.3*	Learning and Development unit	Responsible for training initiatives at corporate level
Unit HR E.1	European Civil Service Law and Social Dialogue unit	Takes care of regulatory and legal aspects
Unit HR.01*	Planning and policy steering unit	Contributes to the shaping of DG policy and ensures the coherence of its action
Unit HR.02*	Luxembourg site coordination	Liaises with DGs in Luxembourg
Unit HR B.1*	Ethics, rights and obligations unit	Welcomes new colleagues; staff rights and obligations
OIB*/OIL*	Offices for Infrastructure (Brussels/Luxembourg)	Takes care of physical facilities
Across the organization		
Well-being correspondent network	Connects all officers responsible for well-being across DGs	Implements and proposes *Fit@work* activities at DG level
Internal Communication Network	Connects all officers responsible for well-being across DGs	Promotes *Fit@work* at DG level
Human Resources Network Resources (RRH)	Connects all HR Heads of Units across DGs	Implements and promotes *Fit@work* at DG level
Staff associations		
Sports and leisure clubs association (SLCA)	Connects all the officially recognized sports and culture clubs of the Commission	Delivers and organizes sporting and cultural activities across the Commission
Local and Central personnel committees	Connects all staff representatives	Represents and negotiates staff interests
Joint Committees		
COPAS and CASS	Joint committees for social actions	Defines and reviews social policy across the Commission

NB: organization chart of the Directorate-General Human Resources and Security, subject to changes.

§10.05 THE KEY ROLE OF THE SLCA IN ENCOURAGING PHYSICAL ACTIVITY

Part of the '*Fit@work* programme' is implemented by empowering the Sports and Leisure Clubs Association (SLCA) to lead sporting and leisure activities that are carried out by established clubs (currently forty-four) and that qualify for formal recognition by the European Commission, in accordance with agreed principles and guidelines. SLCA members are elected by the clubs' presidents. All SLCA members and colleagues running the clubs act on a voluntary basis and are not remunerated.

On a proposal from SLCA, the internal rules are adopted at general meetings while the SLCA manages autonomously, *inter alia*, the distribution of spaces needed for the activities involved. It proposes the allocation to those clubs that have submitted a formal request of the amount of the financial support earmarked annually by the European Commission for this purpose. It also supervises or organizes sport events directly. Any conflict between circles or within a circle is dealt with in the first instance by the SLCA. The Administrative Department intervenes only in case of failure to resolve the conflict at SLCA level. The SLCA is independent from both the employer and the European Commission's Trade Unions.

A club may be created at the request of officials who can demonstrate a demand for a new activity in the field of sport or culture and that the majority of members are officials, retired officials or their family members.

Clubs normally takes the form of a no-profit legal person only when their budget becomes significant. This is normally the case where the club owns costly equipment, such as boats as in the case of a sailing club. In order to obtain formal recognition, the club's articles of association are scrutinized by the SLCA to ensure that its objectives comply with EU general principles and that it does not pursue any political, religious or philosophical goals.[17] Clearly any condition for membership based on nationality, language or level of responsibility within the organization would be totally unacceptable.

Compliance with the rules is checked annually by the SLCA which also pays particular attention to the financial situation of clubs so to avoid any deficit in their accounts. Clubs are self-financed but may benefit from support from the European Commission, in particular for extraordinary expenses or to face unforeseen difficulties.[18] The SLCA can propose to the Administrative Department that the agreement be withdrawn in case of non-compliance with the rules.

The success of the Clubs and the SLCA among the staff members is largely due to their non-bureaucratic nature.[19] The SLCA has been given a major role in the

17. A standard provision in the Club's Statute states that the main goals of the association are those of promoting social, cultural and sporting relations among the personnel and facilitating the integration of new colleagues into the working environment and their family members into the new community. Also retired officials, as already underlined, benefit from the opportunity to keep in touch with active officials by registering with a club.
18. Financial support amounts to approximately 10% of the club's total turnover.
19. Some 3,500 officials either in employment or retired are members of recognized European Commission clubs. The number of officials practising sporting and leisure activities at European

implementation of sports and leisure activities included in the '*Fit@work* programme'. This programme is expected to further increase visibility among staff.

This will be assessed through online staff satisfaction surveys and the organization of physical tests (biometrics) carried out regularly (on a voluntary and anonymous basis) by the SLCA with the assistance of experts in various fields. At the end of a series of physical tests each participant receives a snapshot of his physical condition with tailored recommendations on how to tackle any weaknesses. The organization receives an indication, albeit limited due to the restricted number of participants, of some critical aspects of the physical condition of the staff. Outcomes and future initiatives are discussed amongst the administrative departments concerned, the European Commission Medical Service and the SLCA.

The SLCA's mission is not only to encourage staff to practise physical activity or to engage in social interaction on a regular basis, but also to liaise with the administration and refer the clubs' requests to the management. In order to encourage officials to spend time practising a sport on Commission premises while at work, specific flexitime arrangements need to be devised. To be surrounded by healthy people is in the interest of the employer and of civil society as a whole. Although regular physical activity at work is only one component of the Workplace Health Promotion (WHP) initiatives,[20] there is no doubt that the cost/benefit ratio for the organization is largely positive, as the literature shows.

§10.06 ORGANIZATIONAL CHALLENGES AHEAD

[A] Enhancing the *Fit@work* Activities in the DGs

Fit@work is an ambitious programme as it is intended to reach out to more than 30,000 colleagues across different locations. It is therefore necessary to coordinate the action of DG HR with key stakeholders, in addition to the SLCA. The challenge is at least twofold: to include the initiatives organized at local level in the various DGs, and effectively communicate the initiatives already in place.

In order to include local-level initiatives in the *Fit@work* framework, DG HR cooperates with the Well-being Correspondents' Network (WBCN), which is made up of a contact person for each DG responsible for organizing well-being activities. DG HR regularly meets these stakeholders in order to exchange ideas on new initiatives and the latest topics. As the expression of the reality within the different DGs, the WBCN helps tailor the programme to the specific DG needs, consistent with organizational

Commission premises is however higher as most of the Directorate-Generals have put in place their own programme of well-being. Recently the Administration Department and the SLCA have undertaken to map these activities with a view to ensuring minimum quality standards and to broadening the opportunity for interested officials to attend courses.

20. The European Network for Workplace Health Promotion (ENWHP) 'WHP is a modern corporate strategy which aims at preventing ill-health at work (including work-related diseases, accidents, injuries, occupational diseases and stress) and enhancing health-promoting potentials and well-being in the workforce', in *Luxembourg Declaration on Workplace Health Promotion in the European Union*, 27–28 Nov. 1997 (2007 version).

objectives. At the same time, many DGs run several well-being activities, that can come under the *Fit@work* umbrella (e.g., yoga classes, Pilates, social events). One major challenge is to ensure that such activities are implemented with appropriate quality standards and in a way that addresses potential legal and safety issues. For this purpose, a set of guidelines has been drafted, discussed and circulated across the various DGs in order to share best practices and ensure consistency.

Another key partner in the delivery and buy-in of the *Fit@work* programme is the Internal Communication Network. It is made up of colleagues that are responsible for communication strategies in the different DGs, and coordinated by the DG HR communication unit which in turn liaises with the Steering Committee. The role of both the ICN and the WBCN networks is crucial to promoting the full participation and involvement of EC staff in the *Fit@work* programme. The challenge ahead is to align the network of ICN correspondents with the key messages proposed at organizational level and to cooperate with the well-being correspondent within the same DG. For this purpose, a first joint WBCN and ICN network took place in October 2015. A common working space has been created on the Commission Intranet. Moreover, as the reorganization of DG HR started as of 2016, a stronger link between the central HR communication unit and the ICN correspondents has been formalized.

All well-being related activities performed at DG level in line with these guidelines are to be promoted with the *Fit@work* label and visual identity, using the institutional communication channels.

[B] Increasing the Cooperation Among Different Units and Services

A significant challenge in the coordination of activities also potentially exists among the different DG HR units and services where initiatives at corporate level are worked out. Specific initiatives within the *Fit@work* programme fall under the institutional mandate and specific competences of different units within or outside DG HR. For example, initiatives on teleworking fall within the mandate of a unit which is different from the unit responsible for the arrangements of spaces to be dedicated to *Fit@work* activities. Communication and timing need to be consistent and harmonized across units that are typically used to working autonomously. The prevention of psychosocial risk is a shared responsibility of two units belonging to different Directorates. In order to achieve better cooperation and create synergies among people responding to different hierarchical superiors, a Steering Committee has been created, chaired by the Director responsible for social policy, grouping representatives of the major delivery units and services. It provides political steer and high-level coordination for the programme. In particular, the Steering Committee:

- defines and approves programmes for senior management approval;
- monitors progress of programme activities;
- advises on specific cases;
- liaises with senior management/Vice President Cabinet;
- oversees the communication plan.

The steering committee is a high-level coordination mechanism. However, it does not have hierarchical power over its members. An initial solution for this issue has been to bring together under the same directorate (called Health, Well-being and Working solution) all DG HR units whose mandate is in line with the *Fit@work* general objectives. This change took effect as of 1 January 2016.

[C] Defining Key Performance Indicators

Finally, a third major challenge ahead is the definition and measurement of key performance indicators. The *Fit@work* programme was launched in May 2015, also in response to the feedback received within the 2014 staff survey. While staff satisfaction levels were substantially in line with those recorded in previous years, the item 'the European Commission cares about my well-being' dropped by 14% during the last year. This item is therefore a natural candidate to assess the effectiveness of the overall programme. However, key performance indicators (KPIs) on *Fit@work* should also present some other important characteristics. First, they need to include objective observations and not only on staff perception. Second, they should allow the assessment of the effectiveness of the programme at a higher level of analysis. For example, they should ideally allow measuring the performance of specific sub-areas of the programme. Third, they should be measurable at the level of a single DG. This is because needs in terms of health and well-being vary according to the various DGs and because DGs have considerable autonomy in terms of managerial choices and should regularly report on them. Finally, while a fine-grained set of indicators is desirable, there is also a need to aggregate them in a single '*Fit@work* index' to monitor the progress of the programme at corporate level.

Defining such a set of indicators is a task that presents at least two major challenges. First of all, indicators should be already available, or at least relatively easy to be collected and developed. This is not always the case given the nature of some *Fit@work* activities and the current reporting system within the European Commission. Second, input indicators should be included: the health and well-being of staff members are not only dependent on what the Commission does for them, but also on other factors and personal characteristics outside the control of the Institution. What the European Commission can do is to implement better working conditions and promote a more effective and stress-free management style. It is difficult to assess the extent to which this will enhance levels of health and well-being. These kinds of initiative aimed at creating a better workplace are often difficult to measure in a structured way.

A working group has been established to start a reflection on this topic. At the moment, the solution proposed is to combine five different indicators into an overall index. These five indicators are closely related to the seven areas that make up the *Fit@work* programme: *see* Table 10.2.

Table 10.2 Five Indicators of Well-Being at Work

Indicator	*Area*
Absence rate due to sickness	Physical and mental health
Percentage of staff regularly practising physical activity	Physical activity
Staff satisfaction with regard to work-life balance based on staff survey	Working conditions
Staff satisfaction with infrastructure on the basis of the annual staff satisfaction survey	Physical working environment
Staff satisfaction with management style based on the annual staff satisfaction survey	Supportive working conditions

A further challenge relating to these indicators is to define appropriate targets or benchmarks, to compare the situation at the European Commission with respect to similar organizations and to assess the progress of the programme.

§10.07 CONCLUSION

Fit@work is an ambitious programme, launched in response to a specific need expressed in the staff survey and bearing in mind new trends in the area of workforce management. The richness of the programme and its administrative and organizational complexity pose challenges to management. Organizational tools have been designed that will bring about further initiatives aimed at enhancing staff well-being since *Fit@work* is conceived as a living programme subject to change and improvement.

CHAPTER 11
Company-Level Welfare and Public Policies in Care Services

*Daniela Oliva & Giorgio Luigi Risso**

§11.01 INTRODUCTION

Over the last decade, Italy's welfare system has undergone radical changes. In addition to public welfare, various schemes have been developed, with an important role being played by firms, trade unions, banking foundations and the voluntary sector. In this chapter the focus is on the collaboration between the public authorities and the private sector for managing and providing educational, recreational and care services, while promoting quality employment and the emergence of workers from the informal economy. Further issues include work/family life balance, corporate social responsibility, and policies to promote equal opportunities. It is a vast field where the public social and employment services intersect with the private system and the voluntary or not-for-profit sector. As for the private sector, employers are now seen as important actors in company-level welfare programmes. This is true both of small firms as members of associations and larger firms that offer services of various types to their employees. Their welfare schemes, either autonomously and/or in collaboration with the public system, can be considered to be company-level welfare policies.

This chapter offers an analysis of a programme first implemented in the Province of Turin in the field of care work. The background to this experimentation was the growing demand for family assistance services, the progressive increase in the number of older persons in the population and a rise in the number of migrant workers. The section 11.02 of this chapter focuses on the family assistance projects implemented in

* Daniela Oliva, Director of Training and Labour Policy, Bologna Institute for Social Research; Giorgio Luigi Risso, Employment Services for the Metropolitan City of Turin, now Labour Piedmont Agency.

the Province of Turin (January 2012–February 2014), prompted by the need to tackle widespread irregularities in the employment and to intervene in a sector of the labour market that has developed primarily through informal personal networks. We will be looking at the common lines of the *Assistenza Familiare Reti Integrate* (hereafter: Family Assistance Project), outlining a model developed for the City and Province of Turin in northern Italy.

The next section 11.03 of this chapter examines a project launched in 2007 with the Province of Bologna, funded by the European Social Fund, to enhance conditions for women in the labour market, work-family life balance and the promotion of equal opportunities. This project established a network of firms responsive to these issues (the Gender Community Network) and prepared to collaborate with the public institutions to develop models of shared intervention.

§11.02 THE FAMILY ASSISTANCE PROJECT

[A] Introduction

The integrated system for family assistance gave rise to two different lines of project development: the Family Assistance Project for the City of Turin and the Family Assistance Project for the Province of Turin, taking into account the particular features of each. For the City of Turin, in addition to paying close attention to the resident population it was necessary to take into consideration the city council's social service structure and the network consisting of associations dealing with care work and supplying advisory services to foreign nationals. As for the Province of Turin, due consideration had to be given to the presence and collaboration between Employment Centres and departments managing social services. The Family Assistance Project was developed by planning and implementing shared services, and improving the flow of communication, with integrated network relations and public employment services. Within the limits of the available resources, local helpdesks were opened, training and certification courses funded, contract regularization processes adopted, and support provided for social recognition of care work as a profession.

This system of public governance linked employment services with the public social services on the one hand, and, on the other hand, the system of training, associations, cooperatives and Employment Centres in a framework of safeguards and security for the care workers and the families contacting the helpdesks. In the final experimental stage, the Province of Turin took steps to ensure continuity in the activities through the network of Employment Centres running helpdesks. In implementing the projects, these centres achieved a good level of autonomy and professional standards in the management of this labour market segment. In the course of 2013, the Province of Turin also collaborated with the organizations managing the social services as part of the nationwide Home Care Premium project. Funded by the national social security institute, INPS, the project was designed for public employees and non-self-sufficient members of their families in need of care and assistance, with the assistance of the Employment Centres to match supply and demand. At this point, a new project was launched enhancing the role of the public system in the context of company-level welfare.

This chapter will illustrate the work of the experimental Family Assistance Project which, thanks to the collaboration with the Bologna Social Research Institute, created conditions in the area of the Metropolitan City of Turin (incorporating the City and Province of Turin) for implementing an experimental service for the employees of the Unipol Group within the framework of family assistance for older people and children (family care assistants and childminders, both for extended periods and for occasional and/or emergency needs). The service is part of the broader project for the enhancement of the position of women in the labour market, equal opportunities and company-level welfare (Gender Community Network), which the Province of Bologna has been running for some years.

[B] The Regional Model

In 2010 the Piedmont Region issued a Call for Tenders for the implementation of services in the area of family assistance through the development of local networks, funded with resources from the regional operating programme and the European Social Fund 2007/2013. The Call for Tenders formulated by the Piedmont Region took into account the synergy with the provinces of Piedmont and the system already in place that included public employment centres, private employment agencies, voluntary associations and the private sector. The intention was to bring together employment services, social policies and vocational training in a system of mixed public-private services through the use of European and ministry resources, in addition to regional funding. The model proposed by the Piedmont Region was based on certain principles to be respected in the design of local projects in order to:

- restore dignity to care work, proposing a form of governance for family assistance, providing guarantees for families, placing greater emphasis on attention to the person and relations of trust in the encounter between the two parties, giving due recognition to the professional qualities and competencies, whether formal or informal, of the family care assistants, and supporting access to employment and job security;
- improve and enhance the local supply of personal services, promoting the creation and coordination of a wide range of public and private services in the local areas in the family assistance sector;
- encourage the emergence of irregular labour, creating conditions to match the supply and demand for labour, while facilitating the selection of family care assistants, the consolidation of the area networks and the transition to regular employment contracts.

In addition to consolidating the existing local networks, another important aim concerned the promoting of the employment quality of family assistants and workers in family care services. In this respect, the Region set up meetings with social workers to share information, project lines, operating tools and information technology, while activating procedures for the recognition of the skills of family assistants acquired in informal and non-formal contexts.

The Call for Tenders defined in broad terms a process involving various operations, from the first stage providing for information to a second stage with a range of integrated and customized specialist services promoting regular employment (matching supply and demand), while identifying the appropriate ways to assist the people applying to the helpdesks. For the family care assistants, measures were devised and applied to identify their competencies (including language skills for foreign workers) and their willingness to improve their level of employability. For the families, fact-finding interviews were arranged to obtain information to determine the care needs, the characteristics of the person requiring assistance, and the competencies required of the worker. The next stage consisted of matching supply and demand by identifying the applicants with the appropriate characteristics. On starting work, the workers were not left to their own devices but helped into the family context and made familiar with the local network of services including the social and health services, on the basis of individual supervision and training. The helpdesk also devised an activity to provide job applicants and family care assistants with training, while offering the families advice on tax matters and employment contracts, as well as assistance in completing administrative procedures.

After implementation began on the project, certain complementary schemes were added, with funding from the 2010 Migration Policy Fund. This served to enhance certain aspects of improving the quality of care work (recognition of formal and non-formal skills) and the emergence of irregular employment with incentives for the families in addition to specialist advisory services. As regards the certification of formal and non-formal competencies, a procedure was devised to enhance the position and autonomy of the family care assistants. Subsequently, a training agency specialised in skills certification verified the documentation presented and ascertained the competencies by means of theoretical and practical tests.

Experience was corroborated with a training module on family assistance, for a total duration of fifty hours, serving to obtain certification of the skills acquired. Thanks to the supply of further resources (amounting to EUR 150,000) from the Regional Social Policy Department an economic incentive was introduced for taking part in the training courses. To support the family care assistants who were offered jobs after taking part in the programme, the families hiring them were offered economic incentives to regularise the employment contract. The entire process was subject to continuous monitoring by the Piedmont Region and the Provinces, which constantly verified the progress of the projects and the achievement of the objectives. A total of eight projects were funded and carried out in the various provinces of Piedmont, characterized by a common basis and adaptation to local conditions.

The main elements common to these projects were:

- the presence of specialized helpdesks in the Employment Centres;
- a network of local public-private actors;
- continuity with previous projects;
- the procedures for certification of the skills of the family care assistants;

- incentives for the transition to a regular employment contract.

The terms laid down in the Call for Tenders were adopted also in the Province of Turin, and two different projects were activated, one for the City of Turin, and one for the Province.

[C] The Common Characteristics of the Family Care Projects

The Province of Turin implemented two projects with total funding of about EUR 800,000. The projects derived from previous experiments in this sector, as in the case of the 2006 project *Valorizzare le esperienze lavorative delle assistenti familiari* (VELA) (Enhancing family assistants' work experience) run by the City of Turin. This was followed by a number of significant schemes within the framework of the PARI 2007 Programme of the Piedmont Region and the *Fondi Bindi* (funds provided by the Ministry for Family Policies presided over by Minister Rosy Bindi, with implementation in close collaboration with the social services and the territorial network of the municipalities). This experimental activity led to the creation of integrated services for family care assistants and the families needing assistance, operating on the basis of active labour market policies and promoting quality of employment and the training of workers.

The main aim of the family care projects was the creation, improvement and implementation of the local network to provide high quality services. Coordinated by the Province of Turin, the network operated through dedicated helpdesks with the participation of the Employment Centres, the social services and private agencies active in the family assistance sector (cooperatives, associations and employment agencies). Within this network, the public employment system coordinated the supervision and development activities of the network. The associations, cooperatives and private agencies were responsible for contributing to the development of network and collaborating in the management of the helpdesks.

The social services providing support for integrated management of the local offices. Given the particular characteristics of the area concerned, there was a need to set up two different projects and constitute two associations made up of ten partners for the City of Turin and twenty-nine partners for the Province of Turin.

Nineteen helpdesks were set up for the development of the projects:

- in the City of Turin, the seven helpdesks were run by associations and private labour agencies with particular professional skills in the sector, associated with the two Employment Centres of Turin;
- in the Province of Turin, the twelve helpdesks were set up in the twelve Employment Centres, and managed with the collaboration of cooperatives and employment agencies, with the participation of the social services.

The integrated helpdesks of the City of Turin and of the Province of Turin provided information services, as well as employment services for matching the supply and demand for labour. They were linked through the Piedmont Labour Information System, a common database used by all the Employment Centres.

Given the importance of the quality of care work the aims of the project were pursued through:

- systematic active labour market policies seeking to match the supply and demand for labour;
- action to bring family assistance out of the grey market and ensure social recognition for it;
- action to develop policies for integration and equal opportunities, with particular attention to women from other countries (with targeted actions in reconstructing and further developing vocational paths, knowledge of the Italian language, and information about/guidance towards the services available in the area).

The family care assistants had access to a range of services including guidance, analysis of needs, preselection, identification of competencies, assessment of employability and support in entering the family environment. At the same time, the families concerned benefited from qualified services for matching the supply and demand for labour, advice on procedures to formalise employment, and assistance in employment.

The aim of the actions promoted was to formulate commonly accepted definitions of the standards of the services and performance, enhancing and systematizing the links between the social assistance services and labour services while maintaining public control over the part of the provincial Employment Centres. The aim was also to guarantee not only the quality of the services but also access to them, progressively reducing the gap between the institutions and the citizens.

The family care projects were formally launched in October 2011 (with helpdesk activities starting in January 2012) and concluded, in compliance with the terms of the Call for Tenders, in February 2014. To manage these activities, temporary associations were set up with the Province of Turin playing the leading role.

For the family care project for the Province of Turin, the temporary association, consisting of the provincial Employment Centres and the relevant social services, had the further benefit of various private partners (employment agencies, consortia and associations of social cooperatives). These were selected through a public notice for expression of interest for actors who had acquired experience in managing services for the integration of family care assistants into the labour market.

For the family care project for the City of Turin and the management of the seven help desks, the temporary association consisted of the Turin Employment Centre, the Turin municipal social assistance services, and private partners including employment agencies and voluntary associations.

It is worth stressing that the role played by the social assistance services in the temporary association was of fundamental importance due to their many years of experience in handling services dedicated to home assistance.

For the Turin project, provision was made for an aggregate working time taking into account the density of the population of older persons (Piedmont Region Demographic Trend Database, 2008), while also taking into account the number of domestic workers hired as recorded by the Province of Turing Labour Market Monitoring Office (2009). The geographical distribution of the helpdesks included mountain areas, where four additional reception and information points were established. Coordination of the activities was entrusted to the Coordination Service Centres of the Province of Turin, liaising with the social services in close synergy with all the other public and private bodies participating in the networks.

The ultimate aims of the Projects consisted of:

- inclusion and continuation in the world of work of family care assistants, through enhancement and improving the quality of care work;
- creation and coordination of a number of public and private services in the field of family assistance in the area concerned;
- matching the supply and demand for labour through careful selection of family care assistants in relation to families in need of care services;
- implementation and management of employment relations, and relations between family care assistants and families with advisory services.

The helpdesks mainly provided information and reception services, as well as individual specialist services designed to facilitate access to employment.

The integrated specialist services were designed to meet the needs of users and organized at the level of individual services aimed at establishing employment relations on the basis of guidance and preselection activities as well as ascertaining competencies (including language skills). They also served to match supply and demand, and accompany users into employment, helping them to find appropriate training courses and providing advice on employment contracts.

The service management system available to all the helpdesks was run through the Labour Information System at regional level, with a detailed care work datasheet for the assessment of employability and skills. Among the various services, a decisive role was played by matching the supply and demand for labour. Family care assistants were provided with individual services to draft a résumé of their educational/training and vocational experience, identifying their aspirations, motivations and inclination for this type of work. Appropriate tools were devised to ascertain the competencies of the candidates (care work skills, language skills in the case of foreign nationals), and the level of employability in order to meet the needs of potential employers. For the families seeking care assistants, fact-finding interviews were set up to ascertain the assistance needs, the characteristics of the person to be assisted and the care assistant required. The next step was to put forward a list of qualified candidates with the characteristics required by the families.

At the helpdesks the family care assistants had the benefit of information and guidance services to direct them to the training courses available in the area. The aim was to enhance their skills and qualifications. In addition, the advice service provided the families with support in drafting contracts and dealing with administrative procedures. The aim was to help the families to deal with the administrative procedures to regularise employment, favouring the transition from the informal to the formal economy.

The projects were funded with resources from the Migration Policies Fund 2010 (approximately EUR 322,000), supplementing the regional funds from the Call for Tenders. These supplementary schemes reflect the purpose of the funds, intended to benefit foreign nationals, with help in terms of funding (incentives for making the transition to regular employment) or training (with certification). In particular, these actions concerned two areas for intervention:

- Creating paths for family assistants applying to the helpdesks to obtain certification of their formal and non-formal skills. In methodological terms, the path to recognition and certification of the family care assistants' skills involved a preliminary stage of identification, reception and selection of the workers, with verification of the possession of the minimum requisites. This was followed by ascertainment and validation of the skills; participation in fifty-hour training courses, and finally the entry-level examination for family care assistants relating to the vocational education/training received. Altogether, twenty courses were held, ending in early 2013, with the participation of 312 trainees obtaining certification as family care assistants.
- Provision of economic incentives for employment, promoting the regularization of contracts and helping with the administrative activities. For the economic incentives favouring the transition to regular employment, the Province of Turin involved the social services in the areas outside Turin as partners in provincial project. This was achieved on the basis of previous experience and consolidated collaboration with the Employment Centres outside Turin in the field of care work. The services involved contributed to identifying and providing ongoing support for the families and economic incentives. The system served sixty-five users/families, who hired family care assistants on regular open-ended contracts for a minimum of twenty hours per week, receiving a one-off grant ranging from EUR 700 for part-time to EUR 1,300 for full-time assistants.

[D] Quantitative Results

The project in the City of Turin constituted an example of the shared construction of a system leading to a new welfare model. It is worth noting that the activity in Turin was characterized by the capacity to overcome barriers in bringing together a network of partners (employment agencies and associations), combining efforts to identify the complementary activity areas and to implement an extensive network of services. During the implementation of the project and the helpdesk activities, between January 2012 and February 2014, 14,024 family care assistants (mostly women) made use of the information services, 3084 of them benefiting from individual specialist services. These services included advice on the transition to regular employment, filling in the forms outlining their educational/training and background, providing advice on the regulations and the national agreement for family care assistants, and matching the supply and demand for labour, along with support for moving into employment. About 65% of the family care assistants making use of the services were from outside the EU, while the EU users consisted mostly of Romanians together with some Italians. A total of 799 families applied to the helpdesks for information, and of these 379 made use of the advisory service (concerning contract and administrative procedures) and the matching of supply and demand, with the result that 206 persons were hired, mostly on open-ended contracts. Most of the family care assistants hired were women (179 as compared with nine men) from outside the EU (with a large proportion of Peruvians and Moroccans), over the age of 35.

In the framework of the provincial project, reception and specialist services were implemented at the twelve Employment Centres. The helpdesks were managed with the participation of cooperatives and employment agencies, with the collaboration of the social assistance services. The two years of helpdesk activities saw 6061 family assistants making use of the reception and information services, with over half of these (3862) benefiting from individual specialist activities. In particular, the activity of providing advice in the transition to regular employment consisted of the reconstruction of the vocational skills and educational/training, help with the regulations laid down in the national agreement, and support in finding employment. As expected, most of the workers were from EU countries (2933) – Romanians and Italians – while non-EU citizens accounted for 24%. The number of families making use of the advisory services on administrative procedures and the matching of supply and demand came to 691, resulting in 217 persons being hired, mostly on open-ended contracts (210 women and seven men, 167 EU citizens and fifty non-EU citizens), more than 75% of them over the age of 35.

[E] Considerations on the Experimentation with the Two Projects

The City of Turin and Province of Turin projects were designed as an integrated system with the participation of various parties to ensure a multidimensional approach (public and private services, cooperatives, associations). Thanks to the partnership between public bodies, the voluntary sector and local institutions, a considerable impact was made in the dissemination and transferability of the project. Collaboration between the Province of Turin and the social services served to ensure the transparency of labour market policies and the promotion of equal opportunities. More generally, the approach based on cooperation among the various parties (responsible for taking charge of the users, arranging for their training and eventual employment), tried and tested in the previous projects, was consolidated and adopted throughout the Province. Thanks to the use of shared tools and methods, each of the partners was able to offer quality professional services. With the Piedmont Labour Information System used by all the helpdesks, the workers in the various services had access to the provincial database, thus facilitating the selection of family care assistants, while serving also for monitoring.

The process was designed to impact on the services and local labour market, taking various aspects into account (labour organization models, reconciliation of work and family/private life, extension of the territorial network, promotion of the sector in qualitative terms, enhancement of training), testing a model that can be transferred to other territorial, regional and national contexts. Naturally, the transferability of the project to other contexts can be envisaged where the appropriate conditions are in place, with the right balance between public and private bodies, prior experience and shared resources and targets. In recent years the Province of Turin, with its network of Employment Centres, has invested heavily in collaboration and combined planning of policies and operations in the social and employment field. To be able to replicate the model it will be necessary to create the right conditions and examine the organizational, economic and social context.

In the final considerations it is necessary to take into account certain dynamics typical of care work which may result in negative effects. For example, due consideration should be given to what are perceived to be the mutual advantages in maintaining a certain amount of informal labour (Pasquinelli, Rusmini 2013). In these informal arrangements, which give rise to a moral risk for the parties involved, the workers are not protected in terms of job security, while the families are exposed to the risk of inspections and sanctions. The recourse to informal labour is associated with the increasing economic difficulty experienced by families in bearing the cost of private care, taking into account the ageing of the population and the increasing demand for co-residential assistance for the over-80 age group. As far as the care workers are concerned, there is an increasing supply of labour provided on an hourly basis by Italian women, who have recently entered this market, while foreign nationals are no longer widely available, as many have already found suitable employment (Sarti, 2011).

To regularize informal employment there is a need to develop a system of integrated services (labour and social services) at the national level, to provide information and advice on the transition to regular employment, and to take responsibility for care assistants and families alike. Incentives are needed in the form of tax relief and social security contributions, extending the scope for deductions while introducing economic measures including contributions for those hiring workers on regular contracts. Another point to be stressed is the need to supersede the scant social recognition accorded to the profession through better qualification and effective attestation of the professional role played by family care assistants. In this respect an active labour market policy closely integrated with vocational training is an important factor, promoting recognition of the family care assistants' vocational skills.

What emerges from this overview of the two projects is the need for procedures for certification of non-formal and informal skills, mainly for foreign women benefiting from professional recognition and greater job security. The sustainability of the projects rests essentially on the role of governance of the public system which, drawing on dedicated resources, promotes application of the model to ensure continuity for the helpdesks that are well established in the territory. Another element favouring continuity in the activities consists of the location of the helpdesks, set up in Employment Centres, and thus able to ensure close integration into the daily supply of services. In concluding the experimental stage of the projects, the City and Province (now the Metropolitan Area) of Turin ensured continuity of the activities through its network of Employment Centre helpdesks, which, with implementation of the projects, were able to achieve a high degree of autonomy and professional standards in their approach to this specific segment of the labour market.

§11.03 THE GENDER COMMUNITY NETWORK

[A] The Background

The Gender Community Network is the result of a series of projects funded by the European Social Fund and promoted by the Employment Services of the Province of Bologna. As from 2007, the European Year of Equal Opportunities for All, the Province supported a number of projects aiming to ascertain the occupational conditions of women in local industry, focusing on career paths, management styles and work-life balance. Subsequently, active labour market policies were drawn up, tried and tested with the aim of maintaining and enhancing – albeit in a period of rising unemployment – the role of women in the world of work. These various projects contributed to creating a network (the Gender Community Network) of local firms (many with national and international standing) which, together with the Province of Bologna, ran experimental services both collective (available to the firms concerned) and personalized (for the employees of individual firms).

Since 2012, the Gender Community Network has been associated with the Madreperla project (literally, mother-of-pearl),[1] originally promoted by the Emilia-Romagna Region in 2002 and, subsequently, implemented by the Province of Bologna with the support of the European Social Fund. Madreperla is the name of a database specialized in matching the supply and demand for family care assistants, with a section dedicated to ascertaining assistance needs and a section serving to identify the skills of the family care assistants. The added value of the Madreperla database lies in the fact that it accepts only qualified workers (at both the formal and informal level) assessed by Employment Centres also specialized in the field.

In 2012 the Madreperla database was no longer restricted to the families applying to the Employment Centres in search of family care assistants, but it was structured as a service available to firms in the Gender Community Network in a context where company-level welfare policies converge with policies for work/life reconciliation, the promotion of female employment, and shared public-private welfare policies.

1. The Madreperla Project is associated with the SER.DOM project (Home Services, for the development of employment sources in the field of home services) started in 2001 by the City of Modena and subsequently developed with the collaboration of the Province of Modena Employment Centres.

[B] Services Implemented

Of the services of a collective nature implemented for firms within the framework of the projects promoted by the Province of Bologna, mention should be made of the workshops in firms for the exchange and extension of good practices, networking activities between the Community firms and between the Community and other local organizations (firms, institutions, thematic networks), as well as information and awareness-raising activities and public workshops. The exchange of good practice is promoted by the website www.gendercommunity.net (which, alongside the public section contains an area reserved for firms belonging to the Community)[2] also by means of a periodical Newsletter. However, the core of the services implemented concerns the agreements with the institutions for company-level welfare activities:

(1) The *Care Desk Service* (supplying family assistants for private home care for older people).
(2) The *Care Sharing Desk Service* (providing shared family assistants in condominiums and small neighbourhoods, or where vicinity makes it possible).
(3) The *Metro-Tata Service for childminding services,* usually for at least fifteen hours a week (Tata metropolitana).
(4) Il *Metro-Tata Service to provide childminders and babysitters* for brief periods, unforeseen circumstances or emergencies (Tata on Demand).

The first of the above services is open to all citizens and, in the case of agreements with individual firms (for employees' family members) a procedure is established that entails priority access. It is to be noted that these intermediation services, and also the agreements with the individual firms, are entirely free of charge for the users who incur only the contract drafting costs if the service is in fact provided.

In the context of customized or personalized services, various measures have been adopted to promote the role of women in employment (training, Charter of Values, Ethical Codes promoting diversity, individual career paths, support for women's leadership), as well as workshops looking into issues on the basis of analysis of needs/interests, gender-oriented analysis of the organization, and identification of needs for improving internal policy in terms of equal opportunity, work-life balance and company-level welfare.

[C] The Gender Community Network

The Global Community Network for promoting women in employment collaborates with firms investing in the potential offered by women, work-life balance and company-level welfare, while seeking to involve other potentially relevant bodies and organizations. The community is open to all the firms and institutions intending to:

2. In the reserved area updated documentation is available on: Regulations, Funding Opportunities, Good Practices, Articles and Publications, and a Glossary.

- pay attention to gender issues, work-life balance policies and company-level welfare, as part of the firm's mission, while promoting lifelong learning within the firm;
- promote networking, dialogue among firms and between firms and the institutions not only in the metropolitan area, but also at the national and international level, giving rise to synergies thanks to shared values and the adoption of good practices;
- boost the image and brand of firms and institutions sensitive to gender equal opportunity, work-life balance policies and company-level welfare, giving the issues greater prominence in the area, promoting the involvement of small and medium-sized firms.

Those joining the Community sign the Charter on the Value of Diversity, with which the firms commit themselves to creating and consolidating a community dedicated to positive exploitation of differences (not only of gender) in the workplace, work-life reconciliation, company-level welfare and corporate social responsibility.

One important feature of the Community is its local nature and the close relations that develop between the public and private actors in the local community. However, this focus on the local dimension does not mean restricting the range of action (as will be seen shortly), but only that the Community develops through construction and interaction with other local Communities (Networks), for the purpose of conserving the particular characteristics that distinguish them and allow for more effective action in the areas where they operate.

[D] Results

The Care Desk Service for family assistance for older persons has been operating on an experimental basis in the Province of Bologna since May 2012 with the support of Intesa Sanpaolo-Carisbo. Since 2013 the agreements with the provincial authority have been extended to the ASPPI (*Associazione Sindacale Piccoli Proprietari Immobiliari* – Association of Small Property Owners), CRIF, HERA, Unicredit and Unipol. The Care Sharing Desk Service was set up in 2015 and is run on an experimental basis by ASPPI for local firms. The Metro-Tata Service (Tata Metropolitana), also created in 2015, has been providing two types of service, regular and occasional childminding services, for employees of the Unipol insurance company employed in the province of Bologna. These services are now available to firms in the Gender Community Network.

IRS, the Institute for Social Research, which designed and implemented the services, has also carried out monitoring and evaluation of their utilization by employees of the six firms concluding the agreement. So far thirty-five firms of various sizes, in a variety of sectors, have joined the Gender Community.[3] In addition,

3. Acer, AIAS, Alfa Wassermann, àncora, ASPPI, Azienda Ospedaliera Policlinico Sant'Orsola, Azienda Unità Sanitaria Locale di Bologna, CADIAI, CAMST, CARISBO, Carpigiani, CRIF, Ducati, EmilBanca, Flò fiori, GD Gruppo Coesia, GICO System, Gruppo Hera, IMA; Intesa Sanpaolo, L'aura maioliche, Les libellules, Manutencoop, Maserati, Poste italiane, Schiavina Restauro

sixty-five firms in the province of Bologna, twenty-nine national firms and five regional authorities have taken part in Gender Community Network projects.

[E] Development of the Projects

As mentioned above, in 2013 Unipol signed an agreement with the Province of Bologna to provide its employees with services of a family care assistant for older people. Subsequently, Unipol also agreed to try out the prototype of the Metro-Tata Service for regular and occasional childminding. The restriction of these services to employees in the province of Bologna (where most workers are concentrated) was dictated by the limits on the jurisdiction of the Province (now Metropolitan City) of Bologna. From the outset this factor, which obviously cannot be modified insofar as it depends on institutional powers, represented a limit for all the firms in the Gender Community Network with premises outside the metropolitan area of Bologna. As might be expected, even when the company-level welfare policies derive from autonomous choices (not subject to negotiation with the unions), they are essentially open to all employees, or at least most of them. As a result, Unipol proposed extending coverage of the Gender Community Network to the other metropolitan areas with the highest concentrations of employees. So far, agreements for family assistance for older persons and care services for children (with both continuous and 'emergency' childminding services) have been implemented, outside Bologna, with the Agency AFOLSud, Milan (with competence for the Municipality of San Donato Milanese where Unipol operates, although the service is available for the entire Province of Milan), and with the Metropolitan City of Turin. For 2016 there is a Unipol project to implement further agreements in cities in Italy where the firm is most represented, and to extend collaboration with the public institutions in various fields other than care services.

Given the close attention to local conditions by the Gender Community Network, in each of the new areas collaboration with the Province/Metropolitan City was implemented with the aim of further developing the existing facilities and services and the particular features of the local context. Thus the names of the services were subject to change (the Tata service in Bologna became the Babysitter service in Turin) as well as the procedures for implementation. However, the rationale and the framework of the values outlined above remain unchanged.

In this way, the project of the Metropolitan City of Turin linked up with the Gender Community Network, which extended beyond the area where it was first set up to meet the needs of a company-level welfare overriding the limits laid down by institutional jurisdictions.

[F] Some Considerations on the Gender Community Network

Starting from public governance, by linking various systems (services in the fields of employment, training and social assistance), the projects raised the issue of relations

Costruzioni, Serigrafia76, Società Dolce, Studio Ferrari, Talent's Angels cacciatori di teste, TELECOM Italia, Unicredit, UNIPOL Gruppo, WorkWideWomen, YOOX Group.

with the private sector, and in particular with firms, within the framework of a shared welfare system (something quite different from subsidiarity and/or public-private integration for the supply of services).

The growing demand for care services over the last few years has influenced the supply of company-level welfare, which has to some extent come to overlap with services initially conceived of within a logic of gender equality of opportunity and work/life balance. For such services firms have looked both to the private sector (and this is an area that it is intended to develop) and to the public institutions for a response to the need for a level of qualification for the workers and a system to match supply and demand while dealing with irregular employment. The reasons for this collaboration are to be found not only in the need for safeguards and quality of performance, but also, and more importantly, in the pursuit of conditions for dialogue with the institutions and the territorial context, as in the case of discontinuous activities in the area of company-level childcare facilities.

The activities of the Gender Community Network designed and developed by IRS favoured:

- the involvement of individual firms as local actors in the welfare system;
- the pursuit of direct, disinterested relations with the institutions;
- close links between policies for gender equality of opportunity, corporate social responsibility and welfare in support of workers and their families.

The practice of private home assistance for older persons has developed beyond public control and safeguards and only in the last decade have attempts been made to regulate these activities in terms of: (i) improving employment quality for family care assistants; (ii) specialized intermediation (in general, use of databases, specialist interviews to ascertain the family assistants' skills and identify the needs of the families and older persons); and (iii) involvement of all the workers in the sector, who often have a better understanding of care-work issues than those in the public sector. While the last few years have seen numerous attempts to bring home assistance for older persons back under public control – with some success – it is clear that far less has been attempted in connection with home assistance for children. Childminders are still not generally perceived in professional terms (hence the lack of legal status, and the lack of employment contracts), focusing attention far more on personal acquaintance and trust. However, one of the interesting points is that the meeting point on the one hand between a service of institutional nature dealing with work and training, and on the other hand private firms, came about in the field of care for older people, and only subsequently for children, through alternative and/or supplementary care services such as company-level childcare facilities.

In other words, there is evidence of a convergence (although for different reasons) of interests on the part of these two broad groups in dealing with a policy that eluded (and still largely eludes) public control and, in particular, the institutional bodies that should be most involved, the employment services, in close connection with the social services.

It is also interesting to note the potential of this area of activity and the ways in which it is construed, in particular, at the institutional level. For example, in the national activities of the Gender Community Network and in the Employment Service in Turin, integration with the social services has been pursued, not only for reasons of institutional competence, but also because it results in greater efficiency and effectiveness in implementing social assistance policies. At the same time, in Bologna the Employment Service interpreted it more in the direction of creating better conditions for women working in firms, thus seeing it as a measure for work/life balance.

While the rationale behind developments in this area can be readily grasped (from promoting regular employment and establishing professional qualifications, to the attempt to govern private home assistance), less obvious are the factors that are leading private firms towards convergence on these issues.

Company-level welfare is a complex matter, beginning with the issue of agreement on what exactly it means, or in other words what facilities can come under this heading and what might be more appropriately classified as fringe benefits. In general, it may be said that company-level welfare schemes are aimed at all the employees (as a whole, or those with certain characteristics, such as those with dependent children), while fringe benefits are related to certain organizational positions and cannot be considered provisions of a universal nature. Other classifications highlight the more traditional (supplementary health insurance, recreational services) or innovative (care support services, leisure time services) nature of the facilities. Over and above these distinctions, however, it is worth considering how the range of company-level welfare facilities can be seen to derive from diverse policies and strategies, but also different corporate values, and not simply as a response to the perceived needs of the employees.

The activity of the Gender Community Network is exemplary from this point of view. While the adoption of care provisions for older members of the family was originally designed by firms as a work/life balance measure, it has since developed well beyond this to become a means of collaboration with the local community and institutions. Significantly, the company-level childcare facilities open to users within the area represent a work/life balance measure in the field of care services. Some years ago these services were perceived in terms of work/life balance, but today, after years of rising unemployment and recession, they have taken on the guise of company-level welfare. These firms also engage in other forms of collaboration with local communities (art, environment, participation in socially significant projects). However, it is important to stress that care services for older people and children, traditionally the responsibility of institutions engaged in a range of activities covering education/training, employment and social work, today represent a particularly favourable area for firms interested in collaborating on and sharing in public sector welfare models as a district system (insofar as the local level is favoured over the municipal/metropolitan level).

The challenge for future development in this area lies in seeing the extent to which the Employment Services, which in the cases presented link firms and social services, are able to internalize the increasingly significant presence of firms on the company-level welfare front (not just for care services), and to promote effective sharing of welfare schemes. This also leads to a common view of what the needs of the citizens are, and the degree of coverage of these needs, associated with occupational status. Development in this direction would imply a capacity on the part of the public institutions to monitor and control the welfare measures that the individual citizen can access on the strength of his/her status (occupation, income, personal networks).[4]

§11.04 SOME CONSIDERATIONS ON THE TWO PROJECTS

There is an evident link between the projects outlined above, despite the diversity of their aims, mission, and the geographical environments where they developed. On the one hand, the projects are based on a public-private service model in a network context (operators on the market and in the Turin projects, firms in the Gender Community Network). On the other hand, there is the focus on a particular service representing the core around which these activities have developed, namely care services for older persons and for children.

These are what may be defined as individual demand services, for which both the public and the private sectors construct a supply system based on analysis of the particular needs and the preferences for the possible solutions that may be advanced. Response to these solutions is greatly conditioned by the context and social and cultural models, and only secondly by the economic resources available. As far as the direct users are concerned, these services respond not only to needs for assistance and care, but also to needs of an educational, recreational and social nature. At the same time, as far as the families are concerned, these services respond to the need to reconcile competing demands (with work and/or private life), promoting women's employment (it is mainly women who manage care work), economic compatibility, and cultural/value choices in addressing care work. As far as the institutions are concerned, these are services that offer a wide range of opportunities from the point of view of the public policies that can be brought into play (economic, organizational, for family support, direct intervention). From the point of view of the firms, supplying care services to the families of their employees is a way of responding to various needs, beginning with the need to balance work and family life.

Thus the complex field of care services may be seen to be open to experimentation in devising public-private models of shared policies. This is a varied field of experimentation for the public system (in terms of the emergence and promotion of employment, and in the more specific focus on work, assistance and social-educational aspects), but also for firms, as it enables them to supply a wider range of care services for their employees (traditionally provided as part of company-level welfare), pursuing lines in common with the public system in a context that sees an increasingly strong

4. It is worth noting two recent legislative provisions relating to this issue: Legislative Decree of 15 Jun. 2015, n. 80 "Measures to reconcile care, life and work needs, in implementation of Art. 1, clauses 8 and 9, of the Act of 10 Dec. 2014, n. 183" and the recent enabling act in reform of the public administration "Delegation to the Government in the organization of the public administration," Art. 11 of which provides for promotion of work/life balance for public employees (favouring projects to provide support services for parents).

and common interest in promoting models, approaches and shared activities in the rationale and typologies of intervention.

The experience of the home assistance service for older persons and childminding services for the families of Unipol employees represents a point of convergence of the various forms, focuses and facets of care service. Thus we have a field of application in which other forms of collaboration can be tried and tested with the conviction that, on the one hand, the presence of the public sector represents a guarantee of quality, transparency and legality in the services offered, while on the other hand opening up to organized private actors (not only to the individual citizen) represents an important development for the positioning of the public services, taking control of a traditionally autonomous market.

A particularly interesting point is that with a closely targeted and, on the whole, simple service it is possible to respond to truly pressing needs, and that the public-private collaboration serves to bring home a lesson that is also essentially cultural. In short, the lesson is to reorient the patterns of behaviour of individuals and families towards the goals of the promotion of quality employment, transparency, legality and equal opportunity.

There remains a crucial point in the cases illustrated here, but more generally relevant, namely the question of institutional communication, and indeed of corporate communication. It is undeniable that the patterns of behaviour we wish to see reoriented are deeply rooted. But it is the case that the public bodies, in general, show serious shortcomings in communicating to the citizens, while corporate communication may also be lacking in effectiveness. This critical point is exacerbated by the particular and manifold nature of care services – services the need for which is perceived when it is on the point of becoming urgent.

In other words, most people take no interest in the supply of such services until personal or family needs arise for assistance to older persons or children in the family. When such needs arise the sense of urgency leads the individuals and families to fall back on the socially and culturally predominant approaches based on personal relations. As a result the search for a carer may mean asking the butcher, the baker or the candlestick maker for advice, or looking to friends or family when seeking a childminder. Thus, institutional and corporate communication aimed at encouraging use of care services monitored by the public system must publicize the services systematically and periodically[5] so that when the individual need for assistance arises, families are fully aware of the options available to them.

5. In the Family Assistance Project communication at street level was implemented on an experimental basis with the support of the Municipal Pharmacies.

CHAPTER 12

The Adverse Impact of Unemployment on Mental Health in the Province of Modena, Italy

Tindara Addabbo, Elena Sarti & Fabrizio Starace[*]

§12.01 INTRODUCTION

This chapter addresses the question of mental health, a crucial dimension of well-being, in its connection with work and unemployment during the economic recession.[1] The ongoing recession has given rise to tangible costs in terms of cuts in employment and income in a number of European countries. The uncertainties connected to the increase in unemployment and the spread of precarious employment have been identified in the literature as possible determinants of unfavourable mental health outcomes. This chapter addresses the topic by using local microdata to measure the impact of the crisis on mental health in a specific context. A descriptive analysis based on the 2012 and 2006 Surveys on Income and Living Conditions of Households (ICESmo) in the province of Modena in Northern Italy casts light on a decline in mental health that is more accentuated for women, while multivariate analysis of 2012 microdata points to a gender-specific impact of the length of unemployment on mental health.

* Marco Biagi Department of Economics, Marco Biagi Foundation, University of Modena and Reggio Emilia, Centre for the Analysis of Public Policies (CAPP), tindara.addabbo@unimore.it; Elena Sarti, Marco Biagi Foundation, University of Modena and Reggio Emilia, elena.sarti @unimore.it; Department of Mental Health and Drug Abuse, AUSL Modena f.starace@ausl.mo.it.

1. The authors gratefully acknowledge funding from the Marco Biagi Foundation and the Department of Mental Health and Drug Abuse, AUSL for the Modena Research Project on Work and Mental Health and thank two anonymous referees and the participants at the Human Capabilities and Development Association Conference in Athens for their stimulating comments on previous versions of this chapter. The content is the sole responsibility of the authors.

The existing literature on unemployment and mental health clearly shows a deterioration in individual well-being during periods of unemployment and an enhancement of well-being for those who find a job after a period in unemployment. Health and work both play a crucial role in the definition of well-being. This chapter aims to clarify the link between unemployment and mental health, by focusing on a well-defined institutional context in a country that has been severely affected by the crisis. We focus on the province of Modena that, in addition to the recession, has been affected by a series of earthquakes. All this has had a negative effect on individual mental health, with an effect that appears to be deeper than observed in Italy as a whole.

Our findings show that on average women are more disadvantaged in terms of mental health than men. As expected, unemployment is found to diminish mental health by 6% with a different effect by gender according to its duration. Living in an area of the province suffering earthquake damage negatively affects mental health by 5%.

This chapter is structured as follows. In section 12.02, we refer to the literature on unemployment and mental health and on the effect of natural disasters on mental health. Section 12.03 describes the data analysed in the empirical model, while section 12.04 provides some descriptive statistics. Finally, section 12.05 summarises the main empirical findings of the paper while section 12.06 wraps up the analysis with some concluding remarks.

§12.02 LITERATURE REVIEW

The literature on mental health highlights the adverse effect of joblessness. Among the authors detecting a negative impact of unemployment on mental health, one shows a higher negative impact of unemployment on women's rather than on men's mental health in Greece,[2] where the impact of the recession on mental health is also related to the indirect effect of the cuts in public health services.[3]

The case under examination also focuses on the impact of a natural disaster on mental health. Mental health problems following natural disasters, including earthquakes, have been detected in the literature in relation to the effect of the 2011 Canterbury (New Zealand) earthquake.[4] Their analysis on administrative data on antidepressant or antipsychotic drugs after the Canterbury earthquake shows an increase in the short run of the dispensing of anxiolytics and sedatives/hypnotics, whereas there are no substantial effects in the long run. The effects of the Molise earthquake on the population at different times after the earthquake have been

2. Nick Drydakis, *The effect of unemployment on self-reported health and mental health in Greece from 2008 to 2013: A longitudinal study before and during the financial crisis*, Social Science & Medicine 128, 43–51 (2015).
3. Alexander Kentikelenis, Marina Karanikolos, Aaron Reeves, Martin McKee and David Stuckler, *Greece's health crisis: from austerity to denialism*, Lancet 383 (9918) 748–753 (2014).
4. Ben Beaglehole, Caroline Bell, Christopher Frampton, Greg Hamilton G. and Andrew McKean, *The impact of the Canterbury earthquakes on prescribing for mental health*, 49 (8) Australian and New Zealand Journal of Psychiatry 742–750 (2015).

analysed, showing that the effects on mental health of the population tend to fade out in the long run.[5] Another study looks at the effects of the 2011 earthquake and tsunami in Japan,[6] by using a sample of evacuees taken ten and twenty months after the earthquake and finds a persistence of the negative effect of the earthquake on mental health and self-reported general health. The risk factors associated with mental health disorders after the 2008 Wenchuan (County of Sichuan Province in China) earthquake have been analysed by means of an epidemiological study conducted from December 2008 to February 2009.[7] Among the factors found to be more likely to be associated with mental illness after the earthquake, the study detects lower education levels and calls for an increase in the attention devoted to investment in human capital in China.

In this chapter we concentrate on mental health by examining a specific area of Italy that has been affected by a double shock: an economic recession (and, the associated unemployment) and a natural disaster.

§12.03 DATA

Cross-section data can be used to detect the extent to which unemployment can affect mental health. The context chosen is the province of Modena, in the north-east of Italy. The surveys of the socioeconomic conditions of households living in the province of Modena (ICESmo) were carried out by the Centre for the Analysis of Public Policies at the Marco Biagi Department of Economics (University of Modena and Reggio Emilia). They contain a wealth of information on household variables and individual health (SF-12),[8] making it possible to compute the indices of mental health.

In this analysis we focus on the second and third surveys. The second one (ICESmo2) was carried out in 2006 covering 2,034 households. The third one (ICESmo3) was carried out in 2012 covering 2,020 households. The structure was slightly different from the previous survey as the main aim was to analyse the effects of the economic crisis on living standards. Since during the interviews a series of earthquakes struck the province of Modena, and in particular five municipalities of the nineteen involved in the study, the questionnaire was partly modified to take account of the effect of this natural disaster.

5. Stefan Priebe, Fabio Marchi, Lucia Bini, Martina Flego, Ana Costa, Gian Galeazzi, *Mental disorders, psychological symptoms and quality of life 8 years after an earthquake: findings from a community sample in Italy*, 46(7) Social Psychiatry & Psychiatric Epidemiology, 615-621 (2011).
6. Satoko Nagata, Atsushi Matsunaga and Chie Teramot, *Follow-up study of the general and mental health of people living in temporary housing at 10 and 20 months after the Great East Japan Earthquake*, Japan Journal of Nursing Science, 12(2), 162-165 (2015).
7. Xiaobo Zhou, Lin Kang, Xueli Sun, Hui Song, Wenjun Mao, Xuanyin Huang, Yinghui Zhang and Jing Li, *Risk factors of mental illness among adult survivors after the Wenchuan earthquake*, 48 (6) Social Psychiatry & Psychiatric Epidemiology 907-915 (2013).
8. The SF-12 is a generic measure that provides scales for physical and mental health. Physical and Mental Health Composite Scores (PCS and MCS) are computed using the scores for twelve questions. They range from 0 to 100, indicating the lowest level and the highest level of health respectively.

§12.04 DESCRIPTIVE EVIDENCE

In Europe (excluding Germany) a sharp increase (+ 56.5%) in unemployment was recorded between 2008 and 2013. In Italy the unemployment rate was estimated to be 12.2% in 2013, with a 5.4% increase over 2008. This increase was stronger in the south of Italy, where the unemployment rate is one of the highest in Europe.[9]

The most significant component of the unemployment rate is represented by those who have lost their job: this component was less than half of those seeking work in 2008, while it was more than half in 2013.

According to ISTAT, those making the transition from employment to unemployment increased from 1.6% in the two-year period 2007–2008 to 3.2% in the two-year period 2012–2013, with higher values in the south of Italy. In addition, from 2008 to 2013 the number of individuals seeking a job for more than twelve months doubled, accounting for 56.4% of the total number of unemployed. This situation is even worse for those looking for their first job.

In parallel with those seeking employment, there are 'discouraged workers',[10] estimated to be 35.8% of the total working age population in 2008 and 44.5% in 2013, meaning that there was an increase in both unemployed and discouraged workers in 2013.[11]

The increase in unemployment at the beginning of the economic recession affected men in particular, while about two-thirds of discouraged workers are women, though the number of men in this category is growing fast. Unemployment affects especially the sectors of the population with a low education level, thus widening the gap with those who are more highly educated. Finally, an increase in unemployment was recorded for all age ranges, with higher percentages for those under thirty-five years of age and for parents of small children.

The province of Modena is part of the Emilia-Romagna Region, that is characterised by high income per capita, lower unemployment rates than the Italian average and relatively high employment rates (with a much higher female employment rate than the Italian average). In 2012 the province of Modena was suffering from the effects of the economic recession: the unemployment rate was rising and household income was diminishing.[12]

In May 2012, Modena was hit by another shock: three major earthquakes causing destruction and the loss of human lives in most of the province. On the basis of the ICESmo3 data it is possible to recover information on individual and household variables and to distinguish the areas that were severely hit by the earthquake from

9. ISTAT, *Rapporto Annuale 2014. La situazione del paese*, (2014).
10. According to the ILO, discouraged workers are those 'persons who would like to work and are available to do so, but who do not look actively for work for various reasons [...]. Generally, they are not considered as unemployed in national statistics' (www.ilo.org).
11. ISTAT, *Rapporto Annuale 2014. La situazione del paese*, (2014).
12. Centre for the Analysis of Public Policies (CAPP) *Redditi e benessere delle famiglie modenesi negli anni della crisi. Primi risultati dell'indagine Icesmo3 del 2012*, http://www.capp.unimore.it/site/en/home/icesmo/icesmo3.html.

others. This makes it possible to study the impact on individual mental and physical health.

As Figure 12.01 shows, women appear more concentrated in the lower tail of the index of mental health with respect to men, whereas men show higher mean outcomes in terms of mental health.

Figure 12.01 Mental Health Status by Gender – 25–64 Year Old Age Group[14]

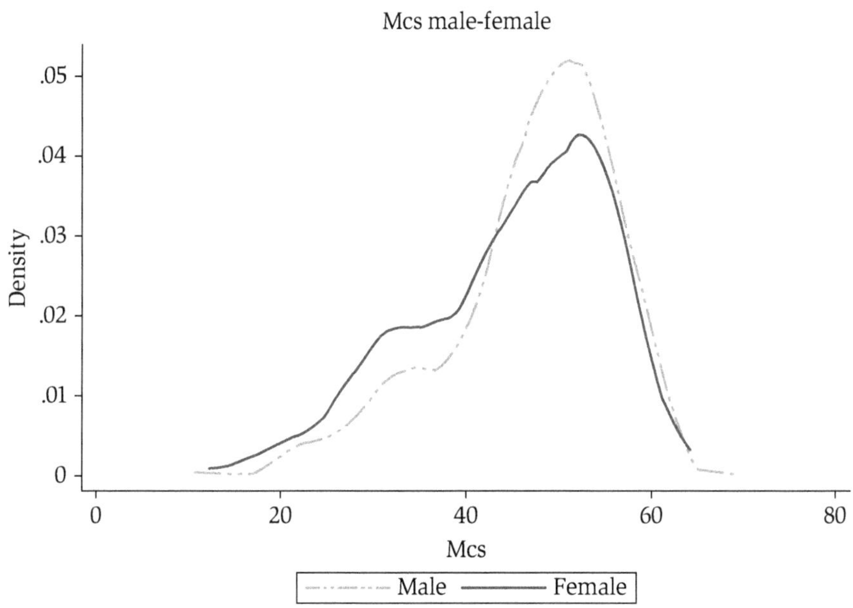

Source: Our elaborations based on ICESmo3 microdata.

In Italy, according to the most recent Survey on Health and Health Services, physical health improved among individuals aged 14 or over from 49.9 in 2005 to 50.7 in 2012, whereas mental health deteriorated, from 49.6 to 48.8.[14]

In this connection, the province of Modena is an interesting case study in terms of the deterioration of the mental health indicators during the economic recession. In fact, by comparing the health data available in ICESmo surveys (2006 and 2012), it may be seen that physical health was stable: 48.8 in 2006 to 48.7 in 2012. On the other hand, the figure for mental health deteriorated more than in Italy as a whole, declining from 48.6 in 2006 to 45.97 in 2012.

We then restricted the sample to those aged 25–64 in Modena, disaggregating by gender. Signs of deterioration of mental health for both men and women can be found

13. Two individuals, who were inactive because affluent, have been excluded from the sample.
14. ISTAT, *La salute e il ricorso ai servizi sanitari attraverso la crisi*, Statistiche Report, www.istat.it (2013).

by analysing the descriptive statistics, while physical health remains fairly stable also in the sample analysed. We then compared the mental and physical health of individuals aged from 25 to 64 in Modena (2012), Emilia-Romagna and Italy (2013) in the most recent surveys. The outcomes in terms of health in Emilia-Romagna were similar to what can be observed in Italy, while the outcomes were worse Modena.

Turning to the gender gap in health outcomes, as shown in Table 12.01, men fare better than women in every context analysed, with a wider gap to the detriment of women in Modena for mental health. Mental health is also the health parameter where the gap between Modena, Emilia-Romagna and Italy is the widest. The mental health of men is 6% lower in Modena than for Emilia-Romagna and Italy as a whole, while women's mental health was lower 8% in Modena than in Emilia-Romagna and Italy. Both men and women show a 3% disadvantage in terms of physical health in Modena with respect to Emilia-Romagna and Italy.

Table 12.01 Physical and Mental Health – Individuals Aged 25–64

	Gender Gap		
	Modena	*Emilia-Romagna*	*Italy*
	(M-F)/F	*(M-F)/F*	*(M-F)/F*
Mental Health	5%	4%	4%
Physical Health	2%	3%	2%

	Modena v. Emilia-Romagna		*Modena v. Italy*	
	Modena / Emilia		*Modena / Italy*	
	M	*F*	*M*	*F*
Mental Health	-6%	-8%	-6%	-8%
Physical Health	-3%	-3%	-3%	-3%

Source: Our elaborations based on ICESmo3 and ISTAT Survey on Health and Health Services 2012 microdata.

§12.05 MULTIVARIATE ANALYSIS

Our empirical strategy makes use of OLS regressions to analyse the effects of unemployment on mental health indices in 2012. In addition, we consider the effect of the series of earthquakes that occurred in 2012 in the area. We make use of a deprivation indicator of unemployment status, and we use the months of unemployment to measure its length. Health is proxied by a set of indicators that are then aggregated according to the SF-12 on mental health, whose increasing values denote better health outcomes.

Our estimations show that women are more disadvantaged on average in terms of mental health, consistent with other studies in countries characterised by high levels of unemployment.[15] According to our empirical study in Table 12.02, the fact of being a woman diminishes the index of mental health by 6%. Ageing has a negative effect on mental health, the effect being similar by gender, whereas being married increases the outcome of mental health only for women. In addition, women with tertiary education have lower outcomes in mental health, whereas living in an area that has been hit by the earthquakes is found to decrease mental health for both men and women by 5%.

According to Icesmo3 data on the length of unemployment, unemployed women aged from 25 to 64 had been unemployed by thirty-one months on average, and men by twenty-three months. By introducing in the model a dummy variable on the definition of unemployment status with regards to its length in 2012 (when there is also a substantial higher likelihood to be in long-term unemployment) it was found that, on average, long-term unemployment negatively affects mental health, reducing it by 6% over the whole sample. However, short-term unemployment (less than one year) has a significant negative effect for men (reducing their mental health by 19%), while long-term unemployment has a negative effect for women (reducing their mental health by 11%).

In short, it seems that the experience of becoming unemployed rather than its duration has a negative effect on the mental health status of men during the economic recession, whereas for women, the longer the period of unemployment, the higher the loss in terms of mental health.

Table 12.02 Multivariate OLS Analysis on Mental Health Outcomes Based on ICESmo3 Data (2012). Individuals Aged 25–64

Variables	*All*	*M*	*F*
Age	-0.0165***	-0.0150**	-0.0169**
	(0.00474)	(0.00638)	(0.00701)
Age Squared	0.000172***	0.000165**	0.000167**
	(5.30e-05)	(7.05e-05)	(7.91e-05)
Female	-0.0584***		
	(0.0135)		
Married	0.0373**	0,03	0.0345*
	(0.0156)	(0.0230)	(0.0209)
High school	-0.0142	0.00641	-0.0361
	(0.0156)	(0.0212)	(0.0228)
Degree or over	-0.0196	0.00634	-0.0491**
	(0.0165)	(0.0208)	(0.0249)
Short-term unemployed	-0.0706	-0.189**	-0.0131
	(0.0513)	(0.0918)	(0.0586)

15. Nick Drydakis, *The effect of unemployment on self-reported health and mental health in Greece from 2008 to 2013: A longitudinal study before and during the financial crisis*, 128 Social Science & Medicine 43–51 (2015).

Variables	*All*	*M*	*F*
Long-term unemployed	-0.0603*	0,011	-0.108**
	(0.0329)	(0.0346)	(0.0476)
Earthquake	-0.0510***	-0.0528**	-0.0500**
	(0.0177)	(0.0253)	(0.0248)
Constant	4.203***	4.141***	4.194***
	(0.101)	(0.135)	(0.150)
Observations	1962	919	1043
R^2	0,25	0,22	0,27

Robust standard errors in parentheses
*** $p < 0.01$, ** $p < 0.05$, * $p < 0.1$
Source: Our elaborations based on ICESmo3 microdata.

§12.06 CONCLUDING REMARKS

As the analysis in this chapter shows, the province of Modena has been affected by the economic recession in significant ways, with negative effects on mental health. This is demonstrated by using microdata available at local level that make it possible to show the effect of employment status on the indicators of health. The effect of being unemployed appears significant, but the effect is different in terms of its duration by gender: becoming unemployed rather than being long-term unemployed negatively affects men's mental health, whereas for women the opposite is the case.

Although severely affected by the recession, the province of Modena is located in a region of Italy characterised by better economic indicators than Italy as a whole. The impact of unemployment on mental health may have been softened by the expectation of more favourable labour market conditions than in other areas of the country facing worse structural problems in the labour market.

Finally, our findings on the negative impact of a natural disaster (the series of earthquakes) that struck various parts of the province Modena can be observed in the data with consequences that are consistent with the literature. A follow-up study on different samples of individuals living in the areas of the district affected by the earthquake[16] would make it possible to identify differences in the moderator effect by personal, family, economic and institutional variables at different times after the earthquake. In addition, it should be possible to analyse the length of the effect on mental health in its interaction with employment status.

16. With reference, for instance, to having been evacuees and for how long, their employment status and the extent of the damage caused by the earthquake to their households.

BCLR - BULLETIN OF COMPARATIVE LABOUR RELATIONS

Vol. Author/Title/Year/ISBN

1. Roger Blanpain, *Individual Employment Contracts: Collective Agreements,* 1970.
2. Roger Blanpain, *Social Planning,* 1971 (ISBN 90-312-0018-2).
3. Roger Blanpain, *Guaranteed Income Funds,* 1972 (ISBN 90-312-0019-0).
4. Roger Blanpain, *Employee Participation at the Level of the Enterprise,* 1973 (ISBN 90-312-0020-4).
5. Roger Blanpain, *Vastheid van Betrekking: Staking en Bezetting,* 1974.
6. Roger Blanpain, *Labour Law and Industrial Relations (International Bibliography),* 1975 (ISBN 90-312-0023-9).
7. Roger Blanpain, *Multinational Enterprises,* 1976 (ISBN 90-312-0024-7).
8. Roger Blanpain, *Worker's Participation in the European Company,* 1977 (ISBN 90-312-0044-1).
9. Roger Blanpain, *Women and Labour,* 1978 (ISBN 90-312-0077-8).
10. Roger Blanpain, *European Conference on Labour Law and Industrial Relations: Multinational Enterprises*, 1979 (ISBN 90-312-0091-3).
11. Roger Blanpain, *Job Security and Industrial Relations,* 1980 (ISBN 90-312-0147-2).
12. Roger Blanpain, Greg Bamber & Russell Lansbury, *Technological Change and Industrial Relations: An International Symposium,* 1983 (ISBN 90-312-0205-3).
13. Roger Blanpain, James Janssen van Raay & A. Moulty, *Worker's Participation in the European Community: The Fifth Directive,* 1984 (ISBN 90-654-4187-5).
14. Roger Blanpain, *Equality and Prohibition of Discrimination in Employment,* 1985 (ISBN 90-654-4215-4).
15. Roger Blanpain, *Restructuring Labour in the Enterprise: Law and Practice in France, F.R. of Germany, Italy, Sweden and the United Kingdom,* 1986 (ISBN 90-654-4283-9).
16. Roger Blanpain & E. Kassalow, *Unions and Industrial Relations: Recent Trends and Prospect: A Comparative Treatment,* 1987 (ISBN 90-654-4294-4).
17. Roger Blanpain & Marco Biagi, *Trade Union Democracy and Industrial Relations,* 1988 (ISBN 90-654-4394-0).
18. Roger Blanpain & Jelle Visser, *In Search of Inclusive Unionism,* 1990 (ISBN 90-654-4439-4).
19. Roger Blanpain, *Flexibility and Wages: A Comparative Treatment,* 1990 (ISBN 90-654-4461-0).

20. Roger Blanpain, Stephen Frenkel & Oliver Clarke, *Economic Restructuring and Industrial Relations in Industrialised Countries,* 1990 (ISBN 90-654-4488-2).
21. Roger Blanpain & Friedrich Fürstenberg, *Structure and Strategy in Industrial Relations,* 1991 (ISBN 90-654-4559-5).
22. Roger Blanpain, Amira Galin & Ozer Carmi, *Flexible Work Patterns and Their Impact on Industrial Relations,* 1991 (ISBN 90-654-4572-2).
23. Roger Blanpain, *Workers' Participation: Influence on Management Decision-Making by Labour in the Private Sector,* 1992 (ISBN 90-654-4600-1).
24. Roger Blanpain, Brian Brooks & Chris Engels, *Employed or Self-Employed,* 1992 (ISBN 90-654-4613-3).
25. Roger Blanpain & Tiziano Treu, *Industrial Relations Developments in the Telecommunications Industry,* 1993 (ISBN 90-654-4642-7).
26. Roger Blanpain & Marco Biagi, *Industrial Relations in Small and Medium Sized Enterprises,* 1993 (ISBN 90-654-4696-6).
27. Roger Blanpain & Marco Biagi, *Participative Management and Industrial Relations in a Worldwide Perspective,* 1993 (ISBN 90-654-4769-5).
28. Roger Blanpain, Jacques Rojot & Hoyt N. Wheeler, *Employee Rights and Industrial Justice,* 1994 (ISBN 90-654-4804-7).
29. Roger Blanpain & Ruth Ben-Israel, *Strikes and Lock-Outs in Industrialized Market Economies,* 1994 (ISBN 90-654-4841-1).
30. Roger Blanpain, Kazuo Sugeno & Yasuo Suwa, *The Harmonization of Working Life and Family Life,* 1995 (ISBN 90-411-0064-4).
31. Roger Blanpain & Laszio Nagy, *Labour Law and Industrial Relations in Central and Eastern Europe,* 1996 (ISBN 90-411-0298-1).
32. Roger Blanpain, *Labour Law and Industrial Relations in the European Union,* 1997 (ISBN 90-411-0527-1).
33. Taco Van Peijpe, *Employment Protection under Strain,* 1998 (ISBN 90-411-0528-8).
34. Roger Blanpain, Takashi Araki & Ryuichi Yamakawa, *The Process of Industrialization and the Role of Labour Law in Asia,* 1999 (ISBN 9-041-1104-7-X).
35. Roger Blanpain & Marco Biagi, *Non-standard Work and Industrial Relations,* 1999 (ISBN 90-411-1117-4).
36. Roger Blanpain, *Private Employment Agencies: The Impact of ILO Convention 181 (1997) and the Judgment of the European Court of Justice of 11 December 1997,* 1999 (ISBN 90-411-1118-2).
37. Roger Blanpain, *Multinational Enterprises and the Social Challenges of the XXIst Century: The ILO Declaration on Fundamental* Principles *at Work, Public and Private Corporate Codes of Conduct,* 2000 (ISBN 90-411-1280-4).
38. Roger Blanpain, Ryuichi Yamakawa & Takashi Araki, *Deregulation and Labour Law: In Search of a Labour Concept for the 21st Century,* 2000 (ISBN 90-411-1370-3).
39. Roger Blanpain, *The Council of Europe and the Social Challenges of the XXIst Century,* 2001 (ISBN 90-411-1543-9).

40. Roger Blanpain, *On-Line Rights for Employees in the Information Society, Use & Monitoring of E-Mail & Internet at Work*, 2002 (ISBN 90-411-1626-5).
41. Roger Blanpain, *The Evolving Employment Relationship and the New Economy: The Role of Labour Law & Industrial Relations*, 2001 (ISBN 90-411-1691-5).
42. Roger Blanpain, *Involvement of Employees in the European Union, Works Councils, Company Statute, Information and Consultation Rights*, 2002 (ISBN 90-411-1760-1).
43. Michele Colucci, *The Impact of the Internet and New Technologies on the Workplace: A Legal Analysis from a Comparative Point of View*, 2002 (ISBN 90-411-1824-1).
44. Roger Blanpain, *White Paper on the Labour Market in Italy: The Quality of European Industrial Relations and Changing Industrial Relations*, 2002 (ISBN 90-411-1841-1).
45. Roger Blanpain, Russell D. Lansbury & Young-Bum Park, *Impact of Globalisation on Employment Relations: A Comparison of the Automobile and Banking Industries in Australia and Korea*, 2002 (ISBN 90-411-1850-0).
46. Roger Blanpain & Antoine Jacobs, *Employee Rights in Bankruptcy:* A *Comparative-Law Assessment*, 2002 (ISBN 90-411-1942-6).
47. Roger Blanpain, Takashi Araki & Shinya Ouchi, *Corporate Restructuring and the Role of Labour Law*, 2003 (ISBN 90-411-1949-3).
48. Roger Blanpain, *Collective Bargaining, Discrimination, Social Security and European Integration*, 2003 (ISBN 90-411-2010-6).
49. Roger Blanpain & Luis Aparicio-Valdez, *Labour Relations in the Asia- Pacific Countries*, 2004 (ISBN 90-411-2239-7).
50. Roger Blanpain & Ronnie Graham, *Temporary Agency Work and the Information Society*, 2004 (ISBN 90-411-2252-4).
51. Roger Blanpain, *The Actors of Collective Bargaining: A World Report*, 2004 (ISBN 90-411-2253-2).
52. Roger Blanpain & Michele Colucci, *The Globalisation of Labour Standards: The Soft Law Track*, 2004 (ISBN 90-411-2303-2).
53. Roger Blanpain, Takashi Araki & Shinya Ouchi, *Labour Law in Motion: Diversification of the Labour Force & Terms and Conditions of Employment*, 2005 (ISBN 90-411-2315-6).
54. Roger Blanpain, *Smoking and the Workplace*, 2005 (ISBN 90-411-2325-3).
55. Roger Blanpain, *Confronting Globalization: The Quest for a Social Agenda*, 2005 (ISBN 90-411-2381-4).
56. Roger Blanpain, Thomas Blanke & Edgar Rose, *Collective Bargaining Wages in Comparative Perspective: Germany, France, the Netherlands, Sweden and the United Kingdom*, 2005 (ISBN 90-411-2388-1).
57. Roger Blanpain & Anne Numhauser-Henning, *Women in Academia & Equality Law: Aiming High - Falling Short?*, 2006 (ISBN 978-90-411-2427-6).
58. Roger Blanpain, *Freedom of Services in the European Union: Labour and Social Security Law: The Bolkestein Initiative*, 2006 (ISBN 978-90-411-2453-5).
59. Roger Blanpain, Frans Pennings & Nurhan Sural, *Flexibilisation and Modernisation of the Turkish Labour Market*, 2006 (ISBN 978-90-411-2490-X).

60. Roger Blanpain & Boel Flodgren, *Corporate and Employment Perspectives in a Global Business Environment*, 2006 (ISBN 978-90-411-2537-X).
61. Roger Blanpain, Shinya Ouchi & Takashi Araki, *Decentralizing Industrial Relations and The Role of Labor Unions and Employee Representatives*, 2007 (ISBN 978-90-411-2583-3).
62. Roger Blanpain, *European Framework Agreements and Telework: Law and Practice: A European and Comparative Study*, 2007 (ISBN 978-90-411-2560-4).
63. Roger Blanpain, Jim Kitay, Leanne Cutcher & Nick Wailes, *Globalization and Employment Relations in Retail Banking*, 2007 (ISBN 978-90-411-2620-1).
64. Roger Blanpain, Russell Lansbury, Jim Kitay, Nick Wailes & Anja Kirsch, *Globalization and Employment Relations in the Auto Assembly Industry: A Study of Seven Countries*, 2008 (ISBN 978-90-411-2698-6).
65. Roger Blanpain & Michele Tiraboschi, *The Global Labour Market: From Globalization to Flexicurity*, 2008 (ISBN 978-90-411-2722-8).
66. Roger Blanpain, Michele Colucci & Frank Hendrickx, *The Future of Sport in the European Union: Beyond the EU Reform Treaty and the White Paper*, 2008 (ISBN 978-90-411-2761-7).
67. Roger Blanpain, Linda Dickens, *Challenges in European Employment Relations: Employment Regulation, Trade Union Organization, Equality, Flexicurity, Training and New Approaches to Pay*, 2008 (ISBN 978-90-411-2771-6).
68. Roger Blanpain, Hiroya Nakakubo & Takashi Araki, *New Developments in Employment Discrimination Law, 2008* (ISBN 978-90-411-2782-2).
69. Roger Blanpain, Andrzej Marian wiątkowski, *The Laval and Viking Cases: Freedom of Services and Establishment v. Industrial Conflict in the European Economic Area and Russia*, 2009 (ISBN 978-90-411-2850-8).
70. Roger Blanpain, William Bromwich, Olga Rymkevich, Silvia Spattini, *The Modernization of Labour Law and Industrial Relations in a Comparative Perspective*, 2009 (ISBN 978-90-411-2865-2).
71. Roger Blanpain, Juan Pablo Landa & Brian Langille, *Employment Policies and Multilevel Governance*, 2009 (ISBN 978-90-411-2866-9).
72. Roger Blanpain, European Works Councils; *The European Directive 2009/ 38/EC of 6 May 2009, 2009* (ISBN 978-90-411-3208-6).
73. Roger Blanpain, William Bromwich, Olga Rymkevich & Silvia Spattini, *Labour Productivity, Investment in Human Capital and Youth Employment: Comparative Developments and Global Responses*, 2010 (ISBN 978-90-411-3249-9).
74. Greg J. Bamber & Philippe Pochet, *Regulating Employment Relations, Work and Labour Laws: International Comparisons between Key Countries*, 2010 (ISBN 978-90-411-3199-7). General Editor: Roger Blanpain.
75. Roger Blanpain, Desislava Nikolaeva Dimitrova, *Seafarers' Rights in the Globalized Maritime Industry*, 2010 (ISBN 978-90-411-3349-6).
76. Roger Blanpain, Hiroya Nakakubo & Takashi Araki, *Regulation of Fixed- Term Employment Contracts*, 2010 (ISBN 978-90-411-3356-4).

77. Roger Blanpain, William Bromwich, Olga Rymkevich & Iacopo Senatori, *Rethinking Corporate Governance*, 2011 (ISBN 978-90-411-3450-9).
78. Roger Blanpain & Frank Hendrickx, *Labour Law between Change and Tradition: Liber Amicorum Antoine Jacobs*, 2011 (ISBN 978-90-411-3424-0).
79. Roger Blanpain, Thomas Klebe, Marlene Schmidt & Bernd Waas, *Trade Union Rights at the Workplace*, 2012 (ISBN 978-90-411-3460-8).
80. Roger Blanpain, William Bromwich, Olga Rymkevich & Iacopo Senatori, *Labour Markets, Industrial Relations and Human Resources Management: From Recession to Recovery*, 2012 (ISBN 978-90-411-4004-3).
81. Roger Blanpain, Hiroya Nakakubo & Takashi Araki, *Systems of Employee Representation at the Enterprise: A Comparative Study*, 2012 (ISBN 978-90-411-4080-7).
82. Roger Blanpain & Frank Hendrickx, *Temporary Agency Work in the European Union and the United States*, 2013 (ISBN 978-90-411-4769-1).
83. Roger Blanpain, Toker Dereli, Y. Pınar Soykut-Sarıca & Aslı en-Tabaı, *Emerging Patterns of Work and Turkish Labour Market Challenges under Globalization: Readings on Labour and Employment Relations*, 2014 (ISBN 978-90-411-4983-1).
84. Roger Blanpain, Pablo Arellano Ortiz, Marius Olivier & Gijsbert Vonk, *Social Security and Migrant Workers: Selected Studies of Cross-border Social Security Mechanisms*, 2014 (ISBN 978-90-411-4770-7).
85. Roger Blanpain & Nikita Lyutov, *Workers' Representation in Central and Eastern Europe: Challenges and Opportunities for the Works Councils' System*, 2014 (ISBN 978-90-411-4746-2).
86. Roger Blanpain, Ulla Liukkunen & Chen Yifeng, *China and ILO Fundamental Principles and Rights at Works*, 2014 (ISBN 978-90-411-4984-8).
87. Roger Blanpain, *The Use of Languages and Employment Relations*, 2014 (ISBN 978-90-411-5606-8).
88. Roger Blanpain, Hiroya Nakakubo & Takashi Araki, *Protection of Employees' Personal Information and Privacy*, 2014 (ISBN 978-90-411-5608-2).
89. Roger Blanpain, Jan Wouters, Glenn Rayp, Laura Beke & Axel Marx, *Protecting Labour Rights in a Multi-polar Supply Chain and Mobile Global Economy*, 2015 (ISBN 978-90-411-5662-4).
90. Roger Blanpain & Stefania Marassi, *Globalization and Transnational Collective Labour Relations: International and European Framework Agreements at Company Level*, 2015 (ISBN 978-90-411-4748-6).
91. Roger Blanpain, Frank Hendrickx & Petra Herzfeld Olsson, *National Effects of the Implementation of EU Directives on Labour Migration from Third Countries*, 2016 (ISBN 978-90-411-6257-1).
92. Roger Blanpain, Frank Hendrickx & D'Arcy du Toit, *Labour Law and Social Progress: Holding the Line or Shifting the Boundaries?* 2016 (ISBN 978-90-411-6747-7).

93. Roger Blanpain & Frank Hendrickx, *Reasonable Accommodation in the Modern Workplace: Potential and Limits of the Integrative Logics of Labour Law*, 2016 (ISBN 978-90-411-6258-8).
94. Roger Blanpain, Frank Hendrickx & Bernd Waas, *New Forms of Employment in Europe*, 2016 (ISBN 978-90-411-6239-7).
95. Roger Blanpain, Frank Hendrickx, Hiroya Nakakubo & Takashi Araki, *The Notion of Employer in the Era of the Fissured Workplace: Should Labour Law Responsibilities Exceed the Boundary of the Legal Entity?*, 2017 (ISBN 978-90-411-8470-2).
96. Elena Sychenko, *Individual Labour Rights as Human Rights: The Contributions of the European Court of Human Rights to Worker's Rights Protection*, 2017 (ISBN 978-90-411-8629-4).
97. William Bromwich & Olga Rymkevich, *Improving Workplace Quality: New Perspectives and Challenges for Worker Well-Being*, 2017 (ISBN 978-90-411-8628-7).